REASONING
WITH THE
CHARTER

REASONING
WITH THE
CHARTER

Leon E. Trakman

Butterworths

Toronto   Vancouver

Reasoning with the Charter
© Butterworths Canada Ltd. 1991

Printed and bound in Canada by John Deyell Company

The Butterworth Group of Companies

Canada
>Butterworths Canada Ltd., 75 Clegg Road, MARKHAM, Ont. L6G 1A1 and 409 Granville Street, Suite 1455, VANCOUVER, B.C. V6C 1T2

Australia
>Butterworths Pty Ltd., SYDNEY, MELBOURNE, BRISBANE, ADELAIDE, PERTH, CANBERRA and HOBART

Ireland
>Butterworth (Ireland) Ltd., DUBLIN

New Zealand
>Butterworths of New Zealand Ltd., WELLINGTON and AUCKLAND

Puerto Rico
>Equity de Puerto Rico, Inc., HATO REY

Singapore
>Malayan Law Journal Pte. Ltd., SINGAPORE

United Kingdom
>Butterworth & Co. (Publishers) Ltd., LONDON and EDINBURGH

United States
>Butterworth Legal Publishers, AUSTIN, Texas; BOSTON, Massachusetts; CLEARWATER, Florida (D & S Publishers); ORFORD, New Hampshire (Equity Publishing); ST. PAUL, Minnesota; and SEATTLE, Washington.

Canadian Cataloguing in Publication Data

Trakman, Leon E., 1947-
>Reasoning with the Charter

Includes index
ISBN 0-409-80896-2 (bound)   ISBN 0-409-90617-4 (pbk.)

1. Canada. Canadian Charter of Rights and Freedoms.
2. Civil rights – Canada – Interpretation and construction.   3. Canada – Constitutional law – Interpretation and construction.   I. Title.

KE4381.5.T73 1991   342.71'085   C91-094408-3
KF4483.C519T73 1991

Sponsoring editor: Fran Cudlipp
Editor: Helen Campbell
Cover design: Brant Cowie
Production: Kevin Skinner

For Dawn

PREFACE

For some years, I have doubted the way judges sometimes approach questions of rights, under the *Charter* as elsewhere. Their analytical conceptions of human rights are often quite unconvincing. As part of the research for this book, I interviewed several judges on the Supreme Court of Canada. My goal was to find out how they thought about such issues. They displayed little unanimity, apart from their broadly liberal orientation towards rights and their desire to shape human rights in the interests of individual liberties. This was limiting; but even more constraining was their apparent lack of consciousness of credible alternatives to liberal jurisprudence.

This book attempts to expose restricted and dogma-ridden views of rights, to criticize them, and to posit different ways of looking at rights in Canada today. Using the *Charter* as a focal point, I argue for a more communal and positive conception of rights. I do so realizing that Anglo-American liberalism has never produced a lasting harmony in Canadian society. Lip-service to a fixed theory of *a priori* individual rights has not done much to satisfy First Nation Peoples. Nor has the *Charter's* Anglo-Canadian tone done much to satisfy the interests of Quebec, as is evident since the demise of the *Meech Lake Accord*. All this speaks for the need for a more communal and positive conception of rights in the future.

I write as an expatriate South African who, twenty years ago, left to seek a new life in a free land. I now find myself providing constitutional assistance to the parties drafting a new constitution for South Africa with guarded hope while I watch the federal structure of Canadian society unravel. I write, too, with the belief that notions of community, affecting aboriginal peoples at Oka as readily as francophile Manitobans, are central to any lasting sense of political life.

This book is also about hope: it is about hope for dialogue between disparate racial, sexual, linguistic and religious groups. It is about trust in a communicative process that accommodates itself to the interests of individuals without succumbing to them. Finally, it is about constitutions, not as aloof bodies of law, but as the cement that unifies disparate visions of the Canadian polity, without seeking to displace those visions. To be truly telling, a constitution is far more than an abstraction. It embodies the conscience of a diffuse people; it voices their beliefs; and it acts as a chamber of their varied dreams.

In preparing this book, I have met with many people, including judges, lawyers and academics. I owe particular thanks for thoughtful commentary to Chief Justice Dickson (as he then was), Mr. Justice Lamer (as he then was), Mr. Justice Estey (as he then was), and Madam Justice Wilson, all of the Supreme Court of Canada. I thank those who encouraged me to write this book, or otherwise read drafts of it: particularly David Beatty, Guido Calebresi, Richard Devlin, Dennis Davis, Ronald Macdonald, Wayne MacKay, Noel Lyon, Dianne Pothier, Albie Sachs, Bob Sedler, Peter Swan, Mary Ellen Turpel and Wade MacLauchlan. I thank, too, Stephen Baldwin and Ken Lenz who acted as readers, Peter Ralph, Janice Spencer, Heather MacKinnon and Dawn Trakman for their editorial work, Kim LeBlanc for typing various drafts, and Gordon James for computer assistance. I am also grateful to the Killam Foundation for the award of a Senior Killam Fellowship, the Social Sciences and Humanities Research Council of Canada for a Release Time Stipend, the Law Foundation of Nova Scotia and the Foundation for Legal Research for research support, and the Dalhousie Law School for its encouragement and support. Far from least, I thank Dawn, Brandon, Laura and Jenna Trakman for enduring my many absences with understanding and patience.

Leon Trakman
Halifax

TABLE OF CONTENTS

Preface vii
Table of Cases xi

CHAPTER 1 INTRODUCTION 1

CHAPTER 2 LIBERATING LIBERTY 7

 State Interests 8
 The Rhetoric of Negative Rights 10
 Form Before Substance: Rights Before Right 16
 Tempered Activism 26
 Affirming Liberty 35
 Re-creating Positive Liberty 41
 Rekindling the Negative Fold 46
 Mediating Among Differences 49
 Conclusion 52

CHAPTER 3 FROM LIBERTY TO COMMUNITY 55

 Rights as Hierarchy 56
 Plural Rights 60
 Correlative Relations 65
 Community Through Expression 72
 Constructing Community 76
 Rationalizing Discourse 79
 Relational Community Revisited 83
 Qualifying Categories 89
 A Dialogic Community 92
 Conclusion 94

CHAPTER 4 PRIVATE RIGHTS, PUBLIC POWER 97

 The Liberal Rationale 98
 A Relational Private 104

Stagnation Through Categorization 110
Private Concentrations of Power 115
An Inferior Private 129
A Transformative Public 133
A Uniform Public 138
Conclusion 140

CHAPTER 5 JUDICIAL DISCOURSE: FACT OR FANCY? 143

Introduction 143
Judicial A Priorism 145
Principles of Hierarchy 153
A Challenge to A Priorism 156
The Absence of Causal Relations 158
Propositions and Suppositions 168
Conclusion 171

CHAPTER 6 MORGENTALER AS ILLUSTRATION 173

On Analytical Rhetoric 174
Rationalized Not Rational Rights 179
Hierarchy as Principle 181
A Priori Social Rights 186
Reconstructing Communal Rights 188
Contingent Rights 192
Conclusion 196

CHAPTER 7 REFLECTIONS 199

EPILOGUE 203

APPENDIX CANADIAN CHARTER OF RIGHTS AND FREEDOMS 205

Index 213

TABLE OF CASES

Abrams v. United States, 250 U.S. 616 (1919) 73, 104
Alberta Reference. *See* Reference re Public Service Employee
    Relations Act (Alta.)
Alberta Union of Provincial Employees v. Alberta (A.G.). *See*
    Reference re Public Service Employee Relations Act (Alta.)
Alliance des Professeurs de Montréal v. Quebec (A.G.) (1985), 21
    D.L.R. (4th) 354, 21 C.C.C. (3d) 273, 18 C.R.R. 195 (Que. C.A.) ..147, 154
Amax Potash Ltd. v. Govt. of Saskatchewan, [1977] 2 S.C.R. 576,
    71 D.L.R. (3d) 1, [1976] 6 W.W.R. 61, 11 N.R. 222 ....18, 57
Andrews v. Law Society of British Columbia, [1989] 1 S.C.R. 143,
    56 D.L.R. (4th) 1, [1989] 2 W.W.R. 289, 34 B.C.L.R. (2d) 273, 91 N.R.
    255, 25 C.C.E.L. 255, 10 C.H.R.R. D/5719, 36 C.R.R. 193 ....8, 9, 14,
    15, 16, 18, 20, 33, 45, 46, 47, 68, 71, 85, 89, 90, 91, 109, 125, 132, 148
Apsit v. Manitoba Human Rights Commn., [1988] 1 W.W.R. 629,
    50 Man. R. (2d) 92, 9 C.H.R.R. D/4457 (Q.B.); affd. [1989] 1 W.W.R.
    481, 55 Man. R. (2d) 263 (*sub nom.* Manitoba Rice Farmers'
    Assn. v. Manitoba Human Rights (Commn.)) (C.A.) 45
Assn. des Compositeurs, Auteurs et Editeurs du Canada Ltée v.
    Keet Estates Inc., [1972] S.C. 315 (Que.) 106
Balfour v. Balfour, [1919] 2 K.B. 571 (C.A.) 129
Basile v. Nova Scotia (A.G.) (1984), 11 D.L.R. (4th) 219, 62 N.S.R.
    (2d) 410, 8 C.R.R. 374 (C.A.); leave to appeal to S.C.C. granted 65
    N.S.R. (2d) 90*n*, 56 N.R. 232*n* 28
Bhindi et al. and B.C. Projectionists, Loc. 348, Int. Alliance of
    Picture Machine Operators of U.S. & Can. (Re) (1986), 29 D.L.R.
    (4th) 47, 86 C.L.L.C. ¶14,052, [1986] 5 W.W.R. 303, 4 B.C.L.R. (2d)
    145, 24 C.R.R. 302 (C.A.); leave to appeal to S.C.C. refused [1986]
    6 W.W.R. lxv, 73 N.R. 399*n* 38
Bichler v. Eli Lilly & Co., 55 N.Y. 2d 571, 436 N.E. 2d 182 (C.A., 1982) .107
Big M Drug Mart. *See* R. v. Big M Drug Mart
Black v. Law Society of Alberta (1986), 27 D.L.R. (4th) 527, [1986]
    3 W.W.R. 590, 44 Alta. L.R. (2d) 1, 68 A.R. 259, 20 C.R.R. 117 (C.A.);
    affd. [1989] 1 S.C.R. 591, 58 D.L.R. (4th) 317, [1989] 4 W.W.R. 1,
    66 Alta. L.R. (2d) 97, 96 A.R. 352, 93 N.R. 266, 37 Admin. L.R. 161,
    38 C.R.R. 193 13

Blainey and Ontario Hockey Assn. (Re) (1986), 26 D.L.R. (4th) 728,
54 O.R. (2d) 513, 14 O.A.C. 194, 10 C.P.R. (3d) 450, 21 C.R.R.
44 (C.A.); leave to appeal to S.C.C. refused 72 N.R. 76*n*, 58 O.R.
(2d) 274*n*, 17 O.A.C. 399*n* 81

Bliss v. Canada (A.G.), [1978] 1 F.C. 208, 77 D.L.R. (3d) 609, 78 C.L.L.C.
¶14,136, 16 N.R. 254 (C.A.); affd. [1979] 1 S.C.R. 183, 92 D.L.R. (3d)
417, 78 C.L.L.C. ¶14,175, [1978] 6 W.W.R. 711, 23 N.R. 527 ....90, 157

Borowski v. Canada (A.G.), [1989] 1 S.C.R. 342, 57 D.L.R. (4th) 231, 47
C.C.C. (3d) 1, [1989] 3 W.W.R. 97, 75 Sask. R. 82, 92 N.R. 110, 33
C.P.C. (2d) 105, 38 C.R.R. 232 ....48, 60, 67, 150, 200

Bregman et al. v. Canada (A.G.) (1986), 33 D.L.R. (4th) 477, 57 O.R.
(2d) 409, 18 O.A.C. 82, 27 C.R.R. 25 (C.A.); leave to appeal to
S.C.C. refused 61 O.R. (2d) 278*n*, 23 O.A.C. 160*n*, 79 N.R. 400*n*, 29
C.R.R. 5*n* 63

B.C. Motor Vehicle Act (Re). *See* Reference re Section 94(2) of
the Motor Vehicle Act (B.C.)

Brooks v. Canada Safeway Ltd., [1989] 1 S.C.R. 1219, 59 D.L.R.
(4th) 321, 89 C.L.L.C. ¶17,012, [1989] 4 W.W.R. 193, 58 Man. R.
(2d) 161, 94 N.R. 373, 26 C.C.E.L. 1, 45 C.R.R. 115 ....90, 133

Brown v. Bd. of Education, 347 U.S. 483 (1954) 35, 163

Brown v. Waterloo Bd. of Commrs. of Police (1982), 136 D.L.R. (3d)
49, 37 O.R. (2d) 277 (H.C.J.); vard. 150 D.L.R. (3d) 729, 43 O.R. (2d)
113, 4 Admin. L.R. 113, 23 B.L.R. 41, 2 C.C.E.L. 7 (C.A.) 106

Caldwell v. Stuart, [1984] 2 S.C.R. 603, 15 D.L.R. (4th) 1, 85 C.L.L.C.
¶17,002, [1985] 1 W.W.R. 620, 66 B.C.L.R. 398, 56 N.R. 83, 6
C.H.R.R. D/2643 131

Canada (A.G.) v. City of Montreal, [1978] 2 S.C.R. 770, 84 D.L.R. (3d)
420, 19 N.R. 478, 5 M.P.L.R. 4 ....63, 151, 165

Canada (A.G.) v. Lavell, [1974] S.C.R. 1349, 38 D.L.R. (3d) 481, 23
C.R.N.S. 197, 11 R.F.L. 333 ....51, 78

Canada (A.G.) v. Law Society of British Columbia; Jabour v. Law
Society of British Columbia, [1982] 2 S.C.R. 307, 137 D.L.R. (3d)
1, [1982] 5 W.W.R. 289, 37 B.C.L.R. 145, 43 N.R. 451, 19 B.L.R. 234,
66 C.P.R. (2d) 1 18

Canada (A.G.) v. Stuart, [1983] 1 F.C. 651, 137 D.L.R. (3d) 740, 82
C.L.L.C. ¶14,201, 44 N.R. 320 (C.A.); leave to appeal to S.C.C.
refused 45 N.R. 531 90

Canadian Disability Rights Council v. Canada, [1988] 3 F.C. 622,
21 F.T.R. 268, 38 C.R.R. 53 (T.D.) 43

Canadian Dredge & Dock Co. et al. v. R., [1985] 1 S.C.R. 662, 19
D.L.R. (4th) 314, 19 C.C.C. (3d) 1, 45 C.R. (3d) 289 105

Canadian Ironworkers Union, No. 1 v. Int. Assns. of Bridge,
Structural & Ornamental Ironworkers Union, Loc. 97 (1979),

45 D.L.R. (3d) 768 (B.C.C.A.) 106, 108

Canadian Newspapers Co. v. Canada (A.G.), [1988] 2 S.C.R. 122,
52 D.L.R. (4th) 690, 43 C.C.C. (3d) 24, 65 C.R. (3d) 50, 65 O.R. (2d)
637n, 32 O.A.C. 259, 87 N.R. 163, 38 C.R.R. 72 .... 27, 30, 113

Canadian Newspapers Co. v. City of Victoria (1987), 46 D.L.R.
(4th) 695, [1988] 2 W.W.R. 221, 20 B.C.L.R. (2d) 217, 34 C.R.R.
170 (S.C.); affd. 63 D.L.R. (4th) 1, [1990] 2 W.W.R. 1, 40 B.C.L.R.
(2d) 297, 46 C.R.R. 271 (C.A.) 42

Cardinal Construction Ltd. v. R. in right of Ontario (1981), 122
D.L.R. (3d) 703, 32 O.R. (2d) 575 (H.C.J.); affd. 128 D.L.R. (3d) 662,
38 O.R. (2d) 161 (C.A.) 109

Cassell & Co. v. Broome, [1972] A.C. 1027 (H.L.) 138

Chaplinsky v. New Hampshire, 315 U.S. 568 (1942) 21, 74

Chaussure Brown's Inc. v. Quebec. See Ford v. Quebec (A.G.)

College of Physicians & Surgeons of Ontario and K (Re) (1985),
16 D.L.R. (4th) 424, 50 O.R. (2d) 14, 7 O.A.C. 39 (Div. Ct.); revd.
36 D.L.R. (4th) 707, 59 O.R. (2d) 1, 19 O.A.C. 51 (C.A.) 112

Court of Unified Criminal Jurisdiction (Re). See McEvoy v. New
Brunswick (A.G.)

Crevier v. Quebec (A.G.), [1981] 2 S.C.R. 220, 127 D.L.R. (3d) 1, 38
N.R. 541 18

Cromer and B.C. Teachers' Federation (Re) (1986), 29 D.L.R. (4th) 641,
[1986] 5 W.W.R. 638, 4 B.C.L.R. (2d) 273, 24 C.R.R. 271 (C.A.) 24, 31

Dartmouth College v. Woodward, 17 U.S. (4 Wheat.) 518 (1819) 116

Denison v. Fawcett (1958), 12 D.L.R. (2d) 537, [1958] O.R. 312 (C.A.) ... 108

Dennis v. United States, 339 U.S. 162, 94 L. Ed. 763 (1950) 109

Director of Investigation & Research, Combines Investigation
Branch v. Southam Inc. See Hunter v. Southam Inc.

Dixon v. British Columbia (A.G.) (1989), 60 D.L.R. (4th) 445, 37
B.C.L.R. (2d) 231 (S.C.); leave to appeal to C.A. granted 43

Dobson v. Winton & Robbins Ltd., [1959] S.C.R. 775, 20 D.L.R.
(2d) 164 109

Dolphin Delivery. See Retail, Wholesale & Department Store
Union, Loc. 580 v. Dolphin Delivery Ltd.

Duckworth v. R., unreported, File No. A-179-81, October 10, 1989
(F.C.A.); leave to appeal to S.C.C. refused 91

Duke v. R., [1972] S.C.R. 917, 28 D.L.R. (3d) 129, 7 C.C.C. (2d) 474, 18
C.R.N.S. 302 19

Edmonton Journal and Alberta (A.G.) (Re) (1983), 146 D.L.R. (3d)
673, 4 C.C.C. (3d) 59, [1983] 3 W.W.R. 141 (sub nom. R. v. G.B.), 24
Alta. L.R. (2d) 226, 42 A.R. 383, 4 C.R.R. 296 (Q.B.) 24

Edwards et al. v. Harris-Intertype (Canada) Ltd. (1983), 40 O.R. (2d)
558 (H.C.J.); affd. 9 D.L.R. (4th) 319, 46 O.R. (2d) 286 (C.A.) 109

Edwards Books. *See* R. v. Edwards Books & Art Ltd.
Entick v. Carrington (1765), 19 State Tr. 1029 .... 18, 122
F.P. Publications (Western) Ltd. and R. (Re) (1979), 108 D.L.R.
    (3d) 153, 51 C.C.C. (2d) 110, [1980] 1 W.W.R. 504, 2 Man. R.
    (2d) 1 (C.A.) 14, 81
Family & Children's Services of Kings County v. E.D. (1988), 86
    N.S.R. (2d) 204, 12 R.F.L. (3d) 104 (C.A.) 46, 52
Ford v. Quebec (A.G.), [1988] 2 S.C.R. 712, 54 D.L.R. (4th) 577, 19
    Q.A.C. 69, 90 N.R. 84 (*sub nom.* Chaussure Brown's Inc. v.
    Quebec), 10 C.H.R.R. D/5559, 36 C.R.R. 1 .... 13, 19, 29, 47, 121, 154
Forsythe v. R., [1980] 2 S.C.R. 268, 112 D.L.R. (3d) 385, 53 C.C.C. (2d)
    225, 15 C.R. (3d) 280, 32 N.R. 520 131
Fowler v. Rhode Island, 345 U.S. 67 (1952) 162
Gay Alliance Toward Equality v. Vancouver Sun, [1979] 2 S.C.R.
    435, 97 D.L.R. (3d) 577, [1979] 4 W.W.R. 118, 10 B.C.L.R. 257,
    27 N.R. 117 122
Geduldig v. Aiello, 417 U.S. 484 (1974) 90
General Electric Co. v. Gilbert, 429 U.S. 125 (1976) 90
Gershman v. Manitoba Vegetable Producers' Marketing Bd.
    (1976), 69 D.L.R. (3d) 114, [1976] 4 W.W.R. 406 (Man. C.A.) 106, 108
Greenya v. George Washington University, 512 F. 2d 556
    (D.C. Cir., 1975) 102
Grimshaw v. Ford Motor Co., 174 Cal. Rptr. 348, 119 Cal. App. 3d
    757 (1981) 108
Grondin v. Ontario (A.G.) (1988), 65 O.R. (2d) 427 (H.C.J.) 43
Guildford v. Anglo-French Steamship Co. (1884), 9 S.C.R. 303 108
H.L. Weiss Forwarding Ltd. v. Omnus et al., [1976] 1 S.C.R. 776,
    63 D.L.R. (3d) 654, 5 N.R. 511, 20 C.P.R. (2d) 93 106
Hadley v. Baxendale (1854), 9 Ex. 341, 156 E.R. 145 138
Haig v. Bamford, [1977] 1 S.C.R. 466, 72 D.L.R. (3d) 68, [1976]
    3 W.W.R. 331, 9 N.R. 43, 27 C.P.R. (2d) 149 138
Harrison v. Carswell, [1976] 2 S.C.R. 200, 62 D.L.R. (3d) 68, 25 C.C.C.
    (2d) 186, 75 C.L.L.C. ¶14,286, [1975] 6 W.W.R. 673, 5 N.R. 523 .. 125, 165
Harvey Foods Ltd. v. Reid (1971), 18 D.L.R. (3d) 90, 3 N.B.R. (2d)
    444 (C.A.) 109
Hedley, Byrne & Co. v. Heller & Partners Ltd., [1964] A.C. 465 (H.L.) 138
Heydon's Case (1584), 3 Co. Rep. 7a, 76 E.R. 637 88
Hunter v. Southam Inc., [1984] 2 S.C.R. 145, 11 D.L.R. (4th) 641,
    14 C.C.C. (3d) 97, 41 C.R. (3d) 97, [1984] 6 W.W.R. 577 (*sub nom.*
    Director of Investigation & Research, Combines Investigation
    Branch v. Southam Inc.), 33 Alta. L.R. (2d) 193, 55 A.R. 291, 55
    N.R. 241, 27 B.L.R. 297, 2 C.P.R. (3d) 1, 9 C.R.R. 355, 84 D.T.C. 6467
    .... 5, 8, 13, 17, 28, 47, 71, 100, 115,
    117, 121, 122, 135, 141, 155, 159, 187, 190, 191

Ins. Corp. of B.C. v. Heerspink, [1982] 2 S.C.R. 145, 137 D.L.R. (3d)
219, [1983] 1 W.W.R. 137, 39 B.C.L.R. 145, 43 N.R. 168, [1982]
I.L.R. 1-1555 153
Irwin Toy Ltd. v. Quebec (A.G.) (1986), 32 D.L.R. (4th) 641, 14 C.P.R.
(3d) 60, 26 C.R.R. 193 (Que. C.A.); revd. [1989] 1 S.C.R. 927, 58 D.L.R.
(4th) 577, 24 Q.A.C. 2, 94 N.R. 167, 25 C.P.R. (3d) 417, 39 C.R.R.
193 ....9, 17, 31, 46, 47, 69, 74, 100, 115, 121, 125, 131, 135, 143, 152, 169
Jabour v. Law Society of British Columbia. *See* Canada (A.G.) v. Law
Society of British Columbia
Lavigne and Ontario Public Service Employees Union (Re) (1986),
29 D.L.R. (4th) 321, 86 C.L.L.C. ¶14,039, 55 O.R. (2d) 449 (H.C.J.);
revd. 56 D.L.R. (4th) 474, 89 C.L.L.C. ¶14,011, 67 O.R. (2d) 536, 31
O.A.C. 40, 37 C.R.R. 193 (C.A.); leave to appeal to S.C.C. granted 57
D.L.R. (4th) vii, 68 O.R. (2d) x, 37 O.A.C. 44n, 102 N.R. 158n, 39 C.R.R.
192n 46, 59, 61
Law Society of Upper Canada v. Skapinker, [1984] 1 S.C.R. 357, 9
D.L.R. (4th) 161, 11 C.C.C. (3d) 481, 3 O.A.C. 321, 53 N.R. 169, 8
C.R.R. 193 ....52, 71, 83, 157
Luscher and Deputy Minister, Revenue Canada Customs &
Excise (Re) (1983), 149 D.L.R. (3d) 243 (B.C. Co. Ct.); revd. [1985]
1 F.C. 85, 17 D.L.R. (4th) 503, 45 C.R. (3d) 81, 57 N.R. 386, 15 C.R.R.
167, 9 C.E.R. 229, [1985] 1 C.T.C. 246 (C.A.) 74
Manitoba Rice Farmers' Assn. v. Manitoba Human Rights Commn.
See Apsit v. Manitoba Human Rights Commn.
McEvoy v. New Brunswick (A.G.), [1983] 1 S.C.R. 704, 148 D.L.R.
(3d) 25, 4 C.C.C. (3d) 289, 46 N.B.R. (2d) 219 (*sub. nom.* Re Court
of Unified Criminal Jurisdiction; McEvoy v. New Brunswick
(A.G.)), 48 N.R. 228 18
McKinney and Bd. of Governors of the University of Guelph (Re)
(1987), 46 D.L.R. (4th) 193, 63 O.R. (2d) 1, 24 O.A.C. 241, 37
C.R.R. 44 (C.A.); affd. 76 D.L.R. (4th) 545, 91 C.L.L.C. ¶17,004,
2 O.R. (3d) 319n (S.C.C.) 38, 102, 115, 159, 163, 203
Miller and Cockriell v. R., [1977] 2 S.C.R. 680, 30 C.R.N.S. 372n 170
Mills v. R., [1986] 1 S.C.R. 863, 29 D.L.R. (4th) 161, 26 C.C.C. (3d)
481, 52 C.R. (3d) 1, 58 O.R. (2d) 543n, 16 O.A.C. 81, 67 N.R. 241, 21
C.R.R. 76 ....160, 178
Morgentaler. *See* R. v. Morgentaler
Naken v. General Motors of Canada Ltd., [1983] 1 S.C.R. 72, 144
D.L.R. (3d) 385, 46 N.R. 139, 32 C.P.C. 138 108
Nantel v. Parisien et al. (1981), 18 C.C.L.T. 79, 22 R.P.R. 1 (Ont.
H.C.J.) 138
New Brunswick Electrical Power Commn. v. Int. Brotherhood of
Electrical Workers, Loc. 1733 (1978), 22 N.B.R. (2d) 364
(Q.B.) 106, 108, 138

Newfoundland Assn. of Public Employees v. Newfoundland
(1985), 85 C.L.L.C. ¶14,020, 53 Nfld. & P.E.I.R. 1, 14 C.R.R. 193
(Nfld. S.C.) 71
Nova Scotia (A.G.) v. Phillips (1986), 34 D.L.R. (4th) 633, 76 N.S.R.
(2d) 240 (sub nom. Phillips v. Nova Scotia (Social Assistance
Appeal Bd.), 26 C.R.R. 332 (C.A.) 48, 81
Oakes. See R. v. Oakes
Ontario Film & Video Appreciation Society and Ontario Bd. of
Censors (Re) (1983), 147 D.L.R. (3d) 58, 34 C.R. (3d) 73, 41 O.R.
(2d) 583 (Div. Ct.); affd. 5 D.L.R. (4th) 766, 38 C.R. (3d) 271, 45
O.R. (2d) 80, 2 O.A.C. 388, 7 C.R.R. 129 (C.A.); leave to appeal
to S.C.C. granted 3 O.A.C. 318 ....29, 74
Ontario Human Rights Commn. v. Borough of Etobicoke, [1982]
1 S.C.R. 202, 132 D.L.R. (3d) 14, 82 C.L.L.C. ¶17,005, 40 N.R. 159,
3 C.H.R.R. D/781 153
Ontario Human Rights Commn. and O'Malley v. Simpsons-
Sears Ltd., [1985] 2 S.C.R. 536, 23 D.L.R. (4th) 321, 86 C.L.L.C.
¶17,002, 52 O.R. (2d) 799n, 12 O.A.C. 241, 64 N.R. 161, 7 C.H.R.R.
D/3102 153
Operation Dismantle Inc. v. R., [1985] 1 S.C.R. 441, 18 D.L.R. (4th)
481, 59 N.R. 1, 12 Admin. L.R. 16, 13 C.R.R. 287 ....2, 11, 17, 18, 19,
26, 38, 46, 48, 49, 58, 102, 117, 143, 165, 169, 170
Phillips v. Nova Scotia (Social Assistance Appeal Bd.). See Nova
Scotia (A.G.) v. Phillips
Printing & Numerical Registering Co. v. Sampson (1875), L.R.
19 Eq. 462 ....104, 105, 118
Prior v. Canada, [1988] 2 F.C. 371, 18 F.T.R. 227, [1988] 1 C.T.C.
241, 88 D.T.C. 6207 (T.D.) 91, 166
Pro Arts, Inc. v. Campus Crafts Holdings Ltd. (1980), 110 D.L.R.
(3d) 366, 28 O.R. (2d) 422, 10 B.L.R. 1, 50 C.P.R. (2d) 230 (H.C.J.) 106
Public Service Alliance of Canada v. R. in right of Canada, [1984]
2 F.C. 889, 11 D.L.R. (4th) 387, 84 C.L.L.C. ¶14,054, 55 N.R. 285,
11 C.R.R. 97 (C.A.); affd. [1987] 1 S.C.R. 424, 38 D.L.R. (4th)
249, 87 C.L.L.C. ¶14,022, 75 N.R. 161, 32 C.R.R. 114 ....100, 112, 127
Qually v. Qually, [1987] 2 W.W.R. 553, 56 Sask. R. 165, 5 R.F.L. (3d)
365 (Q.B.) 12
Quebec Assn. of Protestant School Bds. v. Quebec (A.G.) (No. 2) (1982),
140 D.L.R. (3d) 33, [1982] C.S. 673, 3 C.R.R. 114 (Que.); affd. 1 D.L.R.
(4th) 573, [1983] C.A. 77, 7 C.R.R. 139; affd. [1984] 2 S.C.R. 66,
10 D.L.R. (4th) 321, 54 N.R. 196, 9 C.R.R. 133 ....10, 27, 102, 118, 135
Quebec Protestant School Bds. See Quebec Assn. of Protestant
School Bds. v. Quebec (A.G.) (No. 2)
Rahn v. R., [1985] 1 S.C.R. 659, 19 D.L.R. (4th) 126, 18 C.C.C. (3d) 516,

45 C.R. (3d) 134, [1985] 5 W.W.R. 190, 38 Alta. L.R. (2d) 97, 61
A.R. 56, 59 N.R. 144, 14 C.R.R. 1 19
Reference re Anti-Inflation Act, [1976] 2 S.C.R. 373, 68 D.L.R. (3d)
452, 9 N.R. 541 ....127, 163
Reference re Bill 30, An Act to Amend the Education Act (Ont.),
[1987] 1 S.C.R. 1148, 40 D.L.R. (4th) 18, 22 O.A.C. 321, 77 N.R.
241, 36 C.R.R. 305 47
Reference re Constitutional Validity of Section 12 of the Juvenile
Delinquents Act. *See* Southam Inc. and R. (No. 1) (Re)
Reference re Manitoba Language Rights, [1985] 1 S.C.R. 721, 19 D.L.R.
(4th) 1, [1985] 4 W.W.R. 385, 35 Man. R. (2d) 83, 59 N.R. 321 57
Reference re Public Service Employee Relations Act (Alta.), [1987]
1 S.C.R. 313, 38 D.L.R. (4th) 161, 87 C.L.L.C. ¶14,021, [1987] 3
W.W.R. 577, 51 Alta. L.R. (2d) 97, 78 A.R. 1, 74 N.R. 99, 28 C.R.R.
305 (*sub nom.* Alberta Union of Provincial Employees v. Alberta
(A.G.)), [1987] D.L.Q. 225 ....37, 39, 59, 63, 69,
70, 81, 83, 95, 98, 103, 113, 117, 123, 128, 132, 134, 159, 164, 168, 169, 173
Reference re Section 94(2) of the Motor Vehicle Act (B.C.), [1985] 2
S.C.R. 486, 24 D.L.R. (4th) 536, 23 C.C.C. (3d) 289, 48 C.R. (3d) 289,
[1986] 1 W.W.R. 481, 69 B.C.L.R. 145, 63 N.R. 266, 18 C.R.R. 30,
36 M.V.R. 240 ....15, 18, 23, 26, 29, 32, 57,
58, 158, 165, 177, 184, 190, 191, 193
R. v. Agawa (1988), 53 D.L.R. (4th) 101, 43 C.C.C. (3d) 266, 65 O.R.
(2d) 505, 28 O.A.C. 201 (C.A.); leave to appeal to S.C.C. refused
November 8, 1990 ....77, 81
R. v. Andrews and Smith (1988), 43 C.C.C. (3d) 193, 65 C.R. (3d) 320,
65 O.R. (2d) 161, 28 O.A.C. 161, 39 C.R.R. 36 (C.A.); leave to
appeal to S.C.C. granted June 9, 1989 ....89, 101
R. v. Askov (1990), 74 D.L.R. (4th) 355, 59 C.C.C. (3d) 449, 79 C.R. (3d)
273, 75 O.R. (2d) 673, 113 N.R. 241, 49 C.R.R. 1 (S.C.C.) 70
R. v. Banville (1983), 145 D.L.R. (3d) 595, 3 C.C.C. (3d) 312, 34 C.R. (3d)
20, 45 N.B.R. (2d) 134, 5 C.R.R. 142 (Q.B.)..24
R. v. Big M Drug Mart Ltd., [1985] 1 S.C.R. 295, 18 D.L.R. (4th) 321, 18
C.C.C. (3d) 385, 85 C.L.L.C. ¶14,023, [1985] 3 W.W.R. 481, 37 Alta. L.R.
(2d) 97, 60 A.R. 161, 58 N.R. 81, 13 C.R.R. 64 ....3, 8, 11, 13,
17, 23, 26, 29, 31, 32, 33, 34, 47, 48, 59, 71, 74, 84, 101, 109, 113, 115, 121, 122,
135, 137, 138, 150, 152, 153, 166, 169, 182, 183, 185, 187, 193
R. v. Cancoil Thermal Corp. and Parkinson (1986), 27 C.C.C. (3d) 295, 52
C.R. (3d) 188, 14 O.A.C. 225, 11 C.C.E.L. 219, 23 C.R.R. 257 (C.A.) ...121
R. v. City of Sault Ste. Marie, [1978] 2 S.C.R. 1299, 85 D.L.R. (3d) 161,
40 C.C.C. (2d) 353, 3 C.R. (3d) 30, 21 N.R. 295, 7 C.E.L.R. 53 127
R. v. Doug Rankine Co. and Act III Video Productions Ltd. (1983),
9 C.C.C. (3d) 53, 36 C.R. (3d) 154 (Ont. Co. Ct.) 74

R. v. Edwards Books & Arts Ltd., [1986] 2 S.C.R. 713, 35 D.L.R. (4th) 1,
30 C.C.C. (3d) 385, 55 C.R. (3d) 193, 87 C.L.L.C. ¶14,001, 58 O.R.
(2d) 442*n*, 19 O.A.C. 239, 71 N.R. 161, 28 C.R.R. 1 ....3, 8, 15, 23,
25, 27, 28, 32, 33, 62, 70, 71, 79, 80, 89, 97, 102, 117, 121, 131, 132, 139, 143,
150, 155, 159, 162, 164, 169, 172
R. v. G.B. *See* Edmonton Journal and Alberta (A.G.) (Re)
R. v. Hess, [1949] 4 D.L.R. 199, 94 C.C.C. 57, 8 C.R. 52, [1949]
1 W.W.R. 586 (B.C.C.A.) 145
R. v. Jones, [1986] 2 S.C.R. 284, 31 D.L.R. (4th) 569, 28 C.C.C. (3d) 513,
[1986] 6 W.W.R. 577, 47 Alta. L.R. (2d) 97, 73 A.R. 133, 69 N.R.
241, 25 C.R.R. 63 ....39, 155, 156, 159, 162, 164, 183, 192
R. v. Keegstra (1984), 19 C.C.C. (3d) 254 (Alta. Q.B.) 49, 74
R. v. Keegstra (1988), 43 C.C.C. (3d) 150, 65 C.R. (3d) 289, [1988] 5
W.W.R. 211, 60 Alta. L.R. (2d) 1, 87 A.R. 177, 39 C.R.R. 5 (C.A.);
revd. 61 C.C.C. (3d) 1, [1991] 2 W.W.R. 1, 77 Alta. L.R. (2d) 193
(S.C.C.)....................21, 67, 68, 73, 86, 89, 101, 150, 172, 203-04
R. v. Kopyto (1987), 19 O.A.C. 390 (C.A.) 14
R. v. Le Gallant (1985), 47 C.R. (3d) 170, 18 C.R.R. 362 (B.C.S.C.);
revd. 33 D.L.R. (4th) 444, 29 C.C.C. (3d) 291, 54 C.R. (3d) 46, [1986]
6 W.W.R. 372, 6 B.C.L.R. (2d) 105, 35 C.R.R. 287 (C.A.) 30
R. v. Lerke (1984), 11 D.L.R. (4th) 185, 13 C.C.C. (3d) 515, 41 C.R. (3d)
172, 11 C.R.R. 1 (Alta. Q.B.); affd. 25 D.L.R. (4th) 403, 24 C.C.C. (3d)
129, 49 C.R. (3d) 324, [1986] 3 W.W.R. 17, 43 Alta. L.R. (2d) 1, 20
C.R.R. 31 (C.A.) 98
R. v. Marshall (1983), 57 N.S.R. (2d) 286 (C.A.) 14
R. v. Morgentaler (1986), 22 D.L.R. (4th) 641, 22 C.C.C. (3d) 353, 48 C.R.
(3d) 1, 52 O.R. (2d) 353, 11 O.A.C. 81, 17 C.R.R. 223 (C.A.); revd.
[1988] 1 S.C.R. 30, 44 D.L.R. (4th) 385, 37 C.C.C. (3d) 449, 62 C.R.
(3d) 1, 63 O.R. (2d) 281, 26 O.A.C. 1, 82 N.R. 1, 31 C.R.R. 1 ....3, 12,
13, 14, 32, 33, 46, 47, 48, 50, 51, 55, 60, 62, 68, 86, 136, 147, 150, 173-97, 200
R. v. Noble (1984), 14 D.L.R. (4th) 216, 16 C.C.C. (3d) 146, 42 C.R. (3d)
209, 48 O.R. (2d) 643, 6 O.A.C. 11, 12 C.R.R. 138 (C.A.) 29
R. v. Oakes, [1986] 1 S.C.R. 103, 26 D.L.R. (4th) 200, 24 C.C.C. (3d) 321,
50 C.R. (3d) 1, 53 O.R. (2d) 719*n*, 14 O.A.C. 335, 65 N.R. 87, 19 C.R.R.
308 ....17, 18, 22, 29, 32, 47, 66, 68, 102, 111, 113, 114,
148, 149, 153, 154, 155, 156, 157, 158, 159, 164, 165, 169, 179, 180, 185
R. v. Oquataq (1985), 18 C.C.C. (3d) 440, [1985] N.W.T.R. 240, 13
C.R.R. 370 (S.C.) 30, 131
R. v. Quesnel and Quesnel (1979), 51 C.C.C. (2d) 270 (Ont. C.A.) 14, 81
R. v. Red Hot Video Ltd. (1983), 6 C.C.C. (3d) 331, 6 C.R.R. 169 (B.C.
Prov. Ct.); vard. 11 C.C.C. (3d) 389, 10 C.R.R. 377 (Co. Ct.); affd. 18
C.C.C. (3d) 1, 45 C.R. (3d) 36, 15 C.R.R. 206 (C.A.); leave to appeal to
S.C.C. refused 46 C.R. (3d) xxv 74

R. v. Therens, [1985] 1 S.C.R. 613, 18 D.L.R. (4th) 655, 18 C.C.C. (3d)
481, 45 C.R. (3d) 97, [1985] 4 W.W.R. 286, 38 Alta. L.R. (2d) 99, 40
Sask. R. 122, 59 N.R. 122, 13 C.R.R. 193, 32 M.V.R. 153 ....19, 187, 190

R. v. Turpin, [1989] 1 S.C.R. 1296, 48 C.C.C. (3d) 8, 69 C.R. (3d) 97,
34 O.A.C. 115, 96 N.R. 115, 39 C.R.R. 306 148

R. v. Videoflicks Ltd. (1985), 14 D.L.R. (4th) 10, 15 C.C.C. (3d) 353,
48 O.R. (2d) 395, 9 C.R.R. 193, 34 R.P.R. 97 (C.A.); vard. [1986] 2
S.C.R. 713 (*sub nom.* R. v. Edwards Books & Art Ltd.), 35 D.L.R.
(4th) 1, 30 C.C.C. (3d) 385, 55 C.R. (3d) 193, 87 C.L.L.C. ¶14,001, 58
O.R. (2d) 442*n*, 19 O.A.C. 239, 71 N.R. 161, 28 C.R.R. 1 42

R. v. Zundel (1987), 35 D.L.R. (4th) 338, 31 C.C.C. (3d) 97, 56 C.R.
(3d) 1, 58 O.R. (2d) 129, 18 O.A.C. 161, 29 C.R.R. 349 (C.A.);
leave to appeal to S.C.C. refused 61 O.R. (2d) 588*n*, 23 O.A.C.
317*n*, 80 N.R. 317*n* 49, 68, 86, 150

Resolution to Amend the Constitution (Re), [1981] 1 S.C.R. 753,
125 D.L.R. (3d) 1, [1981] 6 W.W.R. 1, 11 Man. R. (2d) 1, 34 Nfld. &
P.E.I.R. 1, 39 N.R. 1 168

Retail, Wholesale & Department Store Union v. Saskatchewan,
[1987] 1 S.C.R. 460, 38 D.L.R. (4th) 277, 87 C.L.L.C. ¶14,023, [1987]
3 W.W.R. 673, 56 Sask. R. 277, 74 N.R. 321 ....30, 46, 58,
62, 63, 69, 95, 97, 102, 110, 115, 119, 151, 164, 165, 169

Retail, Wholesale & Department Store Union, Loc. 580 v. Dolphin
Delivery Ltd., [1986] 2 S.C.R. 573, 33 D.L.R. (4th) 174, 87 C.L.L.C.
¶14,002, [1987] 1 W.W.R. 577, 9 B.C.L.R. (2d) 273, 71 N.R. 83, 38
C.L.L.T. 184, 25 C.R.R. 321, [1987] D.L.Q. 69 ....9, 17, 38, 56,
63, 69, 73, 95, 97, 100, 102, 103, 110, 113, 128, 155

Roberts v. Hopwood, [1925] A.C. 578 (H.L.) 12

Robertson and Rosetanni v. R., [1963] S.C.R. 651, 41 D.L.R. (2d) 485,
[1964] 1 C.C.C. 1, 41 C.R. 392 42

Roe v. Wade, 410 U.S. 113 (1973) 153

Ronald Elwyn Lister Ltd. v. Dunlop Canada Ltd., [1982] 1 S.C.R.
726, 135 D.L.R. (3d) 1, 42 N.R. 181, 18 B.L.R. 1, 41 C.B.R. (N.S.)
272, 65 C.P.R. (2d) 1 ....104, 105, 118

Rookes v. Barnard, [1964] A.C. 1129 (H.L.) 106, 108, 125, 138

Roth v. United States, 354 U.S. 476 (1957) 74

S. (M.K.) v. Nova Scotia (Minister of Community Services) (1988),
86 N.S.R. (2d) 209 (Co. Ct.); affd. 88 N.S.R. (2d) 418, 19 R.F.L.
(3d) 75 (C.A.) 63

Saskatchewan Dairies. *See* Retail, Wholesale & Department Store
Union v. Saskatchewan

Saumur v. City of Quebec, [1953] 2 S.C.R. 299, [1953] 4 D.L.R. 641,
106 C.C.C. 289 ....34, 134

Schachter v. Canada, [1988] 3 F.C. 515, 18 F.T.R. 199, 52 D.L.R.

(4th) 525, 88 C.L.L.C. ¶14,021, 20 C.C.E.L. 301 (T.D.); affd. [1990]
2 F.C. 129, 34 F.T.R. 80*n*, 66 D.L.R. (4th) 635, 108 N.R. 123, 29
C.C.E.L. 113 (C.A.); leave to appeal to S.C.C. granted November
15, 1990 ....48, 133
Scott and British Columbia (A.G.) (Re) (1986), 29 D.L.R. (4th) 544,
[1986] 5 W.W.R. 207, 3 B.C.L.R. (2d) 376, 26 C.R.R. 120 (S.C.) 43
Section 12 of the Juvenile Delinquents Act (Re). *See* Southam Inc. and
R. (No. 1) (Re)
Seneca College of Applied Arts & Technology v. Bhadauria, [1981]
2 S.C.R. 181, 124 D.L.R. (3d) 193, 82 C.L.L.C. ¶14,117, 37 N.R. 455,
14 B.L.R. 157, 17 C.C.L.T. 106, 22 C.P.C. 130 ....38, 98
Shewchuk and Picard (Re) (1986), 28 D.L.R. (4th) 429, [1986] 4 W.W.R.
289, 2 B.C.L.R. (2d) 324, 24 C.R.R. 45, 1 R.F.L. (3d) 337 (C.A.) 81
Singh v. Minister of Employment & Immigration, [1985] 1 S.C.R.
177, 17 D.L.R. (4th) 422, 58 N.R. 1, 12 Admin. L.R. 137, 14 C.R.R. 13
....17, 19, 71, 85, 112, 160, 177, 180, 192
Skokie v. Nationalist Socialist Party of America, 51 Ill. App. 3d 279,
366 N.E. 2d 347 (1977); vard. 69 Ill. 2d 605, 373 N.E. 2d 21 (1978) 21
Slaight Communications Inc. v. Davidson, [1989] 1 S.C.R. 1038, 59
D.L.R. (4th) 416, 89 C.L.L.C. ¶14,031, 93 N.R. 183, 26 C.C.E.L. 85,
40 C.R.R. 100 ....9, 12, 131, 132
Smith v. Cahoon, 283 U.S. 553 (1931) 156
Société des Acadiens du Nouveau-Brunswick Inc. v. Assn. of
Parents for Fairness in Education, [1986] 1 S.C.R. 549, 27 D.L.R.
(4th) 406, 69 N.B.R. (2d) 271, 66 N.R. 173, 23 C.R.R. 119 ....27, 131
Southam. *See* Hunter v. Southam Inc.
Southam Inc. and R. (No. 1) (Re) (1982), 141 D.L.R. (3d) 341, 70
C.C.C. (2d) 257, 30 C.R. (3d) 72 (*sub nom.* Re Section 12 of the
Juvenile Delinquents Act), 38 O.R. (2d) 748, 2 C.R.R. 84 (*sub nom.*
Reference re Constitutional Validity of Section 12 of the Juvenile
Delinquents Act), 29 R.F.L. (2d) 1 (H.C.J.); affd. 146 D.L.R. (3d)
408, 3 C.C.C. (3d) 515, 34 C.R. (3d) 27, 41 O.R. (2d) 113, 6 C.R.R. 1,
33 R.F.L. (2d) 279 (C.A.) 24
Switzman v. Elbing and Quebec (A.G.), [1957] S.C.R. 285, 7 D.L.R.
(2d) 337, 117 C.C.C. 129 ....72, 83
Tomen v. Federation of Women Teachers' Assns. of Ontario
(1987), 43 D.L.R. (4th) 255, 61 O.R. (2d) 489, 34 C.R.R. 349 (H.C.J.);
affd. 61 D.L.R. (4th) 565, 70 O.R. (2d) 48, 34 O.A.C. 343, 42 C.R.R.
158 (C.A.) 81
Toronto Hockey Club v. Arena Gardens Ltd., [1924] 4 D.L.R. 384,
55 O.L.R. 509 (H.C.); affd. [1925] 4 D.L.R. 546, 57 O.L.R. 610 (C.A.);
affd. [1926] 4 D.L.R. 1, [1926] 3 W.W.R. 26 (P.C.) 108
Trask v. R., [1985] 1 S.C.R. 655, 19 D.L.R. (4th) 123, 18 C.C.C. (3d) 514,
45 C.R. (3d) 137, 54 Nfld. & P.E.I.R. 221, 59 N.R. 145 19

Tremblay v. Daigle, [1989] 2 S.C.R. 530, 62 D.L.R. (4th) 634, 27 Q.A.C.
81, 102 N.R. 81 120

Union Colliery of British Columbia v. Bryden, [1899] A.C. 580 (P.C.) ... 134

University of California v. Bakke, 438 U.S. 265 (1978) 36

Valente v. R., [1985] 2 S.C.R. 673, 24 D.L.R. (4th) 161, 23 C.C.C. (3d)
193, 49 C.R. (3d) 97, 52 O.R. (2d) 779*n*, 14 O.A.C. 79, 64 N.R. 1, 19
C.R.R. 354, 37 M.V.R. 9 131

Walter v. Alberta (A.G.), [1969] S.C.R. 383, 3 D.L.R. (3d) 1, 66 W.W.R.
513 80

Williams v. Settle, [1960] 1 W.L.R. 1072, [1960] 2 All E.R. 806 (C.A.) 106

Wilson and Maxsom v. British Columbia (Medical Services
Commn.) (1988), 53 D.L.R. (4th) 171, [1989] 2 W.W.R. 1, 30 B.C.L.R.
(2d) 1, 41 C.R.R. 276 (C.A.); leave to appeal to S.C.C. refused
November 3, 1988 28

Winnipeg School Div. No. 1 v. Craton, [1985] 2 S.C.R. 150, 21 D.L.R.
(4th) 1, [1985] 6 W.W.R. 166, 38 Man. R. (2d) 1, 61 N.R. 241, 8
C.C.E.L. 105 153

CHAPTER 1

INTRODUCTION

Canadians have often resisted the influence of hierarchy, despite their conservative traditions. Over time, they have sought to sever themselves from the apron-strings of, among others, the United States, the United Kingdom and the federal government. In doing so, they have pondered endlessly over the constitutional nature of their polity, in the presence of perceived threats from within and without. They have realized that, within a post-modern society, they are united through differences in identity and resolve. At the same time, they have appreciated that their differences are sources of national disunity, as the failure of the *Meech Lake Accord* suggests.[1]

Against this complex identity of the Canadian polity, *Charter* liberalism unduly circumscribes social practice. In particular, it imposes the personality of the abstract right-holder upon groups — upon Catholics and Protestants, rich and poor, men and women alike. In protecting the rights of the self directed individual who holds herself out against a single foe, the State, *Charter* interpreters bypass the identity crises of groups within the Canadian polity. They concentrate upon conflicts between individuals and government. They pass over social issues that transcend both.[2]

Those jurists who place their faith in so private a realm devise only a narrow bridge between individual rights and governmental authority. In neglecting the social context in which *Charter* rights manifest themselves, they forget that a "free and democratic society" is not delimited by a fixed divide between individual rights and the interests of government. They bypass the social context in which *Charter* rights are debated.

In this book, I seek to reconcile *Charter* liberalism with the modern needs of Canadian society by arguing that private rights are a subset of the social sphere.[3] To distinguish parental discipline from abuse, and consenting sex from sexual assault, is to make a social, not simply a private

---

[1] The text of the *Meech Lake Accord* is reproduced in P.W. Hogg, *Meech Lake Constitutional Accord Annotated* (Toronto: Carswell, 1988).
[2] For the full text of the *Canadian Charter of Rights and Freedoms*, as enacted by the *Canada Act, 1982* (U.K.), c. 11, Schedule B, Part I, see the Appendix, at 205.
[3] See further, *infra*, Chapter 4.

1

choice. It is to acknowledge that human rights are social products, and that civil society transcends the contest between government and individual, labour union and corporation, husband and wife. Here, the nature of human rights is determined communicatively, through debate aimed at comprehension, including awareness of ethnic, cultural and sexual difference. The purpose is to do more than identify individual rights as they are: it is to contextualize them in light of their prospective social benefits and effects. It is to shift them from a narrow liberal conversation to a multifaceted and human context within a participatory democracy. In short, I argue for open dialogue about the *Charter*.

This post-modern alternative, resting in communicative discourse and social practice, affirms more than the status of the private right-holders. It bases participation in civil society upon cultural history, social attitudes and political experience. It includes, as part of that participation, social discourse about the status of pregnant women who assert the inviolability of their bodies, and merchants who wish to open their businesses on Sundays. Reproductive rights, far from being private in the face of government intervention, are unavoidably public. They represent different qualities within civil life, including changing political idealism itself. Moreover, they are tenable only insofar as those qualities are exhibited through functional dialogue. For courts to fill *Charter* gaps, in short, is to identify characteristics within civil life which constitutional accords, not limited to *Meech Lake*, are unable to determine. Equally, it is to debate broader social ends without doing injustice to narrower, but equally tenable, *Charter* purposes conceived by its drafters.

Thus, *Charter* rights are instruments of political life. However readily their interpreters claim only to redress the private rights of individuals, they associate private rights with pragmatic ideals. They perpetuate the rights of corporations and labour unions through a vision of social virtue, dressed up as an agreement in favour of a right to strike, trade, or rest on Sundays. They treat legislative action and executive privilege, in *Operation Dismantle*,[4] as political statements upon which they are not to comment. Courts are motivated by social ends when they ponder their opposition to or defence of nuclear testing in Canadian airspace, or the right to be presumed innocent of a crime until proven guilty. However much they frame these beliefs as juristic rationality, they respond to social explanations for those beliefs, not to rights *per se*.[5]

To demythologize private rights as the totality of the "good life" under the *Charter* is not to dispute the protection which they give to individuals. However, to restrict those rights to a private sphere, in

---

[4]   *Operation Dismantle Inc. v. R.*, [1985] 1 S.C.R. 441.
[5]   See further, *infra*, Chapter 5.

Morgentaler,[6] *Big M Drug Mart,*[7] or *Edwards Books,*[8] is to risk overshadowing the *Charter's* other communicative functions. It is in respect of these other functions that *Charter* jurisprudence is most in need of development if it is to serve as a vehicle of national reconciliation. It is with those functions that I am concerned.

Charter principles are not carved in stone. Nor do they stand out for their "obvious" justice. Their importance lies in their acknowledgment that any formal instrument of law, inevitably, is an incomplete expression of human understanding. In effect, the text of the *Charter* itself does not constitute law in action; it is only an instrument of those who embark upon social action. Thus, judges are not slaves to the *Charter's* irrefutable logic, or creatures of its inalterable rationality. Like other interactive groups within the polity, they are confined by social discussion about the *Charter*, not by the exclusivity of the literal meaning of its phraseology. For them, the *Charter* is not an "empty promised land", as Albert Camus would have it,[9] but an open terrain for discourse into the quality of rights, including their distributive effects. Here, *Charter* provisions succumb to disparate beliefs, not fixed visions about the "good life". They offer no self-evident superstructure within themselves, nor one indisputable hierarchy upon which to evolve. They provide perforated principles devised and applied within an imperfect polity. Judges idealize *Charter* principles in their image of them. They construct *Charter* rights more as they believe they should than in response to self-evident truths. So impelled, courts cultivate relationships between belief and truth. They embark upon social action through legal discourse; and they replace truth with sentiment about the virtue of constitutionalizing rights.[10]

In arguing for *Charter* jurisprudence beyond both private right-holding and governmental interests, I avoid the nihilist rebellion against all things past. Nor do I adopt Nietzsche's view that moral idealism is dead. My quest is for community through communication. My goal is to ensure that, through such social dialogue, diverse peoples can be "socially situated" within the polity without becoming "socially saturated" by it.[11] Within this framework, *Charter* rights represent unfolding thoughts that affect social action. They are not products of one determinative ideology advanced by one philosopher king, prime minister or premier. No one

---

6   *R. v. Morgentaler*, [1988] 1 S.C.R. 30.
7   *R. v. Big M Drug Mart Ltd.*, [1985] 1 S.C.R. 295, at 344.
8   *R. v. Edwards Books & Art Ltd.*, [1986] 2 S.C.R. 713.
9   *The Rebel*, trans. A. Bower (New York: Vintage Books, 1956), p. 305.
10 See further, *infra*, Chapters 2 and 5.
11 See in general hereon, *infra*, Chapter 3. See too, A.C. Hutchinson, "Talking the Good Life: From Liberal Chatter to Democratic Conversation", in *Law and the Community: The End of Individualism?*, A.C. Hutchinson and L.J. Green, eds. (Toronto: Carswell, 1989), p. 151, at 169.

right or cultural identity is naturally or logically determinative. Each is chosen in light of communicative dialogue about it. Each is ascribed social properties, not assumed to have them in the first place. To effect these ends is to delineate the *Charter's* function according to its use and effect. It is to move the *Charter* beyond the subjects which comprise it. It is to treat its text as open-ended, without one fixed meaning or predetermined application.

Undoubtedly, some will criticize this approach for introducing too much politics into law, for failing to articulate a unified vision of communicative discourse, and for subjugating individual rights in favour of social action.[12] They will envisage the *Charter* as a means of redressing tension between the State and civil society. They likely will fear my approach for submerging that tension within dubious discourse into the status of French Canadians, aboriginal peoples, women, and other disadvantaged groups. I have a direct answer: these debates are unavoidable. They have already occurred and they will likely continue in the future, as much through *Charter* interpretation as outside of it. Judges who strive to be nonpartisan in political life can isolate themselves from such debate only artificially, not in fact. By raising barriers to social conversation, they lose the opportunity to participate in social life. Indeed, they separate the act of judging from the reality of being judged. They cling to a hopelessly outmoded legacy of self-defining rights. They fail to appreciate that

> [t]he *Charter* cannot just be slipped into a new compartment in the legal mind marked *"Charter* law". It must become an integral part of our legal consciousness if it is to take its proper place in our constitutional evolution.[13]

The alternative is to appreciate that, beyond governmental interests and individual rights, are the collective interests of francophone Canadians, Seventh Day Adventists, women, Jews, blacks, and anti-nuclear activists. Each group has a distinctive role to play within a participatory democracy. Each transcends the formal hierarchy of government and individual; and each is constituted as much in its own distinctive image as in terms of stereotyped rights that are ascribed uniformly to it. To construe the *Charter* in light of such communicative action, arguably, is to seek political harmony among diverse peoples. To do otherwise is to foist upon ethnic, linguistic, and religious minorities one dominant unity based on one pervasive conception of human rights. It is to limit communicative discourse to relations of dominance. It is to raise rights above

---

[12]   A parallel debate sometimes is attributed to the "corporatist state". A monolithic power, it consumes the resources of civil society, stifling individual initiative in the process. See further, *infra*, Chapter 4.

[13]   N. Lyon, "An Essay on Constitutional Interpretation" (1988), 26 Osgoode Hall L.J. 95, at 99.

their social ramifications, and ultimately to defeat the ends of substantive justice.

The vision of communicative action advanced above is not just possible under the *Charter*; it is necessary, precisely because of the difficulty to effect constitutional reform by formal and non-dialectic means. Through that discursive vision, the *Charter* serves as a wide-angled lens, indeed, a focal point from which to gaze in upon Canadian society, to observe it in action. It is also an instrument through which to mediate among divergent views about social justice itself.

Undoubtedly, some will argue that to treat the *Charter* as a monitor of social action and a focal point for communal dialogue is unduly idealistic. I defend myself: idealism is the seed of thought, far less its negation. Central to any conception of liberty, both liberal and communitarian, is an idealistic spirit. To critique it, in effect, is to challenge thought itself. To criticize a communitarian conception of liberty, then, is not to quarrel with its abstract presentation, but its collective spirit.

Charter interpreters might still be unwilling to acknowledge this collective spirit in deference to legal tradition itself. After all, Canadian lawyers are schooled in analytical legal positivism,[14] not in moral and social theory. However, for them to perpetuate that tradition — and still expect the *Charter* to provide social justice — is to want their cake and eat it too. They cannot insist that *Charter* principles be self-evident and yet define them in light of their own brand of social action, without committing a tautological error. They cannot impute self-evident rights to autonomous individuals, yet recognize higher interests that derogate from those rights. They cannot have it both ways.

Unity of thought, under the *Charter* as elsewhere, is forever elusive. Like the magician's trick, once you think you have mastered it, you must re-examine your premises. The *Charter* is much the same. The end is not to achieve one determinative good, or one national spirit, to the exclusion of all others. The purpose is to be amenable to communicative discourse, and to reflect upon difference in ideology and methodology in doing so. The goal is to avoid placing *Charter* rights within a constitutional hierarchy that admits of exclusive answers, displacing debate about their divergent virtues. The end is to transcend obvious constitutional principles and rights.

Charter rights are far more than stationary beacons, fixed in time, place and space. "Drafted with an eye to the future", they render the society itself "capable of growth and development over time to meet new social, political and historical realities".[15] Whether the *Charter* makes a positive difference is ultimately up to those who make it grow, or retard it.

---

[14] See further, *infra*, Chapters 2 and 5.
[15] *Hunter v. Southam Inc.*, [1984] 2 S.C.R. 145, at 155.

CHAPTER 2

LIBERATING LIBERTY

In this chapter, I challenge the resort to a wholly negative theory of individual rights under the *Charter*. In its place, I argue for a more positive theory in which rights are conceived of communally rather than individually, collectively rather than personally. Here, judges who embark upon a positive agenda extend rights to groups who are unable to exercise their negative liberties. They affirm rights that would otherwise remain wholly dormant. Arguably, this assertion of community rights is both explicit and implicit in the *Charter*. It is explicit in protecting aboriginal rights under s. 25, in promoting the status of disadvantaged groups under s. 15(2), and in advancing a multicultural heritage in Canada under s. 27. It is implicit in asserting individual liberties under ss. 2 and 7-14, and in recognizing that to protect "everyone's" liberty from government is to affirm liberty as a social interest as well.

Negative concepts of liberty allow the individual only the opportunity to pursue her own ends. They do not pay heed to the internal and external obstacles that impede her from doing so. In particular, they pass over the individual's personal fears and insecurities, along with the extent to which she is forced to submit to others who are not so impeded. As a result, the State receives no mandate to support the individual beyond its duty to protect her opportunity to act freely, however useless that opportunity might be in fact.

Positive liberty, in contrast, does require the State to act in support of the individual. In particular, the State is responsible to provide the individual with the affirmative means of redressing the internal and external obstacles that impede her freedom of action. These affirmative means, most often, require that the State remove obstacles to the enjoyment of the rights of comparably disadvantaged groups and are construed collectively.

This communal conception of rights is far wider than the negative liberty of individuals. It addresses social relations beyond individual and government. It embraces the distinctiveness of groups, along with the unity of individual rights. It recognizes that social interests encompass the needs and interests of individuals and groups. After all, the protection of individual rights is itself a social choice.

STATE INTERESTS

> [The *Charter*] . . . is intended to constrain governmental action inconsistent with . . . rights and freedoms; it is not in itself an authorization for governmental action.[1]

The *Charter* is usually construed as redressing the ills of a dominant dualism: the opposition between State interests and individual rights. Directed at averting the negative effect of State intrusion upon individual rights, it supposedly authorizes defensive action. The individual is free, not to enjoy the benefit of public life, but to thwart government from depriving her of her private rights. Collective action is determined by the legislature or executive: courts are required to affirm that action, not displace it. Judges are responsible to correct injustices done to individuals by the State.[2] With limited exceptions,[3] they are not to advantage disadvantaged groups at the expense of either individuals or the State. Nor are they to redistribute social resources independently of the State.

Commencing with the free individual, liberty also ends with her: the quality of social life is a consequence of her autonomy. Thus, s. 15 of the *Charter* is deemed not to

> . . . provide for equality between individuals or groups within society in a general or abstract sense, nor . . . impose on individuals or groups an obligation to accord equal treatment to others.[4]

Despite the Supreme Court's adoption of a purposive approach to interpretation in *R. v. Big M Drug Mart Ltd.*,[5] its approach towards rights is still largely libertarian. To permit groups to insist upon a Sunday of rest in *R. v. Edwards Books & Art Ltd.*[6] is simply to enforce a plurality of individual rights under the *Charter*, not to redress group disadvantage. That groups might wish to acquire rights not overtly entrenched in the

---

[1] *Hunter v. Southam Inc.* (hereafter referred to as *Southam*), [1984] 2 S.C.R. 145, at 156 *per* Dickson J. (as he then was).

[2] On corrective justice in relation to freedom of expression, see A.A. Borovoy, "Freedom of Expression: Some Recurring Impediments", in *Justice Beyond Orwell*, R.S. Abella and M.L. Rothman, eds. (Montréal: Editions Yvon Blais Inc., 1985), p. 125; S. Braun, "Social and Racial Tolerance and Freedom of Expression in a Democratic Society: Friends or Foes?" (1988), 11 Dalhousie L.J. 471. But *cf.* A.W. MacKay, "Freedom of Expression: Is It All Just Talk?" (1989), 68 Can. Bar Rev. 713; A. Fish, "Hate Promotion and Freedom of Expression: Truth and Consequences" (1989), 2 Can. J.L. & Juris. 111.

[3] As in s. 15 of the *Charter*. See, *infra*, at 27.

[4] *Andrews v. Law Society of British Columbia* (hereafter referred to as *Andrews*), [1989] 1 S.C.R. 143, at 163-64 *per* McIntyre J., dissenting, but speaking for the majority on this point.

[5] (Hereafter referred to as *Big M Drug Mart*), [1985] 1 S.C.R. 295, at 331 *per* Dickson C.J. (as he then was).

[6] (Hereafter referred to as *Edwards Books*), [1986] 2 S.C.R. 713.

Charter is relegated to the status of social morality, awaiting political action. *Consumer and labour groups are entitled to assert the private rights of their members, but may not collectively impose their power upon those members, or others.* Nor are courts to permit consumer or labour groups to assert their collective rights simply because they are dissatisfied with their disadvantaged status as groups.

Poverty, it would seem, is a private not a public ill. That judges might sympathize with the economic plight of the disadvantaged is one thing. That they might use the *Charter* to respond to political or social inequality, without the sanction of government, is quite another. Notwithstanding the liberalizing effect of *Irwin Toy Ltd. v. Quebec (A.G.)*,[7] courts are "concerned with the application of the law".[8] With few exceptions,[9] *they are not responsible to help the poor at the expense of the rich, or to protect the economically powerless from the economically powerful.* For judges to inject redistributive ends into the *Charter* — to redress welfare interests, unemployment and educational need — is to undermine the autonomy of less needy individuals. Judges who dip into the pot of social resources, however well-intentioned, supposedly skew the distribution of those resources. Those who invoke delegated authority from government to do more, over-extend their function as social activists. In the tradition of *R.W.D.S.U. v. Dolphin Delivery*, the court is to protect the right-holder from a transgressing government, not to serve the disadvantaged in general.[10] According to Mr. Justice McIntyre, "Parliament and the Legislatures have a right and a duty to make laws for the whole community".[11] Courts are not to do so in their stead.

However, judges who restrict liberty to *a priori* private rights, regard-

---

7   (Hereafter referred to as *Irwin Toy*), [1989] 1 S.C.R. 927. The relevant issue here was whether ss. 248 and 249 of the Quebec *Consumer Protection Act*, R.S.Q., c. P-40.1 as amended, which prohibited commercial advertising directed at persons under thirteen years of age, infringed s. 2(*b*) of the *Charter*. The majority of the Supreme Court concluded that these sections of the Act did infringe s. 2(*b*) of the *Charter* but could be saved under s. 1, as they were reasonable limits upon freedom of commercial expression.

8   *Andrews, supra*, note 4, at 164 *per* McIntyre J., dissenting, but speaking for the majority on this point.

9   See, *e.g., Slaight Communications Inc. v. Davidson*, [1989] 1 S.C.R. 1038. Here, the Supreme Court decided that a provision which conferred a discretion upon a labour arbitrator to grant relief for infringements of the *Canada Labour Code*, R.S.C. 1970, c. L-1 (now R.S.C. 1985, c. L-2), impliedly gave the arbitrator jurisdiction to make orders placing limits on *Charter* rights. In this wrongful dismissal case, the employer was required, among other obligations, to provide the employee with a letter of reference without referring to the dismissal.

10   *Retail, Wholesale & Department Store Union, Loc. 580 v. Dolphin Delivery Ltd.* (hereafter referred to as *Dolphin Delivery*), [1986] 2 S.C.R. 573, at 597-99. See too, A.C. Hutchinson and A. Petter, "Private Rights/Public Wrongs: The Liberal Lie of the *Charter*" (1988), 38 U.T.L.J. 278. In this case, locked-out employees were restrained by injunction from what was held to be secondary picketing at Dolphin Delivery. The Supreme Court found that the *Charter* did not apply as the case involved private parties and there was no governmental action.

11   *Andrews, supra*, note 4, at 185.

less of the quality and extent of their enjoyment, perpetuate rather than offset social injustice. They limit liberty to freedom from government, at the expense of liberty as access to rights themselves. Their alternative is to address liberty positively. It is to evaluate rights in light of social inequality itself. Here, positive liberty embodies the substantive right to a tenable quality of life, beyond the abstract right to be free from interference from without. In this sense, positive rights openly embrace a political dimension, not an artificial liberal neutrality.[12]

Certainly, negative rights provide important protection from those who would arbitrarily deny individual liberty. Each individual should have the right to be presumed innocent until proven guilty. Each person should have the right to a jury trial, to counsel, and to trial within a reasonable period of time. These negative rights are necessary aspects of public life, especially within the sphere of criminal law. However, public life is not expressed solely through the negative right to be free from State intervention. Liberty is a manifestation of communal life itself. Being free, like the act of voting, is a shared, not wholly sequestered enterprise. To be an individual is to interact with others, not to subsist wholly apart from them.

THE RHETORIC OF NEGATIVE RIGHTS

The liberal assumption that individuals are entitled to a relatively unimpeded exercise of free will is implicit in Canadian jurisprudence.[13] It is readily illustrated in Chief Justice Deschênes' judgment in *Quebec Assn. of Protestant School Bds. et al. v. Quebec (A.G.) et al. (No. 2)*:

> Every individual in Canada should enjoy his rights to the full . . . and if the group numbers 100 persons, the one hundredth has as much right to benefit from all the privileges of citizens as the other ninety-nine. The alleged restriction of a collective right which would deprive the one hundredth member of the group of the rights guaranteed by the *Charter* constitutes, for this one hundredth member, a real denial of his rights. He cannot simply be counted as an accidental loss in a collective operation: our concept of human beings does not accommodate such a theory.[14]

---

[12]   No doubt I am at odds here with strict logicians who argue that positive liberty encompasses merely the right to liberty, while negative liberty requires that no one else undermine it. Both liberties, they would argue, are merely different sides of the same coin. This rationalization of liberty, however, is short-sighted in not taking account of the politics of rights. Indeed, it is the incapacity of the disadvantaged to exercise negative liberties that justifies affirmative action in their favour. Their positive rights are warranted by the very fact that they are unable to effect their negative interests themselves, and therefore, are reliant upon the development of positive rights that affirm their group interests. See further, *infra*, at 35.

[13]   On the roots of this assumption in classical liberalism, see generally, John Locke, *Two Treatises of Government*, P. Laslet, ed. (Cambridge: Cambridge University Press, 1963). See too, L. Clark, "Liberalism and the Living-Tree: Women, Equality and the Charter" (1990), 28 Alta. L. Rev. 384.

[14]   (1982), 140 D.L.R. (3d) 33, at 64-65 (Que. S.C.).

Negative liberty is also at the centre of modern analytic jurisprudence.[15] As a self-willed being, the individual is entitled to exploit her own human resources, indeed to satisfy her dream of unending wealth. The well-being of others is a byproduct of her happiness, not its determinant.[16] Governmental checks upon her are to be kept to a minimum.[17] That she manages her assets unwisely is her own problem. Ignorance, impecuniosity or bad luck is a private and personal affair. The supposition, a mirage, is that she has only herself to blame for the depleted worth of those assets. Like the corporate shareholder, she advances the value of her own personhood only through her own capacity to trade in it wisely and freely. She lives by that capacity, far more than according to social norms that others impose upon her. Her liberty is the foundation of what she is and ultimately can become: it exists above and beyond her social experiences.[18] Thus, the State is responsible to effectuate her interests equally with the interests of all other people in a free and democratic society. In benefiting her, it supposedly benefits civil society as well.[19]

Charter interpretation is deeply embedded in this rhetoric of negative liberty. Liberty, Chief Justice Dickson reminds us, embodies "an absence of coercion or restraint".[20] Madam Justice Wilson adds, liberty amounts to a "right to pursue one's goals free from government restraint".[21] Plurally construed, each individual adds her proportionate share to the plurality of rights in civil society. To protect her individual world, the court

---

[15] On the roots of neoclassical liberalism, see John Stuart Mill, *On Liberty*, E. Rapaport, ed. (Indianapolis: Hackett, 1978). On the impact of liberalism upon property rights, see A. Offer, *Property and Politics 1870-1914: Landownership, Law, Ideology and Urban Development in England* (New York: Cambridge University Press, 1981); F.H. Underhill, *In Search of Canadian Liberalism* (Toronto: Macmillan, 1960). See too, E.V. Mensch, "The Colonial Origins of Liberal Property Rights" (1982), 31 Buffalo L. Rev. 635.

[16] On the self-interested subject, from an economist's perspective, see O.E. Williamson, "Transaction-Cost Economics: The Governance of Contractual Relations" (1979), 22 J.L. & Econ. 233. See further, P.A. Kropotkin, *Mutual Aid as a Factor in Evolution* (Montreal: Black Rose Books, 1989).

[17] See esp., G. Hardin, "The Tragedy of the Commons", in *The Environmental Handbook*, De Bell, Garrett, comp. (New York: Ballantine Books, 1970).

[18] On the philosophical source of her status, see esp., E. Kant, *Critique of Pure Reason*, trans. K. Smith (London: Macmillan, 1961). See also *Big M Drug Mart, supra*, note 5, at 346 *per* Dickson C.J.

[19] See esp., B.A. Ackerman, *Social Justice in the Liberal State* (New Haven: Yale University Press, 1980); L. Snyder, *Justice or Revolution: America's Choice in the 1980's* (New York: Books in Focus, 1979). But see T.J. Lowi, *The End of Liberalism: Ideology, Policy, and the Crisis of Public Authority* (New York: Norton, 1969).

[20] *Big M Drug Mart, supra*, note 5, at 354.

[21] *Operation Dismantle Inc. v. R.* (hereafter referred to as *Operation Dismantle*), [1985] 1 S.C.R. 441, at 516. In this case, the group, Operation Dismantle, argued that the government's decision to allow the United States to test cruise missiles in Canada increased the risk of nuclear war, thereby infringing s. 7 of the *Charter*. The majority of the Supreme Court ordered their statement of claim struck out and their action dismissed as the possible effects of this experimental action could not be predicted with enough certainty. The dissenting members dismissed the claim on different grounds dealing more directly with the merits.

claims to be neutral between her and other right-holders. It enforces her private choices consistently with the private choices of others. It does not try to save her from herself. Nor does it extend her liberty beyond the limits permitted her by the *Charter*.

> The words of Parliament [*i.e.*, the *Charter*] must be given their ordinary meaning, not some fanciful and imaginative scope that would encourage resourceful counsel and sympathetic judges to make up whatever deficiency they perceive in the existing list of protected rights. Security of the person means no more than the right to physical security.[22]

However, judicial passivity towards the exercise of rights is more akin to partiality. In being so passive, courts favour those who are able to invoke their negative liberties to protect themselves over those who are not so able.[23] "Everyone" has fundamental rights and freedoms under the *Charter*; yet only some are able to invoke them. "Everyone" has the right, under s. 7, not to be deprived of the right to life, liberty and security of the person except in accordance with the principles of fundamental justice;[24] yet only some are able to enjoy that right.

Courts that ignore qualitative differences in the enjoyment of negative liberties adopt the rhetoric of formal equality. Negative right-holders are free to erect fences "over which the state will not be allowed to trespass".[25] Courts, in turn, are required to maintain fences equally for all, whether or not those fences protect barren private land. No court is to erect a pervasive "social philanthropy" by which it threatens the right of every right-holder to decide upon the good life for herself.[26] This proposition is supported by a principle of equality. No individual is to have greater liberty than any other to speak, pray, or be heard. No fundamental right is to be better or worse, more or less determinative, than any other. No right-holder is to be free to invoke her fundamental right to freedom above any other person's right.

With few exceptions, courts are to protect private rights equally, regardless of the economic, social or political standing of the individual.[27] For judges to jeopardize the right of big business to commercial free

---

22　*Qually v. Qually*, [1987] 2 W.W.R. 553, at 558 (Sask. Q.B.). See too, *R. v. Morgentaler* (1986), 22 D.L.R. (4th) 641, at 667-68.

23　See D. Sugarman, "The Legal Boundaries of Liberty: Dicey, Liberalism and Legal Science" (1983), 46 Mod. L. Rev. 102.

24　See also, *Charter*, ss. 2, 3, 6, 8-14, 17, 19, 20, 23, 24.

25　*R. v. Morgentaler* (hereafter referred to as *Morgentaler*), [1988] 1 S.C.R. 30, at 164 *per* Wilson J.

26　The hesitance of courts to engage in social law reform resembling "social philanthropy" is well recorded in the literature. See esp. *Roberts v. Hopwood*, [1925] A.C. 578, at 594 (H.L.), *per* Lord Atkinson; P. Fennell, "*Roberts v. Hopwood*: The Rule Against Socialism" (1986), 13 J.L. & Society 401: A. Petter, "Canada's Charter Flight: Soaring Backwards into the Future" (1989), 16 J.L. & Society 151, at 155.

27　One such exception is *Slaight Communications, supra*, note 9. See, in general, P.W. Hogg,

speech[28] or religion[29] is to undermine the rights of everyone else as well. For them to threaten the private allocation of liberty is to prefer the liberty of some at the expense of others. The purpose of each Charter freedom is to be understood "in light of the interests [the right or freedom] was meant to protect",[30] not for some higher social or moral purpose. That commercial free speech is disproportionately accessible to corporations compared to non-corporations, professionals contrasted with non-professionals, is either bypassed, or more hopefully, taken into account under s. 1 of the *Charter*.[31]

Thus, freedom of expression or association, embedded as an *a priori* right in the *Charter*, seemingly determines its own progeny. The court merely identifies and applies it. The result is judicial deference towards both the substance of *a priori* rights and the constitutional means by which they come into existence. As Chief Justice Dickson declared in *Southam*, "[i]t should not fall to the courts to fill in the details that will render legislative *lacunae* constitutional."[32] It is one thing for judges to invoke the *Charter* to protect the liberty of the well-to-do from government. It is quite another for them to invoke the *Charter* to advantage the unpropertied in relation to the well-to-do. To expect the latter is to expect courts to evaluate the normative effect of human rights upon a diffusely endowed, and disparately privileged, population.

Judges who still insist that "[t]he role of the courts is to map out the ... parameters"[33] of a private fence around the individual, envisage only the limited salvation of the poor and ignorant. In protecting the depersonalized right-holder from the State, they pass over the formidable foe of poverty, bias and distrust that resides within individuals and social groups alike. "For ye have the poor always."[34] Few individuals

---

"Is the Supreme Court of Canada Biased in Constitutional Cases?" (1979), 57 Can. Bar Rev. 721, at 722-25. But *cf.*, J.C. Bakan, "Constitutional Arguments: Interpretation and Legitimacy in Canadian Constitutional Thought" (1989), 27 Osgoode Hall L.J. 123, at 123-25; F.L. Morton, "The Political Impact of the Canadian Charter of Rights and Freedoms" (1987), 20 Can. J. Pol. Sc. 31.

28   See *Ford v. Quebec (A.G.)* (hereafter referred to as *Ford*), [1988] 2 S.C.R. 712. On the right of lawyers to associate through business partnerships, see *Black v. Law Society of Alberta* (1986), 27 D.L.R. (4th) 527 (Alta. C.A.), affd. [1989] 1 S.C.R. 591.

29   See *Big M Drug Mart*, [1985] 1 S.C.R. 295.

30   *Ibid.*, at 359.

31   For a critique of the disproportionate exercise of rights in the Western liberal tradition, see esp., J. Habermas, *Legitimation Crisis*, trans. T. McCarthy (Boston: Beacon Press, 1975). It is interesting to note that Karl Marx founded his social critique upon reconstituting, not in rejecting, private rights. See esp. Marx, "Economic and Philosophical Manuscripts of 1884", in *Early Writings*, trans. T.B. Bottomore (New York: McGraw-Hill, 1964); Marx, *Critique of Hegel's "Philosophy of Right"*, trans. J. O'Malley and A. Jolin (Cambridge: Cambridge University Press, 1970).

32   *Southam*, [1984] 2 S.C.R. 145, at 169 (emphasis added).

33   *Morgentaler, supra*, note 25, at 164 *per* Wilson J.

34   Matthew, 26:11, See too, J. Fudge, "Community or Class: Political Communitarians and Workers' Democracy", in *Law and the Community: The End of Individualism?*, A.C.

have the economic and personal resources to mount a Charter challenge. Few, beyond the corporate wealthy and politically agile, have the stomach for the arduous battle up the judicial ladder to the Supreme Court of Canada.[35] Still fewer have the wherewithal to assist their fellows, through courtroom interventions, class actions and the like.[36] For many, fundamental rights are mythical, however apparent they might be to Charter activists. Some suffer because negative liberty, designed to keep the government out of private life, excludes them from public life. They lose because Madam Justice Wilson's "invisible fence",[37] however potentially useful to defend them against the State, isolates them from the enjoyment of their rights.

Courts that maintain this rhetoric, rather than restructure the public-private divide, perpetuate it.[38] Using the jargon of negative liberty, they give civil society little useful meaning beyond the individual's right not to do anything for it. Freedom of the press, along with other negative liberties, evolves into freedom of property.[39] In applying a uniform test of objective competence equally to all, the court provides a safe place for propertied men and women. That Charter rights are biased against aboriginal peoples or women is viewed as unfortunate, but not necessarily determinative. Certainly, some individuals and groups can alter their economic and political status. However, for the poor and uneducated, that alteration is based largely upon the tolerance of others, not limited to judges. No individual is the absolute determinant of her own destiny. No group enjoys its rights in an identical manner to all other groups. As the Supreme Court of Canada recognizes in *Andrews*, to insist that all individuals and groups be treated alike, despite their differences, is to promote social injustice and inequality, not the contrary.[40]

Hutchinson and L.J. Green, eds. (Toronto: Carswell, 1989), p. 57; H. Glasbeek, "The Corporate Social Responsibility Movement — The Latest in Maginot Lines to Save Capitalism" (1988), 11 Dalhousie L.J. 363; S. Beck, "Corporate Power and Public Policy", in *Consumer Protection, Environmental Law, and the Corporate Power: Studies for the Royal Commission on the Economic Union and Development Prospects for Canada*, I. Bernier and A. Lajoie, eds. (Ottawa, 1985), vol. 50, p. 181. See too, J.W. Singer, "The Player and the Cards: Nihilism and Legal Theory" (1984), 94 Yale L.J. 1, at 60-66.

35   See A. Petter, "The Politics of the Charter" (1986), 8 Supreme Court L.R. 473; A.C. Hutchinson and A. Petter, "Private Rights/Public Wrongs: The Liberal Lie of the Charter" (1988), 38 U.T.L.J. 278.

36   See, *e.g., R. v. Kopyto* (1987), 19 O.A.C. 390. There, the Canadian Civil Liberties Association was refused leave to intervene where the accused lawyer was charged with contempt of court in challenging s. 8 of the *Criminal Code* as violating s. 2(b) freedom of expression.

37   *Morgentaler, supra*, note 25, at 164.

38   For critical commentary, see esp., D. Gibson, "The Charter of Rights and the Private Sector" (1982-83), 12 Man. L.J. 213. On the public-private divide, see, *infra*, at 97.

39   See, *e.g., Re F.P. Publications (Western) Ltd. and R.* (1979), 108 D.L.R. (3d) 153 (Man. C.A.); *R. v. Quesnel and Quesnel* (1979), 51 C.C.C. (2d) 270 (Ont. C.A.); H. Glasbeek, "Comment: Entrenchment of Freedom of Speech for the Press — Fettering of Freedom of Speech for the People", in *The Media, the Courts and the Charter*, P. Anisman and A.M. Linden, eds. (Agincourt: Carswell, 1986), p. 111.

40   *Andrews*, [1989] 1 S.C.R. 143, at 164. See too, *R. v. Marshall* (1983), 57 N.S.R. (2d) 286, at 321 (C.A.).

Rendering rights positive does not, in itself, redress such disproportionate treatment among individuals and groups. Nor does it avoid the prohibitive cost of mounting a *Charter* challenge. However, it does encourage governments and courts alike to adopt an affirmative course of action in relation to such basic needs as shelter, literacy and nourishment. For example, a positive right to security of the person might entail welfare benefits, a right to housing and a defence against trespassing.

The difficulty in attaining this affirmative goal is not that judges are inherently passive, but that they feel constrained to be non-activist. Their dilemma is unenviable. For the most part, they respect the principles of representative democracy. They defer to the legislature, subject to the "reasonable limit" imposed upon it by s. 1 of the *Charter*. In the words of Chief Justice Dickson in *Edwards Books*:

> A "reasonable limit" is one which . . . it was reasonable for the legislature to impose. The courts are not called upon to substitute judicial opinions for legislative ones as to the place at which to draw a precise line.[41]

Supporting the judges' deference towards the legislature is faith in objective reason. Judges supposedly apply the *Charter* to legislation by wholly objective means. They "measure the legislative enactment against the requirements of the *Charter*";[42] and in doing so, they rise above their own personal beliefs in the quality of social justice.

> [U]nless the Court can find that choice [of the Legislature] unreasonable, it has no power under the *Charter* to strike it down or . . . to invade the legislative field and substitute its views for that of the Legislature.[43]

Yet, in coupling deference towards legislative authority with judicial inventiveness, judges engage in a delicate balancing act.[44] They observe, somewhat axiomatically, that the "historic decision to entrench the *Charter*" was not taken by the courts, but by "the representatives of the people".[45] Nevertheless, they assume that they are "entrusted" with a "new and onerous responsibility" to effect its representative design.

> It ought not to be forgotten that the historic decision to entrench the *Charter* in our Constitution was taken not by the courts but by the elected representatives of the people of Canada. *It was those representatives who extended the scope of constitutional adjudication and entrusted the courts with this new and onerous responsibility.*[46]

---

41   *Edwards Books*, [1986] 2 S.C.R. 713, at 781-82.
42   *Andrews, supra*, note 40, at 191 *per* McIntyre J.
43   *Ibid*.
44   See esp. *Reference re Section 94(2) of the Motor Vehicle Act, R.S.B.C. 1979, c. 288 as am. by the Motor Vehicle Amendment Act, 1982 (B.C.), c. 36* (hereafter referred to as *Re B.C. Motor Vehicle Act*), [1985] 2 S.C.R. 486, at 497 *per* Lamer J. (as he then was).
45   *Ibid*.
46   *Ibid*. (emphasis added). See too, B.L. Strayer, "Life under the Canadian Charter: Adjusting the Balance between Legislatures and Courts, [1988] Public Law 347, at 366.

In so positing, courts maintain that they do not choose to be active in protecting negative rights: they are constitutionally required to be so. In contrast, they are not to be active in protecting positive liberty on grounds that governments ought to do so themselves, for example, by invoking s. 15(2) or 33 of the *Charter*.

This restrained form of judicial activism compounds its own defects. Judges who insist that each individual is entitled not to share her assets with others, raise her negative liberties above the interests of the communality. In not requiring her to contribute positively towards that communality, they downplay the social dimensions of her individual rights. In effect, they sever her private rights from civil society, attributing no particular quality to civil society beyond her wholly abstract rights as an individual.

My argument is not against the protection of negative liberties under the *Charter*. Rather, I challenge the supposition that, by enforcing only negative rights, courts exhaust their own affirmative responsibilities. The negative rights of individuals do not constitute the totality of liberty. They are but a part of it. To affirm liberty is to invite debate over the moral content of that liberty, beyond the competitive relationship between individual and State. Thus, liberty is meaningless within a social vacuum: it has a distinctly communal component. Applied to equality rights:

> Every strongly held theory or conception of equality is at once a psychology, an ethic, a theory of social relations, and a vision of the good society.[47]

Judges do not decide cases in blissful disregard of moral values and ethical ends.[48] They are far more than simple determinants of rights. They mediate among alternative social means and ends. They are not impartial between the privileged and the underprivileged, however much they pay lip-service to the rhetoric of classical liberalism.

FORM BEFORE SUBSTANCE: RIGHTS BEFORE RIGHT

The distinction between negative and positive liberty can be traced to the reluctance of courts to determine the substantive content of constitutional rights. Courts supposedly protect individuals by examining only

---

[47]   J.H. Schaar, "Equality of Opportunity and Beyond", in *Equality*, J.R. Pennock and J.W. Chapman, eds. (New York: Atherton Press, 1967), p. 238, cited with approval by McIntyre J. in *Andrews, supra*, note 40, at 164.

[48]   M.J. Sandel, *Liberalism and the Limits of Justice* (Cambridge: Cambridge University Press, 1982), p. 12. See too, K. Greenawalt, "The Enduring Significance of Neutral Principles" (1978), 78 Colum. L. Rev. 982; H. Wellington, "Common Law Rules and Constitutional Double Standards: Some Notes on Adjudication" (1973), 83 Yale L.J. 221; A. Mueller and M.L. Schwartz, "The Principle of Neutral Principles" (1960), 7 U.C.L.A. L. Rev. 571. But see R.M. Dworkin, *Law's Empire* (Cambridge, Mass.: Belknap Press, 1986), pp. 114, 400.

the procedures by which the State constrains rights. They follow the traditions of *R. v. Oakes*:[49] they decide whether governmental objectives are proportionately related to the means of effecting them. They do not decide whether those objectives are substantively fair, except in evaluating them in relation to their effects.[50] Thus, the Supreme Court decided, in *Big M Drug Mart*, whether the objective underlying a Sunday pause day was "of sufficient importance to warrant overriding a constitutionally protected right or freedom".[51] It largely conceded the substantive issue of whether the legislative objective was pressing and substantial.

Judges reinforce their reluctance to engage in substantive discourse by relying upon a formal division between judiciary and legislature within a constitutional democracy. Legislatures supposedly enact laws that promote, displace or otherwise limit individual liberties. Courts develop procedures to ensure that those laws are constitutional. Legislatures choose the means of effecting the interests of a free and democratic society under s. 15(2) or 33 of the *Charter*. Courts determine only whether they do so in a manner that is rational and whether the means they use are necessary. Legislatures constrain individual rights. Judges evaluate whether such legislative action is formally legitimate. In each case, courts — unlike legislatures — proclaim what rights are, not how politics ought to effect them.

> While in political science terms, it is probably acceptable to treat the courts as one of the three fundamental branches of Governments, that is, legislative, executive and judicial, I cannot equate for the purposes of *Charter* application the order of a court with an element of governmental action.[52]

Purposefully excluded from the judicial fold are the broader social, religious and political implications of judicial decision-making. Courts, supposedly, do not decide upon the virtue of government searches and seizures in *Southam*,[53] Sunday closing in *Big M Drug Mart*,[54] or the risk of genocide in *Operation Dismantle*.[55] They judge freedom of expression in light of the principles of a liberal democracy in *Irwin Toy*.[56] They do not judge the social virtue of such liberty. Nor do they judge the substantive virtue of governmental policies that restrict refugee status in *Singh*.[57] They assume instead that, just as legislatures ought not to usurp the function of judges by interpreting their own laws, courts ought not to

---

49 (Hereafter referred to as *Oakes*), [1986] 1 S.C.R. 103.
50 *Ibid.*, at 139. On *Oakes*, see, *infra*, Chapter 5.
51 *Big M Drug Mart*, [1985] 1 S.C.R. 295, at 352.
52 *Per* McIntyre J. in *Dolphin Delivery*, [1986] 2 S.C.R. 573, at 600.
53 See *Southam*, [1984] 2 S.C.R. 145.
54 See *Big M Drug Mart*, *supra*, note 51.
55 *Operation Dismantle*, [1985] 1 S.C.R. 441.
56 *Irwin Toy*, [1989] 1 S.C.R. 927, at 973-78.
57 *Singh v. Minister of Employment & Immigration*, [1985] 1 S.C.R. 177.

make decisions of policy if they are to preserve the autonomy of the legislature in law-making.[58] This view is epitomized by Mr. Justice La Forest in *Andrews*:

> [I]t bears repeating that considerations of institutional functions and resources should make courts extremely wary about questioning legislative and governmental choices . . . [59]

This restrained method of interpreting the *Charter* is reinforced by judicial fear of unbridled and injudicious law-making. The Attorney General of Ontario, in written argument in *Re B.C. Motor Vehicle Act*, for example, warned of the "dangers of a judicial 'super-legislature' beyond the reach of Parliament, the provincial legislatures and the electorate".[60] To a similar effect, courts of law pinpoint an alarming breakdown in the division of power between legislatures and judiciaries. They emphasize, even more, that judges who indulge unchecked in policy-making undermine the credibility of the judiciary itself.[61]

In adhering to this cautious stance, judges supposedly protect the individual's right to be heard and represented by counsel,[62] to speak and be heard.[63] They protect the legislature's conception of public safety and social harmony, not their own. So motivated, the Supreme Court in *Operation Dismantle*,[64] claims only to determine the legitimacy of executive action, not its own view of the substantive merit of that action. It reflects in *Oakes*,[65] less the virtue of a drug-free society, than the means of attaining that end through a statutory reverse onus.

Whether or not the Supreme Court believes the legislature's objectives are virtuous, it treats the legislature as the principal composer of its symphony. Claiming to be merely conductors, judges accept the human rights score given them by the *Charter*, without judging its normative

---

[58] Confining judges to process, as distinct from substantive decision-making, is central to John Hart Ely's theory of judging in *Democracy and Distrust: A Theory of Judicial Review* (Cambridge: Harvard University Press, 1980). See too, P.W. Hogg, "The Charter of Rights and American Theories of Interpretation" (1987), 25 Osgoode Hall L.J. 87. For criticism of Ely's thesis, see esp. L.H. Tribe, "The Puzzling Persistence of Process-Based Constitutional Theories" (1980), 89 Yale L.J. 1063: R.M. Dworkin, "The Forum of Principle", in *A Matter of Principle* (Cambridge: Harvard University Press, 1985). But *cf.* P.J. Monahan, "Judicial Review and Democracy: A Theory of Judicial Review" (1987), 21 U.B.C. L. Rev. 87, at 153-59.

[59] *Andrews, supra,* note 40, at 194.

[60] Cited by Lamer J. in *Re B.C. Motor Vehicle Act, supra,* note 44, at 497.

[61] For a discussion hereon, see *Amax Potash Ltd. v. Govt. of Saskatchewan,* [1977] 2 S.C.R. 576, at 590 *per* Dickson J. (as he then was).

[62] See, *e.g., Canada (A.G.) v. Law Society of British Columbia et al.; Jabour v. Law Society of British Columbia et al.,* [1982] 2 S.C.R. 307. But *cf. Crevier v. Quebec (A.G.),* [1981] 2 S.C.R. 220; *McEvoy v. New Brunswick (A.G.),* [1983] 1 S.C.R. 704.

[63] See Justice Dickson's reference in *Oakes, supra,* note 49, at 157-58, to *Entick v. Carrington* (1765), 19 State Tr. 1029, at 1066, where Lord Camden identified the acquisition and use of property as "the great end for which men entered into society".

[64] *Supra,* note 55.

[65] *Supra,* note 49.

content. They restrict themselves to a world of fair and equal treatment for individuals. They do not judge the fairness of the means by which the legislature intrudes upon human rights. Nor do they judge the quality of the individual's views, as propagated in newspapers, only her right not to be denied the opportunity to advertise in them.[66] Typically stated,

> ... the tribunal which adjudicates upon ... rights must act fairly, in good faith, without bias and in a judicial temper, and must give to [the individual] ... the opportunity adequately to state his case.[67]

The court's realm of justice is formal and procedural, not actual and substantive. Judges restrict their activism under the *Charter* largely to form, not substance, and primarily to criminal challenges.[68] They decide, in *Operation Dismantle*, whether those who challenge the power of the executive have a legitimate cause of action or raise a "justifiable issue".[69] Rather than canvass "legislative facts" that impact upon the substantive quality of constitutional rights, they evaluate the impact of "adjudicative facts" upon the "immediate parties".[70] They are far less concerned about whether the individual's claims are worthy or needy than with protecting her *a priori* entitlement to them.[71] They are interested in "the equal subjection of all classes to a common rule", not with how different classes of persons ought to be treated.

> Equality before the law, interpreted as the equal subjection of all classes to a common rule ... does not in itself imply any qualitative view about the sort of law to which all should be subjected.[72]

This strict division of power between legislature and court unduly simplifies the function of both. It presupposes that judges, in interpreting "the law", somehow can avoid substantively reconstituting it. The illusion is that legislative and judicial processes each prevail within its own autonomous sphere. The legislature establishes policies in relation to hu-

---

66 But see *Ford*, [1988] 2 S.C.R. 712, at 764.
67 *Duke v. R.*, [1972] S.C.R. 917, at 923 *per* Fauteux C.J.
68 See, *e.g.*, *Singh*, *supra*, note 57; *R. v. Therens*, [1985] 1 S.C.R. 613; *Trask v. R.* [1985] 1 S.C.R. 655; *Rahn v. R.*, [1985] 1 S.C.R. 659.
69 See *Operation Dismantle*, *supra*, note 55, at 464-67 *per* Wilson J.
70 On the distinction between legislative and adjudicative facts, see K.C. Davis, "An Approach to Problems of Evidence in the Administrative Process" (1942), 55 Harv. L. Rev. 364.
71 See generally, J.I. Laskin, "Evidentiary Considerations under the Canadian Charter of Rights and Freedoms," unpublished address, cited by W.R. Lederman, "Assessing Competing Values in the Definition of Charter Rights", in *The Canadian Charter of Rights and Freedoms*, 2nd ed. by G.-A. Beaudoin and E. Rutushny (Toronto: Carswell, 1989), p. 127, at 157, n. 62.
72 *Per* G. Marshall, "Notes on the Rule of Equal Law", in *Equality*, J.R. Pennock and J.W. Chapman, eds. (New York: Atherton Press, 1967), p. 263. See too, A.V. Dicey, *Introduction to the Study of the Law of the Constitution*, 10th ed. (London: Macmillan, 1960), pp. 192-94.

man rights. The judge interprets them. The supposition is that judges
are not equipped to engage in public discourse, least of all about the
quality of human rights. In Peter Hogg's opinion:

> They [judges] do not necessarily have much knowledge or expertise
> in public affairs, and after appointment they are expected to remain
> aloof from most public issues.[73]

Judges who insist that they correct injustice only, pass over the distributive consequences of their formal actions. They ignore the fact that
the attitudes of "judges . . . on important social and political issues do
not reflect those of the population at large."[74] They insist upon an equal
right to free speech. However, they pass over the unequal ability of
people to speak, listen and understand. They forget that the status of the
poor and uneducated is far more than a coincidental product of a *laissez
faire* system that protects the right to be poor or uneducated. They forget
that they themselves reinforce inequality of status by protecting those
who are best able to benefit from negative and private liberties from
those who are not so able.

To identify the character of substantive justice, then, is to understand
that people, judges included, decide upon its character differently. Justice
is not simply out there, waiting to be observed and experienced. To
comment upon the procedural worth of legislation is to open the door to
its substantive justification. To identify a "valid and desirable social purpose"[75] within legislation is also to judge its content. This inevitable mix
of process and substance is depicted in Mr. Justice McIntyre's claim, in
dissent, in *Andrews*:

> [I]n general terms the *Barristers and Solicitors Act* of British Columbia
> [in restricting admission to the bar to Canadian citizens] is . . . enacted
> for a valid and desirable social purpose . . .[76]

Yet, judges who reckon with disparate views about moral righteousness
and political expediency comprehend the nature of substantive justice
differently. They suppose that the meaning of freedom of expression
and association is formed procedurally; however, the content of each
freedom hinges upon substantive qualities which courts themselves inject
into it. Thus, the right to communicate anti-Semitic statements is justified based upon preferred reactions towards racial dominance and anti-
Semitism. Beyond the abstract right to free expression is the political

---

[73] P.W. Hogg, *Constitutional Law of Canada*, 2nd ed. (Toronto: Carswell, 1985), p. 98. See
too, Hogg, "Is the Supreme Court of Canada Biased in Constitutional Cases?" (1979),
57 Can. Bar Rev. 721.

[74] See P. Brest, "Who Decides?" (1985), 58 S. Cal. L. Rev. 661, at 669. See too, J.A.G.
Griffith, *The Politics of the Judiciary* (Glasgow: Fontana Press, 1981); M. Minow,
"Foreword: Justice Engendered" (1987), 101 Harv. L. Rev. 10.

[75] *Andrews*, [1989] 1 S.C.R. 143, at 187 *per* McIntyre J.

[76] *Ibid.*

value that an interpretative community attaches to disparate conceptions of racial purity, cultural exclusivity, and perhaps, ethnic superiority of Aryan peoples. Of concern, alongside the self-determining right of Keegstra to act at will, is the value that diverse communities, not limited to courts, attribute to so-called "fundamental rights". Of relevance is the manner in which judges mediate among competing images of free speech. Thus, in *Keegstra*, the Supreme Court appropriately recognizes the extent to which truth is politically inspired, while "self-autonomy is . . . derived from membership in a cultural or religious group".[77] Establishing the limits of freedom of expression is undoubtedly a substantive inquiry, not a self-evincing truth that appears, miraculously, from a procedural examination of s. 1 of the *Charter*. Even American courts, despite their absence of an equivalent to s. 1, establish categories of restraint upon speech, not procedurally, but substantively. They circumscribe speech in light of its "lewd", "obscene", "profane", "libelous" or "insulting" nature:

> There are certain well-defined and narrowly limited classes of speech, the prevention and punishment of which has never been thought to raise any Constitutional problem. These include the lewd and obscene, the profane, the libelous, and the insulting or "fighting" words . . . [S]uch utterances are . . . of such slight social value as a step to truth that any benefit that may be derived from them is clearly outweighed by the social interest in order and morality.[78]

Substantive justice transcends *a priori* rights. It supersedes the negative liberties that individuals and groups, Jews and neo-Nazis alike, claim for themselves. The normative worth that judges attach to anti-Semitism is paramount. In *Skokie v. Nationalist Socialist Party of America*,[79] for example, the court decides at what point the substantive value of free expression outweighs the abhorrent nature and effect of a pro-Nazi demonstration. The right to free expression is the product of its mediated suppositions about the satisfactory nature of speech. Those who decide upon the meaning of free speech restrain speech. Those who identify the circumference of liberty circumscribe liberty. Rights never disclose their own normative character.

---

[77]   *R. v. Keegstra* (1990), 61 C.C.C. (3d) 1, at 49 (S.C.C.). On substantive reasons for limiting the right to freedom of expression, see esp., D. Bottos, "*Keegstra* and *Andrews*: A Commentary on Hate Propaganda and the Freedom of Expression (1989), 27 Alta. L. Rev. 461; A. Fish, "Hate Promotion and Freedom of Expression: Truth and Consequences" (1989), 2 Can. J.L. & Juris. 1ll; A.W. MacKay, "Freedom of Expression: Is It All Just Talk?" (1989), 68 Can. Bar Rev. 713; N. Rauf, "Freedom of Expression, the Presumption of Innocence and Reasonable Limits: An Analysis of *Keegstra* and *Andrews* (1988), 65 C.R. (3d) 356.

[78]   *Chaplinsky v. New Hampshire*, 315 U.S. 568, at 571-72 (1942). See too, *Skokie v. Nationalist Socialist Party of America*, 366 N.E. 2d 347 (Ill. App., 1977); affd. in part and revd. in part, 373 N.E. 2d 21 (1978). See too, D.A. Downs, "*Skokie* Revisited: Hate Group Speech and the First Amendment" (1985), 60 Notre Dame L. Rev. 629.

[79]   *Supra*, note 78.

> At some point . . . liberty [of expression] becomes licence and colours
> the quality of liberty itself with unacceptable stain.[80]

Judges endow freedom of expression with political values as much
through their belief in the social ends which that freedom serves, as
through their insistence upon constitutional *a priorism*. They evaluate the
adverse relationship between the expression of Aryan superiority and its
effect upon social security in light of the normative value they attribute
to each. They choose between restricted speech and public harmony in
terms of their mediated conceptions of both. They define the substantive
content of the accused's liberty in Oakes in light of their conceptions of
fundamental rights and freedoms.[81] At no time do judges find substantive rights directly within the private rights of particular Jewish or Nazi
sympathizers. At no time is freedom of expression wholly self-explanatory. As Chief Justice Dickson would have it, judges give voice to

> . . . the values and principles essential to a free and democratic society
> which *I believe* embody, to name but a few, respect for the inherent
> dignity of the human person, commitment to social justice and
> equality, accommodation of a wide variety of beliefs, respect for
> cultural and group identity, and faith in social and political institutions
> which enhance the participation of individuals and groups in society.[82]

Certainly, judges can avoid any hint of subjective nuance. They can
rely upon a spirit of social consensus in which they construe *Charter* rights
in a manner that promotes society's "shared goals".[83] On this view, *Charter* rights reflect the popular ends of society, not the courts' reconstruction
of them. However, this approach is limited. It places too much faith in
consensus about rights. It relies too much upon a rational link between
popular will and the judicial expression of that will. Liberty does not
have an inherently negative meaning in which all courts can agree. Judges
do not protect liberty only from acts of the State. They also affirm the
positive character of liberty in education, housing, employment and welfare. They evaluate more than the legitimacy of statutory holidays, and
more than the legislature's objectives in constituting, terminating or otherwise modifying full employment or welfare programmes. They act,
not simply because Parliament requires them to act, but because they
believe in the worthiness of their actions. They assume a distinctly func-

---

[80]   *Report of the Special Committee on Hate Propaganda in Canada* (Ottawa: Queen's Printer,
       1966), pp. 60-61.
[81]   On such "obviousness" in the context of *Oakes*, see, *infra*, Chapter 5.
[82]   *Oakes*, [1986] 1 S.C.R. 103, at 136 (emphasis added).
[83]   *Canadian Constitutional Law in a Modern Perspective*, J.N. Lyon and R.G. Atkey, eds.
       (Toronto: University of Toronto Press, 1970), p. 70. See too, D. Beatty and S. Kennett,
       "Striking Back: Fighting Words, Social Protest and Political Participation in Free and
       Democratic Societies" (1988), 67 Can. Bar Rev. 573, at 576. But see, *contra*, S. Wright, "The
       Judicial Right and the Rhetoric of Restraint: A Defense of Judicial Activism in an Age
       of Conservative Judges" (1987), 14 Hastings Const. L.Q. 487, at 502.

tional role. They realize that the legislative and executive branches of government cannot develop social and economic policy all by themselves. Policy is also developed by those who interpret it. Thus, judges evaluate Sunday closing laws in light of the social consequences of a common pause day upon employment, recreation and welfare interests. They do so as policy-makers, not simply as protectors of the negative liberty of would-be Sunday shoppers, merchants and employees.[84]

That courts ought to and do engage in social and economic policy-making certainly is not novel in Canadian jurisprudence. That they do so under the *Charter* is equally clear. "The task of the Court", Mr. Justice Dickson claimed in *Big M Drug Mart*, is not simply to choose between the substantive or procedural content of law. It is to secure for persons "the full benefit of the *Charter's* protection".[85] Mr. Justice Lamer (as he then was) emphasized this in *Re B.C. Motor Vehicle Act*:

> The novel feature of the *Constitution Act, 1982* . . . is not that it has suddenly empowered courts to consider the content of legislation. This the courts have done for a good many years when adjudicating upon the *vires* of legislation . . . [T]he *Constitution Act* . . . has extended its scope so as to encompass a broader range of values.[86]

Yet, there is a distinct air of causal restraint to such judicial activism. Judges are causally motivated when they enforce rights on grounds that the exercised right injures no one more than it benefits a legitimate right-holder. The Illinois Supreme Court is causally motivated when it grants neo-Nazis a right to march through Skokie, Illinois on the grounds that this is likely to cause lesser injury to Jews and their supporters than benefit to those who wish to associate freely.

However, the causal relationship remains normative. Judges cannot assume that rights to express views on the mastery of the Aryan race are illegitimate, while marching for the hungry and the needy is legitimate, unless they also choose substantive reasons to justify each cause. For courts to grant a right of expression is to make a moral decision about the virtue of the popular or unpopular cause that underscores it, not merely whether individuals are entitled to exercise it. *Courts* choose the weights to attach to each right and interest. *They* determine when the right to march for the world's hungry outweighs the disruption of traffic and business that arises from that march. They decide, too, when the right to march for a less popular political cause, perhaps for lesbian and gay rights, is somehow less justifiable.

Undoubtedly, judges can couch their qualitative opinions in procedural terms. They can treat procedure as non-dogmatic and fallible, in

---

84 See, *e.g., Edwards Books*, [1986] 2 S.C.R. 713, at 782.
85 *Big M Drug Mart*, [1985] 1 S.C.R. 295, at 344, cited with approval by Lamer J. in *Re B.C. Motor Vehicle Act*, [1985] 2 S.C.R. 486, at 499.
86 *Re B.C. Motor Vehicle Act, supra*, note 85, at 496.

the tradition of Charles Sanders Pierce.[87] They can reconstruct process rights, as John Dewey did,[88] so as to take account of governmental interests. They can even invoke these procedures, in the tradition of postmodernism, to critique legal rights themselves.[89] However, each of these formulations of procedure is based upon normative theory. Each represents an ethical ideal. Each is expressed as faith in a desired condition of life; and each finds its jurisprudential mainstay in beliefs about fairness and justice that are reposited as rights. Judges who disguise these beliefs within causal relations reinforce rather than deny their own role as social engineers. They evaluate more than the procedural relationship between *a priori* rights under ss. 2 and 7 and governmental interests under s. 1. They establish under what political conditions the State is entitled to violate s. 2 and s. 7 rights. They decide, too, why, when and how it may do so. In doing all this, they construct the limits of both the negative world of the individual and the positive obligations of government. As Lawrence Tribe explains, the situation could not realistically be otherwise:

> Any constitutional distinction between laws burdening homosexuals and laws burdening exhibitionists . . . must depend on a substantive theory of which [of the two is] exercising fundamental rights and which [is] not.[90]

Certainly, judges can pretend to "find" a positive legal meaning directly within the phrase "free and democratic society" under s. 1, or "fundamental rights and freedoms" under s. 2. They can assert that "[t]he *Charter* does not purport to confer new freedoms."[91] They can insist, too, that it gives a constitutional guarantee to old freedoms only. However, in doing all this, courts suppose that some neat divide separates "old" from "new". They suppose, further, that this separation somehow is embedded within the *Charter* itself.[92] In reality, judges do not invariably

---

[87]   See P. Wiener, *Evolution and the Founders of Pragmatism* (New York: Harper & Row, 1965).

[88]   See, *e.g.*, J. Dewey, "Logical Method and the Law" (1924), 10 Cornell L.Q. 17.

[89]   See, *e.g.*, R. Rorty, *The Consequences of Pragmatism* (Brighton: Hamstead Press, 1982). While neo-liberals have invoked pragmatism to justify individual rights, postmodernists have advanced a non-individualist structure of rights. Rorty refers to that structure as "post-modernist bourgeois liberalism", in Rorty, "Postmodernist Bourgeois Liberalism" (1983), 80 J. Phil. 583. Even the irrationalist wing of Critical Legal Studies employs pragmatism to demonstrate the imperfections and inconsistencies that are inherent within the liberal order, including, among others, economic freedoms. See, for instance, J.W. Singer, "The Player and the Cards: Nihilism and Legal Theory" (1984), 94 Yale L.J. 1; C. Dalton, "An Essay on the Deconstruction of Contract Doctrine" (1985), 94 Yale L.J. 997; M.G. Kelman, "Trashing" (1984), 36 Stan. L. Rev. 293.

[90]   L.H. Tribe, "The Puzzling Persistence of Process-Based Constitutional Theories" (1980), 89 Yale L.J. 1063, at 1076.

[91]   *Re Cromer and B.C. Teachers' Federation* (1986), 29 D.L.R. (4th) 641, at 659 (B.C.C.A.), *per* Lambert J.A. Lambert J.A.'s argument is generally not accepted by the Supreme Court of Canada.

[92]   See, *e.g., per* Dea J. in *Re Edmonton Journal and Alberta (A.G.)* (1983), 146 D.L.R. (3d) 673, at 676-80 (Alta. Q.B.). *Cf. R. v. Banville* (1983), 145 D.L.R. (3d) 595 (N.B.Q.B.); *Re Southam*

share one universal conception of a free and democratic society. They construe the purpose and effect of ss. 1 and 2 as they think they ought to do. For some, "old" conceptions of freedom are quite "new"; for others "new" conceptions of freedom remain "old". For both, the nature and content of freedom is constructed. Freedom is not a fact in itself.

Judges can argue that they do no more than establish a rational connection between fundamental freedoms and their confinement. They can claim to do no more than separate legitimate from illegitimate legislative action as the *Charter* requires. However, in doing this, they cease to be wholly passive. In establishing a rational connection between, say, the exact saving of $10 million and the dismissal of minority employees from the civil service who collectively earn $10 million, they ignore the cumulative effect of governmental action upon employees and their dependants. They bypass popular — and unpopular — suppositions about race relations within the civil service.

There is no guarantee that judges who take account of substantive rights will produce just results, but there are few guarantees anywhere. Just as a court might regard the right of neo-Nazis to march in a predominantly Jewish suburb as morally offensive, it might conceivably find fault with the right of humanitarians to march for the hungry. Each view can be rationalized. Hunger marches might produce only short-term benefits, without addressing the longer-term deprivation of the hungry. In addition, such marches might encourage paternalism and discourage resourcefulness among the hungry. Conversely, neo-Nazi marchers might be viewed, simply, as a group that is interested in resurrecting pride in the German race. Those who march for the hungry might be envisaged, not as saints who seek salvation for humankind, but as rabble-rousers who aim to disrupt the *status quo*.

Courts that are realistic about different conceptions of the public good appreciate that social and economic inequity reside as much in the mind of the interpreter as in the social condition itself. As Mr. Justice La Forest reflected in *Edwards Books*, "[t]here is no perfect scenario in which the rights of all can be equally protected."[93] Judges attribute diffuse weights to fundamental rights, economic want, social need and political virtue. They prioritize those rights according to mediated beliefs in their political, economic and social contributions to the common weal. Judges are not tied to a neutral proceduralism. They cannot shield themselves from their own humanity, or lack of it. Nor can they ignore their own role as law-makers. After all, legislative and executive branches of government provide only general explanations for substantive action. Courts inevitably add specific qualifications.

Inc. and R. (No. 1) (1982), 141 D.L.R. (3d) 341 (Ont. H.C.J.), affd. 146 D.L.R. (3d) 408 (C.A.).
93   *Edwards Books, supra,* note 84, at 795.

Even when judges choose not to interfere with State action, they fulfil a substantive function. When the Supreme Court insists, in *Operation Dismantle*, that the Cabinet ought to decide upon the virtue of militarizing Canadian airspace, it produces a substantive effect through its own inaction. In asserting that complainants, in opposing cruise missile testing, lack a sufficient cause of action, it presumably takes comfort in its belief that treaty-making power ought to vest in the executive, and that the Cabinet ought to decide upon the security of the realm.[94] Indeed, it is precisely in this regard that Mr. Justice Lamer contended in *Re B.C. Motor Vehicle Act* that

> . . . the principles of fundamental justice are to be found in the basic tenets of our legal system. They do not lie in the realm of general public policy, but in the inherent domain of the judiciary as guardian of the justice system.[95]

Understandably, judges can legitimate their role in politics by claiming that they merely act in compliance with the traditions of democratic liberalism. In the opinion of Chief Justice Dickson, as he then was, they can simply

> . . . *note* . . . that an emphasis on individual conscience and individual judgment . . . lies at the heart of our democratic political tradition.[96]

This assertion *is* tenable: protecting individual rights *is* central to any communal philosophy of rights. However, there is a danger that judges will reduce substantive rights to a political aberration — a private fact — in respect of which they claim to have no status. Loyal to procedural determinism, there is the risk that they will likely thwart the interests of substantive justice itself.

TEMPERED ACTIVISM

Certainly, a procedural review of legislative action can lead to substantive results that are most satisfactory. Procedural challenges, quite successful against administrative tribunals under the *Charter*, could be equally successful against courts of law. Indeed, courts already protect the negative liberty of individuals from criminal responsibility under ss. 2 and 7-14.[97] Similarly, Canadian courts increasingly envisage negative liberty in light of its substantive effects upon the disadvantaged. For

---

[94]   See *Operation Dismantle*, [1985] 1 S.C.R. 441.

[95]   *Re B.C. Motor Vehicle Act, supra,* note 85, at 503.

[96]   *Big M Drug Mart, supra,* note 85, at 346 (emphasis added). Dickson C.J. adds: "The ability of each citizen to make free and informed decisions is the absolute prerequisite for the legitimacy, acceptability and efficacy of our system of self-government."

[97]   This observation traces back to the earliest experiences with the *Charter*. See F.L. Morton and M.J. Withey, "Charting the Charter, 1982-1985: A Statistical Analysis" (1987), 4 C.H.R.Y.B. 65, at 72-73; B.L. Strayer, "Life under the Canadian Charter: Adjusting the Balance between Legislatures and Courts", [1988] Public Law 347, at 356.

example, in *Edwards Books*,[98] the Supreme Court upheld — rather than struck down — a statute providing a common pause day in favour of retail workers. In *Canadian Newspapers Co. v. Canada (A.G.)*,[99] it saved a provision in the *Criminal Code* that permitted sexual assault complainants to request a ban on publication of their names. However, the Supreme Court promoted the well-being of retail workers and complainants in sexual assault cases with the comfortable realization that the legislature agreed. It arrived at substantive results in compliance with Parliament's will, rather than for reasons beyond it.

This same philosophy of tempered judicial activism has constrained the growth of positive liberties as they apply to groups. Courts do not actively argue for laws, schemes and programmes that aim to benefit disadvantaged groups under s. 15(1). Rather, they recognize such schemes as legislatures and administrators decree.[100] They guard the language rights of French Canadians from the English majority, less through affirmative action, than by resisting governmental acts that impact negatively upon such groups.[101] So too, they are negatively active when they preserve legislative schemes that favour aboriginal peoples under s. 25 of the *Charter*; when they sustain benefits bestowed on denominational schools under s. 29; and when they preserve multicultural schemes under s. 27.[102]

Yet, such negative activism remains all too moderate, as even those who laud post-*Charter* jurisprudence acknowledge.[103] It would be hard to suggest otherwise. Some appreciate the harm of *Charter* elitism: that the *Charter* will be unequally invoked, and that judges will use it to protect the advantaged, but not the disadvantaged.[104] The harm in all this is that the spoils of the *Charter* will go to the rich and educated. The disadvantaged will enjoy benefits only according to social conditions that the advantaged create — and perpetuate — for them. Others will stress that courts, in catering to majoritarian interests, will regress into a third chamber of the legislature. They will deteriorate into second-hand monitors of social attitude, guessing at public attitudes in light of limited awareness of them.[105]

---

98 [1986] 2 S.C.R. 713.
99 [1988] 2 S.C.R. 122.
100 See s. 15(2).
101 See *Quebec Assn. of Protestant School Bds. v. Quebec (A.G.)*, [1984] 2 S.C.R. 66; *Société des Acadiens du Nouveau-Brunswick Inc. v. Assn. of Parents for Fairness in Education*, [1986] 1 S.C.R. 549.
102 See further hereon, *infra*, at 35.
103 See, *e.g.*, Strayer, *loc. cit.*, note 97; P.H. Russell, "Canada's Charter of Rights and Freedoms: A Political Report", [1988] Public Law 385; B. Wilson, "The Making of a Constitution: Approaches to Judicial Interpretation", [1988] Public Law 370; R.J. Sharpe, "The Charter of Rights and Freedoms and the Supreme Court of Canada: The First Four Years", [1987] Public Law 48.
104 See, *supra*, at 9.
105 See esp., P.W. Hogg, "Is the Supreme Court of Canada Biased in Constitutional Cases?"

Undoubtedly, the *Charter* might continue to protect vested interests only, however justifiable they might be. In *Edwards Books*, employees were protected from having to work on Sundays.[106] In *Southam*, corporations were able to prevent combines investigation officers from searching their premises for evidence of anti-competitive behaviour.[107] So too, door-to-door sellers who are not permanent residents of a province were successful in challenging legislation that restricted their mobility rights.[108] Medical doctors, too, triumphed against provincial governments that tried to restrict their entry into the medical profession and their mobility as practising physicians.[109] This selective protection of the individual rights of corporations and professionals is less an aberration than a product of partiality towards particularly vocal, but not necessarily truly popular, interests. It is also evidence of the comparative dearth of *Charter* cases dealing with the protection of welfare rights.[110]

No doubt, courts do not plan to protect only the affluent, resourceful, and enduring under the *Charter*. But individuals other than corporations and professions often cannot uniformly mount, finance and survive *Charter* challenges.[111] Nor are judges well placed to remedy such unequal access to the judicial system, save through their grant or denial of leave to appeal. Courts can award court costs to poor plaintiffs. However, unless they construe the *Charter* so as to give rise to a positive right to counsel, they can do little to offset the court costs of the poor. They can do even less about the cost of the individual's loss of work-time, or her stress and aggravation in undertaking a *Charter* challenge.

I do not identify a judicial plot to disregard the plight of the underprivileged. Indeed, in *Edwards Books*, Chief Justice Dickson identified the very serious risk of the *Charter* evolving into the vehicle of the rich, at the expense of the poor:

> In interpreting and applying the *Charter* I believe that the courts must be cautious to ensure that it does not simply become an instrument of better situated individuals to roll back legislation which has as its object the improvement of the condition of less advantaged persons.[112]

(1979), 57 Can. Bar Rev. 721, at 723-26; P. Brest, "Who Decides?" (1985), 58 S. Cal. L. Rev. 661, at 668-69; M. Minow, "Foreword: Justice Engendered" (1987), 101 Harv. L. Rev. 10.

[106] *Edwards Books, supra*, note 98.

[107] *Southam*, [1984] 2 S.C.R. 145.

[108] *Basile v. Nova Scotia (A.G.)* (1984), 11 D.L.R. (4th) 219 (N.S.C.A.); leave to appeal to S.C.C. granted 65 N.S.R. (2d) 90n.

[109] *Wilson and Maxsom v. British Columbia (Medical Services Commn.)* (1988), 53 D.L.R. (4th) 171 (B.C.C.A.); leave to appeal to S.C.C. refused November 3, 1988.

[110] See, *e.g.*, Hogg, *loc. cit.*, note 105.

[111] For critical debate hereon, see P.J. Monahan, *Politics and the Constitution: The Charter, Federalism and the Supreme Court of Canada* (Toronto: Carswell, 1987); P.J. Monahan and A. Petter, "Developments in Constitutional Law: The 1985-86 Term" (1987), 9 Supreme Court L.R. 69; A.C. Hutchinson and A. Petter, "Private Rights/Public Wrongs: The Liberal Lie of the Charter" (1988), 38 U.T.L.J. 278.

[112] *Edwards Books, supra*, note 98, at 779.

In addition, Canadians courts have engaged repeatedly in substantive activism. They have denied effect to warrantless searches on grounds that they invade personal freedoms.[113] The Ontario Court of Appeal has struck down censorship legislation.[114] The Supreme Court has challenged the substantive injustice of absolute liability. In particular, it has declared unconstitutional a provincial law that provides for a minimum period of imprisonment for driving on a highway with an invalid or suspended driver's licence.[115] More sensationally still, it has declared unconstitutional Sunday closing laws on grounds that they violate freedom of conscience and religion under s. 2(*a*) of the *Charter*.[116]

However, these judicial affirmations of positive liberty remain modest. Courts are involved in only a narrow sphere of legislated "politics". They acknowledge that legislated "politics" lie at the centre of French language rights in cases like *Ford*.[117] Yet, they still individualize language rights. They still identify the status of Franco-Quebecers with the legislature's recognition of their disadvantaged past as individuals, far less with the prospective affirmation of their group identity as Franco-Canadians.[118]

This restrictive approach towards judicial law-making underscores the attitudes of judges toward negative liberty. To preserve private rights, supposedly, is simply to protect the group with which each individual is associated. To preserve the rights of individuals is to defend them from other members of that or some other group. Thus, the consumer of banned literature, or the would-be Sunday worker, is not alone. She represents others who are like-minded: her victory is their victory too. In *Oakes*,[119] for example, the accused is not to be denied the right to be presumed innocent. No fair-minded judge ought to accuse, punish or otherwise chastise Oakes, save insofar as punishment is convincingly legitimated in law.

> The ability of each citizen to make free and informed decisions is the absolute prerequisite for the legitimacy, acceptability, and efficacy of our system of self-government. . . . They are the *sine qua non* of the political tradition underlying the *Charter*.[120]

---

113   See, *e.g.*, *R. v. Noble* (1984), 14 D.L.R. (4th) 216 (Ont. C.A.). They have struck down reverse onus provisions in narcotics control legislation on grounds that they violate the presumption of innocence under s. 11(*d*) of the *Charter*. See also *Oakes*, [1986] 1 S.C.R. 103.
114   See *Re Ontario Film & Video Appreciation Society and Ontario Bd. of Censors* (1984), 5 D.L.R. (4th) 766 (Ont. C.A.).
115   See *Re B.C. Motor Vehicle Act*, [1985] 2 S.C.R. 486.
116   See *Big M Drug Mart*, [1985] 1 S.C.R. 295.
117   [1988] 2 S.C.R. 712. For a detailed discussion hereon, see, *infra*, at 40.
118   *Ibid.*
119   *Supra*, note 113.
120   *Big M Drug Mart, supra*, note 116, at 346 *per* Dickson C.J.

Each court, in complying with this negative conception of rights, is assisted by the historical origins of negative liberty. It is protected in its caution by the realization that negative liberty evolved long before the enactment of the *Charter*, indeed, even before Canada became a State.

Yet, in arguing all this, the Supreme Court, among others, finds itself threatened by the limitations that inhere within negative private life itself. In requiring that each individual assert her own rights, it glamorizes negative liberty. It assumes, not only that the individual is able to protect herself by relying upon due process of law, but that the legal system supports her resort to it. Neither assumption is justified at face value. If experience with rape victims is any indication, the individual woman's trust in due process of law is often absent. Many rapes are not reported. In still other cases, the rape victim conceives of herself, less as a victim, than as another accused.[121] Her fear is reinforced by judicial practice. Courts that allow complainants to be cross-examined about their sexual history, do more than infringe or protect the accused's right to a fair trial.[122] They raise the accused's private right not to be falsely accused above a countervailing public interest in the physical and mental well-being of women as a class.

In addition, judges render some negative rights more legitimate than others by dressing them up in private garb. Thus, aided by legislation, they endow the corporation with an artificial personality of its own, quite apart from its shareholders and directors. Yet they place the union's rights behind a private "fence" of its constituent membership.[123] To preserve liberty, in effect, the court protects corporate interests above other "private" interests. To protect women and children from the ills of striking picketers in *R.W.D.S.U. v. Saskatchewan*,[124] it masks the primary beneficiary, the corporate employer, that secures employment on its own terms. Only as an egalitarian fiction do individuals have and enjoy their liberties equally. Only in make-believe are the rights of Ford Motor Company to express itself or associate comparable to the rights of employees or consumers, not to mention single mothers and the unemployed.

Judges who insist that *Charter* rights are predominantly private and negative fail to see that history embraces the *persona* of its times. That history reflects the ideologies of a selective audience that includes, but is

---

[121] See generally, D. Kinnon, *Report on Sexual Assault in Canada* (Ottawa: Canadian Advisory Council on the Status of Women, 1981).

[122] See, *e.g.*, *R. v. Oquataq* (1985), 18 C.C.C. (3d) 440 (N.W.T.S.C.); *R. v. LeGallant* (1985), 47 C.R. (3d) 170 (B.C.S.C.), revd. 33 D.L.R. (4th) 444 (C.A.); *Canadian Newspapers Co. v. Canada (A.G.)*, [1988] 2 S.C.R. 122.

[123] See A. Petter, "The Politics of the Charter" (1986), 8 Supreme Court L.R. 473; A.C. Hutchinson and A. Petter, "Private Rights/Public Wrongs: The Liberal Lie of the Charter" (1988), 38 U.T.L.J. 278.

[124] *Retail, Wholesale, & Department Store Union v. Saskatchewan* (hereafter referred to as *Saskatchewan Dairies*), [1987] 1 S.C.R. 460.

not limited to, judges. Thus, the ancient *Magna Carta* is relevant today in the capacity of courts to adapt its institutional goals to the needs of a modern constitution. To do so, judges modernize the interpretation of "due process", yet somehow frame "due process" in the context of its checkered past.[125] They recognize, on the one hand, that "the *Charter* . . .was not intended as a law which would protect only what existed before it came into force."[126] On the other hand, they appreciate that "the *Charter* does not purport to confer new freedoms"[127] beyond negative and private liberties.

To effectuate constancy, the court finds middle ground between the liberal roots of the *Charter*, and its embodiment within an instrumental modernity. Yet, it is trapped in that very middle ground. If it looks to a too distant past, it risks being accused of being undemocratic and elitist. If it fails to have resort to those historical *travaux*, it risks being denounced for subjectivity. The court's solution, to draw upon a principled liberty that stands above the history of rights, is no solution at all. It becomes unduly emphatic. It supposes that human rights are internally coherent; that they rise above the chronicles of yesterday; that they speak to an inevitable good that is contained within them. Typically,

> [v]iewed in this context, the purpose of freedom of conscience and religion becomes clear. The values that underlie our political and philosophic traditions demand that every individual be free to hold and to manifest whatever beliefs and opinions his or her conscience dictates, provided *inter alia* only that such manifestations do not injure his or her neighbours or their parallel rights to hold and manifest beliefs and opinions of their own.[128]

One can hardly fault judges for attempting to rationalize history in terms of conventional wisdom, even if it is their wisdom. Yet, the history of human rights is an unruly horse. Any attempt to find coherence directly within it, as in judicial precedent, is embroiled among inconsistent rights and disparate explanations for them. The court becomes trapped between an incoherent past and an equally inchoate present.

What is questionable, then, is the belief among judges that private rights have self-evident roots that link their past to their present. To distinguish a private and principled liberty from instrumental experience is to separate the cart from the horse. What prevails in principle exists in experience. Neither exists apart from the other.[129] Principles are dy-

---

[125] On the due process debate surrounding the *Charter*, see, *supra*, at 15.

[126] *Irwin Toy Ltd. v. Quebec (A.G.)* (1986), 32 D.L.R. (4th) 641, at 650 (Que. C.A.), *per* Jacques J.A. Jacques adds that "[s]uch an interpretation would stifle its [the *Charter's*] meaning and scope and it would have no effect."

[127] *Re Cromer and B.C. Teachers' Federation* (1986), 29 D.L.R. (4th) 641, at 657 (B.C.C.A.), *per* Lambert J.A.

[128] *Big M Drug Mart, supra*, note 116, at 346 *per* Dickson C.J.

[129] See hereon, *infra*, Chapter 5.

namic, not fixed. Each is determined more according to cultural norms by which judges guide it than for principled reasons that inhere within it. Indeed, principled reason tolerates a day of rest as much for those who uphold a Friday or Saturday Sabbath as for those who pray on Sundays, whatever *Edwards Books* might suggest.[130] So too, religious freedom is as "fundamental" when it protects everyone's right to work every day of the week as when it stipulates that no one is obliged to work on any particular day.[131]

Certainly, judges consider human experience in evaluating the extent of the negative right to security of the person in *Morgentaler*,[132] or the right to be presumed innocent in *Oakes*.[133] Assuredly, they do not simply find one determinate right that trumps all countervailing experience. However, judges also find as much reason to disagree as to agree upon the meaning of life, liberty and security of the person. They justify a day of rest as freedom of religion in one context as readily as they deny it in another.[134] They decide at what stage an objective relates to concerns that are pressing and substantial in a free and democratic society; and they determine, too, when these concerns ought to be characterized "as sufficiently important" to override a fundamental right or freedom.[135] No principled reason rises above the social ends of the judges themselves. No necessary evidence dictates when they must protect the individual from the State or the State from the individual.

One response to the indeterminacy of human rights is to believe that judges, as delegated law-makers, do no more than they are constitutionally expected to do. They render clear in the *Charter* that which is otherwise unclear. They make convincing what is otherwise unconvincing; and they do so exclusively in response to the requirements of a constitutional democracy. Rather than append their views to liberty, they identify liberty as it is, sheltered in its own private realm. They elaborate upon its meaning, not in response to their own moral sensibilities, but by complying with the democratic requirements of the legislature. As Mr. Justice Lamer argued in *Re B.C. Motor Vehicle Act*, "the decision to entrench the *Charter* ... was taken not by the courts but by the elected representatives of the people of Canada."[136]

Thus, whatever constitutional meaning judges wish to inject into the *Charter*, they can at least root their selective perceptions of fundamental rights and freedoms within democratic theory; and they can duly adapt that theory to accommodate different conceptions of human rights. It is

---

[130]   See *Edwards Books*, [1986] 2 S.C.R. 713, at 812 *per* Wilson J.
[131]   On "everyone's" right to fundamental freedom under the Charter, see, *infra*, at 40.
[132]   [1988] 1 S.C.R. 30.
[133]   [1986] 1 S.C.R. 103.
[134]   *Big M Drug Mart, supra*, note 116, and *Edwards Books, supra*, note 130.
[135]   In *Oakes, supra*, note 133, at 140.
[136]   [1985] 2 S.C.R. 486, at 497.

perhaps with this in mind that Chief Justice Dickson appropriately "recalled", in *Big M Drug Mart*, "that the *Charter* was not enacted in a vacuum and must therefore . . . be placed in its proper linguistic, philosophic and historical context."[137]

Yet it is altogether unclear how judges conceive either of their democratic empowerment or of their responsibility to act in a principled manner. If they construe negative liberties as primarily principled, they are obliged to look back at a history in which principled rights are identified differently.[138] Indeed, it is hard to conceive of the *Charter* in relation to French language rights without the benefit of a controversial, even contradictory hindsight.[139] It is even harder to envisage judges participating in *Charter* debate without embellishing upon the meaning of democratic principle itself. Judges who supplement *Charter* principles add content to the constitutional fountainhead from which they claim to draw those principles. They conciliate among prospective human rights according to their own visions of the social purposes which those rights serve.[140] They do so institutionally, in defining the limits of s. 15 in *Andrews*,[141] s. 7 in *Morgentaler*,[142] and s. 2(*a*) in *Edwards Books*.[143] They do so conceptually, in delineating the reach of life, liberty and security of the person, and perhaps one day, fundamental justice in abortion cases.[144] They insist that they must do so in the interest of justice. However, by so insisting, they carry a constitutional ball that many would rather not have!

Certainly, judges can claim to humanize negative rights. They can allege that to follow constitutional principle, they need to adapt it to each new experience, to each new claim, each new case. However, in so alleging, they open themselves to the criticism that their experiences, far from being uniform in nature, are disjointed, or at worst, manipulated or privileged. They risk being challenged for harmonizing *Charter* rights partially, in favour of particular private interests at the expense of others. Those who adopt an activist stance are likely to be denounced for protecting welfare interests above *Charter* rights,[145] or social assistance and popular education before constitutional principle. Those who redress the uneven effect of principled rights upon corporate and impoverished claimants are likely to be blamed for tampering with *a priori* negative liberties.[146]

---

137 *Big M Drug Mart, supra*, note 116, at 344.
138 See, *supra*, at 45 and 49.
139 On language rights in Quebec, see, *supra*, at 10.
140 On this piecemeal approach towards litigious relations, see, *infra*, at 42.
141 [1989] 1 S.C.R. 143.
142 *Supra*, note 132.
143 *Supra*, note 130.
144 See, *infra*, Chapter 6.
145 See, *supra*, at 8.
146 See, *supra*, at 9.

Any thought of replacing Lockean with post-classical conceptions of liberty likely makes courts fear, not so much that they might be over-ruled, but that they might be accused of either too much or too little activism. Worse still, they worry that their activism might induce them to construct rights in the absence of a determinative methodology. They doubt their democratic right to do so without either public approval or the sanction of the State.

Judges have less activist alternatives. They can find in the *Charter* an originating status that serves as a basis for the extension of human rights *ad-infinitum*. So conceived, "freedom of speech, religion and the inviola-bility of the person"[147] evolve into

> ... *original freedoms* which are at once *the necessary attributes* and modes of self-expression of human beings and the primary conditions of their community life within a legal order.[148]

To have religious freedom, it would seem, is to draw upon a past social and legal order, without being tied to its letter in the present. Religious rights, formally rooted in the past, are de-institutionalized in the present. "Equally protected [under the *Charter*] . . . are expressions and manifesta-tions of religious non-belief and refusals to participate in religious prac-tice."[149]   In effect, the spirit of the *Charter*, not unlike von Savigny's *volksgeist*, or spirit of the people,[150] is snuggled, less against a principled past based on negative liberty, than it is based upon a divergent and adaptive present. The court, in embodying different conceptions of com-munity, adapts the past to the present as a measure of an adaptive unity, constitutionally endorsed.

I have no serious objections to this rhetoric of "open principle", so long as it is conceived of as a means towards a social end. This rhetoric of "open principle" pales, however, when judges decontextualize their de-cisions by supposing that principle justifies itself. Finding themselves caught between their own imaginative interpretation of the *Charter* and self-generated principles of negative liberty that inhere within its text, they take two steps back for each step forward. Indeed, as studies of their decisions through the 1980s suggest, after an initial romance with *Charter* activism, the judiciary retired into an almost comfortable conser-vatism.[151] Only a stone's throw away is the last bastion of judicial conser-vatism — where negative rights, *a priori* in nature, again speak for them-selves.

---

[147]   *Saumur v. City of Quebec*, [1953] 2 S.C.R. 299, at 329 *per* Rand J.
[148]   *Ibid.* (emphasis added).
[149]   *Big M Drug Mart*, [1985] 1 S.C.R. 295, at 347 *per* Dickson C.J.
[150]   See F.K. von Savigny, *Of the Vocation of Our Age for Legislation and Jurisprudence*, trans. Hayward (New York: Arno Press, 1975), p. 24. See too, H. Kantorowicz, "Savigny and the Historical School of Law" (1937), 53 L.Q. Rev. 326; J. Stone, *Social Dimensions of Law and Justice* (Stanford: Stanford University Press, 1966), pp. 86-89, 101-11.
[151]   See further, *infra*, Chapter 5.

Yet, judges who are substantively active *can* move beyond interpretation to more creative methods of allocating *Charter* rights and freedoms. They can judge the allocation of those rights in light of normative qualities which they — and others — inject into them. In doing this, they likely attribute to the *Charter* an increasing positive force in a society that is in need of a more positive vision of group life.

AFFIRMING LIBERTY

At its narrowest, positive liberty is concerned wholly with comparing the status of different groups, evaluating the political conditions that give rise to difference in treatment and reflecting upon the effect of those differences upon each group. Construed parsimoniously, positive liberty is directed only at rectifying imbalances between haves and have-nots; it is not concerned with higher social aspirations. The judge does not consider whether competitive life is good for society, or whether property perpetuates poverty or expands upon social initiative. The court simply ensures that relations of power are not abused: that majorities do not abuse minorities, whites do not enslave blacks, and men do not impoverish women.[152]

This approach, embodying a selective form of affirmative action, provides only a partial — and indeed, temporary — positive life. Disadvantaged groups are free to assert their group identity against those who otherwise might deny or dispossess them of their rights, but only to the extent of that denial or dispossession. Their positive rights as a group approximate the negative liberty of individuals. Both individuals and groups assert their liberty against those who would displace it, whether they be governmental or non-governmental actors. The individual wishes not to be dispossessed of rights she already has. The disadvantaged group seeks access to rights either denied it or not yet accorded it.

The key difference between the liberty of groups and individuals lies in the positive means that are employed to provide disadvantaged groups with the opportunity to acquire rights, notably under s. 15(2) of the *Charter*. However, this difference between the negative liberty of the individual and affirmative action is narrowly circumscribed. Once the rights of disadvantaged groups are affirmed and normalcy resumes, positive liberty presumably returns to its negative and private state. Following the American tradition of *Brown v. Bd. of Education*,[153] the grant of positive liberty aims at correcting prior injustices wrought upon the disadvan-

---

[152]   See in general hereon, D. Beatty, *Putting the Charter to Work* (Kingston and Montreal: McGill-Queen's University Press, 1987); P.J. Monahan, *Politics and the Constitution: The Charter, Federalism and the Supreme Court of Canada* (Toronto: Carswell, 1987); P.C. Weiler, "Rights and Judges in a Democracy: A New Canadian Version" (1984), 18 U. Mich. J. L. Ref. 51.

[153]   347 U.S. 483 (1954).

taged, rather than at redistributing social resources permanently in their favour. The affirmation of minority rights and entitlements to collective resources, therefore, is temporary only. The purpose is not social unity in and through the recognition of difference. The long-term goal is sameness of treatment. The affirmative rights of the group deteriorate, once again, into the private and abstract rights of its membership. Regardless of her racial, sexual or religious identity, the individual eventually returns to her isolated and private state. That social and educational disadvantage perpetuates itself within a class system, despite efforts at rectificatory justice, is dealt with correctively, not distributively. Supposedly, the greater harm is that affirmative rights, rendered permanent, might lead to unremitting paternalism, or in the language of *University of California v. Bakke*,[154] might result in reverse discrimination.

Much of this misses the point. To affirm the liberty of disadvantaged groups wholly by rectificatory design is to effect redistributive social ends only coincidentally. Promoting distributive justice addresses not just an injustice here or there, but the social and economic conditions in which such injustices recur. To endorse affirmative liberty, whether under s. 15(2) or s. 7, is to identify a collective existence beyond disadvantage. It is to affirm a social programme that encompasses more than those things which all of us happen to hold in common. It embraces more than the air we breathe and water we drink, and more than the status of the disadvantaged. Affirmed is the substance of social and political life, well beyond the competitive and exclusionary interests of individuals and groups alike.[155]

Liberty need not be conceived of wholly negatively any more than life need be expressed solely through the isolated human subject. Society is not benefited simply by treating either individuals or groups as distinctive. Virtue flows as much from co-operative social endeavour as through the toiling individual who competes with her fellows to sustain herself. In this sense, liberty is expressed as much through communicative discourse among and within groups as through negative rights by which each community protects its distinctiveness. These communicative norms are not make-believe. They are expressed in no less than the *International Covenant on Economic, Social and Cultural Rights*. There, it is stated that "the widest possible protection and assistance should be accorded . . . the family . . . [as] the natural and fundamental group unit of society".[156] To this it adds "the right of everyone to form trade unions and join the trade

---

154   438 U.S. 265 (1978).
155   See hereon esp. Robert Paul Wolff's distinction between "affective community" ("the reciprocal consciousness of a shared culture") and "rational community" ("that reciprocity of consciousness which is achieved and sustained by equals who discourse together publicly for the specific purpose of social decisions and action"): Wolff, *The Poverty of Liberalism* (Boston: Beacon Press, 1968), p. 187.
156   December 16, 1966, C.T.S. 1976, No. 46,933, U.N.T.S. 3, art. 10.

union of his choice",[157] to have a "free" education in the "elementary and fundamental stages",[158] and to "take part in the government of [each individual's] . . . country".[159] Implicit in these international instruments is the belief that developing schemes to enrich collective rights are inherent responsibilities of nation states, beyond the need to protect the negative liberty of each subject.

Certainly, courts can justify a narrow world that excludes many social purposes and effects from the right to liberty. They can emphasize a rather limited positive sphere in which each individual participates with others exactly as she wishes; and each is free to give less to the group than she takes from it. Here, the individual's liberty confines the polity. Free to assert her religious, ethnic and sexual identity, she is not expected to contribute to the group if she does not wish to do so. The social harm is that, given her negative status, no communal world beckons her. She is concerned solely with protecting her own turf: there is no other community of players beyond her. Negative rights are the centre-piece of her nation state. Participatory democracy plays only a distant role in a liberal state that promotes isolated individualism. In the words of C.B. Macpherson:

> By the time the liberal state was democratized, the demand of the democratic forces was to get into the competition [of the liberal state], not to discard it for any other kind of social order.[160]

This same de-socialization of community occurs elsewhere, notably in relation to employment rights. Courts affirm only a union's right to act on behalf of its members, not its positive contribution to conditions of employment.[161] Claiming freedom from government intrusion in the *Alberta Reference*,[162] the individual supposedly asserts her *Charter* rights as a singular employee, even though she happens also to be part of a union. She is free to act, not so much as a cog in the union's machinery, but as a self-protecting actor. Her communion with others is restricted to the relationship between herself and her foe, more than to her solidarity with other union members. No other machinery of public life exists beyond the adverse relationship between her and the State. Her private status as an individual is reinforced constitutionally. The *Charter* does not impose positive obligations upon the parties to collective labour agreements on grounds that these are private contracts, even when they are

---

157   *Ibid.*, art. 8. These positive norms are further embellished in art. 7, which ensures "a decent standard of living".

158   *Ibid.*, art. 26.

159   *Ibid.*, art. 21.

160   C.B. Macpherson, "The Near Future of Democracy and Human Rights", in *The Real World of Democracy* (Toronto: CBC Publications, 1967), p. 57.

161   See, *e.g.*, *Reference re Public Service Employee Relations Act (Alta.)* (hereafter referred to as the *Alberta Reference*), [1987] 1 S.C.R. 313, at 396-97 *per* McIntyre J.

162   *Ibid.*

regulated by labour codes.[163] Similarly, in *Re McKinney and Bd. of Governors of University of Guelph*,[164] the Ontario Court of Appeal held that the *Charter* does not apply to a university or to its contracts of employment: these too are private, to be regulated by private law.[165] That social actors, notably but not limited to corporations, happen to perform public functions, benevolently or otherwise, is rendered incidental to their private rights.

Judges who restrict the *Charter* to the distinctly negative and *a priori* relationship between individual and government cause a further social ill. They deny meaningful benefit to groups with unpopular interests. Gay rights activists receive rights under the *Charter* only when their adversaries are governments that deny them substantive justice. They get human rights protection when human rights codes deal with sexual orientation as a substantive issue, as in *McKinney*.[166] However, when both the *Charter* and human rights codes are silent, such activists may well receive no substantive remedy, save perhaps under the common law.[167]

For judges to insist that some rights are private is to wish to forge social unity through the individual in spite of the isolated nature of those rights. It is not entirely realistic to suppose, as Madam Justice Wilson did in *Operation Dismantle*,[168] that a "hermit has no need of rights". A hermit, however isolated, is exposed to adulterated air, contaminated food and unclean water. Not even the hermit can be assured of a hermetically sealed lifestyle in the presence of a pervasive social life around her. To envisage her as a single player in a faceless world is to achieve far less than the best of both worlds. She cannot be part of a common weal and yet free herself from it, simply if and when she so wishes. The communality wrought by her liberty is far more extensive than her individual status. She is far more than a periodic hermit. She is also more than a Catholic or Protestant who claims a *Charter* right to freedom of religion and expression.

Nor is communal liberty expressed wholly against a single foe, the State. Individual Catholics or Protestants assert their freedom to pray, associate, demonstrate, and indeed, to live their solidarity. They do so for reasons well beyond their opposition to government. They record a communal design that submerges them in groups, not as mere members, but as participants who shape the community itself. Viewed through the

---

163   *Re Bhindi et al. and B.C. Projectionists, Loc. 348, Int. Alliance of Picture Machines Operators of U.S. & Canada* (1986), 29 D.L.R. (4th) 47 (B.C.C.A.); leave to appeal to S.C.C. refused [1986] 6 W.W.R. lxv.
164   (1987), 46 D.L.R. (4th) 193 (Ont. C.A.).
165   This decision was upheld by the Supreme Court of Canada on December 6, 1990: see 76 D.L.R. (4th) 545. On this private-public division, see generally, *infra*, Chapter 4.
166   *Supra*, note 164.
167   See generally, *Dolphin Delivery*, [1986] 2 S.C.R. 573. But see *Seneca College of Applied Arts & Technology v. Bhadauria*, [1981] 2 S.C.R. 181.
168   [1985] 1 S.C.R. 441, at 488.

prism of social solidarity, they are participants within labour unions, not just labourers, in the same way as corporate managers interact within corporations rather than simply direct them.

Nor is communal life restricted to immediate adversaries, for example, to employers versus employees. Raised above adversarial relations between individuals is the social context in which those relations evolve, including their impact upon others. There, the rights of workers hinge, less upon the aspirations of any one worker, than upon the perceived power of collective bargaining itself. There, the "good life" finds strength, less in a plurality of individuals, than in their collective identity. Thus, collective bargaining reflects social attitudes towards strikes and lockouts, beyond the negative rights of striking workers and opposing employers. Just as the State consists of more than its formal constituents — the Cabinet, the Governor General and the Members of Parliament — labour-management relations move beyond adverse relations between labour and management. As Chief Justice Dickson argued in the *Alberta Reference*, "our Constitution's history [involves] giving special recognition to collectivities or communities of interest other than the government and political parties."[169]

Certainly, I do not suggest that individuals should not enjoy a private world, under the *Charter* as elsewhere. However, to endorse the individual's liberty affirmatively is to espouse her communion with others. It is to extend communal life well beyond particular English or French speaking participants, to the cultural and political life in which such participation occurs. That affirmative world encompasses family, religious, cultural and social attitudes. It embraces cultural visions of marital relations and child-rearing, and religious views of atheism and bigotry. Like it or not, these attitudes are inherent in the manner in which law-makers, courts included, evaluate family, religious and political life. Thus, the Supreme Court requires a parent who adheres to a fundamentalist religion to demonstrate that her children are receiving an appropriate education outside of the public system.[170] In effect, the parent has no right to disregard community standards on account of religious belief.

This is not to say that religious and educational liberties, communally construed, can perfect the operation of the polity. Nor should "everyone" surrender their rights to government so that it might re-order their lives as it wishes. My claim is only that human rights should be perceived more readily through communal contributions towards civil society and less through distinctive right-holders. The individual contributes to the polity through friendship, sociability and generosity of spirit. In that sense, she interacts within a polity that includes her social experiences

---

169 *Supra*, note 161, at 364.
170 *R. v. Jones*, [1986] 2 S.C.R. 284.

and attitudes. That polity, in turn, pays homage to her as a person in terms that it helps to devise for her. However, it does so only by including her.

This proposal, that courts affirm liberty positively, is implicit in the *Charter* itself. It inheres in s. 7 in which *"everyone* has the right to life, liberty, and security of the person".[171] In this sense, liberty is open to "everyone", while the State assumes a positive obligation toward "everyone". Michael Sandel explains that liberty is affirmed communally, when people interact

> . . . less as individuated subjects . . . and more as participants in a common identity, be it family or community or class or people or nation.[172]

This communal notion of liberty is also evident in relation to language rights under the *Charter*. French and English speaking inhabitants of Canada do not receive a possessory right in their languages that prohibits all others from use and enjoyment of either language. To protect French language rights is not simply to protect French language speakers. The effect, rather, is to provide a bilingual framework in which others, not limited to either French or English speakers, can engage. Nothing about ss. 16-20 of the *Charter* categorically compels courts to adopt two solitudes, one for the French and another for the English, at the expense of an otherwise multicultural society. Viewed positively in light of s. 27 of the *Charter*, the assurance of bilingualism is itself an expression of multiculturalism. To encourage non-English and non-French speaking Canadians to share in the richness of these two languages, is not to require that they each sacrifice their own cultures in doing so. The purpose is to encourage sharing within a multicultural society through two languages, not to refute whatever else diverse language users might be, have or want. To suggest that French is only for the French and English is only for the English is an unfortunate — and unnecessary — inference of the "distinct society" clause in the now failed *Meech Lake Accord*. It is unfortunate in that it undermines the very sense of community by which people communicate. It is unnecessary in that it undermines the spirit of s. 23 of the *Charter* by excluding more pervasive social benefits from the ambit of French and English language rights.

No one can seriously dispute that the *Charter* advantages English and French speaking Canadians over other groups. Section 20, for example, provides for a "right to communicate with, and to receive available ser-

---

171   *Charter*, s. 7 (emphasis added).
172   M.J. Sandel, *Liberalism and the Limits of Justice* (Cambridge: Cambridge University Press, 1982), p. 143. See too, P. Selznick, "The Idea of a Communitarian Morality" (1978), 75 Cal. L. Rev. 445; A. Gutman, "Communitarian Critics of Liberalism" (1985), 14 Phil. & Pub. Aff. 308.

vices from, any head or central office of an institution of the Parliament or government of Canada *in English or French"* only.[173] The *Charter* grants no equivalent affirmative right to Poles, Swedes, Germans, and Ukrainians. Viewed cynically, non-French and non-English Canadians are inhibited from full participation in public life, since they face barriers to communicating in their languages of choice. Viewed affirmatively, however, their interests are addressed when more extensive social services are provided through the medium of two, rather than a multitude of languages. However utilitarian this rhetoric of exclusion might seem to be, it is the ultimate dividing line between naked idealism and functionalism.[174] At its most far-sighted, the social end is to envisage language rights as one means, among many others, of extending positive liberty throughout the Canadian *polity*. In issue is the affirmation of a positive sphere of public life that is accessible to "everyone", but not subject to the whim of anyone.

RE-CREATING POSITIVE LIBERTY

> Generally speaking . . . it is dimensional complexity [of groups] which produces such characteristics as endurance and time, stability of identity, systemic interdependence, and relative autonomy, and these play a crucial role in qualifying groups for special status while avoiding the problem of open-endedness.[175]

Communal life is not fixed in formal categories. A religion is not merely an institution to which we each belong and to whose tenets we each adhere. It is one of the varied means through which groups express their affinity for common, and at the same time, disparate ideals. It is also the medium through which they display their constant alongside their changing identities. Nor are religious proclivities expressed solely through formal prayer. As a manifestation of kinship and fellowship, freedom of religion encompasses non-believers, Catholics, Lutherans, Jews and Mohawks alongside zealots, atheists and agnostics. It enshrines a diverse spirituality in which the irreligious stand alongside the religious. Thus, freedom of religion includes both the private life of the devout and

---

[173] *Charter*, s. 20 (emphasis added).

[174] *Cf.* R.A. Macdonald, "Postscript and Prelude — The Jurisprudence of the Charter: Eight Theses" (1982), 4 Supreme Court L.R. 321. Macdonald appropriately links affirmative rights to participatory democracy. He asks (at 346): "Does the restriction enhance the ability of all citizens to participate meaningfully in the process of the State?" However, in addressing the opposition between government and individual, he returns to a somewhat narrower, albeit popular belief, that positive liberty is extolled wholly by government, as distinct from civil society. For a critique of government as the sole repository of public life, see, *infra*, Chapter 4.

[175] F. Svensson, "Liberal Democracy and Group Rights: The Legacy of Individualism and Its Impact on American Indian Tribes" (1979), 27 Pol. Stud. 420, at 434. See too, D.M. Johnston, "Native Rights as Collective Rights: A Question of Group Self-Preservation" (1989), 2 Can. J. L. & Juris. 19; M. McDonald, "Collective Rights and Tyranny" (1986), 56 U. Ottawa Q. 115.

the community of the irreligious. It embraces the right to a secular and a temporal education, to both receive and decline medical treatment.

To downplay this communicative influence upon free will is to create a mystique about others as much as about ourselves. Personal freedoms are also collective. Whether each individual believes in God or the fullness of the human spirit, both individuals and groups are relatively autonomous. Their right to believe is part of a dialectic through which they interact. As part of their social existence, it moves from personal sentiment to public declarations of faith. It embodies their shared values alongside their different conceptions of religious life.

> Freedom of religion goes beyond the ability to hold certain beliefs without coercion and restraint and entails more than the ability to profess those beliefs openly.[176]

Thus, fundamental freedoms, not limited to freedom of religion, are as much expressions of social consciousness as they are personal entitlements. Individuals are not completely free to engage in polygamy. They cannot refuse medical treatment without limit. No grand *Charter* design attributes to anyone an absolute and impregnable religious freedom against all who might displace it. Individuals can dream that they are each autonomous, indeed, self-contained units unto themselves. However, their private worlds are really just those that others allow them to have. When all is said and done, their negative liberties evolve into that which those others, not limited to government, attribute to them in light of an often impermanent social consciousness. In this sense, free will is constrained by the degree of communal tolerance of it. Punishment of one's children *is* subject to community standards beyond private rights.

To highlight private rights, as though they are wholly self-serving, is to pretend that the quality of human life is completely within each individual's control. This is clearly not so. Others, not limited to legislatures, continually constrain individual life. Courts confine the right to life, liberty and security of the person. They evaluate the right to freedom of the press according to their image of its nature and effect. For example, in *Canadian Newspaper Co. v. City of Victoria*,[177] the British Columbia Supreme Court judged the right to use newspaper vending boxes in the city of Victoria under s. 2(*b*) of the *Charter* in light of its own perception of the negative aesthetic effect of doing so:

> In my view these interests [of the City Council in preserving the aesthetics of the city] are sufficient to justify the prohibition against placing coin-operated newspaper boxes on the streets.[178]

---

[176]   *R. v. Videoflicks Ltd.* (1984), 14 D.L.R. (4th) 10, at 35 (Ont. C.A.), *per* Tarnopolsky J.A. But *cf. Robertson and Rosetanni v. R.*, [1963] S.C.R. 651.
[177]   (1987), 46 D.L.R. (4th) 695 (B.C.S.C.); affd. 63 D.L.R. (4th) 1 (C.A.).
[178]   *Ibid.*, at 715 *per* Murray J.

In acting thus, the court embellished conventional mores in light of qualities it deemed to be satisfactory in the social context.

Judges who refuse to intervene in favour of individuals, notably in family life, only believe they are leaving them alone. In fact, they render them alone conceptually, not in fact. They move the family, labour union and corporation from the private to the public realm. Private life acquires a normative dimension. More than a negative liberty, it evolves into a positive determinant of political co-existence. This positive life is depicted most readily in the right to vote. The vote constitutes a means of integrating individuals into communal life rather than separating them from it. It represents modernity in its greatest glory. The individual is free to influence the nature of political life. To this end, the Ontario High Court struck down a section of the Ontario *Election Act* that disqualified inmates in a penal institution from voting in a provincial election on grounds that it violated s. 3 of the *Charter*.[179] Similarly, the Federal Court rendered unenforceable a provision in the *Canada Elections Act* that prevented mentally disabled persons from voting.[180]

Yet, the right to vote falls short of the ideals of a participatory democracy. It is deficient, not in the right itself, but in the democratic action that accompanies it. This defect arises historically, when courts impose property, age and sex restrictions on the right to vote. It still occurs in disqualifying specific categories of persons from voting. For example, in *Re Scott and British Columbia (A.G.)*,[181] the court held that the right to vote, guaranteed by s. 3 of the *Charter*, is subject to reasonable restrictions, including age, mental capacity, residence and registration. More substantively still, the right to vote is formally limited when voters are unable to express themselves equally within a constituency system that weighs votes unequally.[182] These deficiencies in the voting system are accentuated substantively when courts apply a strict standard of proportionality to delimit constituencies in cases like *Dixon v. British Columbia (A.G.)*.[183]

A positive social programme extends beyond the right to vote.[184] It includes the right to be informed of charges against one, and to be represented by counsel in criminal prosecutions. It resides in a co-operative, as in an adversarial community, in an affirmative, not merely a negative community.[185] This broader affirmation of popular liberty, beyond po-

---

[179] *Grondin v. Ontario (A.G.)* (1988), 65 O.R. (2d) 427 (H.C.J.). The court ruled, in addition, that such action was not reasonably justified under s. 1.
[180] *Canadian Disability Rights Council v. Canada*, [1988] 3 F.C. 622 (T.D.).
[181] (1986), 29 D.L.R. (4th) 544 (B.C.S.C.).
[182] For discussion hereon, see, *infra*, at 176.
[183] (1989), 60 D.L.R. (4th) 445 (B.C.S.C.); leave to appeal to C.A. granted.
[184] See, *supra*, at 35.
[185] Some *Charter* commentators, in acknowledging the affirmative language of, *inter alia*, s. 2, nevertheless distinguish *Charter* rights from the somewhat negative phraseology of the American Constitution. However, they tend to conceive of this difference semantically, as a difference of expression, not substance. See, *e.g.*, R.A. Sedler,

litical rights, is grounded in constitutional law itself. It is portrayed in
the realization that *"everyone"* has the right to associate herself with a
distinctly communicative spirit, beyond the looking-glass image of herself.[186]

To affirm this positive conception of social life is to rely upon members of civil society to interact with legislatures, executives, courts and
corporations alike. It is to trust them to associate with francophone and
anglophile Canadians, as with religious and ethnic minorities. It is to
inhibit them from relying upon their own political neutrality, allowing
the bigot, racist and sexist within them to hide behind public inertia. The
affirmation of positive liberty hinges upon the willing participation of
civil society in social discourse. After all, legislatures cannot be expected
alone to affirm the public rights of Jane Q. Public. Legislatures are but
one organ of civil society. They are far less than the sole substantive cure
for all public ills. Political activism is no more restricted to them than
newspapers are confined to reporting the news. Certainly, legislatures
enact laws that redress the disadvantages of aboriginal peoples, women
and the disabled. However, they do not alone direct the positive life of
the polity.

In presenting positive liberty so broadly, I do not suggest that *everyone*
in civil society ought to be treated similarly. Indeed, giving the right to
vote to "everyone" does not ensure that "everyone" in civil society acquires a truly equal say in the life of the polity. Nor does "everyone's"
liberty lead to equality when some have a greater capacity to effect their
liberty than others. Few would suggest that non-aboriginal people are as
concerned as aboriginal people about social programmes that ensure the
survival of aboriginal life. Disadvantaged groups differ in the nature of
their interests and in the means of realizing them. Aboriginal interests
differ from the interests of women, despite the fact that many aboriginal
people are also women. Similarly, the concerns of women differ from
the concerns of the physically disabled, even though many disabled are
also women. In addition, the disabled have claims that diverge from
gays, aged Canadians and immigrants, despite the fact that gays often
are members of these other groups as well. Each group is alike in being
disadvantaged. It is not alike in the type and extent of that disadvantage.

Accordingly, I do not suggest that women be treated like men, or

"Constitutional Protection of Individual Rights in Canada: The Impact of the New
Canadian Charter of Rights and Freedoms" (1984), 59 Notre Dame L. Rev. 1191, at
1220. But *cf.* P. Bender, "The Canadian Charter of Rights and Freedoms and the United
States Bill of Rights: A Comparison" (1983), 28 McGill L.J. 811, at 824-25: M. Manning,
Rights, Freedoms and the Courts (Toronto: Emond-Montgomery, 1982), pp. 249-52; K.
Swinton, "Application of the Canadian Charter of Rights and Freedoms", in *The
Canadian Charter of Rights and Freedoms: Commentary*, W.S. Tarnopolsky and G.-A.
Beaudoin, eds. (Toronto: Carswell, 1982), p. 41.
[186]   See further, *supra*, at 35.

aboriginal people be treated like whites. To be treated identically is to reduce the status of women and aboriginal people in the face of a seemingly higher state of being, that of the male white. Preserving difference is as much a means towards equality as a threat to it. Mr. Justice McIntyre emphasized this in *Andrews:*

> It must be recognized at once, however, that every difference in treatment between individuals under the law will not necessarily result in inequality and, as well, that identical treatment may frequently produce serious inequality.[187]

I do not suggest that every racial group be free to assert its liberties collectively against all other groups in the same way that individuals assert their liberty against the State. To so claim would be to endorse a wholly negative conception of communal life. To shift from negative to positive liberty is to move, not only beyond the isolated individual who insists upon her right to be left alone, but also beyond isolated groups that seek to be left alone. Only in resisting governmental intrusion into private and group life respectively does the negative liberty of groups resemble the negative rights of individuals. To endorse positive life, beyond both, is to accept that differences among races, religions and cultural groups enrich rather than diminish the polity. Indeed, if *Andrews*[188] has any meaning at all, it is that positive life justifies the right to be treated differently as a communal end in itself.

Different groups, quite understandably, have different expectations of themselves, as of others. Aboriginal peoples compare themselves to those who enjoy a more beneficial status in the polity. They find few, if any, groups that have suffered more than they have.[189] Others, not least of all judges, evaluate aboriginal claims in light of the political and economic expectations which those others impute to aboriginal people. They respond to ethnic or sexual differences beyond an abstract society that speaks similarly for all. They shift from a uniform conception of liberty that is enjoyed by everyone, to inimical conceptions of liberty that require reconciliation.

This shaping of the polity takes place discursively, through a social conversation that explores, discovers and reacts to different conceptions of liberty. It reflects a cumulative spirit, based upon understanding, tolerance, reconciliation, and ultimately, the accommodation of difference. It is justified through the unity of separateness as through the unity of sameness. It is reflected in the willingness of those who judge social relations to accommodate different visions of liberty within a tolerant and co-operative polity, without sacrificing difference itself.

---

187   *Andrews*, [1989] 1 S.C.R. 143, at 164.
188   *Ibid.*
189   See, *e.g., Apsit v. Manitoba Human Rights Commn.*, [1988] 1 W.W.R. 629 (Man. Q.B.); affd. [1989] 1 W.W.R. 481 (C.A.), where aboriginal claimants sought privileged access to certain rice permits in light of their historical lack of access.

REKINDLING THE NEGATIVE FOLD

Certainly, negative liberties are necessary. Individuals and groups alike protect themselves under the *Charter* from the government's directions in child-rearing,[190] and from its decisions about advertising.[191] Landed immigrants assert their rights against provincial governments who otherwise would prevent them from practising their professions.[192] The individual, undoubtedly, is a soldier who needs to fight against intrusion. She is a maverick, entitled to protect her own domain. She allows the State to rule over her. Yet, she is justified in fighting it off when it attempts to over-regulate her. The State, quite understandably, is her "obvious" foe under the *Emergencies Act*[193] and elsewhere; it raises its conception of the common good above that of her as an individual. It employs national security to trump her individual rights, and in so doing, it sometimes denies social justice to her, and to others.[194]

However, all this passes over the real status of both individual and State. The State is not a monolithic force that stands alone, for or against human rights. Like the corporation, labour union and individual, it is diverse in its inclinations, needs and actions. It variously represents the foetus in relation to pregnant women, the foster child in relation to her natural parents, along with the sanctity of married life and parental authority. At no stage is the State inextricably bound to any one subject or group of subjects; it selects the social interests it prefers to protect. Courts, in turn, ensure that some State interests prevail, but not all.

Similarly, individual rights are not self-contained entities. They are justified in light of a shared belief in their virtue. Those who regard their rights as self-contained undermine communal life itself. The individual becomes a prisoner of her negative life. She is fixed wholly in her own private world. She is separated from a common endeavour that includes her. Thus, courts, in *Morgentaler*[195] as elsewhere, fail to endorse social interests beyond the pregnant woman's particular right to security. They do not identify freedom of association, in *Saskatchewan Dairies*,[196] with the individual's shared life, only with her separate life. They reduce labour rights to the numerical sum of labourers who hold them, not to the social significance of labour power. They pass over the need to affirm the rights of labour unions so as to avoid labour's ongoing subservience, not simply to the State, but to corporate power itself.[197] They fail to appreciate

---

[190] *Family & Children's Services of Kings County v. E.D.* (1988), 86 N.S.R. (2d) 204 (C.A.).
[191] *Irwin Toy*, [1989] 1 S.C.R. 927.
[192] *Andrews, supra,* note 187.
[193] R.S.C. 1985 (4th Supp.), c. 22.
[194] See *Operation Dismantle*, [1985] 1 S.C.R. 441.
[195] [1988] 1 S.C.R. 30.
[196] [1987] 1 S.C.R. 460. See also *Re Lavigne and Ontario Public Service Employees Union et al.* (1986), 29 D.L.R. (4th) 321 (Ont. H.C.J.). But *cf. Re Lavigne and O.P.S.E.U.* (1989), 56 D.L.R. (4th) 474 (Ont. C.A.).
[197] See further hereon, *infra*, Chapter 4.

that the individual's private world cannot rise above the public world around her.

Those who favour private life fear succumbing to a netherworld of social rights. They dread having to displace the negative liberties of some in order to affirm the positive liberties of others. They fear that, in attempting to reconstitute rights, they will do so only partially. They worry about devising rights they cannot subsequently defend on rational grounds. As Chief Justice Dickson argued:

> It should not fall to the courts to fill in the details that will render legislative lacunae constitutional.[198]

They worry, too, that judges who decide upon the moral sanctity of legislative programmes will decide upon the fate of civil society itself. For example, Madam Justice Wilson asserted in *Reference re Bill 30*:

> . . . it is not the role of the Court to determine whether as a policy matter a publicly funded Roman Catholic school system is or is not desirable. That is for the legislature.[199]

However, these fears of undue judicial law-making fail to reckon that legislative game-plans are not static, waiting to be found. They are revealed differently to different judges. Even when judges concur in their content, they still attribute different weights to them. They construe reproductive rights expansively in *Morgentaler*.[200] At the same time, they strike down provisions in the *Criminal Code* that impede access to abortion facilities.[201] They stress the right to advertise in a language of choice.[202] Yet they restrict the right to advertise as it affects children.[203]

Legislatures provide courts with only general guidelines in relation to constitutional interpretation. They do not offer interpretive sections to clarify the meaning of fundamental freedoms like freedom of conscience, religion, expression and association. They rely on judges to derive those methods themselves. Judges, in turn, construe fundamental rights and freedoms quite differently. They extend privileges to the already privileged, or more openly, to the underprivileged as well.[204] They defend the interests of consumers and producers in *Irwin Toy*,[205] along with the rights of non-citizens to practise law in British Columbia in *Andrews*.[206] Whether they legitimate their action through the *Charter*, a statute, or the common law, they do not apply a uniform method of interpretation to achieve

---

198   *Southam*, [1984] 2 S.C.R. 145, at 169.
199   *Reference re Bill 30, An Act to Amend the Education Act (Ont.)*, [1987] 1 S.C.R. 1148, at 1167-68.
200   *Supra*, note 195.
201   See, *infra*, Chapter 6.
202   See *Ford*, [1988] 2 S.C.R. 712.
203   See *Irwin Toy*, *supra*, note 191.
204   See esp. *Oakes*, [1986] 1 S.C.R. 103, at 135-42; *Big M Drug Mart*, [1985] 1 S.C.R. 295, at 351-55.
205   *Supra*, note 191.
206   *Supra*, note 187.

their ends. The justice of their decisions is *not* equally demonstrable to and for all.

Judges who camouflage their interest in public life within a wholly private theory of rights, diminish both *Charter* rights and their own function, as interpreters, in relation to them.   They define the pregnant woman's right not to be delayed in securing an abortion negatively and competitively, not communicatively.[207] They pass over the social interests that are connected to those rights.[208] Thus, in *Nova Scotia (A.G.) v. Phillips*,[209] judges highlight the individual's rights as a member of a disadvantaged group under s. 15(1).   However, they disregard communal attributes which they might otherwise impute to her.[210] They do not consider, for example, the extent to which her negative liberties are instruments of power or powerlessness. They assert, most simply, that each individual should be equally free to think, feel and act at will: the State should not do so for her.[211]

Courts *can* objectify their social biases. They can subject the competition between State interests and individual rights to objective standards of measurement in cases like *Operation Dismantle*,[212] *Morgentaler*,[213] and *Borowski*.[214] Yet, their decisions hinge upon their willingness to select criteria upon which to base those objective standards in the first place. However well-intentioned, courts cannot help but be their sister's keeper, whether in determining the safety of the hemisphere, or in assessing life within it.[215]

Judges who seek to silence Keegstra or Zundel, therefore, do more than constrain the right of free speech. They carve out the boundaries of good neighbourliness itself. They do so, supposedly, as guardians of the Constitution, but also as protectors of a more elusive welfare of a civi-

---

[207] *Morgentaler, supra,* note 195, at 63-73 *per* Dickson C.J.

[208] See further, *infra,* Chapter 6.

[209] (1986), 34 D.L.R. (4th) 633 (C.A.). In *Phillips,* the court struck down legislation that discriminated against single fathers differently than single mothers. Everyone lost until the legislature amended and reintroduced the programme.

[210] But *cf. Schachter v. Canada,* [1988] 3 F.C. 515 (T.D.), affd. [1990] 2 F.C. 129 (C.A.), leave to appeal to S.C.C. granted November 15, 1990, where the court held that the failure of the *Unemployment Insurance Act* to provide benefits to adoptive as to natural parents was contrary to s. 15(1). Strayer J. refused to render those sections of the Act unenforceable, declaring, instead, that natural and adoptive parents are entitled to the same benefits.

[211] See *Big M Drug Mart, supra,* note 204.

[212] *Supra,* note 194.

[213] *Supra,* note 195.

[214] *Borowski v. Canada (A.G.),* [1989] 1 S.C.R. 342.

[215] For cogent debate upon the extent to which we are *not* our sister's keeper, notwithstanding the claims of deontologic liberals, see A. Gutman, "Communitarian Critics of Liberalism" (1985), 14 Phil. & Pub. Aff. 308; C. Backhouse, "Nineteenth Century Judicial Attitudes Towards Child Custody, Rape and Prostitution", in *Equality and Judicial Neutrality,* S.L. Martin and K.E. Mahoney, eds. (Toronto: Carswell, 1987), p. 271.

lized people. They permit the executive to conclude treaties that allow cruise missiles to fly over Canadian airspace as much because of their belief in national security as for any other reason.[216] They ignore the extent to which they are motivated by moral indignation or outrage by dressing up the right to free speech in juristic terms. However, they cannot displace the need to subjectify reason itself. Nor can they bypass their need to conciliate among social differences in order to reach specific decisions.[217]

MEDIATING AMONG DIFFERENCES

Judges who try to provide social justice enter into a class struggle. They evaluate inequality from the perspective of majorities who abuse minorities, whites who disfavour blacks, men who violate women, and parents who discard their young. They cast *Charter* rights within a non-egalitarian society into a distinctly moral sphere. At their narrowest, they protect collective rights simply because groups of right-holders are not able to protect themselves. They reduce communal life to the interests of oppressing groups. They envisage communal life solely in terms of an over- or under-assertive group. Each group speaks similarly for all within it against all outside of it. Each group, like each individual, competes to speak and be heard in light of the words or actions of other groups.[218] Whites, men and aryans compete with non-whites, women and Jews respectively. That significant segments of society might not want to listen to words of race hatred — allegedly uttered by a Keegstra or Zundel — they transform juridically into the wishes of identifiable groups not to be exposed to the biases of a purportedly master-race. The core intent, "to protect the target groups . . . from serious non-physical injury or reputational injury", they insist, "is a sufficient reason to limit imprudent speech".[219]

This approach is self-limiting. It is rooted in the adversarial domain. The decision-maker elects between identified adversaries, whether they be individuals or groups. She construes social injustice narrowly, so that "the well-being of the society *is simply the sum total of the well-being and happiness of its individual members*".[220] She fixes social relations in the power of one group or individual over another. She highlights the domi-

---

[216] *Operation Dismantle, supra*, note 194.

[217] See, *e.g., R. v. Keegstra* (1984), 19 C.C.C. (3d) 254 (Alta. Q.B.); *R. v. Zundel* (1987), 35 D.L.R. (4th) 338 (Ont. C.A.). For discussion on the mediation of social difference, see esp., *infra*, Chapter 3.

[218] See, *supra*, at 35.

[219] *R. v. Keegstra* (1988), 43 C.C.C. (3d) 150, at 171 (Alta. C.A.). See too, *R. v. Zundel, supra*, note 217, at 364.

[220] *Report of the Royal Commission on Health Services* (the Hall Report, 1964), vol. 1, at 5 (emphasis added).

nance of neo-Nazi over Jew, white over black, man over woman.[221] Equally
importantly, she shifts the competitive realm of the individual to the
equally competitive world of the group.

At its worst, this adverse world of negative rights, is destructive of
communal life. Courts that explore only the competition between the
right to speak and the right not to listen to racist or sexist words, forget
that words have a social dimension beyond speakers and listeners,
whether they be blacks, women or Jews. Indeed, in times of social stress,
"'hate' could mushroom into a real and monstrous threat to our way of
life".[222] Those who protect freedom of speech, regardless of that which
the speaker says, reduce objective rights to the bigotry, sexism and racism
of the speaker. They expect those who are most likely to be hurt by
bigotry to have deaf ears. They fail to realize that it is difficult not to
hear evil in a media-dominated world.

No group of litigants, blacks, women or aboriginal people, can per-
sonalize collective attitudes towards sex, race and religion without also
affecting the social climate around them. Groups of social actors are not
mere bystanders. They affect prayer, fiscal security, family, and the sanctity of the pregnant woman's body. They encompass special interest
groups that lobby for or against nuclear armament, gay and lesbian rights
or the death penalty. Within this wider sphere, social interests move
beyond adverse relations, between the State and pregnant women, producers and consumers, employers and employees. They entertain public
perceptions of hunger, employment and population growth, along with
social reactions towards each. Thus, the pregnant woman's right not to
be compelled to give birth hinges as much upon the perceived availability
of safe and humane abortion facilities as upon the right to foetal life
itself. The nature of foetal rights derives as much from the proposition
that foetal rights are constitutional as from scientific assumptions about
the moment of life.[223]

A competition between rights, as between social interests, is not necessary in itself. Indeed, affirmative action is truer when it resides in social
consciousness, well beyond the adversity between oppressor and oppressed. Rights are more readily protected when judges engage in conversation about difference in the social content of rights, and when they
evaluate the suppositions of those who display and effect those differences. Thus, liberties like free speech under ss. 2 and 7 of the *Charter*, have

[221] On such power relations in relation to sex discrimination, see esp., C. MacKinnon, *Sexual Harassment of Working Women: A Case of Sex Discrimination* (New Haven: Yale University Press, 1979), pp. 149-58; C. Boyle and S.W. Rowley, "Sexual Assault and Family Violence: Reflections on Bias", in *Equality and Judicial Neutrality, supra*, note 215, at 312.
[222] *Report of the Special Committee on Hate Propaganda in Canada* (Ottawa: Queen's Printer, 1966), p. 24.
[223] *Morgentaler*, [1988] 1 S.C.R. 30.

significance for both particular ethnic groups and the polity as a whole. They prevail, not simply as a result of adverse relations between right-holders and ethnic listeners. They evolve through a variety of "speech acts" and "speech effects" that take place within a wider public realm.[224]

I do not claim that affirmative rights completely displace negative rights. Neither the individual's nor the group's "private" world is swallowed up by identification with other people or associations. Those who forget this and interpret the *Charter* in a communitarian light fall into the same trap of static pluralism as those they criticize. Andrew Petter, for example, suggests that

> [t]he extent to which one person's rights and entitlements are expanded is the extent to which the rights and entitlements of others are contracted.[225]

With this statement, Petter rekindles a competitive theory of negative rights, albeit in relation to groups. He simplifies the communality by insisting that each person receive no greater rights than everyone else. Rights are vested either in negative individuals or in negative communities; to expand upon one is to contract the other. There is no growth beyond the static pie, nothing greater than the adversity between communities. Public life, it would seem, is no more than either the collectivity of private persons that constitute it, or the groups that represent it. This misses the point. Identification with the polity does not suddenly displace either personhood or social distinctiveness. Neither individual nor group is reduced to the mere instrument of an abstract and collective voice. Mrs. Lavell, in *Canada (A.G.) v. Lavell*,[226] does not cease to be either a person or an aboriginal person because of her gender or heredity. To so claim is not only to deny distinct status to personhood or group identity; it is to displace any egalitarian dream of an expansive social state. Each group becomes nothing more than its own keeper. Each individual is reduced to her isolated state. Individuals are not cloned according to their social, cultural or ethnic likeness. No matter how similar they appear to be, they speak with different voices as individuals, members of groups, and participants in the polity at large. They are like-minded in some respects and differently minded in others. Thus, no law-maker can seriously suggest that women think alike in all respects. Women do not agree upon the reach of reproductive rights any more than society at large agrees upon the virtue of the death sentence. To suggest, in *Morgentaler*,[227] that those who favour or disfavour reproductive rights are uninfluenced by the opinions of doctors, priests, civil rights activists or

---

[224] On "speech acts" and "speech effects", see, *infra*, Chapter 3.
[225] See A. Petter, "The Politics of the Charter" (1986), 8 Supreme Court L.R. 473, at 474.
[226] [1974] S.C.R. 1349.
[227] *Supra*, note 223.

lawyers is to ignore the impact of communal relations upon them. Law-givers look through a variable prism that encompasses individual, family, government and civil society alike. Exposed to a liberal, almost propertied, conception of rights, they ponder a "new yardstick of reconciliation be-tween the individual and the community".[228] In responding to commu-nal ideals, they take account of diffuse social reactions towards parent-hood, family life and social violence upon individual rights. In justifying parental discipline in a violent society, they distinguish child abuse from commodious family relations.[229] No matter how earnestly they insist upon the objective reach of ss. 2 and 7-14, they inevitably construe *Charter* rights in light of their social attributes.

Rising above liberal and socialist worlds is liberation from both. Nei-ther liberation of private life from the State nor liberation of the State from dominant private groups is a necessary condition of human co-existence. Neither adds anything to society simply by excluding the other. Each is falsely conceived through the static pie of opposing social forces. Neither envisages social interaction that is communicative, con-ciliatory, and ultimately, co-operative. The alternative is to endorse social and economic, or "second generation" rights, along with the "third gen-eration" rights of peoples to self-determination and communal develop-ment. It is to encompass, as substantive justice, the fundamental obligation of the State *and the justice system* to ensure the development of progres-sive standards of living, housing and employment. Phrased positively, everyone *should* have a right to shelter, sustenance and community. These positive rights are conciliatory more than competitive, communicative more than isolated, dynamic more than static.[230]

CONCLUSION

To affirm rights in society is to visualize rights, less as products of the discrete choices of individuals, than as interdependent acts of social groups. Here, communal life speaks in different voices, through the vision of Métis peoples, Catholics, pro-choice groups, and those who oppose cruise testing. The individual is alone only in the observation

---

[228]   *Law Society of Upper Canada v. Skapinker*, [1984] 1 S.C.R. 357, at 366.

[229]   See, *e.g.*, *Family & Children's Services of Kings County v. E.D.* (1988), 86 N.S.R. (2d) 205 (C.A.).

[230]   For an excellent example of the constitutional endorsement of second and third generation rights, see the *Banjul Charter on Human and People's Rights*, adopted by the Organization of African Unity (Doc. CAB/LEG/67/3/Rev. 5, Nairobi, Kenya, June 27, 1981). See further, A. Sachs, "Towards a Bill of Rights for a Democratic South Africa" (1989), 12 Hastings Int. & Comp. L. Rev. 289; Z. Motala, "Human Rights in Africa: A Cultural, Ideological, and Legal Examination" (1989), 12 Hastings Int. & Comp. L. Rev. 373. But *cf.* E. Bondzie-Simpson, "A Critique of the African Charter on Human and People's Rights" (1988), 31 Howard L.J. 643. See too, the ANC Constitutional Committee 1990, *A Bill of Rights for a New South Africa* (Bellville, South Africa: Centre for Development Studies, 1990), p. 29.

that she eats her own meals and breathes her own air. For the rest, she lives alongside others. She eats meals which they provide, directly or otherwise. She breathes air which they share with her, and sometimes contaminate. She has rights, not simply to exclude others from partaking of her food, polluting her air, or sleeping in her bed. She enjoys them as shared entitlements. Thus, the liberated court tolerates pluralism within society, knowing that the recognition of difference is itself a means towards social unity. However, in striving towards a complementary social spirit, it seeks to promote tolerable standards of living, employment and education that rise above the negative human subject. It takes account of the unequal ability of those who interact within the polity, along with the substantive means by which courts can redress that inequality.[231]

I do not dismiss the salient worth of the individual. The exercise of negative liberty does foster communal growth. However, it does not encompass the full gamut of social, economic and political life. Liberty is not determined wholly through a conflict between competing right-holders and groups, including the State. To affirm religious difference is to transcend the adversity between believer and non-believer. To affirm aboriginal rights is to conceive of both aboriginal and non-aboriginal conceptions of rights. Individual rights remain central to the social fabric. However, the individual asserts her rights through her ongoing association with others, not only through her autonomy from them. Co-operation and solidarity are as important to the polity as are competition and autonomy.

Her distinctiveness is not diminished by her participation within groups. Her interaction with other women or aboriginal people does not dictate that she must clone herself upon them. Differences among individuals complement as much as they threaten communal relations.[232] Indeed, a tolerant society identifies rights, not simply with the views of one or another group, but as each reflects upon and responds to the attitudes of individuals within it. The purpose is to debate, understand and reconcile differences among groups and those who interact with them. The goal is to redress through discourse the simmering resentment of Quebec in the wake of *Meech Lake*, and the hostility of First Nation Peoples following the stand-off at Kanasaktakwe and Kahnawake. It is to

---

[231] Roberto Unger typifies the conflict between the negative self and community in his "paradox of sociability". The individual is faced with the choice between keeping herself apart from others, without at the same time being alienated from them. See Unger, *Passion: An Essay on Personality* (New York: The Free Press, 1984); Unger, *Knowledge and Politics* (New York: The Free Press, 1975).

[232] Unger, clearly opposed to liberal conceptions of free choice as the basis of social action, nevertheless highlights the self as central to the social being. (See Unger, *Passion: An Essay on Personality, supra*, note 231, at 300.) However, he depicts the person, less as an autonomous and separate being, than as both a prison and a salvation. Salvation of the person, in particular, flows from the individual's "acceptance of vulnerability", including the risk of being hurt by others (*ibid.*, at 300-02).

affirm a positive social agenda through a co-operative spirit that encompasses mutual respect and assistance, along with regard for the dignity of others.

CHAPTER 3

FROM LIBERTY TO COMMUNITY

> The whole process of socialization . . . is a process in which the
> individual attains to increasing autonomy of action, but it is also a
> process in which the bond between the individual and the normative
> culture is strengthened, because this bond comes to depend less and
> less on any particular relations of the individual.[1]

Outside of language, aboriginal and multicultural rights, the unity of the
Canadian polity is contingent largely upon a self-contained private world.
Individuals have the right to assemble and speak under the *Charter*. Workers, as natural persons, have the right to strike, and corporations, as legal
persons, have the right to engage in business. Each person, in acting for
herself, also acts for the good of all.[2] As John Rawls would have it: "[t]he self
is prior to the ends which are affirmed by it."[3] This private world rests upon
three assumptions. First, human rights are framed within a rational private
hierarchy. Secondly, the common good necessarily flows from this hierarchy.
Thirdly, human rights within the private world hierarchy are non-communal
by nature. The sum total of private rights, rationally conceived and applied,
constitute the common good; there is no higher good beyond them.

My purpose here is to highlight non-competitive theories of community, and to extend them beyond plural right-holders to political life
itself. I contend that liberty is not rivetted in the image of a wholly
private and competitive world. I argue for the construction of a conception
of community discursively; and I claim that this conception, once constructed, should be guided by the interests of both reciprocity and equality. I base this discursive conception of community upon three primary
elements: the recognition of difference in history, culture and social practice; the capacity to converse with others about difference; and the willingness to confront both personal predilection and its denial in terms of
that conversation. These three factors infer, in sum, a readiness to en-

---

[1] R. Munch, "Talcott Parsons and the Theory of Action II: The Structure of the Kantian
     Core" (1982), 86 Am. J. Soc. 709, at 779.

[2] See *R. v. Morgentaler* (hereafter referred to as *Morgentaler*), [1988] 1 S.C.R. 30, as an
     illustration of the dominance of individual over community.

[3] J. Rawls, *A Theory of Justice* (Cambridge: Harvard University Press, 1971), p. 560.

dorse the human dimensions of social conversation, to treat other conversationalists, like oneself, as conversationally imperfect, and to mediate conversational differences constructively in light of those imperfections.

Accordingly, to argue for a realistic conception of community is to judge the manner in which discourse takes place within, and ultimately shapes, that polity. It is to reflect upon the presumed contributions of the trade union towards the polity, beyond the inherent rights of each individual labourer to organize, strike or picket.[4] Thus, conceptions of community are continually created and re-created in light of interests that are not necessarily shared. Discourse about rights involves facing, listening to and addressing others. Conversations about rights are, at best, incomplete and temporary; and their benefits, at best, are instrumental. These conversations influence attitudes. They justify. They persuade. They convince. However, they do not close off alternative conversations. They do not provide definitive solutions for all times.

Judges who restrict conversation to immediate parties who claim the benefit of *a priori* rights to the exclusion of everyone else, unduly restrict complex social relations. They reduce the totality of labour, corporate and family affairs to wholly private rights and relationships at the expense of the social context that surrounds them. They fasten liberty to the individual right-holder as glue adheres to paper; and in doing so, they hinder the ongoing renewal of a transformative liberty. They sometimes forget that the freedom to associate, so central to liberalism, anticipates a communal, not a wholly private life. As Alexis de Tocqueville once claimed:

> . . . [the] most natural privilege of man, next to the right of acting for himself, is that of combining his exertions with those of his fellow creatures and acting in common with them.[5]

RIGHTS AS HIERARCHY

Communal relations are often conceived, not simply correlatively,[6] but also through relations of dominance. Higher right-holders trump lesser right-holders, and dominant relations trump lesser relations. Thus, the relationship between individual and government, as between corporation and union, man and woman, is characterized in light of the status of each right-holder *vis-à-vis* the other. In effect, each right depends upon the social and economic standing of those who possess it; while each relationship hinges upon the status of those who participate within it. Following *R.W.D.S.U.* v. *Dolphin Delivery*,[7] relations between individual

---

4   See hereon, *supra*, Chapter 2.
5   A. de Tocqueville, *Democracy in America*, vol. 1, P. Bradley, ed. (New York: Vintage Books, 1945), p. 203.
6   On correlative relations, see, *infra*, at 65.
7   *Retail, Wholesale & Department Store Union, Loc. 580 v. Dolphin Delivery Ltd.* (hereafter referred to as *Dolphin Delivery*), [1986] 2 S.C.R. 573.

and government are subject to a higher public law hierarchy, notably to the *Charter*. Relations between individuals are subject to a lower private law hierarchy. The supremacy of the public hierarchy is justified on the assumption that, to have a coherent and effective constitutional order, fundamental rights should receive higher constitutional status than non-fundamental rights. This is captured in s. 52 of the *Constitution Act, 1982*[8] in providing that the Constitution

> . . . is the supreme law of Canada, and any law that is inconsistent with the provisions of the Constitution is, to the extent of the inconsistency, of no force or effect.

The modern liberal construction of human rights is oriented around two interrelated hierarchies: a structural hierarchy imposed by the State upon individuals, and a conceptual hierarchy among rights themselves. In *Charter* terms, the authority of individual rights hinges upon the extent of their constitutional endorsement. They are embodied along a spectrum, from fundamental, to legal, to non-legal rights. They exist within an institutional framework that ranges from *Charter* rights to common law rules, to moral precepts lacking the force of law. They are reconciled only as that framework permits. They are authoritative for reasons that inhere directly within them. Thus, relations between legislatures and courts are subject to a pervasive constitutional structure. Each organ of government is subject to the *Constitution*; and in complying with it, each has sovereignty only within its own hierarchical domain:

> The Courts will not question the wisdom of enactments which, by the terms of the Canadian Constitution are within the competence of the Legislatures, but it is the high duty of this [Supreme] Court to ensure that the Legislatures do not transgress the limits of their constitutional mandate and engage in the illegal exercise of power.[9]

A comparable hierarchy seemingly separates public from private life. Private rights are subject to private law; public relations are contingent upon public remedies. Thus, Canadian courts identify a public hierarchy in which the interests of government prevail over individual interests, and a private hierarchy in which fundamental rights trump lesser rights. These separate hierarchies, supposedly, are central to the democratic State. To delineate the "good life", the State requires authority to act within its domain. To protect fundamental liberties, the *Charter* assures the individual of her own sphere, apart from that State. These distinct hierarchies are preserved, in particular, under ss. 1 and 2 of the *Charter* respectively.

---

[8]   Enacted by the *Canada Act, 1982* (U.K.), c. 11, Schedule B.

[9]   *Amax Potash Ltd. v. Govt. of Saskatchewan*, [1977] 2 S.C.R. 576, at 590. See also *Reference re Manitoba Language Rights*, [1985] 1 S.C.R. 721, at 745-46; *Reference re Section 94(2) of the Motor Vehicle Act, R.S.B.C. 1979, c. 288 as am. by the Motor Vehicle Amendment Act, 1982 (B.C.), c. 36* (hereafter referred to as *Re B.C. Motor Vehicle Act*), [1985] 2 S.C.R. 486, at 496-97.

The hierarchy of the State is maintained under s. 1 and the hierarchy of fundamental — and private — freedoms is assured under s. 2.[10]

Courts face particular difficulties in preserving these two distinctive hierarchies. First, they cannot enforce individual liberty and State sovereignty both at the same time. Secondly, they cannot formulate one methodology by which to reconcile these hierarchies. Thirdly, they cannot insist upon the pervasiveness of either hierarchy where neither represents the full expanse of communal life. Communal discourse is more properly enhanced by a willingness to debate difference than by pre-empting debate through hierarchy. Discourse is functional when it evolves reflexively from thoughts, beliefs and attitudes rather than by virtue of some pre-ordained hierarchy.

Yet, the interface between private and public hierarchy is all too evident in constitutional law. The State, it would seem, entrenches individual autonomy under ss. 2 and 7-14. Yet, it asserts legislative authority over the individual, *inter alia*, under ss. 1, 15 and 33. In effect, the State is truly authoritative only in its ability to override the liberty of the individual. The individual is truly free only when she is not restrained by the State. As a result, *Charter* freedoms are reserved to individuals; yet they are subject to the directives of the State under ss. 1, 33 and 52.[11]

At its worst, the State dominates private life. Individuals and groups flourish only through its tolerance of them. The State, as patriarch of communal life, allows them to receive the right to own property and to discipline their children in their private lives, subject to its constraints. However, they cannot use their personal rights for any purpose whatsoever. They cannot decline their dependants schooling, food, or shelter. They cannot redirect family life as they deem fit. They cannot strike in *R.W.D.S.U. v. Saskatchewan*[12] if doing so would have a deleterious effect upon, among others, dairy farmers and consumers. Nor can they deny the executive the right to test cruise missiles in *Operation Dismantle*[13] if they cannot establish a legitimate cause of action. So impelled, the State determines the conditions under which husbands abuse wives, parents abuse children, employers abuse employees, and government directs the citizenry. That employers are free to "manage" the workforce, parents to "manage" their children, or governments to govern, therefore, is the State's concern. Ultimately, the State affects more than the individual: it impacts upon the quality of community life itself.

One means of reconciling private and public hierarchies lies in the belief that individual liberties, plurally construed, are implicitly and un-

---

[10]   See, *e.g.*, W.R. Lederman, "Democratic Parliaments, Independent Courts and the Canadian Charter of Rights and Freedoms" (1985-86), 11 Queen's L.J. 1.

[11]   See *Re B.C. Motor Vehicle Act, supra*, note 9, at 496.

[12]   *Retail, Wholesale & Department Store Union v. Saskatchewan* (hereafter referred to as *Saskatchewan Dairies*), [1987] 1 S.C.R. 460.

[13]   *Operation Dismantle Inc. v. R.*, [1985] 1 S.C.R. 441.

avoidably State interests. Applied to the worker in *Re Lavigne*,[14] the individual is free to institutionalize her bargaining rights because of the authority which the State vests in her. The private good is now fixed in two seemingly complementary hierarchies: first, in the individual's authority over herself, and secondly, in the State's authorization of that authority, in terms of the *Charter*. Following Chief Justice Dickson in *R. v. Big M Drug Mart Ltd.*:[15]

> . . . whatever the situation under that document, it is certain that the *Canadian Charter of Rights and Freedoms* does not simply "recognize and declare" existing rights . . . The language of the *Charter* is imperative.

In effect, the State, in complying with the *Charter*, preserves the private authority of the individual as a limit upon itself. Assisted by the judiciary, itself an institutional hierarchy, the State expects individuals to decide upon the good life for themselves, as they are empowered by the Constitution.

Yet, this complementary hierarchy falls short of its own reconciliatory ends. The individual, placed in a private hierarchy, lacks the freedom to determine her own good precisely because she is governed by an overriding State hierarchy. The labourer is free to unite with others in a labour union, but only insofar as her freedom does not impact negatively upon the interests of employers, consumers, children and the elderly, as the State defines those interests.

Courts simply cannot resolve conflicts between public and private hierarchies by treating State interests under s. 1 of the *Charter* and private rights under s. 2 as naturally commensurate. They cannot comfortably endorse the individual's freedom to strike under s. 2 of the *Charter* if they are to take due cognizance of the State's interest in the product of human labour. Nor can they recognize s. 2 rights within a private hierarchy and s. 1 interests within a public hierarchy without appreciating a public realm that transcends both. The State is not the sole repository of public life under s. 1 any more than fundamental rights are vested unconditionally in the individual under s. 2 or 7 of the *Charter*. To uphold the right of parents to discipline their children is also to reckon with the State's interest in preserving harmonious family life. In each case, the status of private rights **is** a conspicuous part of the politics of government; while politics is a critical component of private life as well.[16]

The modern liberal — somewhat more enlightened than her classical ancestor — undoubtedly recognizes the contradiction between the au-

---

14 See, *e.g.*, *Re Lavigne and Ontario Public Service Employees Union* (1986), 29 D.L.R. (4th) 321, at 380 (Ont. H.C.J.). There, it is stated that being forced to support a union financially violates the right to freedom of association (*per* White J.).

15 (Hereafter referred to as *Big M Drug Mart*), [1985] 1 S.C.R. 295, at 343.

16 See, *e.g.*, *Reference re Public Service Employee Relations Act (Alta.)* (hereafter referred to as the *Alberta Reference*), [1987] 1 S.C.R. 313.

tonomy of the individual and the authority of government.[17] However, her solution is to fall back on a limited vision of democratic life.[18] There, the individual is left unhappily between two poles: she is to choose government to rule over her, yet expect it to oversee her relations with others. She is to be two people: as a private person, she is to complement communal life cumulatively through her relations with others within it, as is endorsed by ss. 2 and 7-14 of the *Charter*. However, she is also a social being, required to succumb to the authority of the State under ss. 1 and 33.

In the section below, I critique this conception of a plural private community on the grounds that it marginalizes the individual, and that it provides for no other conception of civil society beyond that plurality. The alternative is to construct a wider conception of legal and political life. There, the State and the individual co-exist. Each represents a subset of public life. Neither stands alone in its own segregated sphere.[19] Each expresses itself through more than its adversity with the other.

PLURAL RIGHTS

> Liberals have persistently tended to cut the citizen off from the person; and they have placed on their humanistic pedestal a cripple of a man, a man without a moral or political nature; a man with plenty of contractual rights and obligations, perhaps, but a man without moorings in any real community, a drifter rather than a being with roots in species solidarity.[20]

Individual rights that are construed plurally generally give rise to a formal relationship only. Typically, an employee, female or aboriginal is tied to others by a formal relationship of employment, marriage or tribalism that is endorsed by law. At worst, she is subjugated by the group in which she is a member, or by those who dominate it. At best, she is a self-motivated right-holder who determines the quality of her own participation within that group. The result, however viewed, is a marginalized person. Subsumed within the group that surrounds her, the individual is rendered into its creature, yet somehow her own person in terms of it. She preserves her own way of life, but only in accordance with the way of life of others within the formal group.[21] For the court to

---

[17]   See, *e.g.*, Rawls, *op. cit.*, note 3. Rawls' individual is a congenial being who concurs in a social contract from the outset. Ronald Dworkin's autonomous individual is similarly a social animal, responsive throughout to a coherent and communicative discourse. See, in general, Dworkin, *Taking Rights Seriously* (London: Duckworth, 1977). See further hereon, *infra*, at 64.

[18]   This is discussed immediately below.

[19]   See further, *infra*, Chapter 4.

[20]   C. Bay, "From Contract to Community: Thoughts on Liberalism and Postindustrial Society", in *From Contract to Community*, F.R. Dallmyr, ed. (New York: Marcel Dekker Inc., 1978), p. 30.

[21]   The right to an inviolate body, in *Morgentaler*, [1988] 1 S.C.R. 30, and *Borowski v. Canada (A.G.)*, [1989] 1 S.C.R. 342, is rendered immediately resoluble in light of a related right,

protect her is for it to protect the group at large.[22]

The difficulty with this approach is to maintain, without contradiction, a definitive image of the individual as a unique being who is also part of a social group. The individual is meant to interact with other like-minded workers, women or aboriginal peoples. Yet her relations with them are constrained by the State. She is her own person, yet she is subject to a communal identity that others impute to her. An individual, she is also an aboriginal or female who identifies with that group in defending itself from the State.[23] A member of a group, she likely abhors being stereotyped by the State because of that membership. She likely shields her group identity; yet she fears, among other things, that she might be subject to the State's unmitigated patronage because she **is** black, a woman or a member of a religious minority.[24]

The classical liberal remedy is to build communal life wholly through the self-reliant person, not as a member of one or another group. As a result, what is good for the polity rests, full square, upon what is good for individuals who engage in reciprocal relations within it. As such, communal life is nothing more than the consolidation of private relationships. It exists only in the readiness of individuals to engage within it, not in some communal justification for their doing so.[25] Thus, labour unions are composites of workers who contribute to the union, *inter alia*, through their payment of dues to it. The polity, in effect, has no face, no personality, indeed, no being beyond those who constitute it.

---

here, to be born. Determining that a right to personal security is violated is set in the context of the immediate parties to the relationship: pregnant women and foetuses. Lengthy delays in gaining access to abortion and inconsistent rulings of therapeutic abortion committees do *not* move beyond the community of pregnant women or unborn life. By abstracting the claimed right of each from its normative context, the substantive qualities that are associated with it are severed from the external community. The legitimacy of each party's rights is identified only in relation to a competing "other".

[22] See, *e.g.*, Rawls, *op. cit.*, note 3, at 90-96. But see Rawls' second principle of justice, that liberty is subject to the liberty of the least privileged. See esp. J. Rawls, "Justice as Fairness" (1957), 54 J. Phil. 653, at 653-57.

[23] On a similarly "negative" construction of communal association, see *Re Lavigne, supra,* note 14, at 380 *per* White J.

[24] On the feminist critique of conventional-male conceptions of community, see esp., *Equality and Judicial Neutrality,* S.L. Martin and K.E. Mahoney, eds. (Toronto: Carswell, 1987), pp. 269-326 (Sexism in Criminal Law); *Law and the Community: The End of Individualism?,* A.C. Hutchinson and L.J. Green, eds. (Toronto: Carswell, 1989), pp. 119-50, 205-52. See further, C.A. MacKinnon, "Desire and Judicial Power" and "Francis Biddle's Sister: Pornography, Civil Rights and Speech", in *Feminism Unmodified: Discourses on Life and Law* (Cambridge: Harvard University Press, 1987); M. Minow, "Learning to Live with the Dilemma of Difference: Bilingual and Special Education" (1985), 48 Law & Contemp. Probs., No. 2, p. 157. See in general, A.C. Scales, "The Emergence of Feminist Jurisprudence: An Essay" (1986), 95 Yale L.J. 1373.

[25] See *Re Lavigne, supra,* note 14 (*per* White J.). The Union in this case did argue that allowing people to opt out of paying union dues would "prevent them from performing their socio-economic role in society" (at 344). This argument, however, received no apparent consideration by the court.

In enforcing plural rights, decision-makers supposedly do no more than identify social relations that evolve naturally from those relations. They do not evaluate the social interests that underlie fundamental rights. They do not comment upon the substantive nature of employer-employee relations in *Saskatchewan Dairies*,[26] nor upon the virtue of Sunday trade in *R. v. Edwards Books & Art Ltd.*[27] Nor do they consider the quality of reproductive life in *Morgentaler*.[28] Neutral towards private right-holders, they suppose that rights have no value beyond that which right-holders themselves attribute to them.

This conception of democratic responsibility is readily depicted in relation to freedom of association. For Tocqueville, for example, the "right of association . . . appears . . . almost as inalienable . . . as the right of personal liberty".[29] The product of reciprocal relations, each association is a product of individual want. Each relies upon the individual to establish her own associations within it. The individual is **not** obliged to associate with others against her will; nor are others obliged to associate with her. What is good for the whole is a function of what is good for her. In effect, the court sanctifies her autonomy, not some collective being beyond her. It attributes to her no political worth beyond her willingness to participate within the polity. She is free to assemble and speak simply because her rights — duly entrenched in the *Charter* — so provide, not because some greater social purpose permits her to do so. Built on the assumption that human rights apply equally to everyone, little social good supposedly derives from community interests beyond them.

Implicit in this deontologic structure of rights is the belief that individual rights should dictate the nature of collective relations, not the converse.[30] As John Rawls would have it:

> The essential idea is that we want to account for the social values . . . by a conception of justice that . . . is individualistic . . . We do not want to rely on an undefined concept of community, or to suppose that society is an organic whole with a life of its own distinct from and superior to that of all its members in their relations with one another. Thus the contractual conception of the original position is worked out first. From this conception, however individualistic it might seem, we must eventually explain the value of community.[31]

26   *Supra,* note 12.
27   (Hereafter referred to as *Edwards Books*), [1986] 2 S.C.R. 713.
28   *Supra,* note 21.
29   A. de Tocqueville, *Democracy in America,* vol. 1, P. Bradley, ed. (New York: Vintage Books, 1945), p. 203.
30   On deontologic liberalism, see M.J. Sandel, *Liberalism and the Limits of Justice* (Cambridge: Cambridge University Press, 1982), pp. 1-14; A. Arblaster, *The Rise and Decline of Western Liberalism* (New York: Basil Blackwell, 1984), pp. 3-37, 55-94.
31   See Rawls, *A Theory of Justice* (Cambridge: Harvard University Press, 1980), pp. 265-66. Rawls attributes to community a derivative value. Its nature and content exists only in terms of those who function within it. There is no community apart from the subjects who constitute it. Thus, all members of society, acting under a "veil of ignorance",

That individual rights determine the plural nature of human association is apparent in the *Alberta Reference*.[32] There, the majority preserves the individual's right to join and participate in a labour union, but not the liberty of the union itself. Notwithstanding Chief Justice Dickson's distinctly non-liberal dissent, the approach of the majority is both piecemeal and individualistic. The court conceives of the political life of the union through the rights of its members. By restricting communal life to pre-existing right-holders, it ignores the collective dimension of workers' rights, indeed, the whole point of the union. Applying a plural theory to private life, it presumes that individuals ought to be free to relate to one another, but only so long as their actions remain anchored in their own private sphere. Applied to labour-management relations, individuals are free to form labour unions, but not to strike or demonstrate. The act of speaking is personal to the speaker and listener. However, the act of striking or demonstrating transcends the *persona* of both. As Mr. Justice Beetz would have it in *Canada (A.G.) v. City of Montreal*: "[d]emonstrations are not a form of speech but of collective action."[33]

Thus, no matter how fair-minded they are, judges sometimes claim that they cannot redress the wishes of workers to participate in the redistribution of social resources, or the desire of corporations to acquire a more compliant workforce. They cannot render poor workers rich, or extend social empowerment to workers over their bosses. They supposedly mediate between right-holders. They do not impose communal interests upon them. They evaluate rights as they are, not social purposes they believe ought to guide those rights. They regard the communal status quo as predetermined: they do not recompose it after the fact. Notwithstanding the efforts of Chief Justice Dickson and Madam Justice Wilson in the Western labour trilogy, they do not modify the rights of workers and their children. Nor do they amend statutory schemes that impinge upon substantive inequalities in the workforce.[34] They insist that enactments providing for the apprehension of "children in need of protection" apply equally to all children,[35] not to some children before others. That white children are more likely to be employed than black

---

accept individual rights as the totality of the original position. But note that Rawls has moved towards a more open conception of "the good" in his more recent writings. See, *e.g.*, Rawls, "The Domain of the Political and Overlapping Consensus" (1989), 64 N.Y.U. L. Rev. 233; Rawls, "The Idea of Overlapping Consensus" (1987), 7 Oxford J. Leg. Stud. 1.

32   [1987] 1 S.C.R. 313.

33   [1978] 2 S.C.R. 770, at 797.

34   The Western labour trilogy consists of *Dolphin Delivery*, [1986] 2 S.C.R. 573; *Alberta Reference*, [1987] 1 S.C.R. 313; *Saskatchewan Dairies*, [1987] 1 S.C.R. 460. But *cf. Bregman et al. v. Canada (A.G.)* (1986), 33 D.L.R. (4th) 477 (Ont. C.A.), leave to appeal to S.C.C. refused 61 O.R. (2d) 278n.

35   *M.K.S. v. Nova Scotia (Minister of Community Services)* (1988), 86 N.S.R. (2d) 209 (Co. Ct.); affd. 88 N.S.R. (2d) 418 (C.A.).

children, men are more likely to be "bosses" than women, and rich people are less frequently jailed than poor people, raise social not juridical concerns.

Judges who still insist that they merely regulate relations, including relations between the State and individuals, disregard the extent to which others are affected by these relations. They pass over the communal dimension of individual existence and the social content of rights.[36] The harm is that the polity disintegrates into "a plurality of persons, each with his own aims, interests, and conceptions of the good".[37] The loss is that communal life disappears within a sea of fixed rights and duties.

In reality, communal life moves well beyond immediate and reciprocal relations between individuals. It is developed out of disparate attitudes towards the economic and physical conditions of housewives and single mothers. It is constructed out of different social reactions to laws devised by "working" men, factory owners and social welfare organizers. It is justified by functional ends that underlie social relations and by practical means of effecting those ends. As Hutchinson and Petter claim of the right of labourers to organize:

> ... the whole idea and existence of a union is to foster social solidarity and to establish a collective presence that can overcome workers' vulnerability to the greater power of employers. Limiting union rights to those that can be exercised by members individually is to subvert the whole raison d'etre.[38]

This is not to suggest that individual rights and relationships ought to succumb to dominant conceptions of communal life. Indeed, communal life encompasses the individual's hopes, dreams and desires, when she acts alone, as when she acts in concert with others. The *Employment Equity Act*[39] takes account of her desire for fair treatment, in light of communal reactions towards privilege and disadvantage. It contemplates her disadvantaged status as an aboriginal person or a woman, but not as a solitary subject. It reflects upon the status of other women who interact, just as she does, with advantaged white males.

To still insist that civil society be composed wholly out of reciprocal private relations is to advance a distinctly "impoverished conception of communal politics".[40] It is to establish a false pathway from discrete private relations to communal life. To highlight the interface between private rights and discrete relations is to resist any communicative vision

---

[36]   See Rawls, *A Theory of Justice, supra,* note 31, at 192. For a detailed critique of Rawls hereon, see Sandel, *op. cit.,* note 30, at 148-52.

[37]   Sandel, *op. cit.,* note 30, at 1.

[38]   A.C. Hutchinson and A. Petter, "Private Rights/Public Wrongs: The Liberal Lie of the Charter" (1988), 38 U.T.L.J. 278, at 296.

[39]   R.S.C. 1985, c. 23 (2nd Supp.).

[40]   See P.J. Monahan, "Judicial Review and Democracy: A Theory of Judicial Review" (1987), 21 U.B.C. L. Rev. 87.

of the polity beyond both. The individual is a player within a communal play, not the play herself. Her interests do not reside wholly in her opposition to others, including the State. Her position, in part, is a product of her group identity, race, sex, colour, or creed, not simply a consequence of her individuality. Her competitive relations are subsets of communal life as much as embodiments of her personal desires. In no case do her private rights determine the reach of the expedient, righteous, or moral good, all by themselves. In no case do the rights of children, workers or Sunday shoppers subsist in disregard of social attitudes towards them. As much as the individual might wish otherwise, she is alone only in her own mind. Submerged within communal life, her personality acquires meaning through it.

This does not mean that the individual loses her identity to a communal life that engulfs her. It infers only that her identity as a worker, judge or pregnant woman is intertwined with her identity with others. She cannot relate to others unless she is also conceived of as a social being. She cannot be wholly her own person if she is affected by her social relations.

CORRELATIVE RELATIONS

> A political order in which rights consciousness is highly developed is prone to instability unless counterbalanced by norms of duty, obligation and responsibility.[41]

Within a relational community, human interaction, including the act of agreeing, is conceived of as correlative rather than competitive. Emphasis is given, less to the competitive exercise of rights, and more to the correlative relationship between those who hold rights and those who are duty bound by them. Each individual gives to, or takes from, others in light of her correlative rights and the correlative duties she owes others; and each, in contesting the rights of others, claims that her rights ought to be dominant. This is clearly the unexpressed conflict between labour and management in a trilogy of labour cases in Western Canada.[42]

A correlative community is therefore formed by weighing correlative rights against correlative duties. In the tradition of Hohfeld, the individual exercises her rights over those from whom, she claims, she can extract duties.[43] Jewish sympathizers assert their rights against neo-Nazis, while neo-Nazis claim a right to free expression against Jewish sympathizers who would deny it. Each avers that its rights impose correlative

---

[41] A.C. Cairns and C. Williams, "Constitutionalism, Citizenship and Society in Canada: An Overview", in *Constitutionalism, Citizenship and Society in Canada*, A.C. Cairns and C. Williams, eds. (Toronto: University of Toronto Press, 1985), p. 3.

[42] See, *supra*, note 34. See too, *infra*, at 69.

[43] W.N. Hohfeld, "Fundamental Legal Conceptions as Applied in Judicial Reasoning" (1917), 26 Yale L.J. 710; Hohfeld, "Some Fundamental Legal Conceptions as Applied in Judicial Reasoning" (1913), 23 Yale L.J. 16.

duties upon others. Individuals invoke their rights against government. Women assert theirs against men, and ethnic and cultural minorities advance theirs against the majority. In effect, correlative rights encompass adverse and harmonious, discrete and ongoing, conclusive and temporary relations. They reflect the correlative relations of individuals who interact with religious sects, and of religious sects who interact with the State. They embrace the rights and duties of individuals, groups and government alike.

At its worst, a correlative community leads to a static liberty. Individuals and groups employ their rights solely to protect themselves from those who owe them duties. The corporation employs its rights to protect itself from its employees. Oakes uses his right to due process to protect himself from the government.[44] In each case, the legal goal is not to render the relations between particular workers, women, aboriginal peoples and government hermetically sealed; it is to protect correlative rights themselves. The purpose is not to preserve religious practices or business ethics, but specific rights.

Arguably, those who demand that disputes be reconciled through such correlative rights and duties trap themselves in an inert world in which correlative relations supersede social experience.[45] They protect the liberty of a black woman to obtain work, regardless of the political conditions under which she is disadvantaged. They bypass the social conditions under which adverse relations evolve between government and citizen, between white and black, man and woman. They fail to recognize that no one right necessarily prevails. None gives rise to an exactly corresponding duty. In finding a correlation between the individual's rights and the duties of others towards her, they pass over the social conditions under which she exercises her rights in the first place.

In reality, correlative relations are constructed, not self-evident. They do not inevitably protect nuclear freeze from nuclear energy proponents, or Jews from neo-Nazis, or First Nation Peoples from non-aboriginal peoples. Indeed, rights and duties are no more necessarily related to each other than the right to have an abortion is related to the right to be born. Judges may well identify an adverse relationship between workers' rights and employers' duties. However, so long as the social context surrounding those rights and duties is unclear, the virtue of comparing them is equally unclear. Suited to mechanical science, correlative rights lead to formal equality only, not to substantive justice beyond that formality.[46]

---

44   *R. v. Oakes*, [1986] 1 S.C.R. 103.
45   See, *e.g.*, Hohfeld, *loc. cit.*, note 43.
46   See generally Plato, *The Republic*, trans. G.M.A. Grube (Indianapolis: Hackett, 1974), Bk. IV; Aristotle, *Categories*, Chapter 10; and *Topics*, Bk. II, in *The Complete Works of Aristotle: The Revised Oxford Translation*, J. Barnes, ed. (Princeton: Princeton University Press, 1984);

This correlative rhetoric applies to *Charter* rights, deficiencies and all. Judges who insist that communal relations evolve solely through the primacy of rights over duties, confine themselves to a formal process of weighing. Either pro-aboriginal groups receive the right to demonstrate freely in Oka, Quebec, as a measure of their right to associate, or they are duty bound to respect the rights of others who are negatively affected by the exercise of that right. The solution seemingly lies solely in the correlative relationship between rights and duties. This reasoning is questionable. Social justice is the opposite of social injustice only according to the normative values that are injected into it. No unified sentiment confirms the meaning of life, liberty and security of the person. No consolidated vision of rights leads to their inevitable justification, and ratification. The belief that pro-aboriginal groups ought to be free to publish or teach about aboriginal culture hinges upon yet other beliefs: that aboriginal literature is part of freedom of expression, that such literature is worthy of expression, or that the speaker is free to express herself regardless of the content of her expression. To translate such different beliefs into correlative rights and duties is to engage in a leap of faith where doing right for one is the same as achieving the "good" for all.[47] Rights are seldom perfectly and consistently related to duties. Judges diverge over the circumstances in which free speech and free association is in the public's interest.[48] They differ over the precise manner in which life comes into being, and upon the limits of liberty and security of the person. They argue as readily against the existence of a fundamental right to life as in support of it.[49] They diverge over the need to protect seal and whale life in Canadian waters and over the virtue of preserving cult-like practices in the communes of Western Canada.[50] By insisting that correlative rights and duties be evaluated only in relation to each other, they render other conceptions of social life into hollow abstractions. They

---

Aquinas, *Summa Theologica* (New York: McGraw-Hill, 1964); T. Hobbes, *Leviathan*, C.B. Macpherson, ed. (Harmondsworth: Penguin, 1968), Part 1.

[47] On discourse through contrariness, see in general, Plato, *Phaedrus*, trans. W.C. Helmbold and W.G. Rabinowitz (New York: Liberal Arts Press, 1956); *The Republic*, trans. A.D. Bloom (New York: Basic Books, 1968), Bk. V: Aristotle, *Posterior Analytics*, trans. H.G. Apostle (Grinnell, Iowa: Peripatetic Press, 1981), Bk. 1, Chapter 31; J. Locke, *An Essay Concerning Human Understanding*, P.H. Nidditch, ed. (Oxford: Clarendon Press, 1975); D. Hume, *Philosophical Essays Concerning Human Understanding* (Hildesheim: Georg Olms Verlag, 1986).

[48] See *R. v. Keegstra* (1988), 43 C.C.C. (3d) 150 (Alta. C.A.), where Kerans J.A. held that s. 2 of the *Charter* protects both "innocent error and imprudent speech" (at 164); and that "citizens in a democratic society must show a courage and stoicism in the face of abusive exercise of freedom of expression" (at 173).

[49] See *Borowski v. Canada (A.G.)*, [1989] 1 S.C.R. 342.

[50] See in general, C.K. Ogden, *Opposition: A Linguistic and Psychological Analysis* (Bloomington: Indiana University Press, 1967); F.H. Bradley, *Appearance and Reality: A Metaphysical Essay* (Oxford: Clarendon Press, 1966); B. Russell, *An Inquiry into Meaning and Truth* (London: G. Allen & Unwin, 1940), Chapter 20.

reduce the adversity between Andrews, a would-be legal practitioner, and the Barristers' Society of British Columbia to a correlative relationship in respect of which they are neutral.[51] They allow social life, lacking in concrete content, to recede into a netherworld, far removed from the correlative rights and duties of the parties.[52]

Judges who weigh rights and duties correlatively, in reality, erect a normative hierarchy by which they constitute one into a right and the other into a duty. In effect, they choose, not simply between fundamental rights and duties, but between preferred reasons for treating them as rights and duties respectively. They rate s. 2 and s. 7 rights according to variable conceptions of the degree to which those rights are fundamental in fact. They value s. 1 duties according to their diffuse conceptions of the "reasonable limits" of governmental action in "a free and democratic society".[53]

One can hardly expect judges to concur in the benefit of Zundel's right to publish anti-Semitic literature, or Keegstra's right to profess the falsity of the holocaust. There is probably even less agreement upon the social value of the right to life and security of the person than upon that of the right to be born, whatever *Morgentaler* might suggest.[54] Judges do not find rights equally compelling in all respects. The right to freedom of expression of those who challenge the truth of the holocaust is no more a determinant of "the common good" than the duty not to offend holocaust survivors. No matter how earnestly judges deny that they make value judgments about rights and duties, they cannot divorce themselves from social conceptions of good and evil. In cases like *R. v. Keegstra*[55] and *R. v. Zundel*,[56] judges take account of conflicting beliefs in a Zionist conspiracy to perpetuate a holocaust myth. They highlight the social ramifications that arise when employers lock out employees, or employees strike. They reflect diffuse conceptions of religious observance, common pause days and the virtue of Sunday shopping. They display dissimilar visions of the Quebec government's duty to service French Quebec, and the Manitoba government's duty to service English Manitoba. They conceive of rights and duties qualitatively, not simply descriptively.

Thus, the correlative relationship between rights and duties breaks down precisely where it began, with the realization that communal interests give rise to rights and duties only in the court's willingness to so

---

[51]   See *Andrews v. Law Society of British Columbia* (hereafter referred to as *Andrews*), [1988] 1 S.C.R. 143.

[52]   See, *e.g.*, *Morgentaler*, [1988] 1 S.C.R. 30. See also, *infra*, Chapter 6.

[53]   On "reasonable limits" under s. 1, see esp., A. Brudner, "What Are Reasonable Limits to Equality Rights?" (1986), 64 Can. Bar. Rev. 469; P. Rogers, "Equality, Efficiency and Judicial Restraint" (1986), 10 Dalhousie L.J. 139; *Oakes, supra*, note 44, at 138-39.

[54]   See, *infra*, Chapter 6.

[55]   *Supra*, note 48. For extensive discussion hereon, see, *supra*, Chapter 2.

[56]   (1987), 35 D.L.R. (4th) 338 (Ont. C.A.), leave to appeal to S.C.C. refused 61 O.R. (2d) 588n.

construe them in specific relationships. Once the court acknowledges the influence of normative opinion upon it, its decisions represent, less a choice between correlative rights and duties, than an expression of its social interest in one or another rationalization or result. In effect, the court does far more than weigh correlative rights and duties in protecting impressionable children from the ill effects of advertising in *Irwin Toy Ltd. v. Quebec (A.G.)*,[57] or babies from milk deprivation in *Saskatchewan Dairies*.[58] It incorporates a range of social effects into its judgments.

Once judges shift from correlative to *social* relations, the issue is no longer simply about the correlative rights and duties of workers and employers, but about the impact of industrial relations upon both. Rising to the fore is the perceived power of one-sided employment contracts, along with the power of government over labour. The right to strike, picket or lock out shifts from *a priori* rights of individual workers in *Saskatchewan Dairies*,[59] the *Alberta Reference*,[60] and *Dolphin Delivery*,[61] to the social context in which labour unrest occurs. Emphasized is the economic chaos and physical damage that arises from strikes and lockouts, and the fear of unduly empowering workers or employers. Raised, along with the hunger of workers and their dependants, are different perceptions of the worth of the employer's business and the effect of increased prices of goods and services upon the public at large.[62] In each case, the judge takes account of social forces, not merely correlative rights and duties. As Chief Justice Dickson argued in *Saskatchewan Dairies*:

> . . . the relevant question . . . is whether the potential for economic harm to third parties during a work stoppage is so massive and immediate and so focused in its intensity as to justify the limitation of a constitutionally guaranteed freedom . . .[63]

In so enlarging community beyond correlative relations, courts shift their frame of reference to encompass a mediated public life.[64] They identify communal life with a co-operative humanity whose guiding ontology lies in a co-existent state. There, human relations evolve among social beings, not simply correlative right-holders. There, the nature of correlative relations hinges upon the social environment in which would-be right-holders interact, not upon abstract rights.[65] There, judges reflect

---

[57]   (Hereafter referred to as *Irwin Toy*), [1989] 1 S.C.R. 927.
[58]   [1987] 1 S.C.R. 460.
[59]   *Ibid.*
[60]   [1987] 1 S.C.R. 313.
[61]   [1986] 2 S.C.R. 573.
[62]   See, *infra*, at 83.
[63]   *Supra*, note 58, at 477-78.
[64]   On mediation as a process, see, *infra*, at 70.
[65]   See M.J. Sandel, *Liberalism and the Limits of Justice* (Cambridge: Cambridge University Press, 1982). Sandel's analysis is largely directed against the liberal conception of the antecedent self, and in particular, Rawls' claim that the self be able to act as an individuated subject in seeking the good life (at 142-44). Sandel's account is somewhat

upon the nature of law and order, the free market system, and the social context in which both function. They debate French language and aboriginal rights, the right to advertise in French in Quebec, and to trade on Sundays in *Edwards Books*.[66]

Those who engage in such a mediated social discourse, falling short of spontaneous reconciliation, move beyond correlative rights and duties. They find no finite qualities within any one group, and no measurable good within a single formulation of employment, race, or religious sentiment. They realize that, to live as a Catholic, Mormon or Jew is to adopt different kinds of faith with differing degrees of conviction.

Judges who engage in such an open discourse, rather than defeat the ends of adversarialism, encompass it. They observe the adversarial confrontations between legal counsel who debate the language rights of anglophone Quebecers and the reproductive rights of pregnant women. Yet, they are persuaded by more than the adverse rights and duties of specific litigators. They take account of the social ramifications that arise from those rights and duties. They rely upon the services of expert witnesses, public interveners, special masters, and conceivably, professional research services.[67] Their discourse is participatory, communicative, and co-operative. It is participatory in their willingness to provide non-adjudicating parties with access to the courtroom. It is communicative in their readiness to communicate with them, as with the litigants themselves. It is co-operative in their preparedness to construct their opinions in light of that communication. It is co-operative, too, in their readiness to accommodate social interests, for example, the interest of the accused in having a prompt trial in *R. v. Askov*,[68] and the community's interest in ensuring that justice be done.

This shift in emphasis from correlative rights to communal interests is echoed in *Charter* interpretation. As Mr. Justice McIntyre advocated in the *Alberta Reference*:

> The interpretation of the *Charter*, as of all constitutional documents, is constrained by the language, structure, . . . by constitutional tradition, and *by the history, traditions and underlying philosophies of our society*.[69]

---

disputable in the associational frame in which he constitutes the self. By denying credence to any objective self with self-determined rights, he identifies a contingent subject that exists through the community that happens to constitute her.

66   [1986] 2 S.C.R. 713.

67   See in general, P.L. Dubois, *The Analysis of Judicial Reform* (Lexington, Mass.: Lexington Books, 1982), and esp. A. Sarat, "Judicial Capacity: Courts, Court Reform, and the Limits of the Judicial Process", in *The Analysis of Judicial Reform, ibid.*, at 31. See too, K.C. Davis, "Judicial, Legislative, and Administrative Lawmaking: A Proposed Research Service for the Supreme Court" (1986), 71 Minn. L. Rev. 1.

68   (1990), 74 D.L.R. (4th) 355 (S.C.C.) (on the constitutional right for an accused to be tried within a reasonable period of time). See in general, J. Resnik, "Failing Faith: Adjudicatory Procedure in Decline" (1986), 53 U. Chi. L. Rev. 494.

69   *Supra*, note 60, at 394 (emphasis added).

This expansive method of interpretation, however unintentionally advocated, is also implicit in the Supreme Court's endorsement of the "purpose and effects" approaches towards legislation.[70] It is evident in the
perception of judges that *Charter* purposes stretch beyond the immediate
demands of specific right-holders to the interests of the polity at large.[71]

None of this denies a place to correlative rights and duties in communal
life. Individuals and groups interact correlatively every day. They do so
when they claim the right to conduct business on Sundays in *Edwards
Books*,[72] to refugee status in Canada in *Singh v. Minister of Employment &
Immigration*,[73] and to practise law as non-citizens in *Andrews*.[74] However,
their correlative rights and duties in performing these acts stem from the
communal belief that particular rights and duties ought to be granted *ex
posteriori*, not that they exist *a priori*. This sense of community is "strong"
or "weak" in light of normative conviction. Thus, judges are exposed to
a disparate sense of being, feeling and acting. They experience the diverse
attitudes of religious enthusiasts, proponents of cruise missile testing,
and champions of Sunday trade. Indeed, their very capacity to observe,
experience and react to social attitudes evolves out of their understanding that human relations are socially situated, not segregated from society.

This is not to advocate an all-consuming communal life in which judges
reduce all individual goals to common ends. However, communal life
cannot be modeled solely upon adverse relations between individuals
and the State without diminishing itself. Neither individuals nor groups
of right-holders can be the sole repositories of social endeavour.[75] Human
rights and duties do not constitute the totality of the good life: they are
as much products as determinants of that life. Their source lies in faith
that life ought to be lived communally; and that faith is expressed through
a spirit of humanism, political consciousness, and moral sensitivity.[76]
Judges identify this faith with sociability of the human spirit, beyond
abstract mysticism. At their most sociable, they identify positive action
with the State's obligation to dismantle racist and sexist stereotypes. They

---

70   See, *e.g., Big M Drug Mart*, [1985] 1 S.C.R. 295, at 332-33 *per* Dickson J. (as he then was).
71   See, *e.g., Hunter v. Southam Inc.*, [1984] 2 S.C.R. 145, at 157; *Law Society of Upper Canada
      v. Skapinker*, [1984] 1 S.C.R. 357, at 366.
72   *Supra*, note 66.
73   (Hereafter referred to as *Singh*), [1985] 1 S.C.R. 177.
74   [1989] 1 S.C.R. 143.
75   On the development of an extensive, and sometimes communicative, conception of
      freedom of association, based upon international commitments to human rights, see
      A. Brudner, "The Domestic Enforcement of International Covenants on Human Rights:
      A Theoretical Framework" (1985), 35 U.T.L.J. 219. But *cf.* M. MacNeil, "Recent
      Developments in Canadian Law: Labour Law" (1986), 18 Ottawa L. Rev. 83, at 92; and
      Newfoundland Assn. of Public Employees v. Newfoundland (1985), 85 C.L.L.C. ¶14,020, at
      12,090 (Nfld. S.C.).
76   See esp., M. Ferguson, *The Aquarian Conspiracy: Personal and Social Transformation in the
      1980s* (New York: St. Martin's Press, 1980); A. Gorz, *Ecology As Politics*, trans. P.
      Vigderman and J. Cloud (Montreal: Black Rose Press, 1980).

insist that people matter more than things and that rights represent more than the legal byproduct of economic power.[77] They embrace within that faith communal reactions towards human salvation, whether they are expressed by practising Christians, agnostics, or atheists. They realize that "membership" in a community ultimately "can mean nothing other than participation"[78] in it.

COMMUNITY THROUGH EXPRESSION

> The right of free expression of opinion and of criticism . . . and the right to discuss and debate such matters, whether they be social, economic or political, are essential to the working of a parliamentary democracy . . .[79]

Communicative discourse that is viewed relationally hinges wholly upon the "speech acts" of the individuals who engage in it. One party expresses a view, a "speech act", and the other responds. The alternative is to construe discourse more communicatively, not simply as dialogue between parties engaged in correlative relations. In effect, social conversation consists of more than the "speech acts" of related parties.[80] It serves as a measure through which social actors formulate, comprehend, and ultimately, convey their divergent ideologies and beliefs. Acting as a communal influence upon their "speech acts",[81] this conversation guides the very course of freedom of expression.

In classical liberal terms, freedom of expression is simply the right to engage in the free exchange of thoughts and ideas. Following John Stuart Mill, it is a private means towards communal life.[82] To express herself freely, the individual needs to be free. To silence her, in the words of Oliver Wendell Holmes, is to silence the voice of difference itself:

---

[77]   See in general, F. Capra, *The Tao of Physics: An Exploration of the Parallels between Modern Physics and Eastern Mysticism* (London: Wildwood House, 1975); M. Gandhi, *All Men are Brothers* (New York: Columbia University Press, 1959). Economist-philosophers, in turn, critique efficiency-as-progress and "bigness" as goodness. See esp. *The Schumacher Lectures* (1982); E.F. Schumacher, *Small is Beautiful: A Study of Economics As If People Mattered* (New York: Harper & Row, 1975). On "popular education and its social significance, see P. Freire, *Pedagogy of the Oppressed*, trans. M.B. Ramos (New York: Herder & Herder, 1970).

[78]   F. Svensson, "Liberal Democracy and Group Rights: The Legacy of Individualism and Its Impact on American Indian Tribes"(1979), 27 Pol. Stud. 420, at 431. See too, S. Hall and D. Held, "Citizenship" (1989), 33 Marxism Today 16.

[79]   *Switzman v. Elbing and Quebec (A.G.)*, [1957] S.C.R. 285, at 326 *per* Abbott J.

[80]   On "speech forms" and "speech acts", see, *infra*, at 73.

[81]   For a somewhat different distinction between "adjudicative facts" and "legislative facts", see W.R. Lederman, "Assessing Competing Values in the Definition of Charter Rights and Freedoms", in *The Canadian Charter of Rights and Freedoms: Commentary*, 2nd ed. by G.-A. Beaudoin and E. Ratushny (Toronto: Carswell, 1989), p. 127.

[82]   See J.S. Mill, "On Liberty", in *John Stuart Mill: Three Essays* (Oxford: Oxford University Press, 1975), pp. 17-21.

> If all mankind minus one were of one opinion, and only one person
> were of the contrary opinion, mankind would be no more justified in
> silencing that one person, than he, if he had the power, would be
> justified in silencing mankind.[83]

In this liberal tradition, the law-maker is not free to prescribe either
the normative content of the individual's speech or the parties who are
entitled to engage in "speech acts". Communal dialogue, guided by the
"speech form" of language, is inherently competitive. Each actor chooses
between rival forms of expression. Each decides whether to adhere to
one speech form or act over another; and each converses with and listens
to whom she chooses in light of that freedom.

At its most superficial, the individual's freedom of expression is an
end in itself. With the notable exception of the recent decision in *R. v.
Keegstra*,[84] society, supposedly, is most happy when the individual's
expression is least checked. It is least happy when that expression is
most constrained. In competitive terms, communal satisfaction is derived from the maximization of each individual's right to interact freely
within the community. The goal is to promote a "free trade in ideas" by
accepting the "power of thought . . . in the competition of the market".[85]
The aim is to place freedom of expression at the centre of a free society.
This neo-liberal justification for freedom of expression supposes that to
restrict the individual's freedom to express herself is to inhibit her effort
to arrive at truth.[86] As Mr. Justice McIntyre contended in *Dolphin Delivery*:

> Freedom of expression is not . . . a creature of the *Charter*. It is one of
> the fundamental concepts that has formed the basis for the historical
> development of the political, social and educational institutions of
> western society. Representative democracy . . . depends upon its
> maintenance and protection .[87]

Influenced by this classical liberal tradition, judges seemingly identify
the nature of "speech acts" from the language, or "speech form" used. At
the same time, they are neutral as to the content of that speech. They
claim that they are duty bound to enforce the individual's free expression, but not to judge the effect of that expression upon social relations.
As Chief Justice Dickson argued by analogy in relation to freedom of
religion in *Big M Drug Mart*:

---

[83]   *Abrams v. United States*, 250 U.S. 616, at 630 (1919), *per* Holmes J., dissenting.

[84]   In *R. v. Keegstra* (1990), 61 C.C.C. (3d) 1, the Supreme Court of Canada upheld legislation
       restricting freedom of expression in a race hatred case. See further, *supra*, Chapter 2.

[85]   Mill, *On Liberty, supra*, note 82, at 23. See too, A. de Tocqueville, in *Democracy in America*,
       J.P. Mayer, ed. (New York: Doubleday, 1969), pp. 520-24; I. Cotler, "Freedom of
       Association in Canadian Law", in *The Canadian Charter of Rights and Freedoms:
       Commentary*, W.S. Tarnopolsky and G.-A. Beaudoin, eds. (Toronto: Carswell, 1982), p.
       154.

[86]   See, *e.g.*, Mill, *On Liberty, supra*, note 82.

[87]   *Dolphin Delivery*, [1986] 2 S.C.R. 573, at 583.

> The essence of the concept of freedom of religion is the right to
> entertain such religious beliefs as a person chooses, the right to declare
> religious beliefs openly and without fear of hindrance or reprisal . . .[88]

However, in judging the legitimacy of freedom of expression, courts
inevitably make normative decisions about the content of expression.
They are motivated by norms of moral intuition, ethical suasion and
political conviction. They cannot easily skirt the fact that freedom of
expression is a social, not a purely objective condition.[89] As Chief Justice
Dickson proposed in *Big M Drug Mart*: "[a] truly free society is one which
can accommodate a wide variety of beliefs, diversity of tastes and pur-
suits, customs, and codes of conduct."[90] As such, freedom of expression
is distinctly social. It arises within a communicative environment that
includes the opinions of diverse actors, beyond the mutually related parties. Thus, those who corrupt youth through advertisement, in *Irwin Toy*[91]
as elsewhere, do so only insofar as others, not limited to judges, impute
negative attributes to their "speech forms" and "speech acts". Similarly,
displeasure at particular "speech acts" stems, not from incontrovertible
truth about freedom of expression, but from preferred formulations of
that truth.[92]

Thus, judges superimpose a social choice upon Keegstra's freedom of
expression; namely, that he ought to be held legally responsible for his
actions. Restricting his freedom of expression stems, not from his "speech
acts", but from the shared view that his actions are socially deleterious.
He is culpable, not because "his" truth about the holocaust is necessarily
false, but because of the shared conviction that he should not be permitted
to express "his" truth publicly. At issue is not whether people like Zundel
or Keegstra have an inviolate freedom to express themselves, unaffected
by an arbitrary social will. Nor does their social responsibility hinge
upon correlative duties which they owe each and every Jew or Christian
who is aggrieved by their remarks and who seeks their silence. They are

---

[88] *Big M Drug Mart*, [1985] 1 S.C.R. 295, at 336.
[89] Freedom of expression is richly debated in our philosophical literature. See, *e.g.*, J.
Milton, *Areopagitica* (New York: AMS Press, 1971); J. Locke, *Letter Concerning Toleration*,
2nd ed., trans. Popple (New York: Bobbs-Merrill, 1955); Mill, *On Liberty, supra*, note 82,
at 697.
[90] *Supra*, note 88, at 336.
[91] [1989] 1 S.C.R. 927.
[92] On the contingent nature of rights, in particular, in relation to freedom of expression,
see esp. *R. v. Keegstra* (1984), 19 C.C.C. (3d) 254 (Alta. Q.B.); *R. v. Doug Rankine Co. and
Act III Video Productions Ltd.* (1983), 9 C.C.C. (3d) 53 (Ont. Co. Ct.); *R. v. Red Hot Video
Ltd.* (1983), 6 C.C.C. (3d) 331 (B.C. Prov. Ct.); vard. 11 C.C.C. (3d) 389 (Co. Ct.), affd. 18
C.C.C. (3d) 1 (C.A.), leave to appeal to S.C.C. refused 46 C.R. (3d) xxv; *Re Luscher and
Deputy Minister, Revenue Canada Customs & Excise* (1983), 149 D.L.R. (3d) 243 (B.C. Co.
Ct.), revd. [1985] 1 F.C. 85 (C.A.); *Re Ontario Film & Video Appreciation Society and Ontario
Bd. of Censors* (1983), 147 D.L.R. (3d) 58 (Ont. Div. Ct.), affd. 5 D.L.R. (4th) 766 (C.A.),
leave to appeal to S.C.C. granted 3 O.A.C. 318. See also *Chaplinsky v. New Hampshire*,
315 U.S. 568 (1942); *Roth v. United States*, 354 U.S. 476 (1957).

constrained by the belief, now recognized by the Supreme Court in *Keegstra*, that particular forms of speech are more harmful to society than beneficial to the speaker.

The social choices that guide individual rights of expression, therefore, are qualitative. They embody opinion about how individuals ought to express themselves in relation to others. Each freedom is the product, not of the freedom itself, but of faith in the social attributes and consequences that are imputed to it. Thus, social choices evolve out of communal responses to "speech acts", not out of "speech acts" alone. They include a sense of social indignation, outrage, and indifference towards particular "speech acts", beyond the isolated relationship between speaker and listener. They are embodied in the "speech acts" of decision-makers. They are reflected in the reasons judges give for their decisions.

None of this is to suggest that social discourse ought to exclude the perceptions of individual right-holders. Indeed, to do so would be to discourage social activism itself. Free speech is a salient means by which individuals participate in communal discourse. However, that discourse also encompasses diverse social reactions towards the ideas being presented, including the understandings which others, not least of all courts, have of them. Identifying "social facts" about the holocaust, then, is not reserved to sociologists or historians, but to diverse participants in social conversation. In effect, Zundel, Keegstra and the Canadian Jewish Congress each speak in light of social choices in respect of which they, along with others, are participants. None determines the truth about free speech wholly by itself.

Accordingly, judges who view freedom of expression as self-illuminating dodge the communal constraints that are imposed upon free speech, beyond the immediate rights of individuals.[93] Freedom of expression encompasses a sense of purpose, beyond the human agency that expresses it.[94] It includes both "speech acts" and broader "social purposes", beyond immediate correlative relations. This extended discourse derives from the decision-maker's willingness to explore, discover, and ultimately, reflect upon pre-existing conceptions of free expression. It includes her willingness to critique those conceptions, to explore alternatives, and to develop functional methods of effecting those alternatives.

---

[93]   "If it happens that the granting of the group claim also satisfies the claims of individuality or personhood, this is not due to the production of individuality by groups, but to the ultimate common grounding of both individuality and groupness (and sociality) in the structure of the human": R. Garet, "Communality and Existence: The Rights of Groups" (1983), 56 S. Cal. L. Rev. 1001, at 1052.

[94]   On freedom of expression in general, see A.W. MacKay, "Freedom of Expression: Is It All Just Talk?" (1989), 68 Can. Bar Rev. 713; R. Moon, "The Scope of Freedom of Expression" (1985), 23 Osgoode Hall L.J. 331; C. Beckton, "Freedom of Expression", in *The Canadian Charter of Rights and Freedoms: Commentary, supra,* note 85, at 75; C. Beckton, "Freedom of Expression — Access to the Courts" (1983), 61 Can. Bar Rev. 101; S.I. Bushnell, "Freedom of Expression — The First Step" (1977), 15 Alta. L. Rev. 93.

This reformative view of freedom of expression has three particular advantages: it demonstrates that the nature and limit of freedom of expression resides in social commentary. It associates that commentary with participation in social debate; and it offers the court a way to circumscribe freedom of expression without having to sacrifice different conceptions of it.

CONSTRUCTING COMMUNITY

Ferdinand Tonnies has popularized two conceptions of community: *gemeinschaft* and *gesellschaft*. *Gemeinschaft* involves a "natural will . . . [involving] relationships . . . [that] are spontaneous and affective, and . . . are the outcome of interaction between incumbents of status roles". *Gesellschaft*, in contrast, "is that social form in which rational will (*kurwille*) has primacy . . . [and is] chosen and employed in conformity with the norms of rationality and efficiency in both the technical and economic sense".[95] In positing these two extremes, Tonnies establishes two stereotypes that exclude each other. Natural relations of status — supposedly including family and cultural life — somehow are spontaneous and affective, not rational. Rational and efficient communities, supposedly, are not spontaneous or affective.

The problem with this conception of community is that Tonnies relies upon two naturally exhaustive categories. Either community resides in a natural relationship of kith and kin, or in a rational community of commerce and industry. Either society is constituted rationally, or it evolves spontaneously. In each case, social action is founded upon either extreme, less upon their complementary character.[96] In truth, neither extreme speaks for itself. Attitudes towards family life evolve through a combination of rational, efficient and spontaneous forces. Indeed, rational discourse repeatedly renders the family into an efficient rather than a spontaneous factor of production. Conversely, inefficient conduct is rational when it is perceived to satisfy a good that is greater than efficiency.[97]

Accordingly, to insist upon either a rational or a spontaneous conception of community is to assume, quite falsely, that each ought to be viewed differently from the other. In truth, freedom of expression embodies both the spontaneous action of autonomous subjects, and the rational and efficient system by which they make choices. Individuals express themselves by reacting, consciously or otherwise, to a range of

95   See F. Tonnies, *Community and Society*, trans. and ed. C. Loomis (New York: Harper, 1963).

96   See J.R. Gusfield, *Community: A Critical Response* (New York: Harper & Row, 1975), p. 59, quoting Max Weber, *From Max Weber*, trans. H.H. Gerth and C.W. Mills (New York: Oxford University Press, 1946). See further, *infra*, at 89.

97   D.G. Carlson, "Reforming the Efficiency Criterion: Comments on Some Recent Suggestions" (1986), 8 Cardozo L. Rev. 39; D. Kennedy, "Cost-Benefit Analysis of Entitlement Problems: A Critique" (1981), 33 Stan. L. Rev. 387.

ethnic, religious, sexual and cultural norms. To describe their responses as rational or spontaneous is to suggest what is often not known after the fact, that is, their prior intentions. More often than not, communal life is expressed through stereotyped images of rational and spontaneous conduct which others infer *ex post facto*. For example, commercial classes deem the exploitation of woodlands to be economically desirable. Aboriginal peoples consider it a distinct threat to their indigenous cultures. Each stereotype evolves spontaneously. Yet each appears to develop rationally in light of the interests of that group, as distinct from other groups. Aboriginal peoples preserve their land for hunting, fishing, and tribal burial. Lumber companies, supposedly bent on creating employment and profit, deplete resources for gain. Indeed, these are precisely the stereotypes that arose in *R. v. Agawa*,[98] in the vision of aboriginal peoples and conservationists as spontaneous, and industrialists as rational.

Alongside this stereotyping of communities is the perception that each stereotype is self-contained. French Canadians presumably wish to preserve French. English Canadians presumably wish to preserve English. In this sense, each stereotyped community seemingly competes with the others. Each satisfies its own ends only by excluding those others. For example, French Canadians find their cultural identity partly in their separateness from English culture. Canadians find it in their separateness from Americans.

This competitive stereotyping of groups hopelessly oversimplifies communal life. This is particularly so where stereotypes result in everyone within a group being treated as like-minded, notably, in their competition with everyone outside of it. Even more simplistic is the vision of communities that are irreversibly confined to fixed relationships. Aboriginal people from the same nation certainly relate to one another in terms of pre-existing cultures. However, they continually renew these cultures in light of contemporary wisdom. Sometimes, they modernize their cultures willingly; other times, they forcibly resist change. Sometimes, they view ancestral practice as ethnically commendable; other times, they resist it reactively, on grounds that it is primitive. On yet further occasions, they display a proactive consciousness: they reformulate tribal values to accord with — and respond to — Western practice.[99]

None of this is to refute communicative difference grounded in historical practice. Understandably, among First Nation Peoples,

> . . . individuals [still] . . . feel some consciousness of kind which is not contractual, and which involves some common links through primordial or cultural ties.[100]

98 (1988), 53 D.L.R. (4th) 101 (Ont. C.A.).
99 See T.R. Berger, "The Persistence of Native Values", in *Ethnicity and Ethnic Relations in Canada: A Book of Readings*, J.E. Goldstein and R.M. Bienvenue, eds. (Toronto: Butterworths, 1980), p. 82, at 87.
100 D. Bell, "Ethnicity and Social Change", in *Ethnicity: Theory and Experience*, N. Glazer and

However, to formalize communal life only within pre-existing castes, clans and families, is to confine communal life to rationalized structures that resist change. These stereotypes are especially doubtful when they stem from personal idiosyncrasy, disguised as objective fact. They are dubious when they are framed in adversity, in opposing racial, cultural and linguistic groups, in francophones who oppose anglophones, and First Nation Peoples who resist second nation peoples. Consequently, the defect in cases like *Canada (A.G.) v. Lavell*,[101] that deny benefits to aboriginal peoples, lies in the belief that each member of a tribal band is permanently captured by an historical stereotype that exhaustively engulfs her. So too, the *Meech Lake* debate is confined by an unduly narrow conception of "distinct society".

Stereotyped groups exist only because someone — including some group — so defines them, not because they are inherently so. Thus, the rights of English and French speaking Canadians, aboriginal and non-aboriginal peoples, Jews and Gentiles are rationalized according to norms that are applied to them from without, as much as found within them. These norms stem from social discourse itself. They are dependent upon the belief that social co-existence hinges on norms of conduct that groups share, and further, that these norms are not formulated solely by one group to the exclusion of others. In each case, communal life rises above the cloning of Western liberal values, within a white, male and Christian society. In each case, too, the quality of communal life transcends the stereotyped adversity between immediate players.

No typecast image determines the interests of all within it in opposition to all outside it. That members of a particular family or clan do not share beliefs on the sexual revolution goes without saying. That their political aspirations are more compatible with outsiders than with their own family or clan demonstrates the potential for dialogue beyond the stereotyped unit itself.[102] Not all aboriginal peoples think and behave alike. Nor are all aboriginal peoples inextricably locked in a conflict with European capitalism. Thus, communal life evolves, less from a self-evident "spirit of a people" (*volksgeist*) or family, than from the disparate environment in which groups, including law-makers and family members, interact. This wider environment evolves through immediate and historical dialogue; it is as much instantaneous as premeditated. In this sense, Tonnies' conception of spontaneous community is both justified and limited. Fundamental freedoms cannot be determined solely by referring back to a spontaneous culture. Nor can they be decided entirely by rational dis-

---

D.P. Moynihan, eds. (Cambridge: Harvard University Press, 1975), p. 155.

[101]   [1974] S.C.R. 1349. See too, P.W. Hogg, "The Canadian Bill of Rights — 'Equality Before the Law' — A.G. Can. v. Lavell" (1974), 52 Can. Bar Rev. 263.

[102]   See, *infra*, at 80.

covery. They can be determined only by recognizing a link between the two.

None of this is to displace either spontaneous or rational conceptions of community. Rational communication still provides a medium, however tenuous, through which to engage in discourse, including discourse about communal bias and prejudice. Human rights tribunals still respond to prejudice, at least partly rationally, when they evaluate the perceived social effect of Ku Klux Klan activity upon blacks in the United States, or the impact of the Western Guard upon visible minorities in Canada. Yet, administrative tribunals form *ex ante* presuppositions about the nature of prejudice and its impact upon communal life. They express their opinions reactively, through their corrective responses to racial prejudice, not proactively by recasting systemic bigotry into systemic harmony among the races. They rationalize their decisions, more than they are rational. They institutionalize them selectively, more than they derive them spontaneously. The error is to suppose that everyone is able to engage in a rights discourse, indeed, that it is alien to no one. Their fiction — inherited from competitive relations — is that each set of rights ought to prevail over others. Their falsehood is to suppose that Western liberal rights ought to override aboriginal rights in colonized Canada.

In truth, the content of communal life is not neatly settled *ex ante* in light of historic, or conventional relations. The rights discourse, undoubtedly, is alien to some. Nor do courts tidily resolve ideological conflicts in light of stereotypical norms which they apply equally to all. Communal norms are mutable. They have no constant pedigree, no fixed application. Inconsistent norms exist within the Western liberal tradition; they prevail in family, cultural, ethnic and business life, as within the judiciary itself. They affect the nature of social discourse itself, not least of all, the differential power to speak and to be heard. Spontaneous decision-making is not an all-encompassing shield by which decision-makers avoid semiconscious and subconscious biases. Communicative discourse means what it says: it means opening channels of debate without necessarily disregarding past debate; it infers, too, that the *status quo* not be recast automatically into the status *ex post*. This view is not wholly at odds with judicial practice. Indeed, as Mr. Justice La Forest wrote in *Edwards Books*: "[t]here is no perfect scenario in which the rights of all can be equally protected".[103] There is no reason to perpetuate such unequal treatment through a conspiracy of silence in public life.

RATIONALIZING DISCOURSE

Communicative discourse is weighed in light of the background of

---

[103] *Edwards Books*, [1986] 2 S.C.R. 713, at 795.

those who advance and engage in it, not least of all in light of the background of judges themselves. As Peter Hogg remarked:

> [The judiciary's] background is not broadly representative of the population: they are recruited exclusively from the small class of successful, middle-aged lawyers; they do not necessarily have much knowledge of or expertise in public affairs.[104]

Thus, courts evaluate the impact of legislation upon communal ownership of land in light of communal norms which they impute to them.[105] They decline to allow supermarkets to conduct business on Sundays as distinct from Fridays and Saturdays by judging common pause, presumably, from their perspective as Christian or Jew, father or mother.[106] At worst, the communal rights of minorities fall to a lesser plateau precisely because judges render them so. Women fail to participate in discourse about rights because men, not least of all male judges, traditionally dominate the rights discourse. At best, courts realize that no one norm of behaviour ought to govern the ownership or use of property. They appreciate that communities develop behavioural practices in light of the diverse norms, sentiments and attitudes of other communities, along with their own.

Thus, courts frame communal *mores* competitively. Either aboriginal peoples receive the right to tribal land upon which to hunt, fish, pray, assemble or bury their dead; or other communities — presumably including other aboriginal peoples — have the right to earn a livelihood there. Either the court treats the rights of aboriginal peoples as the governing norm, or it grants non-aboriginal peoples the adverse right to exploit tribal lands for economic gain.

Courts that develop norms to govern competing relations between aboriginal and non-aboriginal peoples, therefore, develop norms of coexistence that surmount the discrete norms of any one dominant group. They do not permit one group to apply its own insulated norms to judge the interests of another group. Similarly, they reconcile differences between communities, less according to objective norms of reconciliation, than in light of norms which they regard as justified. They experience, discover and choose norms in light of the intensity of their belief in them, their capacity to accommodate differences in belief in terms of them, and the likely effect of their doing so upon social practice. In the *Alberta Reference*, for example, both Justice Le Dain and McIntyre stress that, in labour relations, the court engages in a "balance of competing interests" that is "delicate", "dynamic and unstable" and upon which "the public

---

104   P.W. Hogg, *Constitutional Law of Canada*, 2nd ed. (Toronto: Carswell, 1985), p. 98. See too, Hogg, "Is the Supreme Court of Canada Biased in Constitutional Cases?" (1979), 57 Can. Bar Rev. 721.
105   See *Walter v. Alberta (A.G.)*, [1969] S.C.R. 383.
106   See esp. *Edward Books, supra*, note 103, at 810 *per* Wilson J.

at large depends for its security and welfare".[107] Chief Justice Dickson highlights, too, that the legitimacy of exemptions from Sunday closing laws involves "balancing . . . the religious freedom of a retail store owner against the interests of his or her perhaps somewhat numerous employees".[108] Each process of balancing is couched in objective terms; yet each is applied subjectively. In punishing the sex offender,[109] the judge stresses retribution in light of the victim's suffering; at the same time, she wishes to avoid making it "embarrassing, inconvenient, damaging [or] . . . dangerous" for witnesses to testify.[110] She evaluates relations among organs of government, ethnic and sexual groups only by adding her own moral viewpoint to their action. In forming opinions about sex offences and sexual equality, she includes her own preferences. She insists that she ought not to police the sexual practices of the nation; yet she judges aberrant sexuality. She claims, at once, that the hungry ought to be fed and that people ought to take care of themselves. Her discourse, like everyone else's, does not lead to one determinative good. She responds to some social ills by perpetuating as much as by resisting them.[111]

Subjective opinion is not restricted to law-makers. It is not limited to adverse relations between government and individual. Absorbed from social attitudes, it is incorporated into institutional — and judicial — practice. Judges perpetuate subjective values when they propose a uniform rule of law to regulate sexual differences.[112] They do so when they judge the peculiarities of aboriginal life according to Western cultural stereotypes.[113] They do so, too, when they treat the norms of a multicultural society as though it were bi-cultural. In each case, they institutionalize intolerance, bigotry, racism and sexism simply by not addressing it, or by attributing to it selected, and selective, qualities.[114]

Yet, decision-makers need not be constrained by unduly subjective opinions. One alternative is for them to construct communal life in light of a common social design that includes, but is not limited to, dominant stereotypes. What the law-giver thinks, does or says is a product of unified reason, not a reflection upon partisan politics. She investigates

---

107   *Alberta Reference*, [1987] 1 S.C.R. 313, at 414.
108   *Edwards Books, supra,* note 103, at 777.
109   See, *e.g., Re F.P. Publications (Western) Ltd. and R.* (1979), 108 D.L.R. (3d) 153 (Man. C.A.); *R. v. Quesnel and Quesnel* (1979), 51 C.C.C. (2d) 270 (Ont. C.A.).
110   *F.P. Publications, supra,* note 109, at 168.
111   On the attitudes of Canadian courts towards sexual equality, see *Re Shewchuk and Picard* (1986), 28 D.L.R. (4th) 429 (B.C.C.A.); *Nova Scotia (A.G.) v. Phillips* (1986), 34 D.L.R. (4th) 633 (N.S.C.A.); *Re Blainey and Ontario Hockey Assn.* (1986), 26 D.L.R. (4th) 728 (Ont. C.A.); *Tomen v. Federation of Women Teachers' Assns. of Ontario* (1987), 43 D.L.R. (4th) 255 (Ont. H.C.J.), affd. 61 D.L.R. (4th) 565 (C.A.). See too, Comment, "Legitimizing Sexual Inequality: Three Early Charter Cases" (1989), 34 McGill L.J. 358.
112   *Ibid.*
113   See, *e.g., R. v. Agawa* (1988), 53 D.L.R. (4th) 101 (Ont. C.A.).
114   See generally, J.S. Auerbach, *Justice Without Law?* (New York: Oxford University Press, 1983).

the social and monetary cost of maintaining life in light of unbiased values that take account of difference, not those which she happens to attribute to that life. She studies the rights of specific francophones and aboriginal peoples in light of cultural traits which are manifest in those groups; and she judges the rights of the terminally ill according to the conspicuous costs of treatment, not what she believes ought to be their fate. Reactive to law, rather than proactive, she responds to legal questions, not social problems.

However, to expect judges to draw upon one universal experience, one vision of life, liberty and security of the person, is to hope for the impossible. It is to render different experiences into instant solutions to often complex social problems. Indeed, it means subjugating diverse human experience to the distinctive norms of one dominant group; and it also means identifying those norms with the court itself. Thus, judges uncover sameness in social, cultural and religious life largely by creating it; and they treat difference in such life as an aberration, not as legally relevant.

Judicial attempts to construct a universal discourse about rights is not *per se* bad or wrong. However, it is bad insofar as it leads inevitably to sameness of treatment. One cannot expect English and French speaking Canadians to agree upon common norms to govern language usage. However, one can expect Canadian courts to develop proactive conventions by which to govern such differences. Rather than treat everyone the same, the aim of these conventions is to accommodate disparate conceptions of rights, including challenges to the rights discourse itself. Thus, any meaningful interface between one community and another rests upon the court's capacity to devise and apply norms of reconciliation between them. Ideally, courts employ these norms to establish the confines of a "distinct society" as a cultural and social unit. They recognize, too, that not all sectors of a society are exactly alike, and therefore, ought not to be treated alike; and they treat sectors of society differently in light of discourse into those very differences.[115]

I do not suggest that, in attempting to derive norms of reconciliation to accommodate cultural and political differences, decision-makers will arrive at an idealized society. Their biases do not cease to be biases because they seek to reconcile normative differences between racial groups. Social experiences do not lead to "the public good" simply because they are widely practised. However, I do suggest that, absent judicial attempts to formulate norms of reconciliation, judges will perpetuate the oldest bias of all: they will use bias as the means to avoid, and ultimately repress, social and political discourse itself.

---

[115]   See, *e.g.*, P.W. Hogg, *Meech Lake Constitutional Accord Annotated* (Toronto: Carswell, 1988), Chapter 2.

RELATIONAL COMMUNITY REVISITED

In a relational community, the nature of the polity is established by the relations between individuals within it. Each determines her own function according to the manner in which *she chooses* to relate to others within it. In effect, communal well-being occurs only through the individual's contribution of her ideals and practices to it within a democratic state. Beyond her relations with others, including government, communal life is devoid of content. Mr. Justice Abbott made this point in relation to freedom of expression in *Switzman v. Elbing and Quebec (A.G.)*:

> The right of free expression of opinion and of criticism . . . and the right to discuss and debate . . . are essential to the working of a parliamentary democracy . . .[116]

This faith in individual autonomy is evident in interpretations of the *Charter*. In effect, the court identifies fundamental freedoms with the freedoms of individuals. In protecting individual rights under the *Charter*, it, supposedly, reconciles the interests of the community as well. As Mr. Justice Estey would have it:

> With the *Constitution Act, 1982* comes a new dimension, a new yardstick of reconciliation between the individual and the community and their respective rights, a dimension which, like the balance of the Constitution, remains to be interpreted and applied by the Court.[117]

Yet, this individualized conception of community fails to provide any realistic sense of communal life beyond the competitive and sometimes selfish interests of related parties, usually, governmental and private ones. No matter how studiously courts base communal life upon autonomous subjects, they either restrict rights and duties to competing actors; or they "reconcile" these in terms of an abstract public will, notably under s. 1 of the *Charter*, that supersedes both competitors. The sham is that these relational rights remain as self-determined means towards an equally self-determined end — the universalization of private rights. Indeed, to find so succinct a means of correlating rights and duties is for courts to offer no clear understanding of the reason for that correlation. It is to cause them to flounder in their own abstractness, indeed, to allow the cup of fundamental rights to deteriorate into "an empty vessel to be filled with whatever meaning we [the judges] might wish from time to time".[118]

Correlative rights, however seemingly fundamental, are far from self-defining. Incomprehensible unless decision-makers are willing to inject normative properties into them, they ensure nothing whatever beyond the abstract right everyone supposedly has to them. They are exhausted

---

[116]   [1957] S.C.R. 285, at 328.
[117]   *Law Society of Upper Canada v. Skapinker*, [1984] 1 S.C.R. 357, at 366-67.
[118]   *Alberta Reference, supra*, note 107, at 394.

artificially, by bequeathing to everyone equal liberty, equal freedom and equal rights. Thus, judges who function within this relational community treat everyone similarly, whether they be white or black, French or English speaking. One variable — race, sex, colour or creed — decides all. The judges render all other factors constant.[119] However, in their attempt to construct a plural society of private actors — all of the same mind — judges likely derogate from sociability itself. They establish a relational meeting-point among diffuse peoples only through a single variable which they choose to isolate, whether it be race, sex, colour, creed or religion. They simulate communal unity where no such unity exists in fact; and they fail to appreciate, as Chief Justice Dickson aptly highlighted in *Big M Drug Mart*, that "the interests of true equality might well require differentiation in treatment".[120]

In reality, no single conception of rights unites everyone, even when everyone is seemingly free to decide upon its meaning for themselves. We are not identical beings with uniform perceptions of life and liberty. Certainly, we are all made of flesh and blood; we all bleed, and try as we might, we all have spiritual infirmities. However, our infirmities are different; we bleed in different ways and to different degrees. Just as we differ as persons, the *corpus* of our rights also differs. We are not absolute determinants of our own being, or of our rights. As communicative beings, both subjects and objects of communal life, we cannot hold ourselves apart from others and still claim to function in association with them. We are forever sub-parts of a community.[121]

This does not suggest that the individual's rights should disappear within the community with which she identifies. She does have rights; and others, including the State, owe her duties. As an individual, she also owes duties towards others. Her personal aspirations are socially significant. She participates in social exchanges; and she influences as much as she is influenced by them. Lon Fuller once remarked: "there are external criteria found in the conditions required for successful group living";[122] and one such influence is the disproportionate effect which particular individuals have upon group life, and the converse.

---

119   For concerns about judges attributing a false unity to rights, see D. Greschner, "Judicial Approaches to Equality and Critical Legal Studies", in *Equality and Judicial Neutrality*, S.L. Martin and K.E. Mahoney, eds. (Toronto: Carswell, 1987), p. 59; M. Eberts, "Risks of Equality Litigation", in *Equality and Judicial Neutrality*, *ibid.*, at 89; Hon. M.R. MacGuigan, "The Protection of Freedom and the Achievement of Equality in Canada", in *Civil Liberties in Canada*, G.L. Gall, ed. (Toronto: Butterworths, 1982).

120   *Big M Drug Mart*, [1985] 1 S.C.R. 295, at 347.

121   See esp., I. Young, "The Ideal of Community and the Politics of Difference" (1986), 12 Social Theory & Practice 1; J. Wallach, "Liberty, Communitarians and the Tasks of Political Theory" (1987), 15 Pol. Th. 581. The Hegelian critique of liberal community is also directed at Christian ethics, in particular, the stress in the Christian tradition of private, as opposed to communal, association. See *Hegel's Philosophy of Right*, trans. T.M. Knox (Oxford: Clarendon Press, 1952), pp. 51-53, 84-85, 231.

122   L.L. Fuller, "Reason and Fiat in Case Law" (1946), 59 Harv. L. Rev. 376, at 379.

Yet, the individual still does not find one relationship or right neatly laid out for her to apply in communal relations. She is impelled by a diffuse sense of belonging, whether as a non-citizen who wishes to practise law in *Andrews*,[123] or a refugee claimant in *Singh*.[124] In seeking to change her legal status, she is not necessarily at one with all other would-be lawyers or immigrants. She is part of a group even though some within it have different motivations for acting that are not necessarily tied to the identity of the group itself.

To ascertain the nature of communal relations is therefore to do far more than identify individual rights and duties. It is to explore the diffuse moral values and social aspirations of those within it. It is to realize that adversarial and correlative relations, rather than manifest all of communal life, constitute but a small part of it. Thus, labour relations redress more than the rights of labourers and duties of employers. They take account of a communal context in which employment rights are exercised. They depict attitudes towards human relations, such as hostility towards Sunday shopping, and intolerance towards immigrants and non-citizen lawyers. No one would doubt that the Supreme Court viewed Andrews as an individual, an immigrant, a non-citizen, a holder of a law degree, and also as a person keen to practise law in British Columbia. However, the court conceivably also viewed him as the object of intolerance in being excluded, as a non-citizen, from practising law in Canada. Thus, for Andrews to be given freedom to practise law in British Columbia is for the Supreme Court to make a statement about the political conditions that govern non-citizens, not simply to comment upon Andrews' s. 2 rights.[125]

The point is that the right-holder's world is complicated by a discursive history, in particular, by the impact of varied cultural conventions upon human co-existence. That history of discourse is reflected in race, gender and social relations, in divisions over their nature, and disparate methods of reconciling those divisions. To limit that history, division and reconciliation to individual relations is to unduly simplify the nature of civil life. The individual's rights do not simply exist in relation to all others, including the State, who owe her duties. Indeed, it is only by establishing an association among disparate attitudes that courts establish the liberty of the subject. Thus, the correlative relationship between Andrews and the Barristers' Society of British Columbia in *Andrews* arises as much from social attitudes towards protectionism in the legal profession as from Andrews' own correlative rights. His relationship with the Barristers' Society is affected far more by the court's perception of inequality than

---

123   [1989] 1 S.C.R. 143
124   [1985] 1 S.C.R. 177.
125   See *Andrews, supra,* note 123.

by his self-evident rights. His rights are explicit only in terms of social properties that are injected into them. Thus, human rights embrace multiculturalism under s. 27 as readily as freedom of speech or association under s. 2. They encompass, under ss. 1 and 15, the sexual, racial, cultural and religious identity of Canadians in general, not merely the individual rights that, all too often, benefit white, anglophone males.

This sense of community does not hinge upon a Rawlsian social contract.[126] Nor does it depend upon courts seeking to make the greatest number of individuals happy, the self-serving dream of majorities. Rather, it is impelled by the social need to co-exist through the tolerance of difference, including difference in the nature of fundamental rights.[127] Within this social context, fundamental freedoms are not neatly expressed through institutional relations between individuals and the State. Nor are they manifest in self-evident relations between right-holders and those who owe them duties. They revolve around a diffuse communal life that is directed, not at uniting everyone within specific relations, but at improving participation in communal life through those relations. They encompass people's rights, the right to health care, education, economic development and environmental protection. They embrace popular interest in national and international peace and co-operation. They are socially dynamic, not closed-ended, politically progressive, not falsely static.

This is not to suggest that such social purposes exclude correlative rights and duties. Certainly, judges delineate the specific rights and duties of pacifists who resist the unbridled right of the executive to declare war, just as they react to the rights and duties of specific social activists in cases like *R. v. Zundel*[128] and *R. v. Keegstra*.[129] However, they embrace more than Zundel's or Keegstra's right to promote the honour of Germany during the Second World War, or the right of Mohawks to draw attention at Oka to their historical suffering. They raise into issue divergent sympathies, for and against hate-mongering. They debate, in *Morgentaler*,[130] the right to life and liberty, to foetal viability, forced parenting, and social upheaval. Rather than dwarf correlative relations within this social frame, they encompass those relations.[131] They formulate these perceptions of fundamental rights and freedoms selectively,

---

[126] See, in general, J. Rawls, *A Theory of Justice* (Cambridge: Harvard University Press, 1971).
[127] For a critique of the liberal construction of the common good, see esp., D. Kennedy, "Form and Substance in Private Law Adjudication" (1976), 89 Harv. L. Rev. 1668; Kennedy, "Cost-Benefit Analysis of Entitlement Problems: A Critique" (1981), 33 Stan. L. Rev. 387.
[128] (1987), 35 D.L.R. (4th) 338 (Ont. C.A.).
[129] (1988), 43 C.C.C. (3d) 150 (Alta. C.A.).
[130] [1988] 1 S.C.R. 30.
[131] For a laudable attempt to overcome the limitations of the subjective self, see I. Murdoch, *The Sovereignty of the Good Over Other Concepts* (London: Cambridge University Press, 1967). Murdoch stresses that moral realism resides, not in what is good *per se*, but in the aspiration to avoid internalizing the self, treating it as separate from others.

not deterministically.[132] They do all this in their everyday speech, as a result of their exposure to the law *stricto sensu*, the media, lawyers, witnesses and one another. They do so by acknowledging that they are both individuals and members of groups.[133]

Judges who participate in this open discourse encompass different dimensions of social life within it. They frame these dimensions formally through hierarchy, conceptually as ideas, and interactively as dynamic participation in social life. They appreciate, too, that hierarchical relations move beyond self-interested individuals to embrace communal dialogue. They understand that correlative rights and duties complement rather than exhaust communal life.

Judges who still insist that communal values are mere products of fundamental rights create an illusion of permanence. They suppose that those rights are eternal. They do not acknowledge the diffuse stature of virtuosity, efficiency and fairness in society, or the extent to which disagreement, as distinct from agreement, facilitates communal discourse.[134] They fail to acknowledge, too, that to preserve aboriginal life is to comment upon disparate attributes which they — and others — inject into that life. To create affirmative action programmes for blacks is, unavoidably, to comment upon black culture. To reflect upon the diminished standing of women in the workforce is for them to see women as an exploited sex. In so commenting upon communal life, judges do not rely upon one single prescience, one "good life". Their conceptions of communal life are markedly diffuse. They give different weights to human suffering in the workforce, family life, and education. They display varied reactions towards the right of pregnant women to reproductive freedom, or of labour to fight management. They employ incommensurate means to redress economic disadvantage and the need for affirmative action. All this is quite understandable. After all, judges form opinions about other people through extended relations with them, as with others. They do not approach each case uniformly. They are armed with different social tools, not one common remedy in which they uniformly agree.

> We all approach our own circumstances as bearers of a particular social identity. I am someone's son or daughter, someone else's cousin or uncle; I am a citizen of this or that city, a member of this or that guild or profession. I belong to this clan, that tribe, this nation . . .[135]

---

[132]   For an elaboration of this in the context of the public-private divide, see, *infra,* Chapter 5.

[133]   On this link between individual and group, see D. Cornell, "Beyond Tragedy and Complacency" (1987), 81 N.W.U. L. Rev. 693, at 696-97; F.I. Michelman, "The Supreme Court, 1985 Term — Foreword: Traces of Self-Government" (1986), 100 Harv. L. Rev. 4.

[134]   See esp. C. McCrudden, "Community and Discrimination", in *Oxford Essays on Jurisprudence,* J. Eckelaar and J. Bell, eds. (Oxford: Oxford University Press, 1987), p. 224; R.D. Parker, "Issues of Community and Liberty" (1985), 8 Harv. J. L. & Pub. Pol. 287.

[135]   A.C. MacIntyre, *After Virtue,* 2nd ed. (Notre Dame, Indiana: University of Notre Dame Press, 1984), p. 223.

A comparable heterogeneity among judges is reflected in their disparate conceptions of *Charter* rights. Judges give different emphases to the
rights of those who wish to pray, speak or associate under s. 2 of the
Charter. They display dissimilar attitudes towards French language rights
under s. 23, the rights of disadvantaged groups under s. 15(2), and
multicultural groups under s. 27. They realize that no single good encompasses all social actors. Help for some amounts to paternalism for
others. To impose a "white man's" standard of education, employment
or living upon aboriginal or black peoples is to accomplish neither corrective nor redistributive justice, only uniform treatment. Democratic
participation in government guarantees to each subject more than the
same treatment; it encourages her to participate in social discourse as an
expression of her autonomy. It enables her to "become" autonomous
through association with others, as distinct from "being" autonomous
from those others.[136]

Correlative rights are part of this dialogic community; yet they are not
conclusive of it.[137] As individuals and groups enjoy communal life differently, they do not all gain equally from it. Thus, communal rights shift
from the private realm of the human being to a vibrant, communicative
world; there, rights are linked to a diffuse range of political, cultural and
religious values. They are socially interactive, not communally inactive.
They are discovered, explored, and ultimately, effected.

Several consequences flow from this broader conception of discursive community. The judge, consciously or otherwise, engages in social
conversation. She moves beyond the correlative rights and duties of
adversaries. She appreciates that human relations are influenced by disparate sympathizers and antagonists. She recognizes, too, that parties to
these relations are subject to divergent attitudes towards intention and
social harm. As a reformist, she may well follow the precepts of *Heydon's
Case*,[138] by constructing a relationship between intended mischief and
social harm. However, she is unlikely always to agree at the outset that
one principled rule should remedy that harm. She is unlikely, too, to
concur with her peers that each ought necessarily to arrive at the same

---

[136]   See esp. hereon, J. Nedelsky, "Reconceiving Autonomy: Sources, Thoughts and
Possibilities", in *Law and the Community: The End of Individualism?*, A.C. Hutchinson and
L.J. Green, eds. (Toronto: Carswell, 1989), p. 223.

[137]   For an account of community reaching constituents of the self, see esp., M.J. Sandel,
Liberalism and the Limits of Justice (Cambridge: Cambridge University Press, 1982), pp.
142-45. For Sandel, the subject is less an individuated self than a participant in a group
or class of subjects who possess a common identity. Sandel's analysis here is largely
directed against the liberal's antecedent self, and in particular, the claim that the self is
able to act as an individuated subject in seeking that good (at 142-44). The deficiency
of Sandel's account lies in the purely contingent terms in which he constitutes the self.
By denying the existence of any objective self with self-determined rights and
obligations, he advocates a wholly contingent subject who exists only by virtue of the
community that happens to constitute her.

[138]   (1584), 3 Co. Rep. 7a.

determination by the same means.[139] Hypothetically, one judge in a case like *Edwards Books*[140] might disallow shopping on Sundays because of a belief that a six-day week is quite enough. Another might agree, but without requiring that day be a Sunday. Yet another might disallow Sunday trade for religious reasons, or because of a belief that shopping on a Sunday undermines family life. Conversely, some judges might treat Sunday as a day to relax through shopping. Others might justify shopping on Sunday to defy all who believe in the contrary. Sympathies and antagonisms differ, as one would expect in a democratic society.

Communal life encompasses diverse opinions of individuals about the nature of life and death, liberty and security of the person. Yet, social issues are not restricted to the whim of immediate parties, including judges. They are wider than the narrow competition between vendors and vendees, mothers and foetuses.[141] The right to life, liberty and security of the person is societally dynamic. It is open to public debate about the social significance of rights, beyond the competitive will of individuals.

QUALIFYING CATEGORIES

Both hierarchical relations and hierarchical rights are suspect for perpetuating substantive inequalities. Thus, in *Andrews*,[142] hierarchical by-laws give fundamental rights to lawyers who are citizens and less than fundamental rights to those who are not. Similarly, hierarchical laws and relations still prevent women from enjoying substantive equality in the workforce. Women are employees; men remain their employers. Men are the "directing minds" of corporations and unions; women are directed. As Colleen Sheppard writes:

> Women experience inequality. Women are disproportionately poor, especially . . . elderly, single mothers of colour, lesbians or divorced. Women are beaten and raped at home and in the streets. Women are harassed as sex objects in the workplace, in universities, at home and in the streets.[143]

---

[139] Cf., e.g., R. v. Keegstra, supra, note 129, per Kerans J.A., and R. v. Andrews and Smith (1988), 43 C.C.C. (3d) 193, per Grange and Kreever JJ.A.

[140] [1986] 2 S.C.R. 713.

[141] See further, infra, at 90. See too, P. Selznick, "The Idea of a Communitarian Morality" (1987), 75 Cal. L. Rev. 445; A. Gutman, "Communitarian Critics of Liberalism" (1985), 14 Phil. & Pub. Aff. 308.

[142] [1989] 1 S.C.R. 143.

[143] N.C. Sheppard, "Recognition of the Disadvantaging of Women: The Promise of *Andrews v. Law Society of British Columbia*" (1989), 35 McGill L.J. 207, at 207. See too, *Report of the Royal Commission on the Status of Women in Canada* (Ottawa, 1970); *Women in Canada: A Statistical Report* (Ottawa: Ministry of Supply & Services, 1985); K. Battle, *Poverty Profile 1988: A Report by the National Council of Welfare* (Ottawa, 1988); *No Safe Place: Violence Against Women and Children*, C. Guberman and M. Wolfe, eds. (Toronto: Women's Press, 1985); C. Backhouse and L. Cohen, *The Secret Oppression: Sexual Harassment of Working Women* (Toronto: Macmillan of Canada, 1978).

The remedy for the abuse of such hierarchical relations between groups is not simply formal, to treat all women, all blacks, or all religious minorities alike. Redressing substantive inequality means supplementing negative and formal hierarchies with positive and open ones. As Mr. Justice McIntyre articulated in his majority decision in *Andrews*:

> [Equality] is a comparative concept, the condition of which may only be attained or discerned *by comparison with the condition of others in the social and political setting in which the question arises.* It must be recognized at once, however, that every difference in treatment between individuals under the law will not necessarily result in inequality and, as well, that identical treatment may frequently produce serious inequality.[144]

This affirmation of equality rights that takes account of social and political differences is quite compatible with the *Charter*. For example, women are entitled to particular protection not accorded men because they, unlike men, are subject to discrimination as a class. "Notwithstanding anything in this *Charter*, the rights and freedoms referred to in it are guaranteed equally to male and female persons."[145] Similarly, s. 15(1) identifies discrimination on the basis of sex and race within a list of prohibited grounds for discrimination.

However, to define discrimination against a *genus*, formally, by treating like cases alike, is to give rise to mechanical jurisprudence. Each member of the *genus*, technically at least, is regarded as a comparable victim of discrimination. Once the characteristics of the group are established, all within it benefit or suffer equally in terms of it. In truth, no *genus* is fixed in itself or in its membership any more than any right has a predetermined scope of operation. Indeed, to maintain otherwise is to deny substantive justice. It is to decline pregnant women the right to claim unique disadvantage under the equal protection clause of the Fourteenth Amendment on grounds that they lack distinctive status, apart from other women.[146] It is to impede Canadian women, at least until recently, from acquiring social insurance benefits for comparable reasons.[147] No group is internally coherent for all purposes; to treat all within it alike is to create a false coherence. It is to resurrect the worst of plural life, one in which equality is idealized only when each person becomes the split image of her neighbour. Such "identical treatment", as Mr. Justice McIntyre points out in *Andrews*, "may frequently produce serious inequality"[148] for imposing hardship upon those who are treated the same in the presence of differences among them.

---

[144]   *Supra*, note 142, at 164 (emphasis added).
[145]   *Charter*, s. 28.
[146]   See *General Electric Co. v. Gilbert*, 429 U.S. 125 (1976); *Geduldig v. Aiello*, 417 U.S. 484 (1974).
[147]   See *Canada (A.G.) v. Stuart*, [1983] 1 F.C. 651 (C.A.); *Bliss v. Canada (A.G.)*, [1979] 1 S.C.R. 183; but today see *Brooks v. Canada Safeway Ltd.*, [1989] 1 S.C.R. 1219; L.A. Turnbull, "Brooks, Allen and Dixon v. Canada Safeway Ltd." (1989), 34 McGill L.J. 172.
[148]   *Supra*, note 142, at 164.

This is not to say that categories of discrimination are worthless. Rather the contrary. Categorizing discrimination on the basis of sex or marital status is an inevitable response to the nature of disadvantage itself.[149] However, to treat each category of persons discriminated against as exhaustive is self-defeating, indeed, plainly unjust. To exclude gays and lesbians as categories of persons who are subject to discrimination under the *Canadian Human Rights Act*[150] is unfair in light of evidence of *de facto* discrimination against them.[151] As *Andrews* aptly illustrates, no category exhausts discriminatory treatment of those who fall outside of its formal confines.[152]

I do not suggest that all categories — women and pregnant women, aboriginal and non-aboriginal peoples — should be collapsed into one. To so insist would be to resurrect a bare-bones liberalism in which all receive like treatment. It would be to overlook that members of subcategories — poor blacks, uneducated women and unemployed aboriginal peoples — often rely on others within the *genus* to defend their interests. Indeed, it would be most unfortunate if Muriel Duckworth, in challenging the federal government's expenditure of tax dollars for military purposes, was denied the right of constitutional challenge simply because she is not a member of a significantly disadvantaged class.[153] However, it would be equally unfortunate if courts placed full trust in fixed categories of disadvantage, refusing to recognize the difference between poor and rich blacks, educated and uneducated women, employed and unemployed aboriginal peoples. The harm in treating each *genus* as exhaustive lies in the supposition that unfair treatment is the problem only of those within the category of discrimination, not a broader social or systemic problem.

Redressing discrimination is accomplished, less by relying upon formal categories of discrimination than by resorting to communal discourse through which diverse groups express themselves. The putative "right" of Jehovah's Witnesses to refuse blood transfusions for their children revolves less around the paternal philosophy of child welfare legislation than around social attitudes towards religion and child care that affect

---

149   *Andrews, supra*, note 142, at 164 *per* McIntyre J.
150   See Bill C-277, *An Act to Amend the Canadian Human Rights Act*, 1st Sess., 33rd Parl., 35 Eliz. II, 1986; Bill C-212, *An Act to Amend the Canadian Human Rights Act*, 2nd Sess., 33rd Parl., 35 Eliz. II, 1986. Both attempts to introduce sexual orientation as a prohibited ground of discrimination died on the order paper.
151   See esp., *Equality for All: First Report to the House of Commons of the Sub-Committee on Equality Rights of the Standing Committee of Justice and Legal Affairs*, 1st Sess., 33rd Parl., 1984-85, pp. 26-31.
152   See *Andrews, supra*, note 142.
153   *Duckworth v. R.*, unreported, File No. A-179-81, October 10, 1989 (F.C.A.); application for leave to appeal to S.C.C. dismissed. See "Peace Activist Wages Fight with Tax Man", *Halifax Mail Star*, April 6, 1989, p. 34. See too, *Prior v. Canada*, [1988] 2 F.C. 371 (T.D.), *per* Addy J.

the interpretation of that legislation. That religious minorities exercise "rights" in competition with religious majorities is less a product of the rights of either group than of the social environment in which those rights are conceived, exercised, and ultimately, judged.

Accordingly, the nature of disadvantage transcends formal categories of persons, whether they be pregnant, unemployed, black, old, or disabled. No formal category addresses the interests of its every constituent. Nor does everyone within the category benefit equally from it. To address disadvantage is to take account of disparities of power, both within and outside of the *genus*. Judges who fail to reflect upon the substantive quality of discrimination also fail to regard the particular needs of the poor, infirm or unintelligent, whenever they fall within some other category. In addition, in considering only formal categories of discrimination, they ignore the social conditions that underlie the status of the disadvantaged.

I do not suggest, here, that courts should create new categories of substantive disadvantage *ad nauseam*. Indeed, for courts to extend categories of preference from those who are black, women or Seventh Day Adventists, to those who are poor, ignorant or overweight, is to create never-ending classes. There is always someone poorer or richer. The result, yet again, is to limit both those within and outside of each category. However, for a court to deny the impact of the social environment upon categories of discrimination is for it to fall somewhere between Scylla and Charybdis, between self-evident rights and the social reconstruction of those rights. It is to create a fixed world in which the formal status of one group trumps the status of another group. No court can ignore the effect of social action upon the status of groups any more than it can suppose that the interests of that group are identical to social interests. Indeed, this view separates the group or *genus* from its social being in relation to yet other groups.[154]

A DIALOGIC COMMUNITY

Within a dialogic community, decisions are the product of observation, discussion and explanation, not clear and convincing proof. Judges reach their decisions, less spontaneously, than through discourse into social practice. They trust less in self-explanation than in normative inference, less in rational discovery than in cultural and social habituation. Thus, they realize that difference in treatment accorded ethnic and religious minorities stems from exploratory discourse into social morality, not from spontaneous discovery; and they engage in exploratory discourse themselves, often quite differently.

This dialogic exploration into social practice is distinctly interactive.

---

[154]   See further hereon, *infra*, at 93.

Decision-makers, not limited to courts of law, interact within it; they do not transcend it. Their participation does not represent the totality of the discourse. No one decision-maker determines all aspects of public debate. No one decides upon the exact relationship between social attitudes and satisfactory legal responses towards them. Thus, judges decide upon the legal significance of social behaviour, not abstractly, but in light of the observations and comments of others who inform them and whom they, in turn, inform. No matter how formal their judicial proceedings, they draw upon the substance of social debate, both within and outside of the courtroom. They observe discrimination at work; they comment upon it; and they decide cases in light of their and other's comments upon it.[155]

This method of decision-making is normative, contextual and prospective throughout. It is normative in that decision-makers arrive at inferred, not necessary decisions about social and ethnical practice. It is normative, too, in that they comprehend, communicate and respond to social practice differently over time. It is contextual in their readiness to discover, absorb, and reflect upon disparate visions of the polity without necessarily diminishing their own discourse in terms of it. Finally, it is prospective in their willingness to address past injustice in the interest of relief which they deem to be socially satisfactory in the context.

The justifications for such discursive inquiry into social attitude and practice are threefold: through it, decision-makers uncover, not truth, but propositions about truth. They decide cases on the basis of ongoing inquiry into social *praxis* without being confined wholly by *a priori* principles of law which stultify that *praxis*. In place of self-evident rules of law, they adhere to normative propositions about social behaviour which they deem to be satisfactory. In place of unequivocal constitutional rights, they identify discursive interests in rights. Exposed to multiple forms of discrimination, they construct rights in light of disparate qualities which they — and others — attribute to them. Thus, they explore, discover, and ultimately, respond to the disadvantages of francophone Canadians and First Nation Peoples by evaluating their unequal access to economic and social resources. They consider the extent to which other groups, not limited to courts of law, perpetuate that inequality. They explore different methods of redressing that inequality; and they decide specific cases accordingly.

Decision-makers who apply this dialogic method of reasoning likely realize that poverty and welfare groups lack the physical and economic resources to engage in open discourse, particularly before courts of law.[156] They appreciate, too, that conversation which encompasses diverse social attitudes, complicates as much as it clarifies public discourse. Yet, by

---

[155]   On dialogic discourse, see further, *infra,* Chapter 5.
[156]   See further, *supra,* Chapter 2.

engaging in public debate, they allow social conversation to become more coherent. By exploring, discovering and responding to the social ill that arises from discriminatory treatment, they render the nature of discrimination less mystical, more intelligible, and ultimately, more accessible to public — and judicial — scrutiny. They explore social attitudes towards positive liberty, including social welfare and public education programmes; and they evaluate different methods of affirming those programmes in law.[157]

Judges who engage in such discourse accommodate disparate social purposes. They debate the right to life in light of diverse religious and social interests; and they reflect upon different implications that stem from those interests. However much they claim to be supplicants within a constitutional democracy, they engage in functional discourse. However abstractly they construe that discourse, they rely upon social conversation to develop it. However principled they purport to be, they explore, discover, and ultimately, respond to functional attitudes towards human virtue. At their most philosophical, they formulate propositions about harmonious, tranquil and productive human relations. At their most discursive, they evaluate social attitudes towards reproductive rights. At their most realistic, they justify their propositions in light of a constructed, not a necessary relationship between fundamental rights and public interests.[158] Their world is dialectic: it includes correlative rights and relations. Yet, it is far wider; it encompasses social conversation itself; it includes ongoing debate about human virtue; it moves well beyond the correlation between right and duty.[159]

None of this is to suggest that judges should surrender themselves to the vagaries of public debate. Nor do I claim that they should recede into an echo chamber of popular — or unpopular — sentiment. Rather, I suggest that, absent social and moral discourse, judges would not develop a truly meaningful pathway from communicative action to judicial practice. They would not be socially responsive in deciding cases.

CONCLUSION

Judges who suppose that what is good for the parts is also good for the whole render communal life unidimensional. They address the rights of First Nation Peoples, French Canadians, employees and women in the context of correlative relations only; and they treat social attitudes that sustain those relations as mere byproducts of them. Their fallacy is to suppose that each communicative act lies within a social vacuum, a "speech act" absent a "social fact". Their shortcoming is to believe that

---

[157]   See, in general, *supra*, Chapter 2.
[158]   See further, *infra*, Chapter 6.
[159]   On correlative rights and duties, see, *supra*, at 65.

each party decides upon the quality of her own participation in communal life in her discrete relations with other equally distinctive parties. Their ruse is to claim that the individual contributes proportionately to the common good, never more, while the polity benefits only to the extent of that specific share. As a result, communal relations never grow beyond the status of those who are immediate parties to them. Correlative rights never mature beyond this plurality of private relationships. The result, as the trilogy of labour cases in Western Canada illustrates,[160] is an abstract good that functions within a vacuous social context. There, public life is restricted to relations of dominance: either government imposes norms of behaviour upon members of civil society, or a corporate gentry asserts its power over consumers and the forces of labour.

In arguing for a discursive community beyond specific relations, I am likely to be criticized for being utopian, or even anti-democratic. In asserting a communitarian ethic based on equality and reciprocity, I will be accused of undue idealism. In asserting a communal good over specific rights, I will be seen to encourage communal directives to overshadow private life. Still others will argue that, rather than subjugate private will to the directives of government, I will subjugate private rights to an amorphous public good, indeed, to a new hierarchy.[161]

My defence is also my key argument. I try, throughout, to move beyond the individual's preoccupation with her rights and private relations to a communal life that the individual shares with others. I wish to direct emphasis, away from immediate relations between instant contestants, to a communal environment in which they interact with others. There, individuals are embroiled within an ongoing dialogue in which no one defines the perimeters of the polity all by herself. Each person is subsumed within the politics of communal life, beyond her correlative rights and duties. Each is a conversationalist who attempts to resolve her problems by seeking to understand the nature of social problems within a participatory democracy. Each is a social monitor who places herself imaginatively in the shoes of others. As a judge, she constructs a creative legal remedy to a social malady. She identifies *Charter* rights, less with immediate rights than with laws that respond to social ends beyond rights. She is concerned about social purposes. She is interested in how those purposes are conceived, conveyed and understood; and she is preoccupied about how to persuade others and be persuaded in terms of them. "The key concept of responsive law", Karl Llewellyn once argued, is to satisfy a "purpose",[162] arguably, a social purpose.

---

160 See the *Alberta Reference*, [1987] 1 S.C.R. 313 (the right to associate does not include the right to strike); *Dolphin Delivery*, [1986] 2 S.C.R. 573 (*Charter* freedoms do not extend to private law actions); *Saskatchewan Dairies*, [1987] 1 S.C.R. 460.

161 For a critique on utopian theory, see esp., R. Unger, *Knowledge and Politics* (New York: The Free Press, 1975), pp. 251-52.

162 K. Llewellyn, *Jurisprudence: Realism and Theory in Practice* (Chicago: University of Chicago Press, 1962), pp. 476-79.

To be truly communicative, courts cannot help but take account of both the human and physical environments in which communicative discourse takes place. To engage in communicative discourse, they need to be empathetic, indeed to be co-operative towards those who sustain the impact of that discourse. In this sense, Western societies have much to learn from traditional communities that have "shared a common commitment to the essence of communal existence: mutual access, responsibility and trust".[163] They have much to uncover about mediation in traditional societies,[164] beyond Western adversity. They have much to gain, too, from an increased consciousness of

> . . . fellowship, integration and cooperation; deep, intense, and intimate ties and relationships; interdependency and solidarity; immersion in and subordination and sacrifice to an organic whole; permanent and otherwise unreserved commitment to an entity larger than . . . [themselves].[165]

---

[163]   J.S. Auerbach, *Justice Without Law?* (New York: Oxford University Press, 1983), p. 4.
[164]   *Ibid.*, at 6-17.
[165]   R.E. Flathman, *The Practice of Rights* (Cambridge: Cambridge University Press, 1976), p. 184.

CHAPTER 4

PRIVATE RIGHTS, PUBLIC POWER

[T]he *Charter*, like most written constitutions, was set up to regulate the relationship between the individual and the Government. It was intended to restrain government action and to protect the individual. It was not intended in the absence of some governmental action to be applied in private litigation.[1]

In their quest to protect the public-private divide, courts sometimes reify the separation between the public and private realms. They restrict public life to relations between different arms of the State, or between the State and identifiable individuals. Thus, they construe the interests of labour unions in *Dolphin Delivery*[2] and *Saskatchewan Dairies*,[3] or supermarkets in *Edwards Books*,[4] as private, not governmental. That these interests might have public ramifications, they treat as a social fact, lacking constitutional status. Thus, in *Dolphin Delivery*, the Supreme Court held that the *Charter* does not apply to "private litigation divorced completely from any connection with government".[5] It held, too, that the *Charter* applies to the common law "only in so far as the common law is the basis of some governmental action".[6]

In this part, I challenge the sometimes strict separation which judges draw between private and public life, and the application of the *Charter* to a narrow public sphere, identified with the State. This judicial approach both unduly simplifies and confuses reality. The *Charter* does not represent merely the apex of public law; it is part of a wider public realm that encompasses so-called private life. A testament to a constitutional spirit,

---

[1] *Retail, Wholesale & Department Store Union, Loc. 580 v. Dolphin Delivery Ltd.* (hereafter referred to as *Dolphin Delivery*), [1986] 2 S.C.R. 573, at 593 *per* McIntyre J. In this case, the Supreme Court considered a *Charter* challenge to a court-ordered injunction aimed at enforcing the common law. The court decided that the common law did not apply to the injunction.

[2] *Ibid.*

[3] *Retail, Wholesale & Department Store Union v. Saskatchewan* (hereafter referred to as *Saskatchewan Dairies*), [1987] 1 S.C.R. 460.

[4] *R v. Edwards Books & Art Ltd.* (hereafter referred to as *Edwards Books*), [1986] 2 S.C.R. 713.

[5] *Supra*, note 1, at 593. See too, at 603.

[6] *Ibid.*, at 599.

it extends beyond acts of government to the community at large. As Chief Justice Dickson argued in the *Alberta Reference*, that public realm is embodied in "our Constitution's history of giving special recognition to collectivities or communities of interest other than the government and political parties."[7]

There is no absolute private world. Individuals are not united, without precondition, against a monolithic State. Nor is the State the sole repository of public life. Private rights, so-called, are implicitly public concerns as well. That a judge or human rights commission might construe discrimination as private to the victim does not render it any less public, any more than the tort of assault is wholly private. Employment discrimination does not cease to be a private wrong because it is remedied by public statute.[8] Nor is Donald Marshall, Jr.'s right to compensation for his false arrest and imprisonment for a murder he did not commit any less public because private compensation was paid to him. That he be compensated for the wrong done to him is surely a public matter. As Dale Gibson observes:

> Since all Canadians, public or private, are subject to the law, the notion that constitutional laws are inherently inapplicable to private conduct [as s. 32(1) might suggest] is no longer supportable, if it ever was.[9]

THE LIBERAL RATIONALE

Liberal-democratic theory has a very private side. "In a society governed by democratic principles it is the individual who is the ultimate concern of the social order."[10] Each person has the right to interact with others, just as she has the liberty to exclude the State from her private life. A rational decision-maker, she is the source of her own identity. Her "right of association . . . appears . . . almost as inalienable . . . as the right of personal liberty."[11] At the same time, the individual's communal identity depends upon her social, economic and cultural association with

---

7   *Reference re Public Service Employee Relations Act (Alta.)* (hereafter referred to as the *Alberta Reference*), [1987] 1 S.C.R. 313, at 364.

8   See *Seneca College of Applied Arts & Technology v. Bhadauria*, [1981] 2 S.C.R. 181.

9   D. Gibson, "The Charter of Rights and the Private Sector" (1982-83), 12 Man. L.J. 213, at 216, cited with approval by Rowbotham J. in *R. v. Lerke* (1984), 11 D.L.R. (4th) 185, at 189-90 (Alta. Q.B.). See too, G. Otis, "The Charter, Private Action and the Supreme Court" (1987), 19 Ottawa L. Rev. 71, at 86-89; B. Slattery, "The Charter's Relevance to Private Litigation: Does *Dolphin* Deliver?" (1987), 32 McGill L.J. 905, at 909-13; R. Howse, "*Dolphin Delivery*: The Supreme Court and the Public/Private Distinction in Canadian Constitutional Law" (1988), 46 U.T. Fac. L. Rev. 248, at 249-53.

10 T.I. Emerson, "Freedom of Association and Freedom of Expression" (1964), 74 Yale L.J. 1, at 4.

11 A. de Tocqueville, *Democracy in America*, P. Bradley, ed. (New York: Vintage Books, 1945), vol. 1, p. 203.

others.[12] In effect, she wears two hats. She is an autonomous right-holder, and a social animal. She expresses her civil liberties as an autonomous subject. However, she decides upon her public — including her criminal — responsibilities as a voting member of the public. Her position is perplexing indeed. In bestowing authority to govern upon the State, as an expression of her own positive liberty, she exercises control over it. In allowing it to exercise authority over her, she undermines her negative liberties in relation to it.[13] Thus, the right-holder is an originator of public life. She is also its private creature. If her public hat does not suit her private life, she must either adjust her private life or seek to modify the nature of her involvement in public life, presumably by voting differently or leaving the jurisdiction. Thus, the individual is free to mount a *Charter* challenge against the State, just as she is free to vote. In her private capacity, she decides how to live her life. The State does not decide for her. In her public life, the State decides all things for her.[14]

Those who assert this vision of an autonomous private realm are advocates of reciprocal private relations.[15] Those private relations are reinforced by a further reciprocal relationship, between government as the political arm of the State, and civil society as a plurality of individual citizens.[16] In effect, all citizens in civil society elect the legislature to act for them. The legislature, once elected, invokes its public power to protect the rights of each person within that civil society.[17] Rather than intrude

12 On this liberal vision of private, see esp., M. Walzer, "Liberalism and the Art of Separation" (1984), 12 Pol. Th. 315; S. Giner, "The Withering Away of Civil Society" (1985), 5 Praxis Int. 247.

13 See further, *supra*, Chapter 2. For classical reflections on liberal democracy, see esp., C.B. Macpherson, *The Life and Times of Liberal Democracy* (Oxford: Oxford University Press, 1977); Tocqueville, *op. cit.*, note 11, vols. 1 and 2; J.S. Mill, *Utilitarianism, Liberty, Representative Government* (London: Dent, 1972).

14 This separation of private from public is linked to the self-determining nature of private rights. See generally, R.M. Dworkin, "Rights as Trumps", in *Theories of Rights*, J. Waldron, ed. (Oxford: Oxford University Press, 1984), p. 153. But *cf.* M.V. Tushnet, "An Essay on Rights" (1984), 62 Tex. L. Rev. 1363.

15 See esp., J. Whitebook, "Saving the Subject: Modernity and the Problem of the Autonomous Individual" (1982), 50 Telos 79, at 84-87. This proportionality among private right-holders overstates the modern liberal claim for autonomy in private life. However, liberal modernists are still preoccupied with the equal opportunity to use rights before equality of access to rights. See esp., J. Rawls, *A Theory of Justice* (Cambridge: Harvard University Press, 1971).

16 See generally, *The Canadian State: Political Economy and Political Power*, L. Panitch, ed. (Toronto: University of Toronto Press, 1977); *Capitalism and the National Question in Canada*, G. Teeple, ed. (Toronto: University of Toronto Press, 1972); R. Miliband, *The State in Capitalist Society* (London: Weidenfeld & Nicholson, 1969); *Imperialism, Nationalism, and Canada*, C. Heron, ed. (Toronto: New Hogtown Press, 1977); E.O. Wright, *Class, Crisis and the State* (London: New Left Books, 1978).

17 See generally, *Canada and the Burden of Unity*, D.J. Bercuson, ed. (Toronto: Macmillan of Canada, 1977); J.A. Porter, *The Measure of Canadian Society* (Toronto: Gage Publishing, 1979). But *cf.* J.A. Porter, *The Vertical Mosaic: An Analysis of Social Class and Power in*

upon the private realm, it underwrites law that preserves the autonomy of that society. This public-private division is embedded in the *Charter*. Sections 2 and 7-14 provide for a private world of family, commercial and professional life. Sections 1, 15(2) and 33, in contrast, stipulate for a very different world of governmental life.[18]

However, this public-private division is rationalized only by an illusion: that the individual, as the freely determined subject, is protected equally from the State by the exercise of her negative liberties; while the State is assured that its public interests are preserved uniformly through public law.[19] In truth, limiting public life to State action excludes violations of human rights from public scrutiny. The victim of family and corporate abuse is denied access to substantive justice if her private law remedies fail, or are simply not available to her. Absent litigation that renders her private rights public, she must rely upon a private law regime that leaves her without a remedy, or with an unsatisfactory one.[20] She must appreciate, following Mr. Justice Mahoney in *Public Service Alliance*, that her "right of freedom of association guaranteed by the *Charter* is the right to enter into consensual arrangements"[21] only. "It protects neither the objects of the association nor the means of attaining those objects."[22]

All this passes over the realization that excluding a private realm from the *Charter* is itself a public election. This is evident in the coalescence of private and public in consumer legislation,[23] in the *Competition Act*,[24] in corporate privacy cases like *Southam*,[25] and in corporate-labour relations cases like *Dolphin Delivery*.[26] Government, as the political arm of the State, decides upon the reach of private rights and freedoms. That it claims to do so democratically, with the consent of the populace at large, is a public claim. That it asserts its right to so govern civil society is the crux of public life itself.

Private life is only truly autonomous when private actors define their

---

Canada (Toronto: University of Toronto Press, 1965). See esp., *Structured Inequality in Canada*, J. Harp and J.R. Hofley, eds. (Scarborough, Ont.: Prentice-Hall, 1980).

[18]   See further, *supra*, at 55.

[19]   See further hereon, *supra*, Chapter 2.

[20]   See, *infra*, at 102.

[21]   *Public Service Alliance of Canada v. R. in right of Canada*, [1984] 2 F.C. 889, at 895 (C.A.).

[22]   *Ibid*. These arguments are highlighted in the realist critique of freedom of contract. See esp., L.E. Trakman, "Frustrated Contracts and Legal Fictions" (1983), 46 Mod. L. Rev. 39; R. Pound, "Liberty of Contract" (1909), 18 Yale L.J. 454; F. Kessler, "Contracts of Adhesion — Some Thoughts about Freedom of Contract" (1943), 43 Colum. L. Rev. 629.

[23]   See esp. the Supreme Court of Canada's treatment of the Quebec *Consumer Protection Act*, R.S.Q., c. P-40.1 as amended, in *Irwin Toy Ltd. v. Quebec (A.G.)* (hereafter referred to as *Irwin Toy*), [1989] 1 S.C.R. 927, *per* Dickson C.J. (as he then was).

[24]   R.S.C. 1985, c. C-34 as amended.

[25]   *Hunter v. Southam Inc.* (hereafter referred to as *Southam*), [1984] 2 S.C.R. 145.

[26]   *Supra*, note 1.

own endeavour entirely by themselves. Once courts insist that the State itself protect the individual's right to be autonomous, they enshrine a peculiarly public interest in that autonomy. They stress the quasi-public obligations of the economically powerful in relation to the economically powerless, and the special fiduciary obligation of the professional who interacts with the non-professional.[27] Indeed, even libertarians who expand upon the private realm treat free enterprise, not simply as a private right, but as a social condition to be enforced by public means.[28] To a similar effect, the Supreme Court contends, in *Big M Drug Mart*, that "[t]he ability of each citizen to make free and informed decisions is the absolute prerequisite for the legitimacy, acceptability, and efficacy of . . . self-government".[29] In identifying "self-government" with State action, the court adopts a distinctly public view of private autonomy.

At their worst, courts that rely upon a formal public-private classification perpetuate dubious ends.[30] They render society "free and democratic" either to protect private property selectively, or equally selectively, to confiscate it for public consumption. Rights are "fundamental" in light of their belief that those rights are being put to a satisfactory *private* use. "Fundamental justice" is "*loosely structured* by . . . constitutional history and contemporary standards of public morality and international law"[31] as they conceive of that "loose structure". Thus, some judges favour freedom of speech, even when invoked "imprudently" to promote hatred.[32] Others insist that wilfully promoting hatred, more than spreading false news, is antithetical to democratic life itself.[33] Each chooses to what extent to believe in a free market-place of ideas within "a relatively stable society of responsible truth-searchers".[34] Each decides when there is a pressing mili-

---

[27]   See further, *infra*, at 104 and 115.

[28]   On critical social theory and the public-private divide, see J. Habermas, *Legitimation Crisis*, trans. T. McCarthy (London: Heinemann, 1976); Habermas, *Theory and Practice*, trans. J. Viertel (Boston: Beacon Press, 1973); H.J. Friendly, "The Public-Private Penumbra — Fourteen Years Later" (1982), 130 U. Pa. L. Rev. 1289.

[29]   *R. v. Big M Drug Mart Ltd.* (hereafter referred to as *Big M Drug Mart*), [1985] 1 S.C.R. 295, at 346.

[30]   On the reconstitution of a public philosophy to replace the primacy of liberal individualism, see W.M. Sullivan, *Reconstructing Public Philosophy* (Berkeley: University of California Press, 1982). See too, R.C.B. Risk, "Lawyers, Courts, and the Rise of the Regulatory State" (1984), 9 Dalhousie L.J. 31. See further, *infra*, at 133.

[31]   N. Lyon, "An Essay on Constitutional Interpretation" (1988), 26 Osgoode Hall L.J. 95, at 118 (emphasis added).

[32]   See *R. v. Keegstra* (1988), 43 C.C.C. (3d) 150, at 164 (Alta. C.A.), *per* Kerans J.A., citing J.S. Mill, *On Liberty*, C.V. Shields, ed. (New York: Bobbs-Merrill, 1956), at 65. See too, A.A. Borovoy, "False News Laws and Freedom of Expression" (1987), 56 C.R. (3d) 77; S. Braun, "Social and Racial Tolerance and Freedom of Expression in a Democratic Society: Friends or Foes?: *Regina v. Zundel*" (1988), 11 Dalhousie L.J. 471.

[33]   See *R. v. Andrews and Smith* (1988), 43 C.C.C. (3d) 193, at 224 (Ont. C.A.), *per* Grange J.

[34]   *R. v. Keegstra, supra*, note 32, at 166 *per* Kerans J.A.

tary threat,[35] a serious hazard to public safety[36] an immediate challenge to public well-being,[37] and a threat to the sanctity of the family.[38] Each declares, too, when language rights ought to be protected, and when doing so gives rise to a "totalitarian conception of society".[39]

In so disclaiming the public nature of private rights, courts sometimes promote formal justice only to produce substantive injustice. They treat publicly held corporations, since they are owned by shareholders, as private, regardless of whether their actions impact negatively upon "the public" at large. In contrast, they maintain that Crown corporations, since they are owned by the State, fall within the public domain, no matter how privately they might act.

The result, that form precedes substance, is confusing. Canadian universities, formally privately owned but substantially funded by government, conceivably are both public and private. Codified systems of law in Quebec presumably are public, while identical common law systems presumably are private. The effect, as Madam Justice Wilson recognizes in *McKinney*, is formal consistency, but substantive injustice.[40] Canadian courts might well entertain a *Charter* challenge to Quebec legislation on the formal grounds that such legislation is public. In contrast, they might deny a *Charter* challenge to an identical common law rule emanating from a province outside of Quebec on the equally formal grounds that common law decisions are private. These uncertainties lead to questionable results. Progressive legislation may be struck down for violating the *Charter*. Regressive common law rules may well prevail. All this cannot help but breed cynicism about the values that underlie the legal system as a whole.

There *are* alternatives. The public sphere need not be restricted formally to legislative or executive action. It can take account of so-called "private law" interests as well as common law rules that impact upon them. This occurs when courts apply *Charter* principles directly to so-called private

---

[35] *Operation Dismantle Inc. v. R.* (hereafter referred to as *Operation Dismantle*), [1985] 1 S.C.R. 441.

[36] *R. v. Oakes* (hereafter referred to as *Oakes*), [1986] 1 S.C.R. 103.

[37] *Saskatchewan Dairies*, [1987] 1 S.C.R. 460.

[38] *Edwards Books*, [1986] S.C.R. 713.

[39] *Quebec Assn. of Protestant School Bds. v. Quebec (A.G.) (No. 2)* (hereafter referred to as *Quebec Protestant School Bds.*) (1982), 140 D.L.R. (3d) 33, at 64 (Que. S.C.), *per* Deschênes C.J.S.C. (as he then was).

[40] On the private or public status of Canadian universities, see esp. *McKinney v. Bd. of Governors of the University of Guelph* (1990), 76 D.L.R. (4th) 545 (S.C.C.), at 640-44 *per* La Forest J., at 593-99 *per* Wilson J., and at 677-79 *per* L'Heureux-Dubé J. *Cf. Greenya v. George Washington University*, 512 F. 2d 556 (D.C. Cir., 1975).
       On the different application of the *Charter* in Quebec compared to the common law provinces of Canada, see *per* Wilson J. in *McKinney, ibid.*, at 558-61. See too, G. Otis, "The Charter, Private Action and the Supreme Court" (1987), 19 Ottawa L. Rev. 71, at 87; J.A. Manwaring, "Bringing the Common Law to the Bar of Justice: A Comment on the Decision in the Case of *Dolphin Delivery Ltd.*" (1987), 19 Ottawa L. Rev. 413, at 444; B. Slattery, "The Charter's Relevance to Private Litigation: Does *Dolphin* Deliver?" (1987), 32 McGill L.J. 905, at 910.

action, or indirectly, when they incorporate those principles by analogy into private law. Indeed, it was authoritatively stated in *Dolphin Delivery* itself that "the judiciary ought to apply and develop the principles of the common law *in a manner consistent with the fundamental values enshrined in the Constitution*".[41]

Thus, the *Charter* has a potentially wide sphere of application. Courts, conceivably, could apply its precepts — directly or by analogy — to big businesses whose financial stability impact, sometimes negatively, upon the public at large.[42] They could invoke it to protect the insured, lacking power and influence in the insurance market, from financial insecurity. They could ensure that the economically powerless receive rights that are comparable to those accorded them under s. 2 of the *Charter* in their relations with the State. In each case, they could do so fully appreciating the insufficiency of private law remedies. They could do so also knowing full well about the inadequacy of public regulation of so-called private action. Indeed, the Superintendent of Insurance and bank inspectors, acting as public regulators, provide only limited protection to individuals who are abused by insurance companies and banks respectively. These bureaucracies *are* under-staffed and under-funded. They *are* ill-equipped to preserve the interests of the consumer and insured, no matter how commonplace the abuse and co-operative the government agency.

To exclude the individual's unhappy private world from the effect of the *Charter* is to expect her, a private actor, to live in a public vacuum. Unprotected from "private" abuse, she is obliged to rely upon an often reluctant State to regulate disparate economic and political power. She is expected to endure the financial insecurity of insurance companies and trust companies. She is to hope, sometimes to no avail, for governments to redress her suffering by public means. She is forced to act alone, to pursue private law remedies, however insufficient they might be.

None of this need be so. The individual's plight can be identified with the plight of others. The communality of individual interests can be defended collectively. The common experience of participants in civil society can give rise to public remedies. As Chief Justice Dickson affirmed in the *Alberta Reference*, "association has always been the means through which political, cultural and racial minorities, religious groups and workers have sought to attain their purposes and fulfil their aspirations".[43] Association is also an important means towards, and manifestation of, public action.

---

41   [1986] 2 S.C.R. 573, at 603 (emphasis added). See too, D. Beatty, "Constitutional Conceits: The Coercive Authority of Courts" (1987), 37 U.T.L.J. 183, at 186-87. But *cf.* P.W. Hogg, "The *Dolphin Delivery* Case: The Application of the Charter to Private Action" (1987), 51 Sask. L. Rev. 273, at 273-77.
42   See esp. W.E. Code, *Final Report of the Inspector on First City Investors* (Edmonton: Government of Alberta, 1989).
43   [1987] 1 S.C.R. 313, at 365-66.

A RELATIONAL PRIVATE

> The concept of equality is, by definition, relational or comparative.
> A person can only be found to be equal in relation to or in comparison
> with some other person . . .[44]

The cornerstone of private life is envisaged as relational: private relations develop between parties who are connected to each other by personal, social, and legal ties, quite apart from their association with the State. To reinforce this private status, each individual exploits or sacrifices her rights in relation to other individuals. This is evident in the classical view of contract law as a "pure" system, based on the symmetrical principles of mutuality, consideration and reliance. The "sanctity of contract", free from a paternalistic State, is part of a *private* bargained-for exchange.[45] Within this private world, *Charter* rights are supposedly unnecessary, indeed, uneconomic and unjust intrusions upon it. Contract laws, sensitive to private relations, ensure the maximization of the private bargain. That insurance, drug and chemical companies, banks and public utilities enjoy a special "private" status is an incident of the free market. That big business acts as a *de facto* government is an expression of private, not public power. Inequality in "private" status remains private, except where legislatures render it public, for example, by redressing the abuse of economic power through anti-trust or consumer laws. "The best test of truth", Chief Justice Holmes suggested in *Abrams v. United States*, "is the power of the thought to get itself accepted in the competition of the market".[46] The individual is expected to enter that competition, not rely on the State to do so for her.

This autonomous private realm is justified economically. Standardized contracts with exclusion and limitation of liability clauses, no matter how imbalanced or unfair, are treated as private because they lead to efficient private — and business — relations. To avoid having to dictate how individuals ought to live, judges apply "private" standards to judge "private" bargains. They accept the content of each bargain as the parties themselves reasonably intend. They regard the social effect of that bargain as incidental to public life, falling short of regulation by public law.[47]

---

[44]   M.H. Friedman, "Equality in the Administration of Criminal Justice", in *Nomos IX: Equality*, J.R. Pennock and J.W. Chapman, eds. (New York, Atheron Press, 1967), p. 250, at 253.

[45]   On the classical foundation of the binding force of obligations in contract, see, *e.g.*, *per* Lord Jessel M.R. in *Printing & Numerical Registering Co. v. Sampson* (1875), L.R. 19 Eq. 462, at 465. See too, *per* Mr. Justice Estey in *Ronald Elwyn Lister Ltd. v. Dunlop Canada Ltd.*, [1982] 1 S.C.R. 726, at 745.

[46]   250 U.S. 616, at 630 (1919).

[47]   See, *e.g.*, F. Kessler, "Contracts of Adhesion — Some Thoughts about Freedom of Contract" (1943), 43 Colum. L. Rev. 629; E.W. Patterson, "The Delivery of a Life-Insurance Policy" (1919), 33 Harv. L. Rev. 198; N. Isaacs, "The Standardizing of Contracts" (1917), 27 Yale L.J. 34; G. Battersby, "Exemption Clauses and Third Parties: Recent Decisions"

Courts, in turn, sanctify the private bargain by attributing democratic components to it. Judges supposedly do not make or unmake contracts. They trust individuals to create their own relations. They expect to stand aside from those relations. To displace the binding force of the private contract by public means is to be undemocratic towards it. Indeed, it is to interfere with the contract itself.[48]

> [If] there is one thing which more than another public policy requires it is that men of full age and competent understanding shall have the utmost liberty of contracting, and that their contracts when entered into freely and voluntarily shall be held sacred.[49]

To perpetuate the private nature of agreements, courts often envisage the rule of law as the means of protecting the relational rights of individuals. They favour peer judgment over justice by a dictatorial State or by equally dictatorial judges.[50]

However, this unity among private individuals only makes sense in a world of relatively equal, trustworthy, and responsible individuals. Formal equality between individuals is suspect in today's corporate economy in which the contract is often an instrument of discriminatory treatment. Reliance upon private law remedies fails, in particular, in the absence of equal access to, and equal treatment in law. Indeed, the very justification for extending *Charter* protection to victims of the "private" bargain rests upon the insufficiency of private law remedies based upon free market principles to remedy inequality of treatment. Thus, judges who recognize the social ramifications of private conduct, increasingly substitute public for private law remedies. They find corporate directors criminally liable for the conduct of those who function as the corporation's "directing mind and will".[51] They condemn "oppressive" and "arbitrary" breaches

---

(1978), 28 U.T.L.J. 75; E.P. Belobaba, "Unfair Trade Practices Legislation: Symbolism and Substance in Consumer Protection" (1977), 15 Osgoode Hall L.J. 327; S.M. Waddams, "Contracts, Exemption Clauses, Unconscionability, Consumer Protection" (1971), 49 Can. Bar Rev. 578.

[48] See L.E. Trakman, "Frustrated Contracts and Legal Fictions" (1983), 46 Mod. L. Rev. 39; Trakman, "Interpreting Contracts: A Common Law Dilemma" (1981), 59 Can. Bar Rev. 241.

[49] *Per* Lord Jessel M.R. in *Printing & Numerical Registering Co., supra,* note 45, at 465. See too, *per* Estey J. in *Ronald Elwyn Lister Ltd., supra,* note 45, at 745.

[50] On juries as public, see generally, J.A. Phillips and T.C. Thompson, "Jurors v. Judges in Later Stuart England: The Penn/Mead Trial and *Bushell's Case*" (1986), 4 Law & Inequality 189; G. Torres and D.P. Brewster, "Judges and Juries: Separate Moments in the Same Phenomenon" (1986), 4 Law & Inequality 171; W.V. Luneburg and M.A. Nordenberg, "Specially Qualified Juries and Expert Nonjury Tribunals: Alternatives for Coping with the Complexities of Modern Civil Litigation" (1981), 67 Va. L. Rev. 887; W.S. White, "Death-Qualified Juries: 'The 'Prosecution-Proneness' Argument Reexamined" (1980), 41 U. Pitt. L. Rev. 353.

[51] See *per* Estey J. in *Canadian Dredge & Dock Co. et al. v. R.,* [1985] 1 S.C.R. 662, where the "directing mind" must act in accordance with the corporate function assigned him (at 685). See too, G. Williams, *Criminal Law: The General Part,* 2nd ed. (London: Stevens, 1961), s. 280.

of faith in consumer transactions.[52] They impose special fiduciary obligations upon big businesses;[53] and they hold employers punitively liable for reckless and tortious breaches of contracts of employment.[54] In each case, they react partially against prejudice and inequality in social and political life. They apply quasi-public remedies to allegedly private transactions. In challenging sexual, linguistic, and religious bias, they move beyond specific relations to the social environment in which those relations are manifest. In regulating the abuse of relations of power, they move beyond strict compensation in contract or tort to quasi-public remedies aimed at punishing and deterring abuse of "private" relations. In deciding upon the limits of private law remedies, they pierce the veil of private life itself.

> [A] jury should be directed that if . . . compensation . . . is inadequate
> to punish him [the defendant] for his outrageous conduct, to mark
> their disapproval of such conduct and to deter him from repeating it,
> then it can award some larger sum.[55]

Thus, courts sometimes apply quasi-public penalties, notably punitive damages, to private transactions for distinctly public reasons. They do so because of the quasi-governmental stature of big business, the subservient status of their subjects, and the momentous public harm that arises from the corporate abuse of individual rights. So motivated, they treat the manufacturers of urea formaldehyde and di-ethyl-stilboestrol (DES)[56]

---

52 See esp., M.A. Catzman, Exemplary Damages: The Decline, Fall and Resurrection of *Rookes v. Barnard"*, [1973] Lectures L.S.U.C. 41; L. Ford, "Damages — Punitive or Exemplary Damages — A Canadian View of *Rookes v. Barnard"* (1965), 4 Alta. L. Rev. 159. See too, *Williams v. Settle*, [1960] 1 W.L.R. 1072 (C.A.); *Assn. des Compositeurs, Auteurs et Editeurs du Canada Ltée v. Keet Estates Inc.*, [1972] S.C. 315 (Que.); *Pro Arts, Inc. v. Campus Crafts Holdings Ltd.* (1980), 110 D.L.R. (3d) 366 (Ont. H.C.J.).

53 On the development of such fiduciary obligations in law, see R. Merkin, "*Uberrimae Fidei* Strikes Again" (1976), 39 Mod. L. Rev. 478; R.A. Hasson, "The Doctrine of *Uberrima Fides* in Insurance Law — A Critical Evaluation" (1969), 32 Mod. L. Rev. 615.

54 See *New Brunswick Electrical Power Commn. v. Int. Brotherhood of Electrical Workers, Loc. 1733* (1978), 22 N.B.R. (2d) 364 (Q.B.). See further *Gershman v. Manitoba Vegetable Producers' Marketing Bd.* (1976), 69 D.L.R. (3d) 114 (Man. C.A.); *Canadian Ironworkers Union, No. 1 v. Int. Assn. of Bridge, Structural & Ornamental Ironworkers Union, Loc. 97* (1979), 45 D.L.R. (3d) 768 (B.C.C.A.).

55 *Rookes v. Barnard*, [1964] A.C. 1129, at 1228 (H.L.), *per* Lord Devlin. For the endorsement by the Supreme Court of Canada of punitive damage awards not only in tort law but also in contract, see *H.L. Weiss Forwarding Ltd. v. Omnus et al.*, [1976] 1 S.C.R. 776. See too, *Brown v. Waterloo Bd. of Commrs. of Police* (1982), 136 D.L.R. (3d) 49, at 65-66 (Ont. C.A.); M.G. Cochrane, "Imaginary Damages for Breach of Contract: Punitive Damages and Damages for Mental Distress" (1984), 5 Adv. Q. 110; B.J. Reiter, "Contracts, Torts, Relations and Reliance", in *Studies in Contract Law*, B.J. Reiter and J. Swan, eds. (Toronto: Butterworths, 1980), p. 235, at 269-72; D.L. Hawley, "Punitive and Aggravated Damages in Canada" (1980), 18 Alta. L. Rev. 485; H. Krasnick, "Punitive Damages in Contract" (1978), 36 The Advocate 11.

56 On the urea formaldehyde controversy in Canada, see D. Cohen, "The Public and Private Law Dimensions of the UFFI Problem" (1983-84), 8 Can. Bus. L.J. 309, 410 (Comment by M.J. Trebilcock, at 438; Comment by A.J. Roman, at 444). On DES litigation, see A.M. Biebel, "DES Litigation and the Problem of Causation" (1984), 51

as aberrant corporate giants, imposing their defective products upon an unsuspecting public. They judge these giants, just as they judge reckless legislators who impose their unfeeling mandate upon the citizenry at large. They appreciate that the special fiduciary obligation of the corporate giant increasingly resembles the fiduciary responsibility of the State. They realize that human subjects increasingly require public protection from those who would purposefully or recklessly divest them of their physical and mental well-being, just as they require *Charter* protection from government.[57]

For courts to construct public responsibility around criminal law is to overstate the capacity of criminal law to remedy abuse of so-called "private" relations. Indeed, it is to ignore the limitations of any criminal justice regime. The State is selective about whom it accuses. Burdens of proof in criminal law are often difficult to satisfy; and the criminal justice system has limited remedies. One alternative is for courts to construct private law remedies that are modeled upon the public responsibility of the State, while not being identical to it. In still protecting civil rights through private action, the court avoids many of the pitfalls of a public trial. It is not circumscribed by the *Criminal Code*. It need not prove its case "beyond a reasonable doubt"; and it is able to develop flexible remedies in civil law to satisfy the needs of each case.[58] This public nature of private law remedies is already evident in the manner in which judges construct a civil law duty of care in products liability and insurance cases.[59] Judges impose special duties of trust and confidence upon organizations who, while being formally private, are economically and socially public. They require large-scale producers to advise their customers about risks associated with, and harm arising from, the use of hazardous products and services. They also require them to exercise reasonable diligence to avert or otherwise mitigate those risks and losses.[60]

Certainly, courts do not do all this lightly. In "determining the extent of liability" in civil suits, they engage in "delicate value judgments and the drawing of fine lines".[61] They hover uncomfortably between compensatory and non-compensatory remedies, between the belief that the

---

Ins. Counsel J. 223; C.T. Davies, "Punitive Damages in DES Market Share Litigation" (1983), 23 Santa Clara L. Rev. 185; Note, "Market Share Liability: An Answer to the DES Causation Problem" (1981), 94 Harv. L. Rev. 668; *Bichler v. Eli Lilly & Co.*, 436 N.E. 2d 182, at 184 (N.Y.C.A., 1982); G.O. Robinson, "Multiple Causation in Tort Law: Reflections on the DES Cases" (1982), 68 Va. L. Rev. 713.

57   See further, *infra*, at 108.
58   See in general, *supra*, note 55.
59   See L.E. Trakman, "The Unharnessed Insurer: A Foreboding Presence" (1981), 31 U.T.L.J. 318; Trakman, "Mysteries Surrounding Material Disclosure in Insurance Law" (1984), 34 U.T.L.J. 421; E.M. Holmes, "Is There Life After Gilmore's Death of Contract? — Inductions from a Study of Commercial Good Faith in First-Party Contract" (1980), 65 Cornell L. Rev. 330. See further, *infra*, at 108.
60   J.G. Fleming, *The Law of Torts*, 6th ed. (Sydney: Law Book Co., 1983), p. 130.
61   *Ibid.*, at 306.

judiciary is responsible only to remedy injustices between individuals and the understanding that they are also to address public harm. They appreciate that statutory remedies governing pollution and acid rain do not redress the full spectrum of harm that arises from environmental waste. They realize, too, that to redress individual wrongs is also to respond to the public implications that arise from those wrongs. In deterring Ford Motor Company, through punitive damages, from knowingly manufacturing defective Ford Pintos, they do more than compensate the innocent consumer or even punish Ford Motor Company.[62] They protect the public's right to know about the risks and harm that stem from insufficient product testing and faulty design; and they allow that public to adopt precautionary and ultimately risk-evasive tactics.

In effect, courts provide consumers with quasi-public protection under the common law against those who would abuse a distinctly public trust, as producers, insurance companies or employers.[63] More positively, they enable those consumers to address their collective concerns by quasi-public means, not least of all by resort to the class action.[64] They caution big business that wanton and reckless negligence or breach of contract can lead to non-compensatory liability on grounds of "oppressive, arbitrary or unconstitutional action", or because "the defendant's conduct has been calculated by him to make a profit . . . which may well exceed the compensation payable to the plaintiff."[65] In doing so, they discharge a fundamentally public and political choice: they punish and deter wanton or reckless abuse of "private" relations. In not doing so, they fall into the trap of trusting in an artificial jurisprudence founded upon pervasive principles of private law.[66]

---

[62]   See *Grimshaw v. Ford Motor Co.*, 174 Cal. Rptr. 348 (1981).

[63]   On the exemplary and, conceivably, punitive liability of employers, see *New Brunswick Electrical Power Commn., supra,* note 54. See further *Gershman v. Manitoba Vegetable Producers' Marketing Bd.* and *Canadian Ironworkers Union No. 1 v. Int. Assn. of Bridge, Structural & Ornamental Ironworkers Union, supra,* note 54.

[64]   On the class action in common law Canada, see esp. *Naken v. General Motors of Canada Ltd.,* [1983] 1 S.C.R. 72; Ontario Law Reform Commission, *Report on Class Actions* (Toronto: Ministry of the Attorney General, 1982). On the class action in Quebec, see R.S.Q. 1977, c. C-25, arts. 999-1051 as amended. See, in general, J.K. Bankier, "The Future of Class Actions in Canada: Cases, Courts and Confusion" (1984), 9 Can. Bus. L.J. 260; W.A. Bogart, *"Naken,* the Supreme Court and What Are Our Courts for?" (1984), 9 Can. Bus. L.J. 280; J.R. Pritchard, "Class Action Reform: Some General Comments" (1984), 9 Can. Bus. L.J. 309; Note, "Cutting the Overhead Costs of Resolving Asbestos Claims: A Time for Action" (1983), 6 J. Prod. Liability 17; J.E. Kennedy, "Class Actions: The Right to Opt Out" (1983), 25 Ariz. L. Rev. 3; A.R. Miller, "Of Frankenstein Monsters and Shining Knights: Myth, Reality and the 'Class Action' Problem" (1979), 92 Harv. L. Rev. 664.

[65]   *Per* Lord Devlin in *Rookes v. Barnard, supra,* note 55, at 1226.

[66]   A long line of cases have denied punitive damages arising out of breach of contract on grounds, *inter alia,* that contract damages are private and compensatory, not public and punitive. See, for instance, *Guildford v. Anglo-French Steamship Co.* (1884), 9 S.C.R. 303; *Denison v. Fawcett* (1958), 12 D.L.R. (2d) 537 (Ont. C.A.); *Toronto Hockey Club v. Arena Gardens Ltd.,* [1924] 4 D.L.R. 384 (Ont. H.C.), affd. [1925] 4 D.L.R. 546 (C.A.), affd.

Judges who insist that they merely protect private rights, seek an impossible dream. They refuse to recognize that the moral philosophy underlying the *Charter* applies to the private as to the public domain. They falter, too, in seeking to protect a "classless" society of equal rightholders, while, at the same time, perpetuating class divisions among those who cannot exercise their rights equally.[67] They fail, as Duncan Kennedy and Peter Gabel would have it, in reducing private life to the "projected image of the unity of isolated people" who are "not engaged in public political life".[68] In treating unequal parties alike, whether they be big or small businesses, aboriginal or non-aboriginal people, men or women, they engender inequality, not equality. As Mr. Justice McIntyre argued in *Andrews v. Law Society of British Columbia*,[69]

> . . . identical treatment may frequently produce serious inequality . . . [I]n the well-known words of Frankfurter J. in *Dennis v. United States*, 339 U.S. 162 (1950), at p. 184:
>
> > It was a wise man who said that there is no greater inequality than the equal treatment of unequals.
>
> The same thought has been expressed in this Court in the context of s. 2(*b*) of the *Charter* in *R. v. Big M Drug Mart Ltd.*, [1985] 1 S.C.R. 295, where Dickson C. J. said at p. 347:
>
> > The interests of true equality may well require differentiation in treatment.[70]

Those judges who appreciate this public context that surrounds private rights extend fundamental rights and freedoms beyond the formal relationship between individual and State. They realize that to endorse a "private" bargain is to construct a political justification for it — in compliance with public order, good morals or plain efficiency. They understand, too, that to treat right-holders equally in private law is comparatively meaningless if they discount the substantive inequalities that prevail in so-called private life.

[1926] 4 D.L.R. 1 (P.C.); *Dobson v. Winton & Robbins Ltd.*, [1959] S.C.R. 775, at 782; *Harvey Foods Ltd. v. Reid* (1971), 18 D.L.R. (3d) 90, at 93 (N.B.C.A.); *Cardinal Construction Ltd. v. R. in right of Ontario* (1981), 122 D.L.R. (3d) 703, at 704 (Ont. H.C.J.), affd. 128 D.L.R. (3d) 662 (C.A.); *Edwards et al. v. Harris-Intertype (Canada) Ltd.* (1983), 40 O.R. (2d) 558, at 572 (H.C.J.), affd. 9 D.L.R. (4th) 319 (C.A.).

[67] The problem is well illustrated by the history of Quebec. See, *e.g.*, E. Bernier, "Sous-Prolétaires Québecois: Class Situation of a Disadvantaged Group", in *Structured Inequality in Canada*, J. Harp and J.R. Hofley, eds. (Scarborough, Ont.: Prentice-Hall, 1980), p. 208; P. Belanger *et al.*, *La division en classes sociales* (Département de Sociologie, Université Laval, 1974); E. Bernier, "Culture de la pauvreté et analyse de classes" (1974), 16 Anthropologica 41.

[68] P. Gabel and D. Kennedy, "Roll Over Beethoven" (1984), 36 Stan. L. Rev. 1, at 35. See too, D. Fraser, "Laverne and Shirley Meet the Constitution" (1984), 22 Osgoode Hall L.J. 783; A.C. Hutchinson and P.J. Monahan, "Law, Politics, and the Critical Legal Scholars: The Unfolding Drama of American Legal Thought" (1984), 36 Stan. L. Rev. 199.

[69] [1989] 1 S.C.R. 143.

[70] *Ibid.*, at 164-65.

STAGNATION THROUGH CATEGORIZATION

> "The *Charter* regulates the relations between government and private
> persons, but it does not regulate the relations between private persons
> and private persons. Private action is therefore excluded from the
> application of the *Charter*."[71]

Judges sometimes construct an "obvious" division between public and
private. Family law is obviously private: criminal law is obviously public.
This approach has at least three problems. First, it renders the normative
content of public and private inevitable. Secondly, it imposes an artificial restriction upon the judge in "obvious" cases, for example, by distinguishing mechanically between parental discipline and child abuse. Finally,
and most importantly, it employs this "natural" distinction between public
and private to close off discussion about purportedly private matters.

The alternative is to subsume the public-private division under the
pervasive veil of public life. The supply of milk, previously associated
with a private relationship between supplier and customer, becomes public
when its disruption impedes the health of children and mothers who are
nursing babies. Of public importance now

> ... is whether the potential ... economic harm to third parties ... is
> so massive and immediate and so focused in its intensity as to justify
> the limitation of a constitutionally guaranteed freedom in respect of
> those employees.[72]

Those who previously insisted that the *Charter* "addresses itself *only* to
laws and relationships between the State and individuals" now reckon
with the public implications of "private" action.[73] Those who "expect a
constitution to empower and regulate the institutions of government, *not
the relationships between private individuals and organizations*"[74] now deal with
the public implications of private relations. Those who distinguish *Charter* rights from State action now weigh State action "against the deleterious
effects of the measures which limit the enjoyment of [those] ... right[s]".[75]

---

[71]   *Dolphin Delivery*, [1986] 2 S.C.R. 573, at 594, *per* McIntyre J., quoting P.W. Hogg,
       Constitutional Law of Canada, 2nd ed. (Toronto: Carswell, 1985), p. 674.

[72]   *Saskatchewan Dairies*, [1987] 1 S.C.R. 460, at 477-78 *per* Dickson C.J.

[73]   F.J.E. Jordan, Senior Counsel, Public Law, Federal Department of Justice, in *Minutes of
       Proceedings and Evidence of the Special Joint Committee of the Senate and of the House of
       Commons on the Constitution of Canada*, First Session of the Thirty-Second Parliament,
       1980-81, at 49 (emphasis added).

[74]   P.W. Hogg, *Canada Act 1982 Annotated* (Toronto: Carswell, 1982), p. 77 (emphasis added).
       Katherine Swinton states this proposition even more explicitly: "[The] Charter of Rights
       is designed to bind government, not private actors", *per* Swinton, "Application of the
       Canadian Charter of Rights and Freedoms", in *The Canadian Charter of Rights and
       Freedoms: Commentary*, W.S. Tarnopolsky and G.-A. Beaudoin, eds. (Toronto: Carswell,
       1982), p. 41, at 44-45. See further, Hogg, *op. cit.*, note 71, at 647, 674-78; J.D. Whyte, "Is
       the Private Sector Affected by the Charter?", in *Righting the Balance: Canada's New
       Equality Rights*, L. Smith, ed. (Saskatoon: Canadian Human Rights Reporter, 1986), p.
       145.

[75]   *Saskatchewan Dairies, supra*, note 72, at 477 *per* Dickson C.J.

They entertain public interest in the workforce beyond the right to strike or picket. They choose whether the harm suffered by third parties out-weighs the benefit to employers or employees; and they reach their deci-sion based on social conceptions of benefit and harm to individual and group alike.

Judges choose where to draw the line between private and public themselves. They construct a welfare state that engulfs private rights, or a libertarian state that preserves those rights, in their own image of both.[76] Yet, they cannot treat corporations and destitute mothers as equally private in light of the substantial differences between the two. They cannot regard fundamental rights as private and yet hope to avoid judging their political and public character.[77] However seemingly impassive they are towards political choice, judges choose between the will of the legislature and the will of individuals. Formally, they do as the *Charter* directs. Functionally, they impute a liberal ideology to it. They shield the individual's private right to trade, associate, or pray under s. 2. They also safeguard the autonomy of the State under ss. 1, 15(2) and 33. They identify the "reasonable limit" of government action in *Oakes*,[78] but only after they have constructed a logical relationship between the object being sought, the means of attaining it, and its social effect.

At their most rhetorical, judges envisage a public-private divide that solves its own mysteries. At their most realistic, they resolve those mys-teries themselves. They engage in political discourse, but somehow they are not wholly under the control of that discourse. They determine that a particular dispute is private or public, but only in light of social conse-

---

76   In more radical versions of "the Welfare State", private life is absorbed into the benevolent State. The public-private divide, however, is retained. Among the more liberal, welfarism is an exception to — not a substitute for — liberal rights. *Cf. The Canadian Worker in the Twentieth Century*, I. Abella and D. Millar, eds. (Toronto: Oxford University Press, 1978); K. Herman, "The Emerging Welfare State: Changing Perspectives in Canadian Welfare Policies and Programs, 1867-1960", in *Social Space: Canadian Perspectives*, D.I. Davies and K. Herman, eds. (Toronto: New Press, 1971), p. 131. On the history of the Canadian Welfare State, see R.C.B. Risk, "Lawyers, Courts, and the Rise of the Regulatory State" (1984), 9 Dalhousie L.J. 31; W.H. McConnell, "The Judicial Review of Prime Minister Bennett's 'New Deal'" (1968), 6 Osgoode Hall L.J. 39. See too, H.L. Wilensky, *The Welfare State and Equality* (Berkeley: University of California Press, 1975). But *cf.* S.D. Clark, *The New Urban Poor* (Toronto: McGraw-Hill Ryerson, 1978).

77   Their dilemma is readily illustrated in scholarly commentary upon private rights. See, *e.g.*, R.M. Dworkin, "Is Law a System of Rules?", in *The Philosophy of Law*, R.M. Dworkin, ed. (London: Oxford University Press, 1977); J. Raz, "Right-Based Moralities", in *Theories of Rights*, J.Waldron, ed. (Oxford: Oxford University Press, 1984), p. 182; Mackie, "Can There Be a Right-Based Moral Theory?", in *Theories of Rights, ibid.*, at 168. Their discomfort is evident in coupling realism with social practices that do not coincide in fact. On the "realist's plight", see W.E. Rumble, *American Legal Realism: Skepticism, Reform, and the Judicial Process* (Ithaca, N.Y.: Cornell University Press, 1968); M.J. Perry, "Taking Neither Rights-Talk Nor the 'Critique of Rights' Too Seriously" (1984), 62 Tex. L. Rev. 1405.

78   [1986] 1 S.C.R. 103.

quences which they attribute to it. They balance private rights against public interests, but only in light of *their* conception of the reasonable limits of a free and democratic society.[79] They realize that there is no pre-existing, natural or inevitable public-private divide.

For judges to insist that the conduct of corporations is always private, while the practices of the College of Physicians and Surgeons of Ontario is always public, is at best to employ artificial reasoning.[80] Private life is *never* wholly depoliticized. No pervasive conception of fundamental rights and freedoms" in s. 2 of the *Charter* outlines, other than abstractly, the confines of the private world. No private condition suddenly displaces political conceptions of the "good life". Privilege is a social, not a private condition. It exists in the disparity between haves and have-nots, between those who can and those who cannot act, whether or not their status is construed as private. It is reflected in the realization that not all rights and freedoms are equally fundamental under s. 2 or equally enjoyed under s. 15 of the *Charter*.

Courts that preserve the public-private division, despite all this, defer to a pre-existing constitutional and social hierarchy. In particular, they claim not to interfere with governmental policy on grounds that it is not legitimate to do so in a constitutional democracy.[81] Chief Justice Dickson so asserted in *P.S.A.C. v. Canada*:

> In my opinion, courts must exercise considerable caution when confronted with difficult questions of economic policy. . . . A high degree of deference ought properly to be accorded to the government's choice of strategy in combatting this complex problem. . . . The role of the judiciary in such situations lies primarily in ensuring that the selected legislative strategy is fairly implemented with as little interference as is reasonably possible with the rights and freedoms guaranteed by the *Charter*.[82]

Thus, courts enforce legislation on grounds that it stems from an authoritative source, and in addition, that it minimally impairs fundamental rights and freedoms. For example, they uphold legislative restrictions on

---

79   See hereon esp., J. Rodger, "On the Degeneration of the Public Sphere" (1985), 33 Pol. Stud. 203: S.I. Benn and G.F. Gaus, "The Public and Private: Concepts and Action", in *Public and Private in Social Life*, S.I. Benn and G.F. Gaus, eds. (New York: St. Martin's Press, 1983); M.J. Horwitz, "The History of the Public/Private Distinction" (1982), 130 U. Pa. L. Rev. 1423; D. Kennedy, "The Stages of the Decline of the Public/Private Distinction" (1982), 130 U. Pa. L. Rev. 1349; K.E. Klare, "The Public/Private Distinction in Labor Law" (1982), 130 U. Pa. L. Rev. 1358.

80   See *Re College of Physicians & Surgeons of Ontario and K* (1985), 16 D.L.R. (4th) 424 (Ont. Div. Ct.); revd. 36 D.L.R. (4th) 707 (C.A.). The legal status of each entity, for example of a government board or multinational corporation, formally circumscribes the perimeters of the public-private divide.

81   *Public Service Alliance of Canada v. Canada*, [1987] 1 S.C.R. 424, at 442 *per* Dickson C.J. See too, *per* Wilson J. in *Singh v. Minister of Employment & Immigration*, [1985] 1 S.C.R. 177, at 218-19.

82   *P.S.A.C. v. Canada, supra*, note 81, at 442.

the right to strike where that same legislation allows for third-party arbitration as an alternative to striking.[83] They uphold statutes that prohibit the publication of names of victims of sexual assault, under s. 1, on the grounds that trials involving sexual assault are still open to the public, thereby leading to minimal interference with the s. 2(*b*) guarantee of freedom of the press.[84]

That we each have a personal and a public life is not in dispute. That the legislature overrides fundamental rights and freedoms, under s. 1 or 33(1) of the *Charter*, is equally obvious. That the judge moves consistently along a principled path from private to public life, or the converse, is far less evident. Judges do not employ any necessary formula to differentiate between private rights that are sacred under s. 2 or 7 no matter what, and public interests that are justifiably advanced by the State under s. 1 or 33(1).[85] Indeed, this lack of a natural divide between public and private is implicit in Mr. Justice McIntyre's difficulty in defining the limits of public life itself.

> [I]t is difficult and probably dangerous to attempt to define with narrow precision that element of governmental intervention which will suffice to permit reliance on the *Charter* by private litigants in private litigation.[86]

If human life embraces both private rights and State interests, an adequate jurisprudence embraces both, not one over the other. Human co-existence, however personal in nature, is part of a "free and democratic society", whether that society is defined as private or public. That co-existence within society is associated with the "respect for cultural and group identity"[87] that is "of sufficient importance to warrant overriding a constitutionally protected right or freedom".[88] It is evident, in the public's regard for family life, in laws that govern child custody, adoption and divorce. It prevails in the positive vision that "any private action acquiesced in by the State can be seen to derive its power from the State".[89]

Law-makers cannot exalt private life in a public vacuum. They cannot raise private rights above State action without evaluating the public con-

---

[83]   See the *Alberta Reference*, [1987] 1 S.C.R. 313, at 380.

[84]   *Canadian Newspapers Co. v. Canada (A.G.)*, [1988] 2 S.C.R. 122, at 125-36 *per* Lamer J.

[85]   The same argument applies to public life. The public interest, identified with ss. 1, 33 and 52, like the private rights under ss. 2 and 7, is far from clear in nature. See further, *supra*, at 55.

[86]   *Per* McIntyre J. in *Dolphin Delivery, supra*, note 71, at 602. For an even more emphatic rejection of the division between public and private under the Charter, see esp., D. Gibson, *The Law of the Charter: Equality Rights* (Toronto: Carswell, 1990), p. 216.

[87]   *Oakes, supra*, note 78, at 136.

[88]   *Per* Dickson C.J. (as he then was), in *Big M Drug Mart*, [1985] 1 S.C.R. 295, at 352.

[89]   P. Brest, "State Action and Liberal Theory" (1982), 130 U. Pa. L. Rev. 1296, at 1301. See too, M.J. Horwitz, "The History of the Public/Private Distinction" (1982), 130 U. Pa. L. Rev. 1423, at 1426-27; L.H. Tribe, "Refocusing the 'State Action' Inquiry: Separating State Acts from State Actors", in *Constitutional Choices* (Cambridge: Harvard University Press, 1985), p. 246.

text in which private right-holders live. Nor can they restrict public life to formal relations between the State and the individual without considering interests that are shared by both. Thus, courts identify the "reverse onus" in *Oakes*[90] with a public vision of the "good life", well beyond the accused's liberty. They evaluate the impact of statutory penalties on the sale and use of drugs upon parents, children and drug addicts who share infected needles. In each case, they embark upon a functional, not a formal public or private conception of the "good life". They choose *when* to treat public interests as commensurate with State interests. They determine, too, *when* to construe private interests as incommensurate with State interests. They are not impelled by inherent logic to do either. Whatever lip-service they pay to their own neutrality, judges embrace disparate views of rights, regionalism, ethnicity, and racial tolerance. They react differently to separate schooling in Quebec, to the plight of ethnic minorities, and to educational rights. They attribute different political weights to national, class and cultural attitudes and to the politics of gender.[91] Their selective politics is illustrated in the changing conceptions of equality before the Supreme Court of Canada.[92] It is present in disparate attitudes towards capital and working classes. It is apparent, too, in divergent reactions towards human suffering and social responsibility.[93]

For the most part, courts accommodate different kinds of public interests, ranging from national security to the well-being of a particular sector

---

[90]   *Supra*, note 78.

[91]   See K. de Jong, "Sexual Equality: Interpreting Section 28", in *Equality Rights and the Canadian Charter of Rights and Freedoms*, A.F. Bayefsky and M. Eberts, eds. (Toronto: Carswell, 1985), p. 493; A.C. Cairns and C. Williams, *The Politics of Gender, Ethnicity and Language in Canada* (Toronto: University of Toronto Press, 1986); A. Duffy, "Reformulating Power for Women" (1986), 23 Can. Rev. Soc. & Anth. 22; M. Boyd, "Sex Differences in the Canadian Occupational Attainment Process" (1982), 19 Can. Rev. Soc. & Anth. 1; W. Roberts, *Honest Womanhood; Feminism, Femininity and Class Consciousness Among Toronto Working Women 1893-1914* (Toronto: New Hogtown Press, 1976).

[92]   See D. Baker, "The Changing Norms of Equality in the Supreme Court of Canada" (1987), 9 Supreme Court L.R. 497; J.M. Vickers, "Equal Theories and Their Results: Equality-Seeking in a Cold Climate", in *Righting the Balance: Canada's New Equality Rights*, L. Smith, ed. (Saskatoon: Canadian Human Rights Reporter, 1986), p. 3; J.M. Vickers, "Majority Equality Issues of the Eighties" (1983), 1 C.H.R.Y.B. 47.

[93]   See in general, M. Robin, "The Working Class and the Transition to Capitalist Democracy in Canada" (1967-68), 47 Dal. L. Rev. 326; S. Langdon, *The Emergence of the Canadian Working Class Movement, 1845-1875* (Toronto: New Hogtown Press, 1975); H.C. Pentland, "The Western Canadian Labour Movement, 1897-1919" (1979), 3 Can. J. Pol. & Soc. Th. 53; I.M. Abella, *On Strike: Six Key Labour Struggles in Canada 1919-1949* (Toronto: James Lorimer & Co., 1975); I.M. Abella, *The Canadian Labour Movement, 1902-1960* (Ottawa: Canadian Historical Assn., 1975); C. Lipton, "Canadian Unionism", in *Capitalism and the National Question in Canada*, G. Teeple, ed. (Toronto: University of Toronto Press, 1972); and towards the aged in particular, see J.F. Myles, "The Aged, the State, and the Structure of Inequality", in *Structured Inequality in Canada*, J. Harp and J.R. Hofley, eds. (Scarborough, Ont.: Prentice-Hall, 1980), p. 320.

of society. They decide which public interests should be construed as private and which should be treated as public. Thus, labour rights have both public and private ramifications. To identify a public interest in collective bargaining is also to identify the interests which the parties themselves have in their own bargain. To protect employers from strike action is to represent both the public interest in employment relations and the wish to protect society from the ills of strike action. Following *Saskatchewan Dairies*:

> . . . public and private interests are not being pitted against each other. . . . [B]eing pitted against each other [in labour-management disputes] are two different kinds of public interest, the public interest in the continuation of services and the public interest in the freedom of workers to associate . . .[94]

Ultimately, public is private, and private is public; and labour rights are both.

PRIVATE CONCENTRATIONS OF POWER

> All human beings are born free and equal in dignity and rights . . .[95]

Courts that adopt a strict public-private ideology, among other things, depoliticize private life. They suppose that, by encompassing the corporation within the private sphere, they demonstrate both the openness of private life and the need for the State to stay at arm's length from it.[96] Indeed, this is precisely one effect of s. 2 of the *Charter*: the corporation receives the protection of s. 2(*a*) in *Big M Drug Mart*,[97] of s. 8 in *Southam*,[98] and of s. 2(*b*) in *Irwin Toy*.[99] The corporation receives a private status in yet other respects. Like other private right-holders, it concludes agreements and commits tortious acts. Like them, it is liable in its own name

---

[94]   *Saskatchewan Dairies*, [1987] 1 S.C.R. 460, at 489. Madam Justice Wilson expands upon her view of public in *McKinney v. Bd. of Governors of the University of Guelph* (1990), 76 D.L.R. (4th) 545, at 583-93 (S.C.C.). In particular, she identifies three tests of governmental action: "the control test" (at 584), "the government function test" (at 587), and "the government entity test" (at 590). In favouring "the government entity test", she focuses "on the question whether an entity performs a task pursuant to statutory authority and whether it performs that task on behalf of government in furtherance of a government purpose" (at 590).

[95]   United Nations General Assembly, Resolution 217 (III) A, December 10, 1948, art. 1.

[96]   See in general, J.A. Porter, *The Vertical Mosaic: An Analysis of Social Class and Power in Canada* (Toronto: University of Toronto Press, 1965): W. Clement, *The Canadian Corporate Elite* (Toronto: McClelland & Stewart, 1975): S. Hall, "The State in Question", in *The Idea of the Modern State*, G. McLennan, D. Held and S. Hall, eds. (Manchester: Open University Press, 1984): R. Weitzer, "Law and Legal Ideology: Contributions to the Genesis and Reproduction of Capitalism" (1980), 24 Berkeley J. Sociology 137.

[97]   [1985] 1 S.C.R. 295.

[98]   [1984] 2 S.C.R. 145.

[99]   [1989] 1 S.C.R. 927. See further, W.D. Moull, "Business Law Implications of the Canadian Charter of Rights and Freedoms" (1983-84), 8 Can. Bus. L.J. 449.

for the consequences of its private actions.[100] Shielded by its articles of in-corporation, it is never more public than the instrument of its creation permits. It has life and existence in light of the subject or purpose for which it was created. In that respect, it is as "private" in its own artificial sphere as any natural person. As Chief Justice Marshall advocated before the Supreme Court of the United States, in *Dartmouth College v. Woodward*:[101]

> A corporation is an artificial being, invisible, intangible and existing only in contemplation of law. Being the mere creature of law, it possesses only those properties which the charter of its creation confers upon it, either expressly or as incidental to its very existence.[102]

A more cynical argument is that the State identifies corporate interests as a second public estate, acting in support of the State, the first estate. Following the socialist critique of the modern state, capital interests are relatively independent of the State, yet media through which the State expresses itself.[103] This co-operation between the State and corporate Canada is depicted in the State's requirement that corporate Canada act as the State's tax collector. In effect, the corporation and the State to-gether appropriate the recently imposed Goods and Services Tax. The individual recedes into the instrument of big business. Compliant with its demands, she accepts its image of "the good life". She buys its cars, insecticides and drugs. Yet, she relies upon the State to protect her from its production of harmful goods and services. She realizes that the State is likely to preserve corporate largesse in its own interests. Yet, she trusts it to protect her rights as well.[104]

The court's role is unenviable throughout.[105] To fend off the criticism that it unduly endorses corporate dominion over private life, the court

---

[100]   See *Gower's Principles of Modern Company Law*, 4th ed. by L.C.B. Gower *et al.* (London: Stevens, 1979).

[101]   17 U.S. (4 Wheat.) 518 (1819).

[102]   *Ibid.*, at 636.

[103]   See, *e.g.*, K. Marx and F. Engels, *Selected Works* (Moscow: Progress Press, 1968), pp. 677-79.

[104]   See A. Fraser, "The Corporation as a Body Politic" (1983), 57 Telos (Fall) 5; *Social Stratification: Canada*, 2nd ed. by J.E. Curtis and W.G. Scott (Scarborough, Ont.: Prentice-Hall, 1979); G. Myers, *A History of Canadian Wealth* (Toronto: James Lorimer & Co., 1972).

[105]   See generally, H. Glasbeek and M. Mandel, "The Legalization of Politics in Advanced Capitalism: The *Canadian Charter of Rights and Freedoms*" (1988), 2 Socialist Studies 84; *Capitalism and the Rule of Law*, B. Fine, ed. (London: Hutchinson Press, 1979). See too, D.L. Bazelon, "Civil Liberties — Protecting Old Values in the New Century" (1976), 51 N.Y.U. L. Rev. 505; I. Nerken, "A New Deal for the Protection of Fourteenth Amendment Rights: Challenging the Doctrinal Bases of the Civil Rights Cases and State Action Theory" (1977), 12 Harv. C.R.-C.L. L. Rev. 297; A.A. Berle, "Constitutional Limitations on Corporate Activity — Protection of Personal Rights from Invasion Through Economic Power" (1952), 100 U. Pa. L. Rev. 933; *Contemporary Canada*, R.H. Leach, ed. (Toronto: University of Toronto Press, 1968); *A Social Purpose for Canada*, M. Oliver, ed. (Toronto: University of Toronto Press, 1961).

must demonstrate its commitment towards distributive, not just corrective justice. In particular, it must uncover some objective reason to publicize abuse of corporate-consumer and corporate-employee relations, even though it traditionally construes those relations as private.[106] If it insists too forcefully on leaving private life alone, it risks being accused of unduly favouring corporate dominance. If it accommodates the interests of disadvantaged groups in public life too readily, it risks having a negative effect upon others who are not so accommodated.

For the most part, courts purport to leave delicate matters of economic and social regulation to the legislative and executive branches of government.[107] Rather than envisage government as dominating private life, directly or through the corporation, they assume that the legislature or executive establishes the limits of public need for itself. Thus, the court obediently enforces the executive's authority to conclude a treaty in *Operation Dismantle*, while claiming that the individual lacks standing to complain.[108] It accepts the executive's sovereign power over national security. That the individual's private security might be adversely affected, it renders secondary. The decision whether or not to constrain public life is for the executive, not the court, to make.[109]

Courts are often equally determined to prevent private actors from dictating the nature of public life to government. They worry that, by linking personal to national security in *Operation Dismantle*, they might license individuals to intervene in matters of State. They desire not to reduce the State to a creature of political factions, unable to act for the communality at large. They conclude that the State should not be subject to popular whim. The right to vote, in effect, should exhaust the right to participate in public life.[110]

However, in concentrating upon a competitive private life in cases like *Southam*[111] and *Edwards Books*,[112] courts treat corporate privilege as the incidental byproduct of private rights. They display less sympathy towards

---

106 See hereon, A.J. Jacobson, "The Private Use of Public Authority: Sovereignty and Associations in the Common Law" (1980), 29 Buffalo L. Rev. 599; M.J. Horwitz, "*Santa Clara* Revisited: The Development of Corporate Theory" (1985), 88 W.Va. L. Rev. 173.
107 See the *Alberta Reference*, [1987] 1 S.C.R. 313, where s. 2(*d*) of the *Charter* was found not to include a guarantee of the right to strike. The Alberta legislation under review, which prohibited strikes, was upheld as not being inconsistent with the *Charter*. The court enforced legislation identified with a public interest in the provision of essential services.
108 *Operation Dismantle*, [1985] 1 S.C.R. 441.
109 *Ibid.*, at 456.
110 See hereon, H. Lessard, "The Idea of the 'Private': A Discussion of State Action Doctrine and Separate Sphere Ideology" (1986), 10 Dalhousie L.J. 107, at 120; S.A. Gavigan, "Law, Gender and Ideology", in *Legal Theory Meets Legal Practice*, A.F. Bayefsky, ed. (Edmonton: Academic Printing & Publishing, 1988), p. 283.
111 [1984] 2 S.C.R. 145.
112 [1986] 2 S.C.R. 713.

workers' rights than regard for the businesses for which they work.[113] Nor has the adoption of the *Charter* radically altered their pro-employer stance.[114] Judges endorse aboriginal treaty rights under s. 35 and minority language rights under s. 23 only selectively.[115] Outside of these right-holders, they generally fail to identify private rights with communal advantage or disadvantage. They do not come to grips with the very conception of group rights.

> A right may be granted to individuals as members of a group without becoming a collective right; thus, the individual exercise of this right militates strongly against it being described as collective. . . . The *Charter* recognizes rights in individuals [not collectives].[116]

Judges who invest private rights so forcibly in the depoliticized individual, bypass her status as a woman, black or member of a religious minority. They pass over the social ramifications of her private rights.[117]

None of this need be so. Whether the individual is discriminated against as an employee or woman is decided in light of public attitudes towards employment and sexual relations. Her suffering is an incident of public life, not private misfortune. Her status is influenced by classes of persons beyond herself, whether they be other women, aboriginal peoples or disabled persons. Most importantly, her private relations are circumscribed by a social context, not a communal void.[118] As E.P. Thompson

---

[113]   See H.W. Arthurs, "The Right to Golf: Reflections on the Future of Workers, Unions and the Rest of Us Under the *Charter*" (1988) 13 Queen's L.J., No. 2, p. 17; J.A. Manwaring, "Legitimacy in Labour Relations: The Courts, the British Columbia Labour Board and Secondary Picketing" (1982), 20 Osgoode Hall L.J. 274.

[114]   See H.J. Glasbeek, "Contempt for Workers" (1990), 28 Osgoode Hall L.J. 1: M. MacNeil, "Courts and Liberal Ideology: An Analysis of the Application of the Charter to Some Labour Law Issues" (1989), 34 McGill L.J. 87; J. Fudge, "Labour, the New Constitution and Old Style Liberalism", in *Labour Law Under the Charter* (Kingston: Queen's Law Journal and Industrial Relations Centre, 1988).

[115]   See hereon, *supra*, Chapter 2.

[116]   *Per* Deschênes C.J.S.C. (as he then was), in *Quebec Protestant School Bds.* (1982), 140 D.L.R. (3d) 33, at 63.

[117]   This unitary preoccupation of lawyers is attributable to the classical view of contracts and torts as "pure" systems of law, logically symmetrical and harmonious in their principles. Thus, "sanctity of contract" is a founding principle in both personal and business transactions. See *per* Lord Jessel M.R. in *Printing & Numerical Registering Co. v. Sampson* (1875), L.R. 19 Eq. 462, at 456, and *per* Estey J. in *Ronald Elwyn Lister Ltd. v. Dunlop Canada Ltd.*, [1982] 1 S.C.R. 726, at 745. The narrowness of these assumptions was clearly recognized by neoclassical "realists". See G. Gilmore, *The Death of Contract* (Columbus: Ohio State University, 1974); C. Woodard, "The Limits of Legal Realism: An Historical Perspective" (1968), 54 Va. L. Rev. 689; K.N. Llewellyn, "A Realistic Jurisprudence — The Next Step" (1930), 30 Colum. L. Rev. 431; I.R. Macneil, "Contracts: Adjustment of Long-Term Economic Relations Under Classical, Neoclassical and Relational Contract Law" (1978), 72 N.W.U. L. Rev. 854.

[118]   For commentary hereon, see M.J. Trebilcock *et al.*, *A Study on Consumer Misleading in the Reform of the Common Law: Proposed Policy Directives for the Reform of the Regulation of Uniform Trade Practices in Canada* (Ottawa: Information Canada, 1976); G. Battersby, "Exemption Clauses and Third Parties: Recent Decisions" (1978), 28 U.T.L.J. 75; E.P. Belobaba, "Unfair Trade Practices Legislation: Symbolism and Substance in Consumer Protection" (1977), 15 Osgoode Hall L.J. 327; S.M. Waddams, "Contracts, Exemption Clauses, Unconscionability, Consumer Protection" (1971), 49 Can. Bar Rev. 578.

writes: "[c]lass is a social and cultural formation . . . [it] cannot be defined abstractly, or in isolation . . . [it] is not a thing, it is a happening."[119]

Thus, individuals and groups alike are entitled to differential treatment under the *Charter* because their social conditions are different. Their s. 2 rights are influenced by the social conditions under which they exercise them. Their constitutional status is not peculiarly their own. Poverty claimants are not alone in their relative incapacity to protect themselves from the dominating influence of big business upon their daily lives. Their s. 2 rights under the *Charter* are all the more fundamental because they are poor, because big business might easily abuse them, and because they have few resources by which to protect themselves from such abuse.

In each case, the capacity to exercise human rights hinges upon the communal qualities that are imputed, sometimes selectively, to it. Equal pay for equal work, education in the language of choice, and admission of minorities to social clubs are all communally endorsed or condemned. None is justified wholly privately. Each is framed in a social context that is wider than the personality of its user.[120] Each has social ramifications that are more pervasive than the individual's right to have an abortion or engage in strike action.[121] Thus, the "distinct society" clause in the failed *Meech Lake Accord* addressed a broad social purpose, beyond the linguistic domination of French speaking Canadians over other groups in Quebec.[122] It sought to extend language rights as an instrument of communication to an ever-widening polity. After all, language rights are far more than the solitary expression of particular francophone or anglophile Quebecers.[123] Language usage *is* social. It is a medium through which groups communicate; it is the source of their culture. It facilitates a multidimensional public discourse.[124] A linguistic culture does not exist in isolation. It functions in association with other cultures. It is a means towards social harmony and national stability, beyond the immediate rights of

[119] E.P. Thompson, *The Making of the English Working Class* (London: Penguin, 1963), p. 9. This concern is somewhat more stridently advocated thus: "If the terms imperialism, racism, sexism and poverty are abbreviated signs for theories of social relationships or social systems which cause the systematic abrogation of basic rights, then imperialism, racism, sexism and poverty can be called crimes according to the logic of our argument": Herman and Julia Schwendinger, "Defenders of Order or Guardians of Human Rights?" (1970), 5 Issues in Criminology 123, at 148.

[120] See *Saskatchewan Dairies*, [1987] 1 S.C.R. 460, esp. *per* Wilson J. in dissent, at 485.

[121] On such collective rights, see S. Lynd, "Communal Rights" (1984), 62 Tex. L. Rev. 1417.

[122] See generally, B. Schwartz, *Fathoming Meech Lake* (Winnipeg: Legal Research Institute of the University of Manitoba, 1987).

[123] See W.S. Tarnopolsky and W.F. Pentney, *Discrimination and the Law in Canada*, rev. ed. (Don Mills, Ont.: Deboo, 1985), pp. 4-79; Schwartz, *op. cit.*, note 122.

[124] However, on language as an instrument of political domination, see G. Pelletier, *The October Crisis*, trans. J. Marshall (Toronto: McClelland & Stewart, 1971); P. A. Linteau et al., *Quebec: A History, 1867-1929* (Toronto: Lorimer, 1983); R. Handler, *Nationalism and the Politics of Culture in Quebec* (Madison: University of Wisconsin Press, 1988).

anglophone and francophone Canadians. It transcends s. 23 of the *Charter*.

The social character of private rights is also evident under ss. 2 and 7 of the *Charter*. Reverberating beyond the particular rights of pregnant women and foetuses, employers and employees, is the need to build a "good society" through rights. In effect, the right to life, to access to abortion services, to strike and to trade are legitimate only according to the political and economic ramifications that are imputed to it.[125] Abortion rights advance more than the cause of women. Foetal rights support more than claims on behalf of the unborn. Both depict the distinctively public nature of private rights. Both demonstrate a Quebec court's conceivable interest in a low birth rate and high unemployment, not just foetal rights, in cases like *Daigle*.[126] Both reproductive and foetal rights take account of nationalism, regionalism, sexual, racial and linguistic identities.[127]

Indeed, even modern liberals associate the individual's rights with the social responsibility to preserve those rights. As John Stuart Mill reminds us: "The most important point of excellence which any form of government can possess is to promote the virtue and intelligence of the people themselves."[128] That the State is bound to protect private rights is rendered into a social, not a purely private function. Indeed, Alexis de Tocqueville reminds us:

> The most natural privilege of man, next to the right of acting for himself, is that of combining his exertions with those of his fellow creatures and of acting in common with them.[129]

However, this form of social activism is limited. The "common good" is made to reside in the State's duty to represent individual interests, not broader social interests. Yet, to provide the individual with a right to associate is to have a positive expectation of the State. It is to rely upon it to provide a supportive framework in which productive human associations can take place. It is to expect it to find a means of overcoming racism, whether towards Mohawks at Oka or oriental people in British Columbia, through group rather than purely private means.

> Human relationships in a community are said to be full, intense, cohesive, and continuous, whereas the individualistic sorts of

---

[125]   This proposition would mean, *inter alia*, reading ss. 1 and 2 together rather than apart. To a similar effect, see Mr. Justice La Forest, "The Canadian Charter of Rights and Freedoms: An Overview" (1983), 61 Can. Bar Rev. 19.

[126]   See *Tremblay v. Daigle*, [1989] 2 S.C.R. 530.

[127]   See P.C. Weiler, "The Evolution of the Charter: A View from the Outside", in *Litigating the Values of a Nation: The Canadian Charter of Rights and Freedoms*, J.M. Weiler and R.M. Elliot, eds. (Toronto: Carswell, 1986), p. 49.

[128]   J.S. Mill, *Utilitarianism, Liberty, Representative Government* (London: Everyman's Library, 1968), p. 193 (emphasis added).

[129]   A. de Tocqueville, *Democracy in America*, P. Bradley, ed. (New York: Vintage Books, 1945), vol. 1, p. 203.

association with which communities are (unfavorably) contrasted produce relationships that are partial, either flat and uninteresting or destructively competitive, and staccatolike in their discontinuities.[130]

One alternative, for courts who wish to avoid normative discourse into communal relations, is to construct two opposing hierarchies. They station human rights at the apex of a private hierarchy which they associate with ss. 2 and 7-14 of the *Charter*. They construct another hierarchy in which the legislature, drawing from ss. 1 and 33 of the *Charter*, stands at the apex. They reconcile clashes between these hierarchies by assuming that the two are naturally bifurcated. All that is public resides in the State. All that is private resides in the individual. Each sphere is self-contained. Each is exhaustive of the common good in its own domain. The individual, free to act at will, satisfies the ends of society through private rights. The State, free to govern society through legislative or executive action, advances the shared ends of society. The judicial protection of private rights is universalized. *Everyone* is *equally* entitled to fundamental freedoms like freedom of expression and association.[131] As the Supreme Court stated in *Irwin Toy*: "[w]e cannot . . . exclude human activity from the scope of guaranteed free expression".[132]

To perpetuate a universal private sphere, the decision-maker congratulates herself on her neutrality towards fundamental rights and freedoms. She insists that private actors are able to regulate themselves in the interests of the polity as a whole. That this action gives rise to a privileged private sphere, she offsets by legitimating reciprocal relations between individuals, to the exclusion of legislative or executive action. "Government bureaucrats", she supposes, defeat the ends of civil society: they unduly regulate reciprocal relations between individuals. She supposes further, *à la* Paul Weiler, that "[t]he immediate parties know best what are the economic circumstances of their relationships, [including] . . . . their non-economic priorities and concerns".[133] She believes, too, that private parties appreciate "what trade-offs are likely to be most satisfactory to their respective constituencies".[134]

However, this sequestering of private relations from their social effects falsely isolates the private agreement from the social trauma or

---

[130] R.E. Flathman, *The Practice of Rights* (Cambridge: Cambridge University Press, 1976), p. 184.

[131] See, *e.g., Big M Drug Mart*, [1985] 1 S.C.R. 295; *Edwards Books*, [1986] 2 S.C.R. 713; *Southam*, [1984] 2 S.C.R. 145; *Irwin Toy*, [1989] 1 S.C.R. 927; *Ford v. Quebec (A.G.)*, [1988] 2 S.C.R. 712; *R. v. Cancoil Thermal Corp. and Parkinson* (1986), 27 C.C.C. (3d) 295 (Ont. C.A.).

[132] *Irwin Toy, supra*, note 131, at 969.

[133] P.C. Weiler, *Reconcilable Differences* (Toronto: Carswell, 1980), pp. 64-65. See too, *Gower's Principles of Modern Company Law*, 4th ed. by L.C.B. Gower *et al.* (London: Stevens, 1979).

[134] Weiler, *op. cit.*, note 133, at 65. This is readily depicted in consumer protection legislation. See *Consumer Protection Act*, R.S.B.C. 1979, c. 65; *Consumer Credit Transactions Act*, S.A. 1985, c. C-22.5; *Consumer Protection Act*, R.S.O. 1980, c. 87.

advantage that flows from it. The "private" agreement of the utility, bank or insurance company influences the public consumption of goods and services. The privately powerful render the powerless impecunious through complex and costly litigation. Relations of power and influence undermine family harmony, market stability and social relations.[135]

Thus, judges who treat liberty as a property right isolate "private" property from its social effects. Rather than judge disproportions in private wealth, they decide only whether that wealth was acquired legitimately. They treat property as the essence of liberty. They permit each individual to have a property interest in her rights; and they protect her enjoyment of those rights only by supposing that her property interest ought to remain private.

> The great end, for which men entered into society, was to preserve their property. That right is preserved sacred and uncommunicable in all instances, where it has not been taken away or abridged by some public law for the good of the whole.[136]

In effect, courts allow property rights to circumscribe fundamental rights and freedoms.[137] They give to the large-scale newspaper a property right to scrutineer and exclude would-be advertisers. That the newspaper might employ that right to prohibit advertisers from propagating unpopular causes, the court construes as secondary. The newspaper has the right to choose with whom to contract. Would-be advertisers cannot insist that it provide them with coverage, no matter how publicly worthy their causes. Following *Gay Alliance Toward Equality v. Vancouver Sun*,

> [t]he law has recognized the freedom of the press to propagate its views and ideas on any issue and to select the material which it publishes. As a corollary to that a newspaper also has the right to refuse to publish material which runs contrary to the views which it expresses.[138]

The legitimacy of the newspaper's right to transact business, therefore, commences and ends where it began, with the newspaper's or the advertiser's property rights. Each does with its own property what private law permits. That the property rights of gays might override the property rights of newspapers and television owners is quite tenable, but only so long as property rights lie at the centre of the liberal hierarchy of rights. The reasoning is distinctly individualistic. To alter property rights by law supposedly is to threaten the fabric of civil society itself. It is to displace the individual's autonomy in favour of some communal good

---

135   See M. Bliss, *Northern Enterprise: Five Centuries of Canadian Business* (Toronto: McClelland & Stewart, 1987); R.M. Kanter, *Men and Women of the Corporation* (New York: Basic Books, 1977).
136   *Per* Lord Camden, in *Entick v. Carrington* (1765), 19 State Tr. 1029, at 1066; cited by Dickson J. (as he then was), in *Southam, supra*, note 131, at 157.
137   See *Big M Drug Mart, supra*, note 131, at 353, and *Southam, supra*, note 131, at 159.
138   *Gay Alliance Toward Equality v. Vancouver Sun*, [1979] 2 S.C.R. 435, at 455.

beyond her. According to Mr. Justice McIntyre in the *Alberta Reference*, "[f]reedom of association means the freedom to associate for the purposes of activities which are lawful when performed alone."[139]

However, by insisting that everyone enjoy liberty equally, the court ignores substantial differences in the quality of property rights. It compares large-scale newspapers who wish to select their advertisers to individuals who wish to choose their friends and business associates. It allows each private right-holder to exercise the power of property in her discrete relations with others.[140] It passes over the realization that a person's status hinges as much upon what she does and is able to do with what she owns as upon what she owns itself. Indeed, what she does with what she owns is often integral to her very identity.

Those who subject fundamental rights to property interests suppose that "men enter into definite relations of production that are indispensable and independent of their will."[141] They suppose, too, that

> [t]he sum total of these relations of production constitutes the economic structure of society, the real foundation, on which raises a legal and political superstructure and to which correspond definite forms of social consciousness.[142]

Their result is to commodify rights, particularly in relation to the underprivileged. They require that the poor prove, as a private matter, that they lack the opportunity to exercise their rights. The reality is that sometimes the poor lack the capacity to complain. They cannot afford to assert their labour rights when they fear dismissal and prospective destitution. They have rights without power. They are damned by the illusion of plural equality. They are doomed by private relations over which they have no real control or influence.[143] Thus, the corporate baron has the power of a medieval lord to dominate private life. Through its economic and political influence, the corporation demonstrates a profound understanding of the market-place, a superior capacity to bargain, and an uncanny capacity to orient that market around its own interests. Largely in control of essential factors of production, it persuades consumers, through advertisement, to purchase the goods and services that it wishes to produce; and it explains its actions as though they are in the

---

139 *Alberta Reference*, [1987] 1 S.C.R. 313, at 409.
140 On this conception of discrete relations in private law, see I.R. Macneil, "Bureaucracy, Liberalism and Community — American Style" (1984-85), 79 N.W.U. L. Rev. 900; L.E. Trakman, "Winner Take Some: Loss Sharing and Commercial Impracticability" (1985), 69 Minn. L. Rev. 471.
141 K. Marx, Preface to *A Contribution to a Critique of Political Economy* (1958), in *Selected Works*, K. Marx and F. Engels, eds. (Moscow: Progress Press, 1968), p. 181.
142 *Ibid.*
143 For a particularly erudite and classic critique of property as a private right, see C.A. Reich, "The New Property", in *Property: Mainstream and Critical Positions*, C.B. Macpherson, ed. (Toronto: University of Toronto Press, 1978).

public's interest. It demonstrates that mass production is efficient. Mass supply reduces the costs of goods and services; it accommodates consumers and workers who otherwise could not afford to buy them. Yet, this concentration of wealth and power in the hands of big business "makes the effect of private actions in certain cases virtually indistinguishable from the impact of governmental conduct."[144]

At her worst, the judge treats big business as a consequence of a free contract, its consensual creation.[145] She masks concentration of economic power under the *Charter* by cloaking private property from the public gaze.[146] Unwilling to play a public role, she avoids discussing the substance of rights. She regards them as external to her inquiry. That the newspaper or television station has the capacity to manipulate the news, she regards simply as extra-legal.[147]

Judges who appreciate this disproportionate effect of wealth upon the exercise of rights sometimes still decline to apply norms of distributive justice to them. They advance "private" explanations for their omission. They claim to decide cases between private litigants on the facts, not on grounds of social policy. They suppose that the executive and legislature, together with the judiciary, simply have no place in this private domain. They purport to give justice to individuals, not to an amorphous polity beyond them.

> In [the] . . . liberal view, no act of the state contributes to, hence properly should participate in, shaping its internal alignments or distributing its internal forces, including inequalities among parties in private.[148]

They insist upon their neutrality towards private life by claiming to decide only as reasonable parties themselves would have decided. They maintain, in effect, that the Hobbesian "warre" is to be fought only between indi-

---

[144] E. Chemerinsky, "Rethinking State Action" (1985), 80 N.W.U. L. Rev. 503, at 510-11. See too, Turkel, "The Public/Private Distinction: Approaches to the Critique of Legal Ideology" (1988), 22 L. & Soc. Rev. 801; E.M. Wood, *The Retreat from Class* (London: Verso Press, 1986).

[145] See esp., W. Bratton, "The 'Nexus of Contracts' Corporation: A Critical Appraisal" (1989), 74 Cornell L. Rev. 407.

[146] See esp., R. Hasson, "What's Your Favourite Right?: The Charter and Income Maintenance Legislation" (1989), 5 J. L. & Soc. Pol. 1; J.C. Bakan, "Strange Expectations: A Review of Two Theories of Judicial Review" (1990), 35 McGill L.J. 439.

[147] On the power of "private" property over the worker in Canada, see esp., H.J. Glasbeek, "Contempt for Workers" (1990), 28 Osgoode Hall L.J. 1; J. Fudge, "Labour, the New Constitution and Old Style Liberalism" (1988), 13 Queen's L.J., No. 2, p. 61. See too, Johnson, "The Development of Class in Canada in the Twentieth Century", in *Structured Inequality in Canada*, J. Harp and J.R. Hofley, eds. (Scarborough, Ont.: Prentice-Hall, 1980): W. Clement, *The Canadian Corporate Elite: An Analysis of Economic Power* (Toronto: McClelland & Stewart, 1975); P.C. Newman, *The Canadian Establishment* (Toronto: McClelland & Stewart, 1975).

[148] C.A. MacKinnon, "The Male Ideology of Privacy: A Feminist Perspective on the Right to Abortion" (1983), 17 Radical America, No. 4, p. 23, at 27.

viduals.[149] Judges are merely to devise the rules of private warfare, not to impose public expectations upon private actors.[150] They bypass the fact that those who declare the rules of the "warre" invariably participate in its battles, however much they claim sideline status.

More realistic judges realize that to treat all private cases alike is to produce substantive injustice. They cannot help but recognize, in cases like *Andrews*,[151] that differences in the make-up of individuals and groups affect the quality of their relationships, including their capacity to bargain with one another. They appreciate that legislatures, in the interests of effective governance, treat different individuals and groups in different ways.[152] They realize, too, that "the making of different provisions respecting such groups, the application of different rules, regulations, requirements and qualifications [to them] . . . is necessary for the governance of modern society."[153] As the late Chief Justice Laskin proposed in dissent in *Harrison v. Carswell*:

> The considerations which underlie the protection of private residences cannot apply to the same degree to a shopping centre in respect of its parking areas, roads and sidewalks. . . . This is a use of theory which does not square with economic or social fact . . .[154]

Some judges perhaps also appreciate that, while the interests of big business and government are distinguishable, their effect upon social experience often is comparable. In particular, the control imposed by big business upon the market resembles government regulation. Both forms of control are products of unbargained relationships; both are peremptory; and both arc often uncompromising. Viewed critically in the context of labour rights, the result is a world dominated more by wealth and influence than by democratic organization. In the words of Karl Klare:

> Public regulation of class struggle through collective bargaining law replicates the role assigned to the state in the classics of liberal political theory, namely to manage and contain conflicts said to inhere in the sphere of social and economic activity . . .[155]

Once courts accept, as in *Irwin Toy*,[156] that large-scale corporate advertisers have the resources to manipulate sectors of society through marketing strategies, they link constitutional remedies to hierarchical relations of power. They apply *Charter* rights according to the normative

---

149   See T. Hobbes, *Leviathan*, C.B. Macpherson, ed. (Harmondsworth: Penguin Books, 1968).
150   See *Rookes v. Barnard*, [1964] A.C. 1129 (H.L.).
151   [1989] 1 S.C.R. 143.
152   See *Andrews, ibid.*, at 168 *per* McIntyre J.
153   *Ibid.*, at 168-69.
154   *Harrison v. Carswell*, [1976] 2 S.C.R. 200, at 207-08.
155   K.E. Klare, "Labor Law as Ideology: Toward a New Historiography of Collective Bargaining Law" (1981), 4 Ind. Rel. L.J. 450, at 456.
156   [1989] 1 S.C.R. 927.

qualities of those rights, not simply the *a priori* fact of their existence. A fundamental right, then, hinges upon the need for and want of it, the ability to exercise it, and the social benefit that derives from it. What is a fundamental freedom depends upon the history, practice and expectation of those who are able to invoke it. What is a justifiable limit upon that freedom hinges upon the level of wealth, education and skill of those who claim it and are affected by its denial. Here, the quality of liberty under s. 2 of the *Charter* moves from an abstract private to a stratified public life that not everyone enjoys equally. The threat to private life stems from a privileged few who use their property to underwrite their version of "private" life at the expense of those who are not so able. Due process of law does *not* confront everyone equally. Here, private rights represent different kinds of public power, and the nature of that power is contingent upon the ability to exercise those rights in the first place.

At its most evasive, private law is no longer consolidated within a single and principled method of legal reasoning. Private life, as "advocated by professed upholders of laissez-faire . . . [now is] permeated with coercive restrictions on individual freedom."[157] Law-makers who trap themselves in this coercive realm reorient the status of big business away from equal to special treatment, and away from free enterprise to economic hierarchies. They legitimate economic power in "private" transactions by tolerating the methods of persuasion and intimidation that are employed by large-scale producers to attract consumers, and sometimes, to deceive them. They subject human endeavour, less to functional equality, than to big business' resort to law in its own interests;[158] and they justify their action, first and last, by insisting that private property performs an efficient social function.[159]

Certainly, those who control vast armies of labour can provide their employees with improved work conditions, medical services, pension benefits, and the opportunity to engage in corporate government. They can allow workers to participate in management decisions, as members of boards of directors, consultants to management, and the like. Similarly, they can require corporations with the ability to cause considerable harm to the public at large, to apprise their customers of the risks atten-

---

[157]   See R. Hale, "Coercion and Distribution in a Supposedly Non-Coercive State" (1923), 38 Pol. Sc. Q. 470, at 470-72. See too, M.R. Cohen, "Property and Sovereignty" (1927), 13 Cornell L.Q. 8.

[158]   Interestingly, Marx contends that private liberty is based, not on the association among individuals, but on their separation from one another. See esp., K. Marx, "On the Jewish Question", in *Writings of the Yong Marx on Philosophy and Society*, 1st ed., trans. L.D. Easton and K.H. Guddat (Garden City, N.Y.: Doubleday, 1967), p. 326.

[159]   See "Symposium on Efficiency as a Legal Concern" (1980), 8 Hofstra L. Rev. 485. But see, *contra*, esp. D. Kennedy and F. Michelman, "Are Property and Contract Efficient?" (1980), 8 Hofstra L. Rev. 711. But see M.J. Trebilcock, "Communal Property Rights: The Papua New Guinean Experience" (1984), 34 U.T.L.J. 377.

dant upon the use of hazardous products. Moreover, they can deny abusers the protection otherwise available to them under ss. 2 and 7-14 of the *Charter*, or their equivalent.

However, to expect comparatively poor customers to sue sophisticated and wealthy foes, who are unwilling to subject their products to stringent safety tests, is to rely on legal procedures in the absence of truly substantive remedies.[160] Absent legislative or executive intervention, the large-scale polluter escapes liability no matter how extensive the loss or worthy the claimant. Alternatively, it is held civilly accountable only to moneyed victims who are able to prove their loss in the face of difficult burdens of proof. Impeded by impecuniosity or lack of initiative, or both, the claimant who has limited resources is hindered in establishing the public nature of her "private" suffering. Consumers at large are unable to intercede on her behalf for lack of a direct interest in her "private" relationship.[161] Only in the last resort is the corporate abuser or those who act as its "directing mind and will" held criminally liable.[162]

This is not to suggest that government, as the distributive arm of the State, and judges, as its alleged agents of interpretation, invariably fail to protect consumers, employees, and the insured. Indeed, in *Reference re Anti-Inflation Act*, the federal government intervened directly in employment relations to combat high inflation, albeit at the expense of labour; and the Supreme Court legitimated its action.[163] The risk is more subtle. It is that governments might ignore the interests of would-be claimants on the spurious grounds that their sufferings are self-inflicted, unavoidable, or able to be redressed by alternative means. Either such consumer claims fail to fit the political platform of the government of the day, or they do so only through individualized self-help. Thus, the poor are supposed to educate themselves, while the resourceful are trusted to satisfy their own needs by their own means. Consumer groups are relied upon to protect consumer interests. Labour unions are expected to repel

---

[160] See L.E. Trakman, "Winner Take Some: Loss Sharing and Commercial Impracticability" (1985), 69 Minn. L. Rev. 471.

[161] On the unsatisfactory resolution of environmental issues at common law, see G. Hardin, "The Tragedy of the Commons" (1968), 162 Science 1243; J.H. Dales, "Pollution Rights", in *Pollution, Property and Prices* (Toronto: University of Toronto Press, 1968), p. 77; P.S. Elder, "Environmental Protection Through the Common Law" (1973), 12 West. Ont. L. Rev. 107; J. Sax, "Environment and the Courts of Law", in *Ecology Today* (Sept. 1971). For examples of legislation, see *Clean Air Act*, R.S.A. 1980, c. C-12; *Environmental Protection Act*, R.S.O. 1980, c. 141; *Clean Air Act*, R.S.C. 1985, c. C-32; *Canadian Environmental Protection Act*, R.S.C. 1985, c. 16 (4th Supp.).

[162] See esp. *per* Dickson J. in *R. v. City of Sault Ste. Marie*, [1978] 2 S.C.R. 1299, at 1331; G. Williams, *Criminal Law, The General Part*, 2nd ed. (London: Stevens, 1961), s. 280. Arguably, punitive liability in civil actions should follow a similar course, so long as the punitive conduct of corporate employees or agents can be imputed to a corporation where its "directing mind and will" is reasonably aware of and able to avert the harm arising from the conduct of such employees and agents.

[163] [1976] 2 S.C.R. 373. See too, *P.S.A.C. v. Canada*, [1987] 1 S.C.R. 424.

the excesses of employers, and "have-nots" to organize in competition with "haves".

However, for the have-nots to defend themselves is for them to over-come their deference to authority. To be free is for them to learn to think and behave freely. It is to withstand conceptions of freedom that others impute to them, supposedly in their own interest. Indeed, if we are to believe Chaim Waxman's *The Stigma of Poverty*:

> . . . to escape from their poverty, they [the poor] must be taught to change their behavior and values. Since their values and patterns of behavior have been internalized over generations through socialization, the change will, of necessity, be a slow and difficult process.[164]

Judges who disregard these obstacles faced by the poor, reduce equality to a mere formality. In declining to comment upon the social climate that surrounds poverty, they typecast freedom abstractly, not substantively. Lacking a means of changing the position of the poor, they perpetuate the structure that gives rise to poverty, not the contrary. They pass over inequali-ties that stem from economic situation, as distinct from social structure.[165]

> To effect a change insofar as poverty is concerned, the situationalists argue, requires not changing the poor themselves, but rather changing their situation by correcting the restrictive social structure.[166]

I do not claim that individuals should sacrifice their personal rights. However, to insist that personal property is the cornerstone of the "good life", no matter what, is to benefit those who already have property at the expense of those who do not.[167] It is to raise ownership above use. It is also to diminish the social significance of property in the face of the right to have it. Courts that acknowledge that property is not equally distributed cannot ignore the disadvantaged status of those who do not

---

[164]   C.I. Waxman, *The Stigma of Poverty* (New York: Pergamon Press, 1977), pp. 26-27.
[165]   See *Dolphin Delivery*, [1986] 2 S.C.R. 573, *per* McIntyre J.
[166]   Waxman, *op. cit.*, note 164, at 26-27. On this "situational solution", see W.I. Gillespie, *The Redistribution of Income in Canada* (Agincourt, Ont.: Gage Publishing Ltd., 1980); L.A. Johnson, *Poverty in Wealth*, rev. ed. (Toronto: New Hogtown Press, 1977); L.C. Thurow, *Generating Inequality: Mechanisms of Distribution in the U.S. Economy* (New York: Basic Books, 1975); L. Tepperman, *Social Mobility in Canada* (Toronto: McGraw-Hill Ryerson, 1975); S. Gilbert and H.A. McRoberts, "Differentiation and Stratification: The Issue of Inequality", in *Issues in Canadian Society*, D. Forcese and S. Richer, eds. (Scarborough, Ont.: Prentice-Hall, 1975); *Readings on Social Stratification*, M.M. Tumin, ed. (Englewood Cliffs, N.J.: Prentice-Hall, 1970); A.K. Sen, *On Economic Inequality* (Oxford: Clarendon Press, 1973); W.G. Runciman, *Relative Deprivation and Social Justice* (Berkeley: University of California Press, 1966); F. Parkin, *Class Inequality and Political Order* (London: MacGibbon & Kee, 1971); A. Beteille, "The Decline of Social Inequality?", in *Social Inequality*, A. Beteille, comp. (Harmondsworth: Penguin, 1969); S.I. Benn, "Egalitarianism and the Equal Consideration of Interest", in *Justice and Equality*, H.A. Bedau, ed. (Englewood Cliffs, N.J.: Prentice-Hall, 1971), p. 152; S. Ossowski, *Class Structure in the Social Consciousness*, trans. S. Patterson (London: Routledge & Keigan Paul, 1963).
[167]   See, *e.g., per* McIntyre J. in the *Alberta Reference*, [1987] 1 S.C.R. 313.

have it. Poverty, first and last, is a social ill. Only in a truly egalitarian world does official neutrality towards private property make sense. The unified protection of property rights is a far cry from democratic action. Nor are public remedies, such as those in the *Charter*, uniformly available to all who cry out against intervention by the State.[168]

AN INFERIOR PRIVATE

Government, as the political arm of the State, inevitably restrains private life. It expropriates private homes to build highways and bridges. It taxes income earners and welfare claimants. It bestows different status upon professionals, artisans, and unskilled labourers. In each case, it limits private rights in light of a public good that it associates with stable government, effective management of the environment, and sometimes, the fair distribution of social resources. However, in insisting that it must distinguish between public and private life, it perpetuates the false image that it alone decides upon the reach of each. If parents do not abuse their children and husbands do not abuse their wives, then, it supposes, family life is private. It fails to realize that, in adopting this passive approach towards family life, it renders the family doubly private. Leaving the housewife and mother untouched by public life, it implicitly accords her a subordinate status in private life. Her supposedly feminine qualities, like affectivity and intimacy, assets in private life, are reduced to public liabilities.[169]

Those who argue against the politicization of the family worry about depersonalizing the home. They fret, too, that were women to be admitted more openly into public life, they might receive less status at home. At their most paternalistic, they are disturbed that women might be required to endure life within an unsympathetic — public — workforce. They worry that women not be reduced to mere factors of production, to ancillary roles, to be dismissed from employment first in the event of economic hardship.

Yet they fail to realize that family life is already politicized. Indeed, the very stereotype which they invoke to keep the housewife in private life becomes part of the politics of public life. They render the woman's material well-being into a "triviality" of family relations, in the tradition of *Balfour v. Balfour*.[170] They reduce her life after children, and her life after marriage, into a very private affair. The home, they envisage, is a

---

168 For a critique, *inter alia*, of corporate capitalism as the embodiment of democracy, see R.A. Dahl, *A Preface to Economic Democracy* (Berkeley: University of California Press, 1985); J. Cohen and J. Rogers, *On Democracy* (Harmondsworth: Penguin, 1983).

169 See hereon, *supra*, Chapter 2. See too, C.A. MacKinnon, "Making Sex Equality Real", in *Righting the Balance: Canada's New Equality Rights*, L. Smith, ed. (Saskatoon: Canadian Human Rights Reporter, 1986), p. 37; MacKinnon, *Sexual Harassment of Working Women* (New Haven: Yale University Press, 1983).

170 [1919] 2 K.B. 571 (C.A.).

predominantly female workplace: there, women are isolated from other workers, indeed treated as non-workers.[171] Marginalized by bonds of marriage, they are allowed to succeed publicly only at the expense of their femininity. For them to acquire status within public life, they are expected either to adopt a male-like *persona*, or to accept less within a largely unsympathetic market.[172] In entering the common workforce, they are appreciated, not for their résumé of accomplishments as household managers, but for their immediate productivity in business or government.[173] They are deemed to lack a significant past as housewives and mothers; or worse still, to have an unenviable past.[174] Even more bothersome, their "public" protests are largely ignored.[175]

By publicizing the individual's world, the court detaches the individual from private isolation. It acknowledges that, in doing so, it addresses mass market manipulation as a social ill. It does not reduce the individual to an object of that market.[176] Nor does it insist that she receive

---

[171] See D.E. Smith, *The Everyday World as Problematic: A Feminist Sociology* (Toronto: University of Toronto Press, 1987); K.T. Bartlett, "Feminist Legal Methods" (1990), 103 Harv. L. Rev. 829; D. Spender, *Man Made Language*, 2nd ed. (London: Routledge & Kegan Paul, 1985); P. Armstrong and H. Armstrong, *The Double Ghetto: Canadian Women and Their Segregated Work* (Toronto: McClelland & Stewart, 1984), p. 90.

[172] See esp., H. Braverman, *Labor and Monopoly Capital* (New York: Monthly Review Press, 1974), pp. 272-77. For a social critique, see C. Pateman, "Feminist Critiques of the Public/Private Dichotomy", in *Public and Private in Social Life*, S.I. Benn and G.F. Gaus, eds. (New York: St. Martin's Press, 1983), p. 281, at 284-85. But *cf.* F.E. Olsen, "The Family and the Market" (1983), 96 Harv. L. Rev. 1497, at 1500-01.

[173] See, *e.g.*, P. Connelly, *Last Hired, First Fired* (Toronto: Canadian Women's Educational Press, 1978); S. Ostry, *The Female Worker in Canada* (Ottawa: Queen's Printer, 1968).

[174] For feminists' commentary hereon, see Pateman, *loc. cit.*, note 172, at 284-85. *Cf.* Olsen, *loc. cit.*, note 172, at 1500-01.

[175] The literature on this protest of women against dominant male institutions is enormous. See, *e.g.*, *Feminism in Canada*, A. Miles and G. Finn, eds. (Montreal: Black Rose Books, 1982); R. Schwartz Cowan, *More Work for Mother* (New York: Basic Books, 1983); L. Berneria and G. Sen, "Class and Gender Inequalities and Women's Role in Economic Development — Theoretical and Practical Implications" (1982), 8 Feminist Studies 157; *Access to Power: Cross-National Studies of Women and Elites*, C. Epstein and R. Coser, eds. (London: G. Allen & Unwin, 1981); M. Boyd *et al.*, "Status Attainment in Canada" (1981), 18 Can. Rev. Soc. & Anth. 657. See too, M. Barrett, *Women's Oppression Today* (London: Verso Editions, 1980); *A Not Unreasonable Claim: Women and Reform in Canada*, L. Kealey, ed. (Toronto: Canadian Women's Educational Press, 1979); P. Chesler and E. Goodman, *Women, Money and Power* (New York: William Morrow & Co., 1976); *Women at Work: Ontario 1850-1930*, J. Acton *et al.*, eds. (Toronto: Canadian Women's Educational Press, 1974); C.M. Hill, "Women in the Canadian Economy", in *International Unions and the Ideology of Class Collaboration*, G. Teeple, ed. (Toronto: University of Toronto Press, 1972); C. Wright Mills, "Women The Darling Little Slaves", in *Power, Politics and People: The Collective Essays of C. Wright Mills*, I.L. Horowitz, ed. (New York: Oxford University Press, 1963), p. 339. See too, *infra*, at 189, note 95.

[176] Habermas provides an excellent historical-social analysis of the decline of private and the growth of public institutions. Public encompasses dominant commercial interests that, in effect, relegate the individual to a commodity within a mass media market. See esp., J. Habermas, *The Structural Transformation of the Public Sphere*, trans. T. Burger (Cambridge, Mass.: MIT Press, 1989). See too, P.U. Hohendahl, "Critical Theory, Public Sphere and Culture: Jurgen Habermas and his Critics" (1979), 16 New German Critique 89.

instruction from it "under penalty of starvation".[177] The court's goal is to promote a communal domain in which big business can no longer hide beneath the veneer of private life. The aim is to shift from narrow theories of corrective justice towards distributive ends. The method of doing so is to move away from the rights of discrete individuals towards collective interests that are expressed through social relations. This is clearly the Supreme Court's intent in cases like *Irwin Toy*.[178] In effect, the individual — here, the child — remains central in this public inquiry; but she is now a social being, not a depoliticized right-holder. Her *Charter* rights are social constructions. They are no longer instruments which she alone invokes in a solitary relationship with the State.

Courts that adopt this approach incorporate private into public life without displacing either.[179] They place the rights of pregnant women and foetuses, strikers and their employers, into the public sphere. Women who claim to have been sexually harassed, like aboriginal persons who allege discrimination, are viewed as making *public* assertions about their most personal injuries.[180] Their suffering reflects their collective disadvantage, without ceasing to be personal. The court considers the anguish of the group alongside that of its victims. In short, it is not that s. 15(2) of the *Charter* shifts equality rights from individuals to groups: it is that substantive inequalities embody the interests of both.[181]

This same public interest in human rights justifies shifting emphasis from the rights of big business and their workers to a supportive — as well as an antagonistic — public sphere. Here, the court addresses the interests of civil society alongside the s. 1 interests of the State. It protects consumers from producers who might otherwise render them impecunious just as it protects those same consumers from government itself. It ensures that a diffuse people receive economic and social security as an expression of their collective right to self-determination.

Thus, free will is personal to both individual and group. It is a political statement about how life in business ought to be lived.[182] It is used to

177   R. Hale, "Coercion and Distribution in a Supposedly Non-Coercive State" (1923), 38 Pol. Sc. Q. 470, at 475. See too, P. Gabel and D. Kennedy, "Roll Over Beethoven" (1984), 36 Stan. L. Rev. 1, at 35.
178   [1989] 1 S.C.R. 927. See too, *Slaight Communications Inc. v. Davidson*, [1989] 1 S.C.R. 1038.
179   On the importance of extending equality to disadvantaged groups, see *Big M Drug Mart*, [1985] 1 S.C.R. 295, at 337-38; *Société des Acadiens du Nouveau-Brunswick Inc. v. Assn. of Parents for Fairness in Education*, [1986] 1 S.C.R. 549, at 579; *Caldwell v. Stuart*, [1984] 2 S.C.R. 603, at 626.
180   See, *e.g., R. v. Oquataq* (1985), 18 C.C.C. (3d) 440 (N.W.T.S.C.); *Forsythe v. R.*, [1980] 2 S.C.R. 268; *Valente v. R.*, [1985] 2 S.C.R. 673.
181   See, *e.g., Edwards Books*, [1986] 2 S.C.R. 713, at 779.
182   Habermas addresses this view of free will by repoliticizing public life, and by constituting it into an autonomous order. From that order, individuals acquire their private rights. This approach entails both rejecting the classical domination of public life by particular bourgeois interests and repudiating the State's control over and manipulation of that public life. See J. Habermas, "The Public Sphere", in *Jurgen Habermas on Society and Politics*, S. Seidman, ed. (Boston: Beacon Press, 1989). Habermas'

establish when the public interest in the workforce outweighs the constitutional rights and freedoms of individual workers and employers, notwithstanding Mr. Justice McIntyre's assertions in the *Alberta Reference*.[183] Judges who appreciate this public character of free will protect substantive equality with the full realization that s. 15 of the *Charter* is "designed to protect those groups who suffer social, political and legal disadvantage in society".[184] They ingrain the status of the worker upon the very face of the public realm. They render life in the workforce more accessible to public scrutiny in cases like *Slaight Communications*,[185] and less isolated than "private" rights.

Judges who are so forthright recognize the need to evaluate rights in light of their unequal endowment. In *Edwards Books*, Chief Justice Dickson explicitly stated, in his evaluation of s. 1 of the *Charter*:

> In interpreting and applying the *Charter* I believe that the courts must be cautious to ensure that it does not simply become an instrument of better situated individuals to roll back legislation which has as its object the improvement of the condition of less advantaged persons.[186]

Their fear is realistic. Certainly, to extend the public realm to better encompass the interests of the disadvantaged is not without peril. Judges who stress the unequal quality of private life risk being accused of subjectivity. In highlighting the unequal effect of private rights upon social relations, they reinforce the accusation that they are biased. Moreover, groups that lack the sophistication to engage in meaningful private discourse might be equally limited in public discourse. If they are confused or intimidated by "private" discourse dominated by large-scale producers, they might similarly be troubled by public discourse into products liability. In addition, to enhance the individual's disadvantaged status in public life is not necessarily to provide her with the means of redressing her personal suffering there. To publicize the effect of products misfeasance upon her is to demonstrate a shared interest in her suffering. It is not to assure her of the effectiveness of that discourse, or that she will benefit in terms of it. That large-scale producers continue to produce defective products, despite an expanding discourse into public liability,

---

"solution" is utopian in two respects: in the belief that such an autonomous public order can exist, and in addition, that private rights and State interests can co-exist in terms of it without undermining it. See further, Heller, "Past, Present and Future of Democracy" (1978), 45 Social Research 867, at 883-84.

183   [1987] 1 S.C.R. 313. McIntyre J. states (at 397): "By . . . combining together, [workers] cannot create an entity which has greater constitutional rights and freedoms than they, as individuals, possess."
184   *Andrews v. Law Society of British Columbia*, [1989] 1 S.C.R. 143, at 262 *per* Wilson J.
185   *Supra*, note 178. See further hereon, *supra*, Chapter 2. For an excellent critique of the blurring between private and public in an era of large-scale industry and concentrated corporate wealth, see M.J. Horwitz, "The History of the Public/Private Distinction" (1982), 130 U. Pa. L. Rev. 1423, at 1427-28.
186   *Edwards Books, supra*, note 181, at 779.

attests to the insufficiencies of public law — like private law — as an instrument of social change. It does not provide all who suffer with the equal opportunity to redress their suffering collectively.[187]

Nevertheless, courts that reflect upon the social nature of autonomy place a communal worth upon the use of power and property. They also limit the insularity of private life. In each case, they render communal dialogue multi-faceted, not closed-ended. They consider economic liberties in light of their social ramifications, not simply as vehicles that protect employee, consumer or minority rights. They expose the harsh work conditions of employees, the oppression of religious minorities, and the economic proclivities of consumers. Not restricted to the lone individual or group, they unveil an ever-widening sphere of distributive justice. They enshrine the freedom of speech, association and assembly of the powerless, beyond the powerful.[188] They reckon with reformation and rehabilitation, beyond retribution and deterrence. Equally importantly, they ensure that their neutrality towards public life does not regress into indifference towards human anguish, toil, and ultimately, suffering.

A TRANSFORMATIVE PUBLIC

A transformative public life is diffuse. It embraces federal-provincial relations, social relations among bilingual and multicultural groups, and the collective rights of underprivileged Canadians[189] and aboriginal peoples.[190] It includes the disparate ideologies of various classes, castes, races, and creeds, family, religious and social groups. It encompasses a people's right to economic and social development, to self-determination, to environmental protection, and to domestic and international peace and security. More than the composition of different communities, it is the essence of what we all are, how we came into being, and how we participate as different peoples within a diffuse social milieu. Public debate revolves, not around differences amongst groups *per se*, but around the effect of diffuse ideas about social relations upon them. Thus, groups react differently to the quality of relations between the sexes in sexual assault cases, and to the connection between mother and child in child abuse cases. They react according to their diffuse cultural, religious and ethnic heritages; and they convey their reactions by disparate means of communication.

---

187 See *Brooks v. Canada Safeway Ltd.*, [1989] 1 S.C.R. 1219; *Schachter v. Canada*, [1990] 2 F.C. 129 (C.A.).

188 See H. Glasbeek, "Comment: Entrenchment of Freedom of Speech for the Press — Fettering of Freedom of Speech of the People", in *The Media, the Courts and the Charter*, P. Anisman and A.M. Linden, eds. (Toronto: Carswell, 1986), p. 101; A.C. Hutchinson, "Talking the Good Life: From Free Speech to Democratic Dialogue" (1989), 1 Yale J.L. & Liberation 17.

189 See the *Charter*, ss. 15(2) and 6(4).

190 *Ibid.*, s. 25.

For *Charter* interpreters to satisfy these diffuse needs is for them to recognize that democratic rights, however seemingly private, are products of a purposive discourse into the social ends that are served by those rights. That discourse encompasses the interests of Jehovah's Witnesses not to be harassed by provincial officials in distributing religious literature, and Chinese not to be denied the right to work because of their oriental status.[191] As a medium of communication, it is forever reconstructed by the groups that define and are defined by it. It is forever an expression of their history, culture and inclination.

Judges who engage in such public discourse move beyond the formal legitimacy of equal rights. They address the systemic discrimination which formally equal rights effect upon diffuse groups. They seek a common good that is sometimes unified by an unfathomable vision of social justice. They appreciate, too, that the nature of justice reflects the normative ends of those who affect and are affected by it. Their diffuse conception of public life is reflected in *Charter* jurisprudence itself. Chief Justice Dickson stressed in the *Alberta Reference*:

> It would . . . be unsatisfactory to overlook our Constitution's history of giving special recognition to collectivities or communities of interest other than the government and political parties. Sections 93 and 133 of the *Constitution Act, 1867* and ss. 16-24, 25, 27 and 29 of the *Charter*, dealing variously with denominational schools, language rights, aboriginal rights, and our multicultural heritage, implicitly embody an awareness of the importance of various collectivities in the pursuit of educational, linguistic, cultural and social as well as political ends.[192]

Thus, the *Charter's* purpose is not to reduce public life to its lowest common denominator, to one typecast order of public and private life. Social and political groups are simply too vast to be fixed in either an all-encompassing State, or an all-consuming civil society. They are too complex to be associated with one conception of the political good to the exclusion of all others. Peter Russell aptly expressed this open vision of *Charter* rights in 1983:

> It would be a pity if adoption of a constitutional charter of rights blunted our capacity to recognize that the state is not the only centre of power in our society capable of restricting freedom or equality or of abusing rights.[193]

Nor are the political complexities of public and private life resolved wholly by formal means. Indeed, for courts to treat the commercial power of big business as private, while construing the commercial power

---

[191]   On discrimination against Chinese subjects in Canada, see *Union Colliery of British Columbia v. Bryden*, [1899] A.C. 580 (P.C). On discrimination against Jehovah's Witnesses, see *Saumur v. City of Quebec*, [1953] 2 S.C.R. 299.

[192]   *Alberta Reference, supra*, note 183, at 364 *per* Dickson C.J., dissenting in part.

[193]   P.H. Russell, "The Political Purposes of the Canadian Charter of Rights and Freedoms" (1983), 61 Can. Bar Rev. 30, at 50.

of municipalities as public, is for them to nitpick about formality. Each entity is part of the public world, whether or not judges formally so constitute it. To maintain otherwise is to feign substantive difference in deference to formality. It is to give meaning to the "good life" in the image of a unidimensional public realm, but in disregard of differences within it.[194] It is to posit a public realm that purports to be colour-blind and asexual in disregard of sexual, religious, and ethnic differences.

The law is not impartial between groups. Judges do not protect all French speaking Canadians, corporations, and religious groups equally. They make normative assessments about the virtue and social effects of language rights in *Quebec Protestant School Bds.*,[195] economic interests in *Southam*[196] and religious claims in *Big M Drug Mart.*[197] They are probably motivated differently in determining whether doctors ought to have the right to extra-bill. They likely attribute disparate constitutional worth to the relative income of doctors and the costs of their services to society at large. Certainly their views are influenced by social policy. Judges are concerned about maintaining the public repute of the medical profession. They are also interested in constraining medical abuse in the public interest.[198] They realize that doctors form private relations with their patients. Yet, they also appreciate that those relations give rise to public responsibility. After all, medical doctors affect the quality of medical services within civil society, just as they impact upon the health of particular patients. Like the labour union and corporation, doctors dwell in a communal world, and courts cannot help but comprehend this fact.[199]

---

[194] Unger, despite his insights in *Knowledge and Politics* (New York: The Free Press, 1975), and *Passion: An Essay on Personality* (New York: The Free Press, 1984), fails to take account of the reconstitution of the State to include voluntary associations within the rubric of quasi-State. This is especially so in light of governmental efforts in the latter part of the twentieth century to integrate voluntary associations into its administrative bureaucracy. This is evident, not simply in the creation of Crown or State corporations, but in the regulatory machinery that governments use to control, *inter alia*, commercial adventurism. See further *Irwin Toy*, [1989] 1 S.C.R. 927.

[195] (1982), 140 D.L.R. (3d) 33 (Que. S.C.).

[196] [1984] 2 S.C.R. 145.

[197] [1985] 1 S.C.R. 295.

[198] On the extra-billing controversy in Ontario, see "Angry Ontario doctors fight ban on extra billing" (1986), 32 Canadian Family Physician, at 461-79; "The best medicine (Should Canadians tolerate extra-billing by doctors?)", in *Saturday Night*, Fulford, ed., vol. 101(7), July 1986, pp. 5-6; "Open-ended doctors' strike called in Ontario fight over extra-billing", *Globe and Mail*, Toronto (Metro Edition), June 10, 1986, pp. A1, A2; "Defiant doctors battle on as extra-billing outlawed", *Toronto Star*, June 21, 1986, pp. A1, A14; "Doctors' extra-billing protest brings 3,000 to Queen's Park", *Toronto Star*, May 8, 1986, pp. A1, A9; "Ontario doctors' groups split over extra-billing law as MPPs start hearings", *Globe and Mail*, Toronto (Metro Edition), March 5, 1986, p. A3; "Stop 'rhetoric' on extra-billing Peterson urges doctors' leader", *Toronto Star*, January 27, 1986, p. A1; "Elston yields nothing in talks with doctors on extra-billing ban", *Globe and Mail*, Toronto (Metro Edition), January 23, 1986, p. A1; "Ontario tables legislation: doctors face fines for extra-billing", *Globe and Mail*, Toronto (Metro Edition), December 20, 1985, p. A1.

[199] But *cf.* Unger, *Knowledge and Politics, supra*, note 194, at 274. Unger identifies the gradual erosion of private action, coupled with the growth of public institutions — notably

This interface between private and public life is also evident in relation to reproductive rights. Reproductive freedom is private only in the immediate sense that the woman herself exercises it. It is public in the expectation that she ought to have that freedom according to an image of life and liberty that she and others share. Conversely, protecting life *in utero* highlights, not simply the right to be born, but the expectation of others that birth ought to follow pregnancy. That expectation is distinctly public. It was public, in 1803, when abortion was subject to capital punishment under *Lord Ellenborough's Act*.[200] It is still public today in attempts to criminalize abortion practices. In issue is not simply the right to have an abortion, but a shared belief in the inviolability of pregnant women, or alternatively, in the sanctity of foetal life. Begetting or constraining foetal life is a collaborative venture that encompasses public attitudes. It is not restricted to private rights, whatever pro-choice or pro-life movements claim.[201]

Courts cannot preserve private life unless they are also willing to reflect upon the public implications of doing so. They cannot grant private privileges unless they consider the communal consequences. The right to report the news, for example, is not simply private. It impacts upon political life, including voting practices. There is no absolutely objective method of news reporting and no necessarily true content in new reports. Individuals are influenced, wittingly or otherwise, by what they are told. They may well read the newspaper in private and vote in public. However, both of their actions are related. Both are public. Both encompass group sentiment, along with the thoughts and feelings of the individuals who express them.

Just as public life has a collective identity, individuals adopt some of that identity for themselves. Thus, a pregnant woman is no less a member of a religious or a cultural group — and no less able to influence or be influenced by it — than she is an individual who wants to have an abortion. Her right to have an abortion is integral to her participation in a society that rewards or damns her in light of her exercise of that right. It entertains diffuse conceptions of family life and varied visions of political and religious attitude. Only superficially is "her" right restricted to personal liberty.

Judges cannot help but realize that unaddressed social interests fester. Courts that turn a blind public eye to wife beating, child abuse and corporate excesses, on the grounds that each is private, help to promote public mischief. Their reluctance to redress consumer disquiet evolves into consumer dissatisfaction with their economic neutrality. In contrast,

---

corporations and labour unions. These institutions compete with government in the regulation of civil affairs.

200   43 Geo. III, c. 58 (U.K.).

201   For discussion on the right to have an abortion in the context of *R. v. Morgentaler*, [1988] 1 S.C.R. 30, see, *supra*, Chapter 1.

judges who treat private injuries as public harm respond to that mischief. They impose exemplary duties of care upon manufacturers of harmful goods as much in the public interest as to protect consumers who are immediately affected.[202] They redress the wanton dismissal of employees as much to rectify unfair labour practices as to respond to the injuries of particular employees.[203] They consider more than the private rights of producers and consumers, employers and employees. They draw upon diverse visions of public life, upon different human ideals and beliefs in free choice. Like the College of Physicians and Surgeons, they justify the right of general practitioners to practise complex surgery in light of their medical education, diagnostic ability and experience. That their opinions have public ramifications is unquestionable. After all, the limit of each surgeon's rights reflects, not unanimity about free choice, but the communicative environment in which public health is debated. The judge appraises the doctor's liberty to perform surgery, not simply from the perspective of the professional's own life, but in light of wider social expectations of the medical profession as healers of the flesh. Here, "[f]reedom . . . is subject to such limitations as are necessary to protect public safety, order, health, or morals, or the fundamental rights and freedoms of others."[204] Only by raising such expectations above a wholly private vision of the surgeon's responsibility do courts of law and administrators construct a realistic view of public life itself.

Judges who identify private relations with public interests ultimately formulate those relations in light of public attributes which they impute to them. In addressing the power of big business, they evaluate more than particular relationships. They consider the source and impact of that power upon social experience itself. They place each commercial venture in a political context, beyond the immediate parties to the "bargain".

I do not maintain that the opinions of groups should displace the preferences of individuals. Indeed, one ingredient of group life is the personalities of those who constitute it. The group is not unified by one common ideology any more than individuals within the judiciary are united by one common outlook towards life. No group, least of all judges, can assume that its particular formulation of liberty is good in itself. Nor do individuals cease to have personal opinions because they are judges, women, aboriginal peoples or Jehovah's Witnesses. Individuals affect groups differently, just as they are influenced differently by those groups. They help to give groups their identities. At the same time, they receive their identity, in part, from those groups.

Judges inject selected visions of public order, social harmony and eco-

[202] See in general, *supra*, note 52.
[203] See further, *supra*, notes 54-55.
[204] *Per* Dickson J. in *Big M Drug Mart, supra*, note 197, at 337.

nomic efficiency into their conception of private rights. They impose onerous fiduciary duties upon litigants with special talents and skills.[205] They subject manufacturers with "extra-ordinary" knowledge of impending economic and social hardship to "extra-ordinary" remedies; and they circumscribe the impact of corporate power upon public life.[206] Courts are not alone in imposing fiduciary obligations upon big business. Legislatures, too, impose special obligations of the utmost good faith upon them.[207] They express their concern about the excesses of big business through anti-trust legislation like the *Competition Act*, and statutory and common law rules that govern the sales of goods and services. They realize that wealth is a source of privilege, and a reason for imposing greater responsibility upon those who control others through its use.[208]

A UNIFORM PUBLIC

Those who propagate a uniform public realm[209] highlight the common properties of public life. They seek uniformity of treatment as a means towards social, political, and ultimately, legal coherence. They develop constitutional practices which, as Dworkin would have it, are "understood or applied or limited . . . in accordance with . . . [coherent] purposes or principles".[210] They conceive of judges as means of "impos[ing] order" in the presence of social disorder.[211]

Yet, public life is stifled once universal conceptions of right and "the good" are recast into the "structural conditions" that govern each and every case.[212] No exhaustive structural condition separates normal from abnormal, acceptable from unacceptable, just from unjust behaviour.[213] The "larger objects" of diversity and tolerance in the *Charter*, to which Mr. Justice Dickson referred in *Big M Drug Mart*,[214] are not equally evident for

---

[205] See, *supra*, at 106, note 53.

[206] See *Hadley v. Baxendale* (1854), 156 E.R. 145; *Hedley, Byrne & Co. v. Heller & Partners Ltd.*, [1964] A.C. 465 (H.L.); *Haig v. Bamford*, [1977] 1 S.C.R. 466.

[207] See further, *supra*, note 53.

[208] On the reliance on "wealth" in determining the availability and quantum of exemplary and punitive damages, see esp. *Cassell & Co. v. Broome*, [1972] A.C. 1027 (H.L.); *Rookes v. Barnard*, [1964] A.C. 1129 (H.L.). On "willfullness" as a justification for extenuating liability beyond compensation, see esp. *New Brunswick Electrical Power Commn. v. Int. Brotherhood of Electrical Workers, Loc. 1733* (1978), 22 N.B.R. (2d) 364 (Q.B.); *Nantel v. Parisien et al.* (1981) 18 C.C.L.T. 79 (Ont. H.C.J.).

[209] See J. Cohen, "Why More Political Theory?" (1979), Telos 70, at 71.

[210] R.M. Dworkin, *Law's Empire* (Cambridge, Mass.: Belknap Press, 1986), p. 47.

[211] *Ibid.*, at 273.

[212] See B. Langille, "Revolution Without Foundation: The Grammar of Scepticism and Law" (1988), 33 McGill L.J. 451.

[213] Habermas constitutes public formally, by defining democracy, at least initially, in universal terms. However, he ultimately faces the inherent risk of internal contradiction in doing so. See esp., J. Habermas, "The Public Sphere: An Encyclopedia Article" (1974), 3 New German Critique 49.

[214] [1985] 1 S.C.R. 295, at 344.

all to see. Ultimately, someone defines the perimeters of constancy and acceptability in public life. Inevitably, judges "choose between eligible interpretations" in light of different, not uniform conceptions of "political morality".[215]

This is not to suggest that each sphere of public life is autonomous, or that judges treat it as such. White Canadians are not entitled to build skyscrapers or cultivate the soil as of right any more than aboriginal societies are entitled to hunt unchecked upon it. To claim that European Canadians have a right to administer all of Canada, whether by treaty, cession, or conquest, is to treat their sovereignty as a natural entitlement. Conversely, to claim that First Nation Peoples have a greater title to Canadian lands due to their ancestry is to forget that others use those lands as well. In each case, the solution lies, less in title, use, or numerical superiority than in the social justification for rights.[216] Within this open public discourse, legitimate claims to land hinge upon qualities that decision-makers select for them, not upon features that inhere within them. What is sentiment about land, they render into public entitlement. What is opinion about the use of land, they reduce to fact, or better still, into mediation about fact.

In so reconstituting public life, courts elect, not simply between the State and plural right-holders, but among preferred conceptions of public life. Their circumference of that life incorporates so-called private legacies, involving large-scale corporations, labour unions, and families. Yet, they shift their emphasis from a competition between individual and State to an association between them. They attribute to human association a wider collective presence than simple relations between parties and the State. They seek neither to balance the interests of government against private rights, nor to evaluate private transactions in relational terms. They embrace the personality of groups, including the degree of their outrage at those who threaten the moral fibre of the polity, in *Edwards Books* as in *Irwin Toy*.[217]

This extended public realm is neither novel nor revolutionary. Corporations already are treated formally as public or private according to the role that the State plays in relation to them, whether as Crown corporations, publicly held, or close corporations. Similarly, family life is public in the economic function and legal responsibility that is attributed to breadwinners, child-rearers, and housekeepers. So too, the life of labour unions is public in the indisputable role that collective bargaining plays in political life. The world is not conveniently carved up into a representational structure in which the one part is public and the other private. David Trubek aptly put it thus:

---

215 Dworkin, *op. cit.*, note 210, at 273-74.
216 On justified reason, see, *infra*, Chapter 5.
217 See, *e.g.*, *per* Dickson C.J. in *Edwards Books*, [1986] 2 S.C.R. 713, at 779.

> The point is not to say that object is better than subject, public than
> private, female than male, rather, the point is to do away with a
> representational structure that seems to force us to such choices
> because it carves the world up this way. Indeed, the desire to
> transcend, deconstruct, the dualism may be what distinguishes the
> radical from the liberal voice.[218]

For judges to deny all this is for them to forget that public life stations
both government and individual will under its unfolded umbrella. Within
this expanded polity, individuals engage in public life without necessary
privilege. They speak without succumbing to the patriarchy of an all-
seeing State.[219] They rely upon judges to protect their right to participate
in municipal government, in the schooling of their children and maintenance of social programmes. Here, judges serve as far more than forces
of constraint upon unbridled State action or unconstrained free will. They
debate French language rights and sexual and racial discrimination. They
take part in social dialogue itself; they observe it; they foster it; they
make policy choices in terms of it.

This approach resembles Jurgen Habermas' history of social ordering.
In his conception of bourgeois public, he separates the public sphere
from both the State and private life. His assumption is that social interaction takes place among participating citizens who have general access
and equal right to engage in the social order. Free from both bureaucratic
privilege and private status, their participation in public life includes
their entitlement to contract freely. However, they interact in accordance
with the social and political conditioning of the market, not merely as
negative actors bent on excluding the State.[220] They rely upon a supportive social and legal climate, a tolerance of difference, and a capacity to
reconcile difference without exploiting it. This is the essence of a
multicultural society in which cultural harmony embraces cultural distinctiveness. It is also a formula for social action within a stratified
Canadian polity.[221]

CONCLUSION

Canadian courts, led by the Supreme Court, have adhered to a distinctly propertied conception of private rights in recent years. They have
endorsed, less the liberal interpretation of private rights, than the protec-

---

[218] D. Trubek, "Taking Rights Lightly: Radical Voices in Legal Theory" (1984), unpublished paper, quoted in E.M. Schneider, "The Dialectic of Rights and Politics: Perspectives from the Women's Movement" (1986), 61 N.Y.U. L. Rev. 589, at 598.

[219] See esp., J.L. Cohen, *Class and Civil Society* (Amherst: University of Massachusetts Press, 1982); R. Hale, "Coercion and Distribution in a Supposedly Non-Coercive State" (1923), 38 Pol. Sc. Q. 470.

[220] See Habermas, *loc. cit.*, note 213.

[221] See, *e.g.*, D. Sanders, "Article 27 and Aboriginal Peoples of Canada", in *Multiculturalism and the Charter: A Legal Perspective* (Toronto: Carswell, 1987), p. 155.

tion of special interests which they have construed as private. This is evident, *inter alia*, in the reluctance of courts to interfere with corporate interests in cases following *Southam*.[222] It is perpetuated in their insistence that courts protect private rights neutrally, rather than propertied interests selectively.

In making wide claims for the public realm, I do not claim that a private sphere ceases to exist. Moments of endearment remain personal to those who cherish them. Personal beliefs do not become public property in a manner that displaces the human subject. However, I do propose that the *Charter* cannot be insulated from even the most personal of moments. After all, the boundary between the sanctity of parental authority and child abuse is a matter of construction, not fact. To seclude the corporate tortfeasor from public scrutiny is to dupe an often aggrieved public. To allow mass producers of goods to advertise their wares widely in the national media is to allow them to influence the Canadian way of life, indeed, to re-create much of it in their own image of it. To claim that they do all this privately is to do more than free them from public reprobation. It is to erect a *Charter of Rights and Freedoms* that stands, less for substantive justice for those in need of its protection, than for a formal and adverse relationship between individual and State.

To extend the operation of the *Charter* beyond this narrow relationship between individual and State is to recast it in the image of a diffuse polity. The *Charter* is not the individual's handmaiden, available at her beck and call. It is a key towards remedying the abuse of private and public power. It addresses the interests of State, corporation, labour union and individual alike. That it happens to benefit such diffuse interests is surely a desirable windfall, not a handicap.

No doubt some will quarrel with my absorption of much of private life and government into an expanded public realm. Both the radical right and the liberal centre likely will wish to exclude the State from private life, or at least restrict it. Libertarians will claim that the market, not government, should direct personal life.[223] Critical Legal Scholars will construe the liberal State as an unhelpful intruder in social life, as they conceive of it.[224] The economic conservative will direct the State to protect private wealth, while the socialist will seek to protect those who are

---

[222] [1984] 2 S.C.R. 145.

[223] See T. Nagel, "Libertarianism Without Foundations" (1975), 85 Yale L.J. 136.

[224] Critical Legal Studies, as a loose movement, identifies an inextricable link between civil society and capitalism. Its members generally distrust a sense of "private" that is expressed through market freedom. See, *e.g.*, D. Kennedy, "The Role of Law in Economic Thought: Essays on the Fetishism of Commodities" (1985), 34 Am. U. L. Rev. 953, at 965. They fail, with limited exceptions, to perceive of other constructions of civil society in which private rights can exist in a reconstituted form. See hereon, *supra*, at 41, for my discussion of "super-liberalism" as a means of linking "private" rights to human association, or in Isaiah Berlin's terms, a means of enhancing "positive liberties". See I. Berlin, *Four Essays on Liberty* (London: Oxford University Press, 1969), p. 118.

subjugated by that wealth.[225] I do not quarrel with any of these groups on this particular issue. My main objection is, not to any of their philosophies, but to their use of those philosophies as singular means towards an all-consuming good. Each agenda is dogmatic. Each admits of no other besides itself; and each fails for precisely that reason.

According, I separate the reconstruction of the public-private division from both individualist and socialist extremes. Public life embodies a changing, not a static consciousness. Social actors conceive of distributive inequalities — starvation, ill health, and personal security — diffusely. In each case, the public-private divide serves their beliefs: the liberal's faith in an autonomous self and the socialist's regard for collective rights. The divide exists for reasons which they impute to it, not for reasons that inhere within it. It is *they* who accommodate an expanded public realm in deciding cases. It is *they* who mediate among alternative conceptions of public life in doing so; and it is *their* discernment of that life which prevails, however privately they conceive of it.

---

[225]   See in general, C.B. Macpherson, *Democratic Theory* (Oxford: Oxford University Press, 1982); M. Walzer, *Spheres of Justice* (New York: Basic Books, 1983).

CHAPTER 5

JUDICIAL DISCOURSE: FACT OR FANCY?

INTRODUCTION

> Knowledge as an experiential process has radically different implications from knowledge imagined to be a mirroring of some independent reality or an incision into an unchanging process.[1]

Judges do not comprehend the total universe. They do not identify every attitude towards advertising in *Irwin Toy*[2] as it affects children, or militarism in *Operation Dismantle*[3] as it impacts upon national security. Their attitudes are varied. They react inconsistently to the evidence presented to them. They do not agree upon all issues under consideration. Nor do they predict the future accurately. They cannot know that treating Sunday as a day of rest in *Edwards Books*[4] will improve the quality of life for unemployed or under-employed Canadians. Nor can they be sure in *Operation Dismantle*[5] that testing cruise missiles over Canadian airspace will help to avert nuclear catastrophe, or incite it. In legal — as in social — dialogue, they lack the benefit of exhaustive constitutional principles that lead to determinative results. Their appreciation of material "fact" is partial. Their scrutiny of legislative practice is limited; and their truth about human rights, far from being absolute, is contingent upon "a plurality of standards of rationality which remain radically incommensurable".[6] Thus, the "disciplinary rules" of the judiciary as an "interpretative community" are quite open in constitutional cases.[7] Judges sometimes resort to the loosest of "structural conditions"[8] in deciding cases; and their

---

[1]   P.E. Rock, *The Making of Symbolic Interactionism* (Totowa, N.J.: Rowman & Littlefield, 1979), p. 70.
[2]   *Irwin Toy Ltd. v. Quebec (A.G.)* (1986), 32 D.L.R. (4th) 641 (Que. C.A.).
[3]   *Operation Dismantle Inc. v. R.*, [1985] 1 S.C.R. 441.
[4]   *R. v. Edwards Books & Art Ltd.* (hereafter referred to as *Edwards Books*), [1986] 2 S.C.R. 713.
[5]   *Supra*, note 3.
[6]   R.J. Bernstein, *Beyond Objectivism and Relativism* (Oxford: Basil Blackwell, 1983), p. 8.
[7]   O.M. Fiss, "Objectivity and Interpretation" (1982), 34 Stan. L. Rev. 739.
[8]   See B. Langille, "Revolution Without Foundation: The Grammar of Scepticism and Law" (1988), 33 McGill L.J. 451; Langille, "The Jurisprudence of Despair, Again" (1989),

constitutional rulings are scientifically "coherent" more because they — and others — so infer than for reasons that inhere within their reasoning itself.[9] This contingent nature of human affairs is not surprising. Even "elegant" scientific theories, despite their popularity, give rise to contingent knowledge only. As Thomas Kuhn warned, scientific theory is subject to variable, not strict proof, to probability, not algorithmic certainty, to argument, not its exclusion.[10]

Modern liberals recognize this contingent nature of knowledge in communication and understanding. They appreciate that theories of reasoning rest upon imperfect conceptions of the human personality. For example, H.L.A. Hart appreciates that "[s]hadows often obscure our knowledge."[11] Ronald Dworkin acknowledges that "liberalism does not rest on any special theory of personality"[12] that renders legal rights inevitable; and Bruce Ackerman reflects, more generally, that the very nature of liberalism and its effect upon decision-making is "of a highly controversial character".[13]

I advance three primary contentions here. Judicial decisions, not restricted to constitutional law, evolve from chosen premises which I refer to as suppositions and propositions. Judges decide cases in light of premises which they deem to be most satisfactory and in respect of which others, not limited to litigants, derive juristic satisfaction. Finally, judicial determinations are adequate only according to normative ends and means which judges impute to them, not which they prove by scientifically accurate methods. Thus, truth is contingent upon premises which courts select and thereafter justify in light of preferred suppositions and propositions. Those premises are obvious only in the belief that they serve satisfactory ends.[14]

I do not suggest that the judicial world of decision-making is so tentative that the quasi-scientific reasoning of courts has no meaning. Nor is

---

23 U.B.C. L. Rev. 549. But *cf.* J.C. Bakan, "Constitutional Arguments: Interpretation and Legitimacy in Canadian Constitutional Thought" (1989), 27 Osgoode Hall L.J. 123, at 185-91; A.C. Hutchinson, "That's Just the Way it is: Langille on Law" (1989), 34 McGill L.J. 145.

9   See R.M. Dworkin, *Law's Empire* (Cambridge, Mass.: Belknap Press, 1986), pp. 46-52. See too, D. Beatty, *Putting the Charter to Work* (Kingston and Montreal: McGill-Queen's University Press, 1987).

10   See esp., T.S. Kuhn, *The Structure of Scientific Revolutions*, 2nd ed. (Chicago: University of Chicago Press, 1970).

11   H.L.A. Hart, "Definition and Theory in Jurisprudence" (1954), 70 L.Q. Rev. 37, at 37.

12   R.M. Dworkin, "Liberalism", in *Public and Private Morality*, S. Hampshire, ed. (Cambridge: Cambridge University Press, 1978), p. 143.

13   B.A. Ackerman, *Social Justice in the Liberal State* (London: Yale University Press, 1980), p. 361.

14   See R.J. Coombe, "Same as it Ever Was: Rethinking the Politics of Legal Interpretation" (1989), 34 McGill L.J. 603; D.L. Cornell, "Institutionalization of Meaning, Recollective Imagination, and the Potential for Transformative Legal Interpretation" (1988), 136 U. Pa. L. Rev. 1135.

communicative discourse within the judiciary lacking in moral direction. Judges, like most of us, do agree upon fundamental moral values, albeit framed in liberal terms. They agree that life, liberty and property have individual and social worth; and they often concur in the methods of identifying that worth, not least of all through the *Charter*. Yet, like the rules of grammar, their legal rules are incomplete. They do not explain, in and of themselves, exactly whether, how and when preferred legal structures ought to be applied in the future. Nor are judges guided by universal principles of rationality in deciding what values to attribute to those structures in particular cases.

In law, as in linguistics, truth hinges upon communicative media which judges employ to convey and comprehend propositional thoughts. Courts do not conclude, perfectly rationally, that legislation governing advertising in French in Quebec is bad, while legislation providing for bilingual signs is good. They offer preferred, not obvious suppositions. In place of a fixed human technology, they learn, experience, expose, test and retest opinions by justifying their decisions, not proving them as a scientific fact. They learn that what appears to be true in 1950 is not true in 1990. They appreciate that, whether or not "Marxism exercises a strange power over its adherents", it is the product of suppositions about the social reprobation of capitalism, not truth itself.[15]

Accordingly, no self-explanatory divide separates necessary from contingent assumptions of "fact". Judicial decisions are contingent upon the nature of the document defining their legal authority, the methods courts use to propagate their opinions, their motivations in doing so, and the perceived social consequences of their actions. The adequacy of their decisions hinges upon the perceived sufficiency of their reasoning, the satisfaction which others derive from them, and the social effect of the remedies they choose. Richard Bernstein sums up their contingent state as

> . . . [a] dialogical model of rationality in which there is choice, deliberation, interpretation, judicious weighing and application of "universal criteria", and even rational disagreement as to which criteria are relevant and most important.[16]

JUDICIAL A PRIORISM

The law of "singing reason", as Karl Llewellyn once coined it,[17] is nowhere more surely housed than in rational legal discourse.[18] Each judge is expected to combine *a priori* principles of law with rational methods of

15 See *R. v. Hess*, [1949] 4 D.L.R. 199 (B.C.C.A.)
16 Bernstein, *op. cit.*, note 6, at 172.
17 See K.N. Llewellyn, *Jurisprudence: Realism in Theory and Practice* (Chicago: University of Chicago Press, 1962).
18 For classical studies of rationality, see M. Weber, *Economy and Society: An Outline of*

reasoning to arrive at just results. This method, in the Kantian tradition, is supposed to be detached from any political interest which judges might have in the results. Their decisions are "correct", "wise", "fair", "just" or "reasonable" according to underlying norms that reflect "a core of settled meaning" within them.[19] To incorporate dominant social interests into rights, supposedly, is to undermine them. It is to sacrifice the "best" legal solution in light of other potential ones.[20] Most importantly, it is to unsettle the political and economic orders by resort to unprincipled methods of reasons that destabilize established conceptions of right.[21]

Thus, natural lawyers seek reasoned truth through a divinely inspired will[22] or by resort to teleologic reasoning from ends to means.[23] Analytical positivists seek truth through positive law,[24] in particular, by constructing "principles, policies and standards" within a coherent and rational system of law.[25] These they legitimate in light of "rules of recognition"

Interpretative Sociology, G. Roth and C. Wittich, eds. (New York: Bedminster Press, 1968); M.F. Scheler, Formalism in Ethics and Non-Formal Ethics of Values, trans. S. Frings and R.L. Funk (Evanston: Northwestern University Press, 1973). On rationality in economics as the precursor to its study in the social sciences, see "Rational Behaviour as a Basis for Economic Theories", in Rationality and the Social Sciences, S.I. Benn and G.W. Mortimore, eds. (London: Routledge & Kegan Paul, 1976), pp. 196-222.

[19]   See H.L.A. Hart, "Positivism and the Separation of Law and Morals" (1958), 71 Harv. L. Rev. 593. For a critique of such core meanings in general, see R. Rorty, Philosophy and the Mirror of Nature (Princeton: Princeton University Press, 1979), pp. 361-63; A.C. Hutchinson, "The Three 'Rs': Reading/Rorty/Radically" (1989), 103 Harv. L. Rev. 555.

[20]   Faced with such indecision, Ronald Dworkin would be disappointed indeed. See esp., R.M. Dworkin, Taking Rights Seriously (London: Duckworth, 1978), pp. 82-112. See too, Dworkin, "Political Judges and the Rule of Law", Maccabaean Lecture in Jurisprudence (London: The British Academy, 1978).

[21]   For an excellent study hereon, see M. Minow, "Foreword: Justice Engendered" (1987), 101 Harv. L. Rev. 10, at 54-55. See too, P. Brest, "Interpretation and Interest" (1982), 34 Stan. L. Rev. 765; S.A. Scheingold, The Politics of Rights (New Haven: Yale University Press, 1974).

[22]   The natural law source of rational discourse is difficult to determine, even in abstract and spiritual terms. For natural lawyers in the tradition of St. Thomas Aquinas, the foundation of rationality lies in the eternal law, and this eternity is expressed in God's will. See Aquinas, Summa Theologica, Part II, in vol. 19 of Great Books of the Western World (Toronto: Encyclopedia Britannica, 1982), pp. 994-96. Alternatively, rationality derives from man's innate capacity to reason, both individually and in groups. Innate reason, sometimes conceived of as "intuition", is doubtful as a guide to legal decision-making for two principal reasons: first, intuition differs among people; and secondly, being internalized, it can be disguised in nature and application. See, e.g., M.V. Tushnet, "Anti-Formalism in Recent Constitutional Theory" (1985), 83 Mich. L. Rev. 1502, at 1532.

[23]   On occasion, reason is portrayed teleologically, as the search for such ends as social harmony and co-operation. The ultimate end, for modern coherence theorists for example, is social harmony through coherent methods of reasoning. But cf. J.W. Singer, "The Player and the Cards: Nihilism and Legal Theory" (1984), 94 Yale L.J. 1, at 35-36. This teleologic approach conflicts with instrumental methods of reasoning. See N. Lyon, "The Teleological Mandate of the Fundamental Freedoms Guarantee: What to Do with Vague but Meaningful Generalities" (1982), 4 Supreme Court L.R. 57.

[24]   See further, J. Austin, The Philosophy of Positive Law, R. Campbell, ed. (London: J. Murray, 1911).

[25]   H.L.A. Hart, "Problems of Legal Reasoning", in Law in Philosophical Perspective, J.

which serve as "common public standards of official behaviour".[26]

The link between natural thought and positive law is evident in judicial attempts to render reasoning universally coherent. The supposition is that judges ought to reflect an "innate pre-existing thinking process common to all people or, at the very least, to everyone in our culture";[27] and further, that they ought to embroil themselves in a "decision procedure that is theoretically capable of producing agreement".[28] Here, no rationally compelling account of societal good is formulated that favours one party over another,[29] save only as "community consensus", rationally construed, itself directs.[30] Unity in the legal system is traced to a judicial process that applies equally to all, not to some interests that override others.[31] Justice "admit[s] all possible values and ends",[32] not one preferred end over others.

Thus, judges, supposedly, are not directly interested in child-birth, population control, or feminist theory in cases like *Morgentaler*.[33] Their debate is not about the relationship between abortion and social life: it is about rights *per se*, about the rights of pregnant women and foetuses under s. 7, s. 1 and conceivably s. 2 of the *Charter*.[34] For the rest, they are supposedly impartial among social interests they cannot perfect into rights by rational means. They are not affected by religious zeal, feelings of

---

Feinberg and H. Gross, eds. (Belmont, Cal.: Wadsworth Publishing Co., 1977), pp. 145-46. See, in general, Hart, *The Concept of Law* (New York: Oxford University Press, 1961); Langille, "The Jurisprudence of Despair, Again", *supra*, note 8; N. MacCormick, *H.L.A. Hart* (London: Edward Arnold Ltd., 1981), pp. 21-23.

[26] See H.L.A. Hart, "Problems of Philosophy of Law", in vol. 6, *Encyclopedia of Philosophy*, P. Edwards, ed. (New York: Macmillan, 1967), p. 268. See too, N. MacCormick, *Legal Reasoning and Legal Theory* (Oxford: Clarendon Press, 1978), p. 103 (proposing that "fact" and "truth" in law be construed in relative rather than absolute terms); J. Raz, *Practical Reason and Norms* (London: Hutchinson, 1975); *The Is-Ought Question*, W.D. Hudson, ed. (London: Macmillan, 1969); F.S.C. Northrop, "Law, Language and Morals" (1962), 71 Yale L.J. 1017, at 1031. But *cf.* M. Mandel, "Dworkin, Hart, and the Problem of Theoretical Perspective" (1979), 14 L. & Soc. Rev. 57. See in general, O.M. Fiss, "The Varieties of Positivism" (1981), 90 Yale L.J. 1007; J.L. Coleman, "Negative and Positive Positivism" (1982), 11 J. Leg. Stud. 139.

[27] Singer, *loc. cit.*, note 23, at 33. But see J. Stick, "Can Nihilism Be Pragmatic?" (1986), 100 Harv. L. Rev. 332.

[28] Singer, *loc. cit.*, note 23, at 25-26.

[29] See, *e.g.*, *Alliance des Professeurs de Montréal v. Quebec (A.G.)* (1985), 21 D.L.R. (4th) 354, at 364 (Que. C.A.).

[30] See Minow, *loc. cit.*, note 21, at 68.

[31] See, for instance, K. Greenawalt, "The Enduring Significance of Neutral Principles" (1978), 78 Colum. L. Rev. 982; H. Wellington, "Common Law Rules and Constitutional Double Standards: Some Notes on Adjudication" (1973), 83 Yale L.J. 221; A. Mueller and M.L. Schwartz, "The Principle of Neutral Principles" (1960), 7 U.C.L.A. L. Rev. 571. See further, R.M. Dworkin, *Law's Empire* (Cambridge, Mass.: Belknap Press, 1986), at 400.

[32] M.J. Sandel, *Liberalism and the Limits of Justice* (Cambridge: Cambridge University Press, 1982), p. 12.

[33] *R. v. Morgentaler* (hereafter referred to as *Morgentaler*), [1988] 1 S.C.R. 30.

[34] See, in general, on *Morgentaler*, *infra*, Chapter 6.

outrage or compassion for life itself.[35] "The business of the court", it would seem, is "neither more nor less than that of declaring the meaning of a law in respect of a contingent occurrence."[36] The responsibility of the court is to devise universal precepts that override particular ones, necessary inferences that override contingent ones, and objective facts that trump subjective opinions.[37]

This reliance upon objective and principled reasoning is evident in *Charter* jurisprudence. It is implicit in the Supreme Court's decision in *Oakes* that the legislative objective be "rationally connected" to the means of attaining it, and further that the least drastic means be used.[38] It is depicted, further, in the rational belief that like cases ought to be treated alike, while similar cases should be construed similarly. The moral worth of this approach is attested to in the now classical belief that to apply fundamental rights equally to all is to be fair to all.

> We hold these truths to be self-evident, that all men are created equal, that they are endowed by their creator with certain inalienable rights, that among these are life, liberty and the pursuit of happiness.[39]

Nor is this universality of human reason restricted to legal theory. Modern-day liberals, like John Rawls and Lawrence Kohlberg, emphasize the universality of reason as the embodiment of the very coherence of life.[40] Indeed, even their critics, in denying universality to individual

---

[35] See esp. Dworkin, *op. cit.*, note 31, at 254-57.
[36] M.J. Oakeshott, "The Rule of Law", in *On History and Other Essays*, M.J. Oakeshott, ed. (Oxford: Basil Blackwell, 1983), p. 147.
[37] See G.C. Christie, "Objectivity in the Law" (1969), 78 Yale L.J. 1311.
[38] *R. v. Oakes* (hereafter referred to as *Oakes*), [1986] 1 S.C.R. 103, at 139.
[39] *Declaration of Independence*, Representatives of the United States of America, Congress Assembled, July 4, 1776. But *cf. Andrews v. Law Society of British Columbia*, [1989] 1 S.C.R. 143, at 163-64; *R. v. Turpin*, [1989] 1 S.C.R. 1296, at 1334, where the court held that s. 15 of the *Charter* does not require "that the criminal law apply equally throughout the country".
[40] See J. Rawls, *A Theory of Justice* (Cambridge: Harvard University Press, 1971), p. 47. This transcendental moral order is far less evident in Rawl's recent works. See, for instance, Rawls, "Kantian Constructivism in Moral Theory: The Dewey Lectures 1980" (1980), 77 J. Phil. 515.
    Not unlike Rawls, Kohlberg maintains that "[t]he two principal justice operations are the operation of equality and reciprocity": L. Kohlberg, *The Philosophy of Moral Development* (San Francisco: Harper & Row, 1981), p. 201. "Reflective equilibrium" occurs when one tests one's principles against one's considered judgments until they are balanced at the higher stages of moral development. In North America, for instance, Kohlberg believes that equilibrated judgment occurs at stage 5, the social contract stage, which yields a set of procedural principles upon which substantive obligations are based (at 161-62). However, only at stage 6, the justice as fairness stage, are moral judgments likely to be universal.
    Kohlberg, like Rawls, is criticized from the left for adopting the false consciousness of Western Liberalism. See E.V. Sullivan, "A Study of Kohlberg's Structural Theory of Moral Development: A Critique of Liberal Social Science Ideology" (1977), 20 Human Development 352. Others have attacked him on the grounds that bias emanates from his western cultural value-system. See E.L. Simpson, "Moral Development Research" (1974), 17 Human Development 81. Further criticism has come from ethical and cultural

rights, recognize the influence of universal reason upon the construction of human rights. Richard Bernstein, for all his objections to objectivism, identifies "universal criteria" somewhere between relativism and objectivism, with reasoned decision-making.[41] Roberto Unger, notwithstanding his critique of the self-evident axioms that underlie liberal jurisprudence, draws attention, almost religiously, to "eternal" truths that guide the decisional process.[42]

This reliance upon universal principles of reasoning is also apparent in the link Canadian courts draw between State interests under s. 1 and fundamental rights and freedoms under s. 2 of the *Charter*. Adopting a two-step approach, they prescribe rights according to their "fundamental" nature under s. 2. Thereafter, they constrain them, rationally, in the interests of a "free and democratic society" under s. 1.[43] In so deciding, they insist that legislative restrictions "should impair 'as little as possible' the right or freedom in question", and that its measures be "necessary", not "arbitrary, unfair or based on irrational considerations".[44] At the same time, they defer to the supremacy of Parliament in setting policies to govern human rights.[45] Fearful of being accused of law-making, they adhere to a distinctly principled method of reasoning. They assume that first principles ought to guide them; and that they ought to apply these principles rationally to specific cases so as to arrive at the "best" legal results. Their governing principle is *dictum de omni et nulla* — whatever is attributed to the governing principle is also attributed to that which is contained under it. Once they recognize the first principle, for example that "everyone" has the right to security of the person, they endorse the specific right to security in terms of it. The more pervasive principle circumscribes the particular right. To have personal security is to have reproductive freedom.[46]

This principled approach towards rights, supposedly, enables courts to limit the influence of normative opinion upon them. They find the source of rights in the individual's "rational being", not in some greater social good which they — or others — impute to her. This principled

---

relativists who deny Kohlberg's principle of universality, and who reject his moral rationality because it disregards moral emotion and is reflective of male-oriented values: C. Gilligan, *In a Different Voice: Psychological Theory and Women's Development* (Cambridge: Harvard University Press, 1982).

41 See R.J. Bernstein, *Beyond Objectivism and Relativism* (Oxford: Basil Blackwell, 1983), p. 172.

42 See R. Unger, *Knowledge and Politics* (New York: The Free Press, 1975), p. 238. In his book, *Passion: An Essay on Personality* (New York: The Free Press, 1984), however, Unger reconceives of truth in light of human nature (at 43-46). *Cf.* A.C. MacIntyre, *After Virtue*, 2nd ed. (Notre Dame: University of Notre Dame Press, 1984).

43 See, *e.g.*, *Oakes, supra*, note 38, esp. at 139.

44 *Ibid.*, at 139.

45 See, *infra*, at 154.

46 See, *e.g.*, *Oakes, supra*, note 38.

conception of constitutional rights is evident in both *Morgentaler*[47] and *Borowski*.[48] In *Morgentaler*, the Supreme Court affirms the right to have an abortion. In *Borowski*, in insisting that it decide only the issue of standing, the court avoids discussing foetal rights. In each case, it views abortion rights as principled, and foetal rights as not. In effect, the court employs an "essentially cognitive" process.[49] Through its resort to "doctrines, institutions and decisions of positive law, it engages, more [in] . . . the discovery than . . . the making of law".[50] The instruments of its cognition reside in "the doctrines, institutions and decisions of positive law",[51] not in normative predilection. The truth content of its decisions resides in the scientific rigour it employs to identify those predilections, not in prophetic insight.

In perceiving of *a priori* characteristics in rights, Canadian courts supposedly free themselves from responsibility to reflect upon social interests beyond them. In concentrating upon Zundel's[52] and Keegstra's[53] right to free speech, they avoid having to deal with the history of anti-Semitism. In considering whether a right to free speech exists in a specific case, they deal only with its consistent application in comparable cases, not its communal impact. They contend that to deny freedom of expression to one, no matter how unpopular the cause, is to threaten the freedom of everyone else. To impede one party's freedom to pray, trade or assemble, is to impede the rights of others as well. So impelled, they force the social good to reside, not in moral indignation or outrage, but in the consistent application of the right itself. "The foundation of individual liberty", indeed, its "matrix . . . in a true democracy",[54] therefore lies in a freedom that is equally available to all, not to some above all others.

Constitutional principles, supposedly, are based on underlying suppositions and propositions that are true in themselves. Thus, in *Big M Drug Mart*, the ambit of s. 1 is deemed to be "obvious".[55] In *Edwards Books*, the court considers it "self-evident" that a parent should "have regular days off from work in common with their child's days off from school".[56] In each case, the court deems the legal result to be the product of an

---

47 *Supra*, note 33.

48 *Borowski v. Canada (A.G.)*, [1989] 1 S.C.R. 342.

49 See E.J. Weinrib, "Legal Formalism: On the Immanent Rationality of Law" (1988), 97 Yale L.J. 949, at 957.

50 *Ibid.*

51 *Ibid.*, at 972.

52 *R. v. Zundel* (1987), 35 D.L.R. (4th) 338 (Ont. C.A.).

53 *R. v. Keegstra* (1988), 43 C.C.C. (3d) 150 (Alta. C.A).

54 C. Beckton, "Freedom of Expression in Canada — How Free?", in *The Canadian Charter of Rights and Freedoms: Initial Experiences, Emerging Issues and Future Challenges* (Ottawa: Canadian Institute for the Administration of Justice, 1984), p. 149. See too, Beckton, "Freedom of Expression — Access to the Courts" (1983), 61 Can. Bar Rev. 101.

55 *R. v. Big M Drug Mart Ltd.* (hereafter referred to as *Big M Drug Mart*), [1985] 1 S.C.R. 295, at 344.

56 *Edwards Books*, [1986] 2 S.C.R. 713, at 770 *per* Dickson C.J. (as he then was).

almost self-evident structure. "Obvious" principles lead to "obvious" determinations; and normative beliefs subserve to a structure that personifies those principles in law. Judges, supposedly, are not to be influenced by moral supposition.[57] They are not simply to do what their "political and ethical views command".[58] They are not to assume the "creative role of the reader".[59]

Judges who adopt this principled method of reasoning contend that interpretation involves the art of construing, not "constructing" law.[60] They suppose, further, that their decisions are products of a direct relationship between law and fact.[61] This self-evident structuring of rights is illustrated in their method of distinguishing between material and immaterial facts. For example, they distinguish between free speech and other forms of social action, including demonstrations, by treating each case as materially different on the facts and therefore in law. As Mr. Justice Beetz explained in *Canada (A.G.) v. City of Montreal*:

> Demonstrations are not a form of speech but of collective action. They are of the nature of a display of force rather than an appeal to reason; their inarticulateness prevents them from becoming part of language and from reaching the level of discourse.[62]

This art of distinction, ultimately, is a formidable means of judicial evasiveness. The court need not admit that, in distinguishing between material and immaterial facts, it limits particular freedoms itself: the distinction seemingly does so for it. For example, in *R.W.D.S.U. v. Saskatchewan*,[63] freedom of association seemingly excludes the right to strike. To be free to associate involves only the *act* of associating, not acts, like striking, that are consequent upon it.

The risk of a judge adopting such principled distinctions is that, in her attempt to avoid political discourse, she likely will re-embrace legal formalism. Fundamental freedoms will become unavoidable incidents of pre-structured rights, subject only to the very general principles embodied in s. 1 of the *Charter*. The judge will distinguish between different methods of acting and different consequences that flow from them. She

---

57   See generally, M.E. Gold, "The Mask of Objectivity: Politics and Rhetoric in the Supreme Court of Canada" (1985), 7 Supreme Court L.R. 455.

58   S. Levinson, "Escaping Liberalism: Easier Said Than Done" (1983), 96 Harv. L. Rev. 1466, at 1471.

59   O.M. Fiss, "Objectivity and Interpretation" (1982), 34 Stan. L. Rev. 739, at 744.

60   S. Fish, *Is There a Text in This Class?* (Cambridge: Harvard University Press, 1980), p. 327.

61   On "identical" fact patterns and legal analogy, see esp., M.P. Golding, *Legal Reasoning* (New York: A.A. Knopf, 1984), pp. 101-11; J. Raz, *The Authority of Law* (New York: Oxford University Press, 1979), pp. 201-05. But *cf.* W.E. Raney, "Justice, Precedent and Ultimate Conjecture" (1909), 29 Can. Law Times 454.

62   [1978] 2 S.C.R. 770, at 797.

63   *Retail, Wholesale & Department Store Union v. Saskatchewan* (hereafter referred to as *Saskatchewan Dairies*), [1987] 1 S.C.R. 460.

will regard her decisions as scientific. Most importantly, she will detach them from sentiment, just as she will separate reason from desire, coercion from freedom, and public from private. Her underlying goal will be to resolve conflicts in terms of, not outside of law.[64] Her purpose will be to raise law to the level of coherent jurisprudence, beyond liberal idealism.[65] To shield herself from value judgments and unprincipled reason, she will insist upon the predictability of law as the means towards social stability;[66] and she will believe that "if law is to be of any value as an instrument for the realization of human purposes, it must contain certain rules concerning the basic conditions of social life".[67]

Thus, courts will suppose, in John Austin's words, that "the existence of law is one thing; its merit or demerit is another".[68] They will rescue legal decisions "from the battleground of power politics" by shifting them to "the forum of principle".[69] They will happily become creatures of a hierarchy of principle for fear of negating them.[70] That they differ over the limits of certainty, they will resolve through interpretation. That judges evaluate human purposes subjectively in *Big M Drug Mart*[71] or *Irwin Toy*,[72] they will reframe in objective terms. That they conceive of language rights partially, they will recast into a principled inference of fact.

Those who adhere to such a hierarchical method of interpretation unduly constrain constitutional interpretation. They bypass the fact that *Charter* principles are general, and that human judgment is integral to the interpretation of general principles. They overlook the extent to which human judgment both precedes and post-dates analytical reason.

---

[64]   For an excellent demonstration of liberal dualism as an "art of separation", including the separation between private and public, see M. Walzer, "Liberalism and the Art of Separation" (1984), 12 Pol. Th. 315.

[65]   See generally, K.J. Kress, "Legal Reasoning and Coherence Theories: Dworkin's Rights Thesis, Retroactivity, and the Linear Order of Decisions" (1984), 72 Cal. L. Rev. 369; M. Hanen, "Justification as Coherence", in *Law, Morality and Rights,* M.A. Stewart, ed. (Boston: Kluwer, 1983), pp. 67-92. On "necessary condition" as the underpinning of scientific rationality, see C. Hempel, "Scientific Rationality: Analytic vs. Pragmatic Perspectives", in *Rationality Today* (Ottawa: University of Ottawa Press, 1979).

[66]   See generally, D.J. Boorstin, *The Mysterious Science of the Law: An Essay on Blackstone's Commentaries Showing How Blackstone, Employing Eighteenth-Century Ideas of Science, Religion, History, Aesthetics and Philosophy, Made of the Law at Once a Conservative and a Mysterious Science* (Cambridge: Harvard University Press, 1941). See further, *supra,* at 9.

[67]   H.L.A. Hart, "Problems of Philosophy of Law", in vol. 6, *Encyclopedia of Philosophy,* P. Edwards, ed. (New York: Macmillan, 1967), p. 264. See too, Hart, *The Concept of Law* (New York: Oxford University Press, 1961), p. 189.

[68]   J. Austin, *The Province of Jurisprudence Determined,* H.L.A. Hart, ed. (London: Weidenfeld & Nicolson, 1954), p. 184. See too, Hart, *op. cit.,* note 67, Chapters VIII and IX.

[69]   R.M. Dworkin, *A Matter of Principle* (Cambridge: Harvard University Press, 1985), p. 71.

[70]   See further, *infra,* at 153 and 181.

[71]   [1985] 1 S.C.R. 295.

[72]   [1989] 1 S.C.R. 927.

PRINCIPLES OF HIERARCHY

Almost rhetorical is the assumption of many Canadian judges that they should not enter the bedrooms of the nation, or determine the quality of religious, economic or cultural life. They suppose that private rights are subject to the directives of a free and democratic State, whether under s. 1 or 33 of the *Charter* or under s. 52 of the *Constitution Act, 1982*. They suppose, too, that the State cannot displace those rights with impunity.[73] Motivated by a reasoned divide between private rights and State interests, they claim to find the law as it is; and they maintain a strictly rational construction of rights in light of that "fact".[74]

Thus, judges avoid delving into normative ideology. They do not challenge the substantive virtue of the *Lord's Day Act*. They evaluate only the principled relationship between the legislature's objective, the means it employs to attain that objective, and the societal effect of its doing so.[75] They organize human rights within a hierarchy of principles. At the apex, they place constitutional principles. They position *Charter* rights below those principles, and non-*Charter* rights yet lower.[76] Thus, they envisage a somewhat formal structure of rights: within it, State interests under ss. 1 and 33 trump fundamental rights,[77] while *Charter* rights like freedom of expression, assembly, and association[78] trump non-*Charter* rights. They invoke the wording of s. 52 of the *Constitution Act, 1982* to demonstrate that the *Charter* is *the* supreme law. They insist, on a literal interpretation of it, that it eclipse all other laws; and they restrict both human rights and governmental action in terms of it. They are far less ready to follow the example of cases like *Roe v. Wade*,[79] in which the Supreme Court of the United States held that the right to privacy included a woman's right to terminate her pregnancy.[80]

---

73 *Oakes*, [1986] 1 S.C.R. 103.
74 In etymological terms, both the words "rationality" and "reason" derive from the Greek word *reri*, to consider. Both infer the presence of contemplation and deliberation; however, the nature of that contemplation or deliberation can be variously determined according to an overriding source, functional quality, purpose, or effect.
75 See *Big M Drug Mart, supra*, note 71.
76 On the quasi-constitutional nature of human rights that are not rendered explicitly fundamental by the *Charter*, see *Ontario Human Rights Commn. v. Borough of Etobicoke*, [1982] 1 S.C.R. 202; *Ins. Corp. of B.C. v. Heerspink*, [1982] 2 S.C.R. 145, at 157-58 *per* Lamer J.; *Winnipeg School Div. No. 1 v. Craton*, [1985] 2 S.C.R. 150; *Ontario Human Rights Commn. and O'Malley v. Simpsons-Sears Ltd.*, [1985] 2 S.C.R. 536, at 546-47.
77 Section 33(1) specifically empowers legislatures to declare legislation operative "notwithstanding a provision included in section 2 or sections 7 to 15 of this Charter."
78 *Charter*, s. 2(*b*), (*c*) and (*d*), respectively.
79 410 U.S. 113 (1973).
80 The extent to which the American Constitution was created in reaction to hierarchy — against British domination — is illustrated in Article 1 of the Constitution. There, reference is made to prohibiting suspension of the writ of *habeas corpus* (Art. 1, s. 9(3)) and to requiring proof of treason and the limits of forfeiture (Art. 1, s. 10(1)). The rejection of the colonial mantle is also present in the various constitutional amendments. The Third Amendment, for example, prohibits the quartering of soldiers in private

So impelled, judges try to discover whether legislative interests comply with s. 33, without substantively reviewing legislative policy.[81] For example, they assert that

> [s]ection 33 lays down requirements of form only, and there is no warrant for importing into it grounds for substantive review of the legislative policy in exercising the override authority in a particular case.[82]

They rationalize this hierarchical structuring of *Charter* rights according to democratic principles. Citizens elect governments to act for them; and governments circumscribe citizen rights in exercising the authority that is vested, democratically, in them. Cynically expressed, the constitutional regime, itself the product of a representative democracy, ultimately constrains that very democracy.[83] Governments limit fundamental rights and freedoms as a consequence of their democratic empowerment by civil society. Courts respect that empowerment. As was stated in *Oakes:*

> It may become necessary to limit rights and freedoms in circumstances where their exercise would be inimical to the realization of collective goals of fundamental importance. For this reason, s. 1 provides criteria of justification for limits on the rights and freedoms guaranteed by the *Charter*.[84]

Thus, courts allegedly do not judge the social effects of Sunday shopping upon religious observance and community life, except indirectly, in deciding upon the benefits provided by Sunday laws. They interpret the *Lord's Day Act*. They accept that the legislature, as the democratic appointee of the people, decides that drug trafficking is heinous.[85] Rather than circumscribe its judgments, they establish only the extent of its authority to make those judgments in the first place. In *Oakes*, they decide whether "the [legislative] means chosen are reasonable and demonstrably justified",[86] whether the legislative objective "relate[s] to concerns which are pressing and substantial in a free and democratic society",[87] and whether the legislative means are "rationally connected to that objective".[88] They contend that, to be objective in "balancing" fundamental rights and State

---

homes; the Fourth Amendment confines the writs of assistance; while the Fifth Amendment provides for a grand jury indictment.

[81] See, *e.g.*, *Alliance des Professeurs de Montréal v. Quebec (A.G.)* (1985), 21 D.L.R. (4th) 354 (Que. C.A.).

[82] *Ford v. Quebec (A.G.)*, [1988] 2 S.C.R. 712, at 740.

[83] See the *Charter*, ss. 3-5 (democratic rights). See too, D. Greschner and K. Norman, "The Courts and Section 33" (1987), 12 Queen's L.J. 155.

[84] *Supra*, note 73, at 136.

[85] *Ibid.*

[86] *Ibid.*, at 136-41.

[87] *Ibid.*, at 138-39.

[88] *Ibid.*, at 139.

interests, "[t]here has to be a form of proportionality between the means employed and the ends sought to be achieved".[89]

Yet, no matter how objective courts purport to be, they often take on the cause of the people or the government. They interpret the *Charter* expansively, rendering it into a "people's" constitution. They interpret it restrictively so as to give government a free hand in public ordering. In both cases, they rise above naked impartiality. They acknowledge, in *Edwards Books*, that they exercise a discretion in balancing "the religious freedom of a retail store owner against the interests of . . . sometimes numerous employees".[90] They do so despite their reluctance "to substitute judicial opinions for legislative ones as to the place at which to draw a precise line."[91] They appreciate, too, that "many competing pressures", including diverse "sociological and economic forces",[92] impact upon their decisions. However much judges defer to a principled method of reasoning, they move "away from words, and towards . . . values".[93] They carve an imperfect balance among conflicting economic and social interests in deciding upon the relationship between means and ends, and ends and effects. They adopt a preferred rather than a mechanical balance between the individual and the State.

I do not disregard the readiness of judges to reason creatively under the *Charter*. Nor do I doubt their ability to justify their authority to do so by constitutional means. Indeed, to balance fundamental rights and State interests under the *Charter*, judges cannot help but shift constitutional practice from a textual past to a contextual future. As Justice Dickson stressed in *Southam*:

> A constitution . . . is drafted with an eye to the future. . . . It must be capable of growth and development over time to meet new social, political and historical realities . . .[94]

Rather, I doubt the supposition that judges can disguise their creativity within a strictly logical discourse. I question their ability to render incommensurate values commensurate by scientific means. I suspect their capacity to repress their normative reactions towards such social attitudes and practices as religiousness, free trade and Sunday pleasure. I question the existence of a timeless balance between private rights and government interests.

---

89 *R. v. Jones*, [1986] 2 S.C.R. 284, at 315. On this "weighing of competing interests", see *Oakes*, *supra*, note 73, at 139; *R.W.D.S.U. v. Dolphin Delivery*, [1986] 2 S.C.R. 573, at 589-90.
90 *Edwards Books*, [1986] 2 S.C.R. 713, at 777 *per* Dickson C.J. (as he then was).
91 *Ibid.*, at 782.
92 *Ibid.*, at 796-97 *per* La Forest J.
93 N. Lyon, "An Essay on Constitutional Interpretation" (1988), 26 Osgoode Hall L.J. 95, at 103.
94 *Hunter v. Southam Inc.*, [1984] 2 S.C.R. 145, at 155 *per* Dickson J. (as he then was).

A CHALLENGE TO A PRIORISM

The problem with strictly rational methods of constitutional review is the spuriousness of whole-hearted faith in predictive tools by which courts decide specific cases. This objection is especially evident when judges balance fundamental rights and State interests that are quite unlike each other. Thus, in *R. v. Jones*,[95] the Supreme Court simulates an objective basis upon which to compare two different means of effecting the State's interest in the "efficient education of the young": public education and religious education at home. The State's interest in public education raises issues that are different in kind from religious education at home. To choose between them is for the court to construct a skewed justification in favour of one or the other *ex post facto*. It can choose between home and public education only by supposing that the one is more socially desirable, economically efficient or politically expedient than the other. This supposition, far from being objective, is rooted in the court's own vision about more and less desirable formulations of social co-existence.   In short, the court's ultimate balance is based on values beyond the immediate rights and interests before it.

Judges establish a rational synthesis between fundamental rights and State interests only by constructing premises upon which to justify their normative choices. They rarely act under the influence of a wholly schematic logic. They do not simply identify one determinative right or one overpowering State interest. Thus, no matter how explicit the legislative preamble, judges render the legislature's objective determinative by treating it as such.   Once they identify other objectives, such as drug reform programmes and occupational retraining in cases like *Oakes*,[96] they shift attention away from obvious objectives and means of satisfying them. Accordingly, judges choose between the presumption of innocence and the heinousness of drug trafficking by reflecting upon a diverse array of social values. They decide, in the tradition of *Smith v. Cahoon*,[97] that trucks carrying seafood should be exempt from the regulation that all trucks over five tons must install new brakes. They temper the legislature's general interest in public safety with a specific interest in reducing trucking costs. They consider a diverse array of public objectives and means of effecting them, not perfectly commensurate ends and means.[98]

Once the balancing of rights and interests encompasses diverse public objectives, the process of rational comparison acquires disparate dimensions. It is rational for the legislature not to have as its objective the

---

[95]   *Supra*, note 89.
[96]   *Supra*, note 73.
[97]   283 U.S. 553 (1931). See J.H. Ely, "Legislative and Administrative Motivation in Constitutional Law (1970), 79 Yale L.J. 1205, at 1237.
[98]   Ely, *loc. cit.*, note 97, at 1237-39.

dispossession of the hungry or incapacitated. It is also rational for it not to dispossess the wealthy, even in the interests of the poor. Judges do not develop strictly analytical norms by which to compare State interests with private rights. They establish norms of comparison as tools of choice, not as necessary instruments with which to decide specific cases.[99] Nor do judges treat individual liberty as fundamental and at the same time, reconcile it with the countervailing interests of the State.[100] They balance fundamental rights and State interests in light of norms beyond both. They construct different connections between governmental objectives and the means of effecting them. They give those objectives and means different meanings in different contexts. They realize, throughout, that one objective or means does not necessarily exclude others.

Thus, it is somewhat questionable to claim that courts uncover a logical connection between relevant and irrelevant distinctions, as Mr. Justice Pratte did in the pre-*Charter* case of *Bliss v. Canada (A.G.)*:

> When a statute distinguishes between persons so as to treat them differently, the distinctions may be either relevant or irrelevant. The distinction is relevant when there is a logical connection between the basis for the distinction and the consequences that flow from it; the distinction is irrelevant when that logical connection is missing.[101]

There is no necessarily logical connection between an objective and a social effect. To provide pregnant women with unemployment benefits does not hinge upon an essential link between the legislature's objective of benefiting them and the social effect of doing so. Rather, the court justifies that result in light of other potential objectives and other means of effecting them. It chooses among competing objectives of promoting family life, benefiting pregnant women and saving money. It identifies different means of satisfying those objectives. Thus, its conception of "rational connections" is self-evident because it so construes them. Its "interpretative attitude", contrary to Dworkin,[102] is founded as much upon a desired outcome as upon reasoned principle itself.

The problem with any whole-hearted reliance upon the "rational connection" between a legislative objective and the means of attaining it is not just that the interpretative community of judges might be unable to agree upon the nature of that relationship. It is that they might conceive of its quality quite differently. Most often, the logical connection between legislative objectives, means and consequences, notwithstanding *Oakes*,[103] is the product of particular — and often competing — interests in them.

---

99   See *Law Society of Upper Canada v. Skapinker*, [1984] 1 S.C.R. 357, at 384.
100   See hereon, *supra*, Chapter 4. On the perceived distinction between private and public objectives, see R. Rorty, "Mind-Body Identity, Privacy, and Categories" (1965), 19(1) Review of Metaphysics 30.
101   [1978] 1 F.C. 208, at 214 (C.A.).
102   R.M. Dworkin, *Law's Empire* (Cambridge, Mass.: Belknap Press, 1986), pp. 47-53.
103   [1986] 1 S.C.R. 103.

Thus, judges impute general, and often unclear, objectives to Parliament. Given the legislature's diverse constituencies, they do not know its precise objective in differentiating between the rights of pregnant women and other persons in employment. Nor do they know whether its preferred means will effect its ends. Those judges who universalize *Charter* principles and legislative objectives decide by imputing characteristics to them. They rely upon particular rather than general, qualified rather than unqualified principles about the limits of a free and democratic society. Their assumption, that human rights like freedom of speech and association speak for themselves, is distinctly pseudo-logical. Their promise of "objective and manageable standards" by which to balance *Charter* rights against State interests, *à la Re B.C. Motor Vehicle Act*,[104] are at best justified. Their faith in "principles of fundamental justice" as "basic tenets of our legal system",[105] inevitably, falls short of objective truth.

This absence of an exclusive relationship between legislative objectives, means and effects lies at the centre of any critique of strict analytical jurisprudence. At issue is not so much the lack of scientific tools of reasoning by which courts identify government objectives that are of "sufficient importance" to warrant overriding constitutionally protected rights.[106] Of overriding concern is the extent to which some Canadian judges rely upon unrealistic methods of justifying legislative objectives, means and social effects. In doubt, too, is the degree to which they resort to a false symmetrical relationship between cause and effect in order to arrive at less than symmetrical ends.

Undoubtedly, judges can identify, and exclude, "wrong" solutions. Intentional murder is a reprehensible act: few would deny this. However, judges are far less likely to justify their decisions about the legal consequences of guilt by strictly causal means than by inferred supposition. They are far more likely to arrive at satisfactory determinations about criminal liability in constitutional cases than at "best" solutions, however much Ronald Dworkin might suggest to the contrary.[107]

THE ABSENCE OF CAUSAL RELATIONS

Once judges accept the inadequacy of analytical reason in constitutional interpretation, the centre of gravity in their inquiry moves perceptibly away from self-evident "connections" between legislative objectives, means and effects to the sufficiency of social explanations for them. Legal rights increasingly embody political discourse; and judges delineate hu-

---

[104]   *Reference re Section 94(2) of the Motor Vehicle Act (B.C.)* (hereafter referred to as *Re B.C. Motor Vehicle Act*), [1985] 2 S.C.R. 486, at 502-03.
[105]   *Ibid.*
[106]   See *Oakes, supra,* note 103, at 137.
[107]   See, *e.g.,* Dworkin, *op. cit.,* note 102, at 408-09.

man rights, in cases like *Oakes*,[108] in light of that discourse. So motivated, they react to social attitudes towards rights, less to rights themselves. They follow less than a compelling legal logic when they decide that particular shopkeepers, would-be workers and shoppers ought not to have a right to trade on Sundays in *Edwards Books*.[109] Their deductions are products of inferences which they deem to be satisfactory in a particular social context. They are not independent statements of fact. Their conclusions are deduced from suppositions which they deem to be "reasonable", not from their lack of alternative suppositions. As LaBrie, already in 1949, commented on constitutional interpretation, judges evaluate each legislative objective in light of diverse conceptions of its "wisdom", not one uniform conception of the public good.[110] Judges react to the *Charter* in a comparable manner. As the Supreme Court argued in *Oakes*, they decide whether a legislative objective is of "sufficient importance" to override a protected right, not whether that objective is "necessary".[111] They require that the means employed to attain that objective impair rights and freedoms "as little as possible",[112] not that it exclude all other means.

In construing the *Charter* so realistically, the Supreme Court implicitly acknowledges that judges attribute social, not strict analytical values to legislative objectives. This is not surprising. After all, the Supreme Court announced already in 1984 in *Skapinker*, that Canadian courts have indulged in "broad, liberal and purposive" interpretation of the *Charter* in "countless cases".[113] More specifically, Mr. Justice McIntyre reflected in the *Alberta Reference*, that judges cannot help but consider extrinsic sources in interpreting the *Charter*; and he included among these, "the nature, history, traditions, and social philosophies of our society".[114] Suppositions about the social effect of legislation unavoidably impact upon the manner in which judges interpret that legislation. Judges react, consciously or otherwise, to religious sentiment, racism and sexism; and to legislative attempts to regulate such anti-social practices. They reflect upon the degree of fanaticism of individuals, religious groups and welfare workers in deciding upon the limits of the s. 2 right to provide a religious education at home in *R. v. Jones*.[115] They override fundamental rights and

---

[108]   *Supra*, note 103.
[109]   *Supra*, note 90.
[110]   See F.E. LaBrie, "Canadian Constitutional Interpretation and Legislative Review" (1949), 8 U.T.L.J. 298, at 298-99.
[111]   *Oakes, supra*, note 103, at 139.
[112]   *Ibid*. This conceptual method of reasoning is especially evident in La Forest J.'s majority decision in *McKinney v. Bd. of Governors of the University of Guelph* (1990), 76 D.L.R. (4th) 545, at 647-54 (S.C.C.).
[113]   *Supra*, note 99, at 365-68. See too, *Hunter v. Southam, supra*, note 94, at 156.
[114]   *Reference re Public Service Employee Relations Act (Alta.)*, [1987] 1 S.C.R. 313, at 403-04.
[115]   *Supra*, note 89.

freedoms for reasons far more complex that the existence of a countervailing State interest under s. 1.

In truth, judges construct various kinds of bridges between the State's interest in a free and democratic society and fundamental rights.[116] They display disparate attitudes towards the State's interest in refugees in *Singh*. They adopt diverse attitudes towards the right of immigrants to gain access to and participate in the Canadian polity.[117]

Each "rational connection" between objective and means of effecting it is the product of an often malleable link between inferred fact and desired result. The connection is neither formulated mechanically *ex ante*, nor inextricably linked by rational means to one decisive objective or legislative purpose. It stems from multiple attitudes and beliefs; and politics, unavoidably, is part of that connection. Thus, judges do not envisage legislative objectives in light of any *necessary* opposition between goodness and evil. They view social ills selectively. They determine the "reasonable limits" of legislation governing drug trafficking, immigration, and restrictions on Sunday trade according to varied conceptions of a just, humane and sympathetic society. They interpret legislation governing foster parenthood in light of diffuse attitudes towards child care and child abuse. They envisage the nature of security in "family, social life and work," in *Mills v. R.*,[118] according to the disparate idealization of it. However much they try, they cannot repress their "underlying philosoph[ies] of life".[119] They are not clothed with the capacity to move deductive logic to immaculate conception, so as to arrive at "self-evident" solutions.[120] They cannot be sure that harsh criminal penalties will likely deter people like Mr. Oakes from selling drugs. Nor can they be certain that denying members of religious communities the right to educate their children at home will undermine public education. They can be sure only that it will reduce the number of pupils who study in traditional schools. Judges lack the capacity to anticipate social outcomes with any

---

[116]   See G.V. La Forest, "The Canadian Charter of Rights and Freedoms: An Overview" (1983), 61 Can. Bar Rev. 19.

[117]   *Singh v. Minister of Employment & Immigration*, [1985] 1 S.C.R. 177.

[118]   [1986] 1 S.C.R. 863, at 919 *per* Lamer J.

[119]   B.N. Cardozo, *The Nature of the Judicial Process* (New Haven: Yale University Press, 1963), pp. 11-12.

[120]   Ronald Dworkin is accused, somewhat too readily, of invoking mechanical methods of reasoning directed at "clear" cases. See J.W. Singer, "The Legal Rights Debate in Analytical Jurisprudence from Bentham to Hohfeld", [1982] Wisc. L. Rev. 975, at 1015. While Dworkin rejects H.L.A. Hart's conception of "unclear" cases (see, for instance, Dworkin, *Taking Rights Seriously* (Cambridge: Harvard University Press, 1977), p. 111), he does not advocate a mechanical process of reasoning from precedent. He acknowledges that different weights can be given to different opinions, and that precedents vary in significance according to their "gravitational" weight. See too, Dworkin, "Law as Interpretation" (1982), 60 Tex. L. Rev. 527, at 545. This is clearly posited throughout his more recent work, *Law's Empire* (Cambridge, Mass.: Belknap Press, 1986).

degree of certainty. They decide only after they have reflected upon the indeterminate environment that surrounds them. They establish legal coherence only by looking beyond analytical reason to imperfect legal principles;[121] and they conceptualize those principles as judicial practice only by shifting from "systematic . . . principles" and "technical . . . rules" to "policies [that] express preferences".[122]

This vision of judges acting as social engineers rather than mechanics is by no means unique in jurisprudence. School upon school of legal thought — from legal realist[123] to social behaviouralist[124] — has challenged juridical attempts to construe law as a preferred legal science. Together, members of these schools have displayed scepticism towards logical symmetry in law that excludes normative belief.[125] They have been joined in their scepticism even by traditional theorists. Neil MacCormick has stressed the value of non-deductive reason, albeit based upon both consistency and legal coherence.[126] Richard Wasserstrom has identified a non-deductive method of judicial reasoning which he construes as "reasoning by justification", as distinct from reasoning by proof.[127] Edward Levi, in his classic work, *An Introduction to Legal Reasoning*, has contended, even more explicitly, that legal rules are "never clear".[128] Post-legal realists, in turn, have cast doubt upon the technical rigour of analytical reason, notably the art of distinction in decision-making.[129] Pragmatists

---

121   See further, I. Tammelo, *Modern Logic in the Service of Law* (New York: Springer Verlag, 1978).

122   N. Lyon, "An Essay on Constitutional Interpretation" (1988), 26 Osgoode Hall L.J. 95, at 123-24.

123   On American legal realism, see J.H. Schlegel, "American Legal Realism and Empirical Social Science: From the Yale Experience" (1979), 28 Buffalo L. Rev. 459; W.L. Twining, *Karl Llewellyn and the Realist Movement* (London: Weidenfeld & Nicholson, 1973); K.N. Llewellyn, *The Common Law Tradition: Deciding Appeals* (Boston: Little, Brown, 1960); Llewellyn, *The Bramble Bush* (New York: Oceana Publications, 1951); Llewellyn, *Jurisprudence: Realism in Theory and Practice* (Chicago: University of Chicago Press, 1962).

124   See R. Pound, *Social Control Through Law* (Hamden, Conn.: Archon Books, 1968).

125   See, *e.g.*, O.W. Holmes, *The Common Law* (Boston: Little, 1881); R. Pound, "Mechanical Jurisprudence" (1908), 8 Colum. L. Rev. 605.

126   N. MacCormick, *Legal Reasoning and Legal Theory* (Oxford: Clarendon Press, 1978), pp. 100-28.

127   R. Wasserstrom, *The Judicial Decision* (Stanford, Cal.: Stanford University Press, 1961), pp. 138-68. See too, H.L.A. Hart, *The Concept of Law* (New York: Oxford University Press, 1961); D. Beatty, *Talking Heads and the Supremes: The Canadian Production of Constitutional Review* (Toronto: Carswell, 1990).

128   E.H. Levi, *An Introduction to Legal Reasoning* (Chicago: University of Chicago Press, 1949). See too, S.J. Burton, *An Introduction to Law and Legal Reasoning* (Boston: Little Brown, 1985), p. 32. (Burton concurs with Levi.)

129   For somewhat over-extended criticisms of deductive reasoning in common law decision-making, see Singer, *loc. cit.*, note 120, at 1015; P. Westen, "On 'Confusing Ideas': Reply" (1982), 91 Yale L.J. 1153, at 1163. For a critique of deductive logic in the common law system in general, see S.J. Burton, "Comment on 'Empty Ideas': Logical Positivist Analyses of Equality and Rules" (1982), 91 Yale L.J. 1136, at 1140-46; A. Wilson, "The Nature of Legal Reasoning: A Commentary with Special Reference to Professor MacCormick's Theory" (1982), 2 Leg. Stud. 269.

have presented functional alternatives to analytical reason.[130] Critical Legal theorists have identified the subjective effect of liberal ideology upon analytical reason.[131] Irrationalists have highlighted the inherent inconsistency in all purportedly rational theories of reason.[132]

All this is quite understandable. Judges are not united by an absolute condition of life, thought or practice. Their thoughts and deeds are contingent upon their different capacities to observe, as much as the different objects they observe. Like Heisenberg's particles in motion, the presence of differently motivated observers extends the distance between the act of observing and the subject-matter being observed.[133] Similarly, the more diverse the subject-matter being observed, the more likely is the observation of it to be diverse. Thus, judges observe and react to political, economic and social "facts" differently. Not unlike parents, they observe and react differently to child abuse. They render their observations objective by assuming that others are likely to observe the comparable subject-matter similarly. These others may well be proven to be like-minded. However, this does not mean that the shared opinion is wholly objective.

Certainly, some judges will resist open theories of judicial interpretation. They will earnestly avoid judging the quality of either legislative objectives or fundamental rights and freedoms on grounds, inter alia, that "[i]t is no business of courts to say what is a religious practice or activity for one group."[134] However, they will find it impossible to observe religious practices without also reflecting upon the substantive value of those practices. They will be unable to demand that legislation not interfere "with profoundly personal beliefs"[135] without reflecting upon the qualitative worth of those "beliefs". Indeed, as the late Chief Justice Laskin reminds us: "[t]he constitution is as open as the minds of those who are called upon to interpret it; it is as closed as their minds are closed."[136] Courts cannot claim to be neutral and detached from the subject-matter before them if they are to attribute values to that subject-matter. They

---

[130]   On this tradition of pragmatism, see W. James, *Pragmatism and the Meaning of Truth* (Cambridge: Harvard University Press, 1975); R. Rorty, *Consequences of Pragmatism* (Brighton, Eng.: Harvester Press, 1982).

[131]   See esp., J.W. Singer, "The Player and the Cards: Nihilism and Legal Theory" (1984), 94 Yale L.J. 1.

[132]   Some members of the Critical Legal Studies movement have sought to demonstrate imperfections and inconsistencies that inhere within the liberal order. See C. Dalton, "An Essay on the Deconstruction of Contract Doctrine" (1985), 94 Yale L.J. 997; M.G. Kelman, "Trashing" (1984), 36 Stan. L. Rev. 293; Singer, *loc. cit.*, note 131, at 25-30.

[133]   See W. Heisenberg, *The Uncertainty Principle and Foundations of Quantum Mechanics*, W.C. Price and S.S. Chissick, eds. (New York: Wiley, 1977), p. 118.

[134]   See, *e.g.*, *Fowler v. Rhode Island*, 345 U.S. 67, at 70 (1952); *R. v. Jones*, [1986] 2 S.C.R. 284, at 295: "a court is in no position to question the validity of a religious belief" (*per* La Forest J.).

[135]   *Edwards Books*, [1986] 2 S.C.R. 713, at 759 *per* Dickson C.J.

[136]   B. Laskin, "Test for the Validity of Legislation: What's the Matter?" (1955-56), 11 U.T.L.J. 114, at 127.

are not mere administrators of the law. They cannot be neutral towards either religious practices or the State's regulation of them, and yet claim to find some rational basis for deciding between them.

Those judges who still rely strictly upon "rational connections" between law and fact, opinion and decision, likely trap themselves behind their own dogma. They claim that past facts are already determined; while the future consequences that arise from those facts need merely be identified in a coherent manner. Yet, they trust in Dworkin-like principles of coherence to link past to present in the absence of real coherence.[137] They invoke analogy to justify their decisions, despite the lack of obvious similarities among cases.[138] They draw reasonable inferences of fact, without agreeing upon the limits of reasonableness itself.[139] To render a variable past into a certain present, they are distinctly selective in relation to both. To arrive at coherent determination, they employ different brands of practical reason[140] and different conceptions of material fact.[141] They diverge widely upon the nature and effect of the social ills of the "separate but equal" doctrine in *Brown v. Bd. of Education*.[142] They recognize the need for anti-inflation hearings. Yet, they do not agree upon the extent of social harm that arises from inflation. Nor do they agree upon the means of arresting it.[143] They decide on the basis of sensory stimuli, not incontrovertible fact. They are motivated by elitism, popularism and generosity of spirit, not by verity itself.

Certainly, judges acknowledge that they have ideological predispositions. However, they usually claim that these are responses to the demands of the legal order itself, not their own moral order. They claim that even though freedom of association advances

---

[137] See R.M. Dworkin, *Taking Rights Seriously* (Cambridge: Harvard University Press, 1977), pp. 22-26.

[138] See Levi, *op. cit.*, note 128.

[139] See V.A. Wellman, "Practical Reasoning and Judicial Justification: Toward an Adequate Theory" (1985), 57 U. Colo. L. Rev. 45.

[140] See, *e.g.*, K.J. Kress, "Legal Reasoning and Coherence Theories: Dworkin's Rights Thesis, Retroactivity, and the Linear Order of Decisions" (1984), 72 Cal. L. Rev. 367; M. Hanen, "Justification as Coherence", in *Law, Morality and Rights*, M.A. Stewart, ed. (Boston: Kluwer, 1983), pp. 67-92.

[141] These different conceptions of material fact are readily displayed in *McKinney v. Bd. of Governors of the University of Guelph* (1990), 76 D.L.R. (4th) 545 (S.C.C.), especially in the different weights that are attributed to mandatory retirement as the basis of discrimination according to age. See esp. *per* La Forest J. at 646-47, *per* Wilson J. at 607-10, and *per* L'Heureux-Dubé J. at 679-82. See generally, M.P. Golding, *Legal Reasoning* (New York: A.A. Knopf, 1984), at 101-11; J. Raz, *The Authority of Law* (New York: Oxford University Press, 1979), pp. 201-05.

[142] 347 U.S. 483 (1954).

[143] See *Reference re Anti-Inflation Act*, [1976] 2 S.C.R. 373, where the court used, *inter alia*, the federal government's White Paper entitled, *Attack on Inflation*, being the policy statement of the Minister of Finance tabled in the House of Commons on October 14, 1975; the Consumer Price Index from Statistics Canada; a study by Professor Lipsey and telegrams from a large number of economists who supported him; and a speech by Mr. Gerald Bouey, then Governor of the Bank of Canada, delivered September 22, 1975.

... many group interests and, of course, cannot be exercised alone, it is nonetheless a freedom belonging to the individual and not to the group formed through its exercise.[144]

They choose between State interest and private rights only after they have adopted an ideological rationale in support of either. Thus, they propose that free choice ought to belong to the individual, not the collectivity, and that social justice is best served thereby. They suppose, in *Oakes*, that the "deleterious effect" which State action has upon the individual is outweighed by the importance of the legislative objective;[145] and they appreciate that private rights cannot exist within a social vacuum, any more than collective rights can bypass individual rights.[146] They conclude only after they have formulated propositions to support their suppositions.

Judges who still insist that, through analytical reason, they can render private rights comparable to State interests create a false image of judging. They treat the freedom to trade on Sundays under s. 2 of the *Charter*, and the State's interest in a common pause day under s. 1, as analytically comparable. However, in doing so, they ignore the incommensurate nature of individual rights and group interests.[147] They analyze to what extent governmental objectives in ensuring the continued supply of goods and services in *Re Public Service Employee Relations Act* ought to trump private rights.[148] They act similarly in deciding to what extent the legislature ought to be free to avert drug trafficking in *Oakes*,[149] or to preserve family and religious life in *Edwards Books*.[150] They assume that a "balance between two competing concerns must be found"[151] on the assumption that they can do so conclusively by some discoverable means. However, they do all this in light of the realization that private autonomy is not directly reconcilable with, or "rationally connected" to State interests. They choose, not simply between the right to speak out against State

---

144   *Reference re Public Service Employee Relations Act (Alta.),* [1987] 1 S.C.R. 313, at 397 *per* McIntyre J. However, Justice McIntyre goes on to find that because there is no analogy between one employee stopping work and a strike, there is no right to strike within the meaning of freedom of association (at 410). *Cf. per* Dickson C.J. (as he then was), where he finds that "the refusal to work by one individual does not parallel a collective refusal to work. The latter is *qualitatively* rather than quantitatively different" (at 367).
145   *Oakes,* [1986] 1 S.C.R. 103, at 140.
146   See, *e.g., per* Wilson J. in *Saskatchewan Dairies,* [1987] 1 S.C.R. 460, at 486-87, where she acknowledges that there will always be some measure of economic harm to the public as a result of a strike. She adds, further, that the effectiveness of the strike as a negotiating tool depends upon that harm. She goes on to find that s. 2(*d*) freedom of association embraces the right to strike and should only be overridden when there is a "serious threat to the well-being of the body politic or a substantial segment of it" (at 487), not simply to prevent economic harm to a particular sector.
147   But *cf. Edwards Books,* [1986] 2 S.C.R. 713.
148   *Re Public Service Employee Relations Act, supra,* note 144.
149   *Supra,* note 145.
150   *Supra,* note 147.
151   *R. v. Jones, supra,* note 134.

action or be restrained from speaking in *Canada (A.G.) v. City of Montreal*,[152] but between allowing free speech while decrying demonstrations that often accompany that speech. In each case, the court does not select simply between a governmental interest and the private rights of the accused. It selects, instead, between very different conceptions of the social good. It chooses between averting trafficking in drugs and ensuring society's fair treatment of criminal offenders in *Oakes*,[153] and between the private right of labour to picket milk suppliers and the private rights of Saskatchewan consumers to receive an uninterrupted supply of milk in *Saskatchewan Dairies*.[154] As a result, judges conceive of Mr. Oakes's *Charter* rights in light of diverse conceptions of retribution and deterrence under the *Criminal Code*. So too, they render the s. 7 rights of abused children contingent upon diffuse attitudes towards security of, and harmony in, family life. They are not impelled by one pervasive good, or by one uniform means of effecting it. They are motivated by different social practices, as by dissimilar constructions of them.

Jurists who seek to avoid debating social practice imperil their own logic. They divide law from politics in the heritage of *Harrison v. Carswell*;[155] yet, they rely upon politics to achieve their legal ends. They admit that matters of a "political or foreign policy nature may be properly cognizable by the courts"; yet they insist in cases like *Operation Dismantle*, that the plaintiff's interests, no matter how politically justifiable, are too "uncertain, speculative and hypothetical" to serve as the basis for a judicial cause of action.[156] In excluding law from public policies that resemble politics, they simulate their capacity to decide cases on the basis of analytical reasoning alone. They overstate the division between judicial process and substantive law-making. In particular, they render doubtful their assumption that

> [t]he task of the Court is not to choose between substantive or procedural content *per se* but to secure for persons "the full benefit of the *Charter's* protection" . . . under s. 7, while avoiding adjudication of the merits of public policy.[157]

No matter how seemingly plain the statutory objective and the means of effecting it, judges cannot be sure of the exact social effect of legislative action. No uniform rationality dictates that cruise missile testing over Canadian airspace is good or bad. Nor can judges be expected to have a consistent belief in the precise worth of family life or parental discipline. Certainly, judges can justify policies that underlie legislative action. They can also rationalize the adequacy of the legislature's methods of satisfy-

---

152 [1978] 2 S.C.R. 770, at 797.
153 *Supra*, note 145.
154 *Supra*, note 146.
155 [1976] 2 S.C.R. 200.
156 *Operation Dismantle Inc. v. R.*, [1985] 1 S.C.R. 441, at 459.
157 *Re B.C. Motor Vehicle Act*, [1985] 2 S.C.R. 486, at 499 *per* Lamer J.

ing those policies. However, in doing this, they engage in political action itself, not in neutral decision-making.

This is not to suggest that judges purposefully manipulate law or fact. It is only to claim that their analytical jurisprudence is informed and modified by social and economic policy. Courts cannot know exactly how a particular woman feels when she is raped, or how an aboriginal feels as a "token" employee in a white school or business. They can understand prejudice only in light of their knowledge about, and understanding of, work conditions and racist and sexist practices; and they can evaluate legislative objectives in light of that knowledge and understanding. After all is said and done, their analytical determinations, unavoidably, are subject to inter-subjective beliefs. Thus, judges evaluate whether Quakers ought to be exempt from paying income taxes that support military expenditure in light of beliefs, not limited to their own, in patriotism and social service.[158] They justify or deny a Sunday pause day, in *Big M Drug Mart* and *Edwards Books*,[159] in part, in light of belief in the quality of religious and cultural life. In no case does either analytical reason or belief establish the whole truth, all by itself. Instead, judges decide upon the legitimacy of Sunday pause days in light of varying kinds and degrees of faith. They realize that not everyone is a practising Christian; that some religious minorities "pause" on Fridays and Saturdays, not Sundays; and they likely include these considerations within their observations.[160] Judges are not all directed towards one truth by identical faith, experience, background or education. They follow different pathways. They display different attitudes, opinions and inclinations towards parental care, public education and business ethics. Their determinations are not brought about by an inner sensibility that is peculiarly their own. Their consciousness of human want includes — and excludes — the consciousness of others. Their reaction towards individual liberty reflects social reactions. Their conception of good and evil embodies communal experience.

Thus, judges do not reach decisions independently of either faith or reason. Whether or not they are persuaded by popular faith in deterrence and punishment, they nevertheless decide upon the limits of culpability in light of a loosely structured relationship between knowledge and faith, fact and the construction of fact.[161] They decide what happens to cruise missile testing in light of the social value which they place upon the authority of the executive, national security, and the threat of a nuclear

---

158   *Prior v. Canada*, [1988] 2 F.C. 371 (T.D.).
159   *Big M Drug Mart*, [1985] 1 S.C.R. 295; *Edwards Books*, [1986] 2 S.C.R. 713.
160   On the relationship between knowledge and belief, see E. Gill, *The Necessity of Belief* (London: Faber & Faber, 1936); W. James, *The Will to Believe* (Cambridge: Harvard University Press, 1979).
161   On equally loose connections in science, see L. Laudan, *Progress and its Problems* (London: Routledge & Kegan Paul, 1977), pp. 61-74. See too, T.S. Kuhn, *The Structure of Scientific Revolutions*, 2nd ed. (Chicago: University of Chicago Press, 1970), pp. 260-62.

holocaust. They combine their judicial distinctiveness with analytical reason by linking social experience to decision-making.

Courts may well frame their decisions in terms of doing justice between immediate parties. They may well raise the individual's rights above the State's, or the State's interests above individual rights. Realistically, however, they envisage human rights in a communal context that includes individuals, community groups and the State alike. They conceive of justice as prescient, not categorical. Their conceptions of equity are discursive, not self-defining. Judges face, address and listen to others delineating the limits of just treatment. They place themselves in the shoes of others; and they modify or retain their opinions about justice in light of their relationships with those others. However they decide, they attribute the "rational" content of foetal life conversationally, not in an abstract setting of self-delineating rights. Their opinions reflect selected premises and normative explanations for them. They propose that life *in utero* has normative worth beyond both the pregnant woman's right to personal security and the foetus' right to exist. They propose that life *in utero* advances family life, even if two out of three babies are born to single, teenage mothers. Their suppositions and propositions are satisfactory in light of their reactions towards cultural attitude and social practice. That judges are likely to justify the nature of foetal rights differently goes without saying. The normative rationale for a right to life is not necessarily consistent. Indeed, from Aristotle to John Locke, the value of life has rested upon varied conceptions of human bondage, salvation and the procreation of the human species.[162] In each case, disdain for human bondage hinges upon the quality of belief in it, and only through that belief, upon the justification for it. For some, wives are "enslaved" by their husbands, employees are "enslaved" by work conditions and poor wages. For others, human bondage is far more restrictive in scope of application; as such, it excludes both wives and employees. For both, decisions are derived from ongoing conversation into moral virtue, human kindness, and justifiable punishment. In no case does inevitable logic establish the value of life, a livable wage, or a tolerable work condition.[163] Nor does inevitable logic establish a "rational connection" between life, language and the authority of the State.[164]

Certainly, courts can identify selected properties of life — a pulse rate, a heartbeat — or a particular quality of life. They can define the quality of "essential services", for example, of firefighters as those "whose interruption would endanger the life, personal safety or health of the whole

---

[162] For a clear discussion on the influence of ideology, politics and metaphysics on truth, see D. Cohen and A.C. Hutchinson, "Of Persons and Property: The Politics of Legal Taxonomy" (1990), 13 Dalhousie L.J. 20.

[163] See Cohen and Hutchinson, *ibid.*

[164] See esp., Sir I. Jennings, *The Law and the Constitution*, 5th ed. (London: University of London Press, 1959), p. 43.

or part of the population".[165] However, they can do so only by having resort to the loosest "sense of orderliness".[166] After all, they still have to decide what public services are "essential", under what conditions and subject to what limits. They cannot reach these determinations solely by analytical means. They cannot resolve them by moving from strict *a priori* principles to determinative results. They cannot be certain about social values that are themselves uncertain.

PROPOSITIONS AND SUPPOSITIONS

Reasoned decisions are justified by two contingent propositions: that the judge believes the premises underlying her decisions are satisfactory; and that those who interpret her decisions, not limited to other judges, are satisfied by them. Thus, Mr. Oakes, retried in another setting, might be subject to a reverse onus according to the dual propositions: that he ought to be deterred from and punished for trafficking in drugs, and that failing to do so likely would have a deleterious social effect. These propositions are derived from the judges' beliefs that Oakes' acts are heinous. Informed by communal reactions to drug trafficking and drug use, these propositions might be variously strong or weak. They are likely to be stronger, for example, when they relate to drug sales to minors than when compared to sales to adults. They are likely to be weaker when the costs of drug rehabilitation are borne by private agencies than when they are supported by public funds. In each case, judges justify their propositions in light of normative beliefs which they attribute to drug trafficking, beyond mere description. These normative beliefs are inferred, *inter alia*, from evidence that drug trafficking and drug usage are socially harmful, that the accused contributed to that social harm, and that such harm was justifiably averted by the legislative means adopted. Each decision is determinative, not because it leads to a "correct" decision *à la* Dworkin,[167] but because it is considered to be a satisfactory product of discourse into social values. It is satisfactory, too, when it is perceived to contribute towards social ends that include, but are not limited to, the specific parties.

This method of justified reasoning reflects the norms of post-legal realism. Judges justify their decisions in light of changing social *mores*. They view drug laws as being in a state of flux, along with flux in society itself. They employ creative methods of interpretation to give meaning to that flux; and they resort to satisfactory propositions in justifying that

---

[165]   *Reference re Public Service Employee Relations Act (Alta.)*, [1987] 1 S.C.R. 313, at 375 *per* Dickson C.J. (as he then was), citing *Freedom of Association and Collective Bargaining: General Survey by the Committee of Experts on the Application of Conventions and Recommendations*, Report III, Part 4B, para. 387 (Geneva: I.L.O., 1983).

[166]   *Re Resolution to Amend the Constitution*, [1981] 1 S.C.R. 753, at 805-06.

[167]   R.M. Dworkin, *Taking Rights Seriously* (Cambridge: Harvard University Press, 1977).

meaning.[168] Thus, judges establish "rational connections" between the ills of drug trafficking and drug use in light of suppositions and propositions about each. They rely upon justified not necessary suppositions, adequate not essential propositions. They suppose that drug trafficking is evil, and that the presumption of innocence is fundamental in a democratic society. They propose that failing to regulate drug trafficking by particular punitive and deterrent means likely encourages it; and they arrive at a preferred "scheme of justice"[169] by reconciling these suppositions and propositions with alternatives, notably, under s. 1 of the *Charter*.

To reconcile competing "schemes of justice", judges are likely to struggle, less to slay the monster of uncertainty, than to come to terms with it. They will realize that the absence of a perfectly coherent solution is, less a social ill, than a positive influence upon decision-making itself.[170] They will appreciate that debating different suppositions and propositions likely promotes human understanding more than the contrary. Through such debate, judges embrace competing social outlooks. They come to appreciate the absence of a self-evident relationship between harsh penalties imposed upon drug traffickers and the curtailment of the drug trade. They find no essential link between the enforcement of Sunday pause days and the advancement of religious faith. They find no categorical divide between public harm and public benefit in *Big M Drug Mart*,[171] *Irwin Toy*,[172] or *Operation Dismantle*.[173]

At their best, judges will construct thoughtful propositions based on reasonably informed suppositions. They will propose satisfactory, not necessary relationships between legislative objectives, means and effects in cases like *Re Public Service Employee Relations Act*.[174] They will recognize that "fundamental" rights adequately, rather than necessarily, override the interests of the State within a "free and democratic society" in *Oakes*.[175] They will appreciate that the public's right to receive essential goods is only imperfectly comparable to the right of specific employees to withhold their services in *Saskatchewan Dairies*.[176] They will not arrive at incontrovertible determinations. Judges cannot know that their propositions, or the suppositions upon which they base them, are indisputably worthy. As Chief Justice Dickson observed in *Operation Dismantle*, the risk

---

168 See *Edwards Books, supra*, note 159, at 768 *per* Dickson C.J.
169 *Ibid.*, at 809 *per* Wilson J.
170 See B.N. Cardozo, *The Growth of Law* (Westport, Conn: Greenwood, 1970), and esp. "Introduction: The Need of a Scientific Restatement as an Aid to Certainty", in *Selected Writings of Benjamin Nathan Cardozo*, M.E. Hall, ed. (New York: Falton, 1975), pp. 186-87.
171 *Supra*, note 159.
172 [1989] 1 S.C.R. 927.
173 *Supra*, note 156.
174 *Supra*, note 165, at 374-75.
175 See *Oakes*, [1986] 1 S.C.R. 103.
176 [1987] 1 S.C.R. 460.

of nuclear confrontation is not "possible to prove . . . one way or the other".[177] Propositions and suppositions are not indisputably obvious. However, they need not be obviously so in order to be satisfactory. To propose a communal conception of property rights is for judges to construct a satisfactory, not a necessary justification for those rights. To accommodate aboriginal rights under the *Charter* is for them to adopt preferred suppositions about those rights, not to uncover one determinative formulation of them.

Suppositions and propositions are not always easily formed. Judges are likely to agonize over the perimeters of legislation that restricts access to abortion-on-demand. They are likely to draw a tenuous link between science and ethics, realizing that "[t]here cannot be such a thing as an ethical science".[178] They are also likely to debate, endlessly, whether the death sentence invariably is "cruel and unusual" under ss. 214 and 218 of the *Criminal Code*, or is so only under particular social conditions.[179] However, their beliefs, no matter how sincere, informed and convincing they are, are not necessarily shared by others. Their commitment to moral decency is likely to be viewed by others as a resort to moral indecency. Their conception of probable social harm is likely to amount to no or only possible harm in the minds of others.[180]

I do not claim that judges should not strive for virtue and truth. Indeed, judges derive a satisfactory vision of "the good life" precisely through such a search. They do so substantively, in recognizing individual alongside communal rights, and in protecting private wealth alongside social welfare. They do so procedurally, in insisting upon an efficient regime of policies, principles, standards and rules of law. Nor do I claim that this discursive method gives rise to a decision that is more readily justified than any other. Indeed, to raise one justification — one proposition or supposition — over another is to presuppose that the premises underlying it are satisfactory, not that they are necessary. It is to allege that they are just, fair and reasonable, not that there are no other alternatives to them.

What is satisfactory, ultimately, is the product of a mediated consensus about the satisfactory nature of the ends it serves and the adequacy of the means invoked to justify it. That consensus stems from the quality of the discourse itself. It includes the capacity of those who are engaged in discourse to mediate among different suppositions and propositions to accommodate different means and ends, and to express them in a satisfactory manner.

Accordingly, I agree with those who insist that the justification for a

---

177   *Operation Dismantle, supra*, note 156, at 453.
178   A.J. Ayer, *Language, Truth and Logic*, 2nd ed. (London: V. Gollancz, 1946), p. 112.
179   See, *e.g., Miller and Cockriell v. R.*, [1977] 2 S.C.R. 680.
180   On comparable decision-making according to probability in philosophy and science, see K.R. Popper, *The Logic of Scientific Discovery* (New York: Basic Books, 1959).

decision hinges upon the manner in which courts discover, explore and apply different ends and means to particular cases.[181] I agree, too, that they do so by having resort to social discourse, not limited to their face-to-face exchanges of thought, ideas and inclination. I concur, further, that they do so both constructively and destructively. To conciliate over difference is also to reject premises that are deemed to be unsatisfactory.

CONCLUSION

There are two central objections to the strict application of deductive logic and legal analogy to *Charter* interpretation: first, the indeterminacy of law itself; and secondly, the need to recognize the normative content of legal precepts in order to derive satisfactory conclusions from them. Once methods of reasoning are conceived of as indeterminate, no one legal method becomes compelling. No social object or means remains fixed. Thus, the adequacy of judicial suppositions and propositions hinges upon the capacity of judges to accommodate cultural, social and political differences in their decisions. The justification for a decision stems from the openness of the discourse that surrounds it. The openness of that discourse, in turn, hinges upon the willingness of those who engage in it to consider a community of interest groups that impact upon it, beyond the immediate litigants or their legal counsel.

Judges who cling to strict analytical principles of law unify heterogeneous premises within a single whole, in disregard of real differences. They draw together under one veil different conceptions of fundamental rights and freedoms, downplaying those conceptions of justice they consider inadequate or undesirable. They believe in faith. Yet, they accord different values to faith-healing and non-violence. They do not always acknowledge that realistic debate into human rights lacks a unified framework or method of expression. They do not accept that *Charter* discourse varies according to the way in which constituent players within it interact, mediate differences in attitude, opinion and belief, and ultimately, arrive at conciliated determinations.

Certainly, judges cannot reduce religious, political and cultural beliefs to the status of concrete principles that stand for all time. They cannot form rational opinions about legislation that outlaws the practices of Mohawks and Quebecers, Mormons and Seventh Day Adventists, without also reflecting upon different suppositions and propositions about how these groups ought to be treated. For judges to pretend that they uncover constitutional facts as they are is to deny the effect of public

---

[181]   See, *e.g.*, D. Beatty and S. Kennett, "Striking Back: Fighting Words, Social Protest and Political Participation in Free and Democratic Societies" (1988), 67 Can. Bar Rev. 573, at 576-77; D. Beatty, *Talking Heads and the Supremes: The Canadian Production of Constitutional Review* (Toronto: Carswell, 1990).

opinion upon them. To claim that substantive inquiry into freedom of speech, association and religion, while "necessary", should still be "avoided wherever reasonably possible"[182] is to pass over disparate suppositions that underlie that freedom. Judges who insist upon a wholly rational state of being, principled in all respects, enter into a discursive void. Worse still, they indulge in a sham of indifference towards conversation. They marginalize difference in favour of a false unity. They typecast the demands of First Nation Peoples and francophile Canadians within a superficial image of both.

Judges who still insist upon a mechanical jurisprudence, likely pass over the relationship between supposition and axiom, proposition and fact, reason and belief.[183] They ignore that their justified reasoning is the product of more than the "connection" between a rational past and a rational present. Their alternative is to justify fundamental rights and freedoms selectively, not to pretend to be neutral towards them. It is to place satisfactory boundaries around faith, not to find these boundaries within self-evident rules of application.[184]

This is not to suggest that reasoned analogy and judicial precedents are valueless, only that they are satisfactory, not necessary. Their legal and political value is imputed, not inherent. It is useful, not compelling. Thus, judges justify their decisions according to explanations which they justify, not obvious proofs. They draw upon inferred, not necessary suppositions. They reconcile their differences selectively, not according to necessary syllogisms and obvious paradigms. As Thomas Kuhn[185] and Feyerabend[186] would have it, judges engage in both empirical and normative discovery. They have "good", seldom compelling reasons for their decisions. That others might construe their reasons as "bad" goes without saying: satisfactory explanations for decisions are not necessarily shared. Nor would it be realistic to expect otherwise.[187] To engage in discourse is to incorporate an ongoing state of difference into decision-making. For law to change as society changes is for judges to house both in continually changing opinion. It is to recognize that both express themselves through diverse conceptions of life, personhood, and community practice. It is never to be satisfied with a past opinion, but always to look to the effect of ongoing discourse upon present and future decisions.[188]

---

182 *Edwards Books*, [1986] 2 S.C.R. 713, at 780.
183 On the interface between reason and belief, see E.J. Bond, *Reason and Value* (New York: Cambridge University Press, 1983).
184 See, *e.g.*, *R. v. Keegstra* (1988), 43 C.C.C. (3d) 150 (Alta. C.A.).
185 T.S. Kuhn, "Notes on Lakatos", in *Boston Studies in the Philosophy of Science*, vol. III, R.S. Cohen and R.C. Buck, eds. (Dordrecht, Holland: Reidel Publishing, 1970), p. 144.
186 P. Feyerabend, "Against Method: Outline of an Anarchistic Theory of Knowledge", in *Minnesota Studies in the Philosophy of Science*, vol. 14, M. Radner and S. Winokur, eds. (1970).
187 See T.S. Kuhn, *The Structure of Scientific Revolutions*, 2nd ed. (Chicago: University of Chicago Press, 1970).
188 On this pragmatic state, see esp., D. Hume, *A Treatise of Human Nature*, L.A. Selby-Bigge, ed. (New York: Clarendon Press, 1978).

CHAPTER 6

MORGENTALER AS ILLUSTRATION

> [T]here is a problem, for the Court must clothe the general expression of rights and freedoms . . . with real substance and vitality. How can the courts go about this task without imposing at least some of their views and predilections upon the law?[1]

When judges treat constitutional rights like liberty and security of the person as *a priori,* they make three questionable assumptions: that the nature of *a priori* rights is self-evident; that those rights are graduated according to a discoverable hierarchy, with the *Charter* at its apex; and that justice is achieved by the neutral application of those principles to specific cases.[2] Absent one of these assumptions, the neatly stacked house of cards comes tumbling down, and the judge must find another way to play the rights game.

This chapter is a critique of these three assumptions. Rather than having a fixed meaning, *Charter* rights mean what their interpreters say they ought to mean. Thus, judges formulate suppositions and advance propositions about the reproductive rights of pregnant women. They suppose that the *Charter* should be construed in light of a "constitutional tradition . . . and [the] underlying philosophies of our society";[3] and they give meaning to those traditions and philosophies according to what they deem to be reasonably satisfactory in the circumstances. They contend, too, that courts are ill-equipped to evaluate "complex and controversial programmes of public policy".[4] Yet, they propose that, in interpreting legislative programmes, they should give them meaning.[5] In short, judges render *a priori* rights into *ex post* constructions which they reconceive as rights. They reformulate pre-existing interests in light of supposed and proposed qualities which they impute to them *ex post facto.*

This reconstruction of rights is evident in *Morgentaler 1988.* The facts of

---

1   *R. v. Morgentaler,* [1988] 1 S.C.R. 30 (hereafter referred to as *Morgentaler 1988*), at 139 *per* McIntyre J.

2   See further, *infra,* at 181.

3   *Reference re Public Service Employee Relations Act (Alta.),* [1987] 1 S.C.R. 313, at 394.

4   *Morgentaler 1988,* at 46 *per* Dickson C.J.

5   On judicial propositions and suppositions, see, *supra,* Chapter 5.

that case, briefly stated, are that several doctors were charged with intent to procure abortions under s. 251 of the *Criminal Code*. The main issue was whether s. 251 of the Code infringed upon the right to life, liberty and security of the person under s. 7 of the *Charter*. Although different reasons were given for that decision, the majority of the Supreme Court concluded that s. 251 of the *Criminal Code* violated s. 7 of the *Charter* and could not be saved by s. 1.

I do not dispute the decision itself: to do so would be to confront the Supreme Court at its most progressive. My aim is to critique a hierarchical order of constitutional rights which the court, despite its courageous stand on reproductive rights, adopts. I argue that *Charter* rights are justified according to satisfactory, as distinct from necessary qualities. The *Charter* is the instrument of a wider social discourse about reproductive freedom, not simply an authoritative determinant of specific rights. Finally, that wider discourse encompasses non-judicial actors, including but not limited to judicial interveners.[6]

ON ANALYTICAL RHETORIC

Judges who adhere to the rhetoric of analytical legal positivism[7] orient rights around a strict positivism. In this positive order, all legal rights, fundamental and otherwise, dwell within an authoritative regime of principles. Higher principles of law trump lower ones: *Charter* rights trump legislated interests; statutory rights supersede common law ones.[8] Thus, courts endorse the constitutional right to security of the person. They do not make law. They do not decide whether the right to security of the person is socially valuable. For Mr. Justice Beetz, for example, "examining the content of the rule by which Parliament decriminalizes abortion is the most appropriate first step in considering the validity of s. 251".[9] Thereafter, the court merely decides whether the legislative rule is constitutional in terms of the *Charter*, nothing more. As was claimed in *Morgentaler 1988:*

---

6   I employ this analysis, *supra*, Chapter 4.

7   J. Austin, *Lectures on Jurisprudence*, 5th ed. by R. Campbell (London: J. Murray, 1885); H. Kelsen, "The Pure Theory of Law" (1934), 50 L.Q. Rev. 474; (1935), 51 L.Q. Rev. 517; H.L.A. Hart, "Positivism and the Separation of Law and Morals" (1958), 71 Harv. L. Rev. 593. See too, F.C. DeCoste, "Retrieving Positivism: Law as Bibliolatry" (1990), 13 Dalhousie L.J. 55.

8   See R.M. Dworkin, *A Matter of Principle* (Cambridge: Harvard University Press, 1985), pp. 82-112; *Taking Rights Seriously* (Cambridge: Harvard University Press, 1977), Chapters 3-4; "Political Judges and the Rule of Law" (1980), 64 Proceedings of the British Academy 259. But see Dworkin, *Law's Empire* (Cambridge: Belknap Press, 1986), pp. 87-113.

9   *Morgentaler 1988*, at 87.

It is not necessary in this case [*Morgentaler 1988*] to determine whether th[at] right extends further, to protect either interests central to personal autonomy, such as a right to privacy, or interests unrelated to criminal justice.[10]

By affirming the legislature's authority over reproductive freedom, judges adopt the stance of rational actors: they evaluate the constitutionality of alternative means of accomplishing the legislature's objectives. If they are to preserve democratic rights, they are not justified, as a non-elected body, to tamper with them.[11] If they expect Parliament not to act "so manifestly unfair[ly] . . . as to violate the principles of fundamental justice",[12] they are not to violate the fundamental principles of democracy themselves. So impelled, judges deny their own right to debate the politics of abortion rights "on the basis of how many judges . . . favour 'pro-choice' or 'pro-life'."[13] They do not engage in discourse about abortion policy in contravention of "sound principle and the rule of law [as] affirmed in the preamble to the *Charter*".[14] As Mr. Justice Beetz would have it, "Parliament has recognized that circumstances exist in which an abortion can be procured lawfully."[15] The court obediently follows suit, subject only to the higher principles of the *Charter*.

Each constitutional right to reproductive freedom supposedly rises above public opinion that might otherwise favour or constrain it. "The law has long recognized that the human body ought to be protected from interference by others."[16] Social attitudes and political practices are extra-legal. They are not to influence courts; and if they do, their effect is to be minimized. Judges are not to be partial actors. They are not to perpetuate preferred social attitudes towards reproduction.

This apolitical vision of judging unduly formalizes constitutional law in disregard of its functional application. Constitutional rights are not objects to be re-created by operation of law.[17] Courts are to evaluate them in light of their *ex ante* characteristics, not according to *ex post* authority which judges inject into them.[18] For the Ontario Court of Appeal in *Morgentaler*, "[a] woman's only right to an abortion at the time the

---

10   *Morgentaler 1988*, at 56 *per* Dickson C.J.
11   For detailed discussion hereon, see, *infra*, at 179.
12   *Morgentaler 1988*, at 110 *per* Beetz J.
13   *Ibid*., at 139 *per* McIntyre J.
14   *Ibid*.
15   *Ibid*., at 86.
16   *Ibid*., at 53 *per* Dickson C.J.
17   *Ibid*., at 109-10 *per* Beetz J.
18   For critical commentary on this priority of the right over the good, see esp., M.J. Sandel, *Liberalism and the Limits of Justice* (New York: Cambridge University Press, 1982); A. Arblaster, *The Rise and Decline of Western Liberalism* (Oxford: Basil Blackwell, 1984); A. Gutman, "Children, Paternalism and Education: A Liberal Argument" (1980), 9 Phil. & Pub. Aff. 338. See too, C.E. Baker, "Sandel on Rawls" (1985), 133 U. Pa. L. Rev. 895.

Charter came into force would . . . appear to be that given to her by s-s.
(4) of s. 251 [decriminalizing abortion]."[19] All further rights, following
H.L.A. Hart's "rules of recognition",[20] constitute mere moral expectations.
They lack legal status. As Mr. Justice McIntyre stated in *Morgentaler 1988*:

> . . . the task of the Court in this case is not to solve nor seek to solve
> what might be called the abortion issue, but simply to measure the
> content of s. 251 against the Charter.[21]

Accordingly, the Supreme Court supposedly does not itself recast the
foetal claim to life into a constitutional right to life. As Chief Justice
Dickson would have it:

> . . . foetal interests may well be deserving of constitutional recognition
> . . . [but] Parliament has failed to establish either a standard or a
> procedure whereby any such interests might prevail over those of
> the woman in a fair and non-arbitrary fashion.[22]

This judicial deference toward legislative authority, understandable in
a democratic society, is dysfunctional when it is rigidly applied. The
court presupposes that legislatures make laws, while courts interpret
them. Yet, it passes over the near impossible act of separating interpretation from law-making. To interpret a law is to give it a meaning it did
not have beforehand, indeed, to make law for the present. Despite this,
the court relies upon a restrictive conception of democracy. Parliament,
democratically elected, records the will of the populace; courts, not being
democratically elected, do not. All this presupposes that legislators are
truly representative of the population at large, that they both reflect and
effect its popular will. The proposition itself is seriously questionable.
The constituency system of representation, known as the Westminster
model, does not lead to proportionate representation. The candidate with
the greatest number of votes is elected regardless of the number of votes
cast for the other candidate.[23] Doubtful, too, is the supposition that legislatures, once elected, perpetuate a plural good. Modern history demonstrates that legislatures prioritize the public interest as much in response

---

19   *R. v. Morgentaler* (1985), 22 D.L.R. (4th) 641, at 666, cited with approval in *Morgentaler
      1988*, at 86 *per* Beetz J.
20   See H.L.A. Hart, *The Concept of Law* (New York: Oxford University Press, 1961).
21   *Morgentaler 1988*, at 138 *per* McIntyre J., cited with approval by Dickson C.J. at 46. See
      too, *per* Beetz J. at 88-89. See further hereon, D. Pothier, "Developments in Constitutional
      Law: The 1987-88 Term" (1989), 11 Supreme Court L.R. 41, at 46; A.J. Petter and P. J.
      Monahan, "Developments in Constitutional Law: The 1986-87 Term" (1988), 10 Supreme
      Court L.R. 61, at 70.
22   *Morgentaler 1988*, at 76.
23   The "first past the post" Westminster rule presupposes that the first candidate over
      the post is elected. All other candidates, having received fewer votes, are not elected.
      Under proportionate representation, candidates are chosen in proportion to the total
      number of votes cast.

to political favouritism as to accommodate a truly popular will. They choose to whom to speak and listen. They reflect a political conscience that is selective, not all-embracing. They embrace reproductive rights in light of preferred credos, including their own.

Similarly doubtful is the belief that judges ought never to make law on the grounds that law is circumscribed by a higher constitutional order. No hierarchy of rights, however entrenched in the *Charter*, is self-propelling. No philosophy of rights circumscribes rights, once and for all, for everyone within a free and democratic society. To construct a principled hierarchy of rights is for courts to debate, consciously or otherwise, the history, attitudes and practices of different groups within the polity, including women, pregnant women and disabled women. It is to explore, discover, react to and mediate among differences in perception. In *Morgentaler 1988*, for example, the judges protect pregnant women from invasions of their liberty and personal security only by constructing the substantive content of their rights. They suppose, as Mr. Justice Beetz did, that "'[s]ecurity of the person' *must include* a right of access to medical treatment"[24] only after they have supposed what must be so in fact. Those who propose, in *Singh*, that "it is incumbent upon the Court to give meaning to each of the elements, life, liberty and security of the person"[25] resort as much to their discursive conceptions of substantive justice as to their definitive embodiment within the *Charter*. They argue, in *Morgentaler 1988*, that "[l]iberty in a free and democratic society does not require the state to approve of the personal decisions made by its citizens"[26] only after they themselves have drawn a line between decisions that are personal and decisions in which the public is directly interested.

Judges who disguise their participation within the political process bypass the impact of their own supplementary morality upon constitutional law-making. They assert, too emphatically, that reproductive rights under the *Charter* rise above political morality; but they forget that the constitutional significance of reproductive rights is the product of their interaction within the polity in the first place. They engage in an unduly formal discourse. They insist upon a permanent, rather than temporary, divide between forms of law-making and their substantive reconstruction. They judge forms of law, not the complex social issues that impact upon those forms.

Certainly, judges can construct a necessary relationship between constitutional rights and legislative action within a representative democracy. It seems appropriate, for example, for Madam Justice Wilson in

---

24   *Morgentaler 1988*, at 90 (emphasis added).
25   *Singh v. Minister of Employment & Immigration*, [1985] 1 S.C.R. 177, at 205 *per* Wilson J., affirmed in *Reference re Section 94(2) of the Motor Vehicle Act (B.C.)*, [1985] 2 S.C.R. 486, at 500 *per* Lamer J., and in *Morgentaler 1988*, at 89 *per* Beetz J.
26   *Morgentaler 1988*, at 167 *per* Wilson J.

Morgentaler 1988 to leave to the "informed judgment of the legislature . . . [t]he precise point . . . at which the State's interest in the protection [of the foetus] becomes 'compelling'".[27] However, legislative action is conceived, as much as it is construed, in light of judicial insight into social habit, attitude and practice.[28] For example, Madam Justice Wilson adds social content to both foetal rights and State action when she claims: "[i]t seems to me . . . that it [the State's interest in protecting the foetus] might fall somewhere in the second trimester."[29] By choosing the second trimester, Madam Justice Wilson implicitly makes a decision of substance that rises above the legislature's conception of reproductive rights. She finds satisfaction in that choice, not in the compelling logic of an all-seeing lawmaker.[30] She might have explored, observed and reacted to social and medical practice differently. She might have arrived at a different moment of conception. She might have argued that the State's interest in foetal life arises at the time of conception, during the first or third trimester, or at birth. Quite appropriately, she made a normative election which she might as easily have avoided doing.

Judges can no more squeeze definitive traditions or policies out of a legislative sponge than they can find those traditions or policies neatly arranged within some popular will. Courts are not instruments of a preordained legislative will. They act as forces of social and political propulsion themselves. They investigate and discover the social conditions under which security of the person ought not to be restricted to "physical integrity".[31] They decide when security of the person justifies "[legal] protection against 'overlong subjection to the vexations and vicissitudes of a pending criminal accusation'".[32] They deliberate over when delays in securing abortion services have "profound consequences on the woman's physical and emotional well-being".[33] However hesitatingly, they wet the legislative sponge through communicative discourse. However cautiously, they immerse themselves in the debate about reproductive autonomy. For example, they decide under what conditions reproductive rights are private by drawing a line between reproductive freedom during the first trimester, and the State's interest in foetal life during the second trimester. They know that their choices are cast in clay, not stone. They know, too, that their decisions are satisfactory, as much according to

---

27   *Ibid.*, at 183.
28   *Ibid.*, at 110-11 *per* Beetz J.
29   *Ibid.*, at 183.
30   For the criticism that analytical legal positivism falls short in defining its own scope of application, see in general, S.J. Burton, *An Introduction to Law and Legal Reasoning* (Boston: Little, Brown, 1985). See further, *supra*, Chapter 5.
31   *Mills v. R.*, [1986] 1 S.C.R. 863, at 919-20 *per* Lamer J., affirmed in *Morgentaler 1988*, at 55 *per* Dickson C.J.
32   *Ibid.*
33   *Morgentaler 1988*, at 57 *per* Dickson C.J.

their ability to gauge public attitudes as upon their formal authority as judges.

RATIONALIZED NOT RATIONAL RIGHTS

Charter rights that are treated as *a priori* lead, quite falsely, to rational outcomes. Following *R. v. Oakes,*[34] the Supreme Court regards each *Charter* right as rationally connected to the end that derives from it. Similarly, in *Morgentaler 1988*, it finds truth in a causal relationship between the *Charter's* text and the specific constitutional rights of each pregnant woman, and it concludes that there is only one rational solution that arises from the text. Instead of giving s. 7 rights the meaning it thinks they ought to have, it grounds *Charter* rights in a self-revealing logic. Each s. 7 right is causally linked to principles that are embedded within the *Charter*. Each legal decision derives systematically from the causal relationship between that principle and a particular right.

Consequently, the Supreme Court construes the pregnant woman's right not to be interfered with in seeking an abortion as the rational byproduct of her constitutional right to security of the person.[35] Rationally conceived, her right is also rationally applied to others. As Chief Justice Dickson would have it, her reproductive freedom is necessary, not simply for her as an individual, but for other women in similar circumstances as well. A "profound interference" with her bodily integrity, in effect, violates the personal security of other women as well.[36] Each right-holder therefore receives only as much as the constitutional principle underlying her right justifies. No one receives more or less than any other comparable right-holder.

Judges who place undue reliance upon the rational reason for rights risk passing over the distinction between *rational reason for rights* and *rationalized reason*. "Life", "liberty" and "security of the person" do not have rational meanings that exist *ex ante*. Their meanings are rationalized *ex post*. This occurs when judges impute social qualities to them in light of norms which they consider to be satisfactory and in respect of which others derive satisfaction. For example, in *Morgentaler 1988*, the majority maintained that s. 251 of the *Criminal Code* was unsatisfactory, *inter alia*,

---

[34]   [1986] 1 S.C.R. 103.

[35]   This approach stems, in some measure, from the idealism of natural law. The idealist builds into law an ideological superstructure around the autonomy of individuals. For this coupling of moral idealism with principled legal reasoning, see R.M. Dworkin, *Taking Rights Seriously* (Cambridge: Harvard University Press, 1977), Chapters 3-4; Dworkin, *A Matter of Principle* (Cambridge: Harvard University Press, 1985); Dworkin, "Political Judges and the Rule of Law" (1980), 64 Proceedings of the British Academy 259. But *cf.* M. Weber, *Economy and Society*, G. Roth and C. Wittich, eds. (Berkeley: University of California Press, 1978).

[36]   *Morgentaler 1988*, at 57 *per* Dickson C.J.

because it gave rise to unequal access to abortion services.[37] It rationalized that result. The decision was not rational in itself.

   This rationalization of rights according to explanations that are deemed
to be satisfactory, rather than necessary, is well endorsed in Canadian
jurisprudence. In *Singh*, Madam Justice Wilson rationalized the extent to
which "it is incumbent upon the [Supreme] Court to give meaning to
each of the elements, life, liberty and security of the person, which make
up the 'right' contained in s. 7."[38] Judges rationalize the "minimum content" of rights,[39] their "broadest implications",[40] and some intermediate
status between them. They decide, in *Morgentaler 1988*, when "[t]he full
ambit of this constitutionally protected right will . . . be revealed".[41]
They rationalize rights in light of suppositions and propositions which
they formulate about them. They evaluate reproductive rights in light of
the psychological effect of compulsory child-birth upon pregnant women.
They reflect upon rights in terms of their perceived social costs and
economic benefits.

   Similarly, judges rationalize an expansive or restrictive construction of
legislative interests for reasons which they deem to be satisfactory. Rather
than prove the limits of "fundamental justice" under the *Charter*, they rationalize it selectively. For example, in *Morgentaler 1988,* the Supreme
Court rationalizes both the legislative objectives of s. 251 of the *Criminal
Code* and the means of effecting them. Chief Justice Dickson rationalizes
his conviction "that the means chosen to advance the legislative objectives
of s. 251 do not satisfy . . . [the test in] *Oakes*".[42] Mr. Justice Beetz rationalizes his view that s. 251's infringement of the security of the person of
pregnant women "violates the principles of fundamental justice".[43] Both
establish the relationship between security of the person and substantive
justice liberally, not literally. Both circumscribe reproductive rights, less
through perfectly rational principles of liberty and security of the person,
than through a constructed vision of social justice, whatever the rhetoric
of *R. v. Oakes* might suggest.[44]

   Certainly, judges can give words like life and liberty analytical characteristics. They can distinguish between entrenched and unentrenched
rights, and between unentrenched and moral rights. They can also establish a hierarchy of rights; and they can give to each — to life, liberty, and
security of the person — a precise worth within that hierarchy. They can
insist that each right is valued in proportion to the value of some other

---

37   See, *supra*, at 174.
38   *Supra*, note 25, at 205.
39   *Morgentaler 1988*, at 89 *per* Beetz J.
40   *Ibid.*, at 51 *per* Dickson C.J.
41   *Ibid.*, at 89 *per* Beetz J.
42   *Ibid.*, at 75.
43   *Ibid.*, at 121.
44   See *Oakes, supra*, note 34. For detailed discussion of *Oakes*, see, *supra*, Chapter 5.

right, or conversely, some other duty. However, their rational structure of rights is justifiable only in light of the normative premises that underlie the structure itself. They can conclude that life without liberty is less valuable than life with liberty only after they have chosen the premises upon which to justify the value of each. They can rationalize each premise, but only according to the desirability of the suppositions which they impute to it; and they can maintain those suppositions only in light of the value which they — and others — place upon them. For example, judges can rationalize the opinion that life commences at birth only by refuting the alternative supposition that birth commences at conception.

Reproductive rights are not immaculately sown in legislative fields. Nor can judges reap those fields all by themselves. However, they can no more dispel the effect of social attitudes upon their construction of rights than birds can fly without wings. They can evaluate *Charter* rights by strictly analytical means only by passing over the extent to which they justify those rights in light of the interests of real people with real foibles and real infirmities. Those judges who adhere to a strict analytical su-perstructure of rights, attribute, at most, suppositional and propositional value to them. Those who circumscribe rights functionally, resort to rationalized, not necessary, explanations for their action.[45]

HIERARCHY AS PRINCIPLE

Judges sometimes claim that rights should be pyramided according to a pre-existing constitutional hierarchy with the Charter at its apex.[46] The *Charter*, understandably, serves as the constitutional fountainhead: all rights are subject to its overriding authority. For example, in *Morgentaler 1988*, they "recognize . . . [the] circumstances . . . in which an abortion can be procured lawfully",[47] in light of the higher principle of security of the person. They assume the stance of innocent bystanders. They trace the *Charter* principles embodied in s. 7 to the specific right of pregnant women to bodily integrity.[48] They suppose that they are bound to con-struct constitutional rights as the hierarchy of constitutional rights de-mands. They propose that to move beyond that hierarchy is to threaten the medium by which *Charter* principles evolve into legal rights. "In my opinion", Chief Justice Dickson asserts in *Morgentaler 1988*, "it is neither

---

[45]   See, *supra*, Chapter 5.

[46]   Mr. Justice Ewaschuk, then E.G. Ewaschuk, Q.C., once wrote: "On balance, the Charter should be viewed as a Canadian product which entrenches most safeguards already recognized by statute or at common law and which can work in the context of existing rules and procedures." See "The Charter: An Overview and Remedies" (1982), 26 C.R. (3d) 54, at 90.

[47]   *Morgentaler 1988*, at 86 *per* Beetz J.

[48]   See, *e.g., ibid.*, at 88 *per* Beetz J.

necessary nor wise . . . to explore the broadest implications of s. 7".[49] Indeed, nothing "so early in the history of Charter interpretation",[50] he claims, compels otherwise.

In adopting this hierarchical approach towards rights, judges are to act as instruments of the *Charter*, not as constraints upon legislative and executive sovereignty. "Generally speaking", Chief Justice Dickson explains, courts do not provide remedies for "administrative inefficiencies".[51] They do so only "when denial of a right as basic as security of the person is infringed by the procedure and administrative structures created by the law itself".[52]

This constitutional hierarchy also dictates the moral content of rights. For example, reproductive autonomy is to reside in analytical reason, not in moral speculation.[53] In the tradition of John Austin, courts are not to debate the "merits or demerits" of constitutional law.[54] As Mr. Justice McIntyre would have it, they are to "confine themselves to such democratic values as are clearly found and expressed in the *Charter* and refrain from imposing or creating other values not so based".[55] They are to trace human rights from constitutional axioms to their legislative application under, *inter alia*, the *Criminal Code*.[56] "A right recognized in the Charter is 'to be understood . . . in the light of the interests *it was meant to protect*'";[57] and such interests are to be identified with the *Charter* itself, not with moral expectations beyond it. Envisaged in majority, as in dissent:

> [T]he task of the Court . . . is not to solve nor seek to solve what might be called the abortion issue, but simply to measure the content of s. 251 against the *Charter*.[58]

Similarly, constitutional rights are to be evaluated in light of their objective as distinct from their subjective attributes. According to Mr. Justice Beetz,

> . . . rules unnecessary in respect of the primary and ancillary objectives which they are designed to serve, such as some of the rules contained

---

49   *Ibid.*, at 51. However, Dickson C.J. does add: "I do not think it would be appropriate to attempt an all-encompassing explication of so important a provision as s. 7 so early in the history of *Charter* interpretation."
50   *Ibid.*, at 51 *per* Dickson C.J.
51   *Ibid.*, at 62 *per* Dickson C.J.
52   *Ibid.*
53   See, *supra*, at 53.
54   J. Austin, *Lectures on Jurisprudence*, 5th ed. by R. Campbell (London: J. Murray, 1885).
55   *Morgentaler 1988*, at 137-38.
56   See, *e.g., ibid.*, at 88-89. See too, *R. v. Big M Drug Mart Ltd.*, [1985] 1 S.C.R. 295, at 344, where the status of the accused was treated as irrelevant on grounds that the charge was unconstitutional.
57   *Morgentaler 1988*, at 52 *per* Dickson C.J., quoting *Big M Drug Mart*, *supra*, note 56, at 344 (emphasis added).
58   *Morgentaler 1988*, at 138 *per* McIntyre J.

in s. 251, cannot be said to be rationally connected to these objectives under s. 1 of the *Charter*.[59]

To this Mr. Justice McIntyre adds:

> [T]he courts must not, in the guise of interpretation, postulate rights and freedoms which do not have a firm and reasonably identifiable base in the *Charter*.[60]

In effect the *Morgentaler* court orients human rights around a *Charter* science.[61] It subjects legislation, including the *Criminal Code*, to the guiding light of the *Charter's* own logic. It limits interpretation to scientific principle. "The goal of *Charter* interpretation is to secure for all people 'the full benefit of the *Charter's* protection'."[62] To attain this goal, the substance of human rights' protection is to be found in the *Charter's* internal design. As Mr. Justice McIntyre supposed, "[t]he decisions made by judges . . . must be plausibly inferable from something *in* the *Charter*",[63] not from something outside of it. To be credible, interpretation of the *Charter* is to be purposive. "[T]his Court", Chief Justice Dickson asserted, "has held consistently that the proper technique for the interpretation of *Charter* provisions is a 'purposive' analysis" of rights.[64] To effectuate that purposiveness, the court is to uncover its inherent meaning, not to re-create that meaning injudiciously.

This decontextualization of *Charter* rights cannot be applied too rigidly. After all, judges resort to purposive interpretation of the *Charter* only selectively. They suppose that the "means chosen to achieve an important objective [are] . . . rational, fair and not arbitrary" as *they* construe rationality, fairness and objectivity.[65] They decide when "the effects of the limitation upon the relevant right or freedom [are] . . . out of proportion to the objective sought to be achieved" as *they* explore, discover and respond to such proportions.[66] The Supreme Court supposes, in *R. v. Jones*,[67] that an administrative and procedural structure is "so manifestly unfair . . . as to violate the principles of fundamental justice"[68] only by inferring what is "manifestly unfair" in fact. No scientific principle reveals precisely what degree of wrongfulness is "manifestly unfair". Courts do so dialectically, notably by comparing the treatment accorded pregnant

---

59 *Ibid.*, at 82.
60 *Ibid.*, at 136. McIntyre J. does acknowledge that "a measure of interpretation of the *Charter* will be required in order to give substance and reality to its provisions" (at 136).
61 See in general hereon, H. Kelsen, "The Pure Theory of Law" (1934), 50 L.Q. Rev. 474; (1935), 51 L.Q. Rev. 517.
62 *Morgentaler 1988*, at 51 *per* Dickson C.J., quoting *Big M Drug Mart, supra*, note 56, at 344.
63 *Ibid.*, at 141 (emphasis added).
64 *Ibid.*, at 51-52.
65 *Morgentaler 1988*, at 74 *per* Dickson C.J.
66 *Ibid.*
67 [1986] 2 S.C.R. 284.
68 *Ibid.*, at 304, cited in *Morgentaler 1988*, at 72 *per* Dickson C.J.

women in the different provinces of Canada. They test and retest suppositions about the legitimacy of administrative and procedural structures
governing abortions. They converse about justified ways to explain those
suppositions, and they verify their suppositions by selecting reasons in
support of them. They do all this by talking and listening. They do not
find purposive solutions by observation alone.

Judges cannot have it both ways. They cannot suppose, as John Austin did before them,[69] that the highest purpose of law is obedience to the
precepts of constitutional law, if they themselves repeatedly circumvent
those principles. Nor can they identify constitutional precepts with
Parliament's will, if they treat Parliament's will as unclear and in need of
judicial elaboration. Judges who insist that they interpret the purposes
of the *Charter* solely as they are, can hardly decide exactly what those
purposes ought to mean *ex post facto*.[70] Nor can they reorient reproductive rights around a higher law that is scientifically revealed to them, if,
all the while, they inject disparate conceptions of humanity into that
order. In attempting to achieve both ends, they likely strain the very
scientific hierarchy of constitutional principle they seek to perpetuate.[71]
Either they wait endlessly for the legislature to provide principles upon
which they, judges, can arrive at solutions; or they employ scientific
rhetoric to extend existing principles of law to new situations. Judges
who insist that constitutional law, like breakfast porridge, be prepared
only by legislative chefs, forget that the scientific link between a hierarchy
of constitutional principles and human rights is illusive at best. The
Charter does not have one common design that is wholly self-revealing,
despite the general language used in s. 1. Nor do courts reconstruct
Charter principles into logically consistent patterns of thought. Purposefully or otherwise, they subject constitutional principles to incommensurate explanations. They treat *Charter* rights, less as the product of a scientific free will, than in light of their mediated responses to economic self-
interest within a free market. In each case, they render the *Charter* into a
creature of social action, not the embodiment of truth.

This lack of a self-evident constitutional hierarchy is evident in the
very manner in which judges construe *Charter* rights. However restrictive
they purport to be, they condemn and at the same time, acquiesce in
legislative encroachments upon human rights. They resort to a liberal or
conservative vision of legislative sovereignty. They do not find one de-

---

[69]   Austin, *op. cit.*, note 54.
[70]   On such objective methods of interpretation, see O.M. Fiss, "Objectivity and
        Interpretation" (1982), 34 Stan. L. Rev. 739; B. Langille, "Revolution Without Foundation:
        The Grammar of Scepticism and Law" (1988), 33 McGill L.J. 451; D. Beatty, *Putting the
        Charter to Work* (Kingston and Montreal: McGill-Queen's University Press, 1987).
[71]   See *Reference re Section 94(2) of the Motor Vehicle Act (B.C.)*, [1985] 2 S.C.R. 486 (esp. *per*
        Lamer J.).

terminative *Charter* purpose in *Big M Drug Mart*[72] or one self-revealing interpretation of the rights of the accused in *Oakes*.[73] Thus, the *Morgentaler* judges justify or condemn administrative regulations that govern reproductive rights according to their assessment of the social ill that stems from those regulations. They conclude that "an administrative structure . . . which result[s] in an additional risk to the health of pregnant women, is manifestly unfair" only after they have determined that which ought to be treated as "manifestly unfair"[74] in the first place. They identify fundamental injustices done to pregnant women, less with obvious standards of ill-treatment accorded them, than with differing perceptions of their suffering.[75] In place of an absolute right to reproductive freedom, they preserve a satisfactory freedom. This they do temporarily, not conclusively, partially, not completely.[76]

Realistic judges do what they cannot avoid not doing. They see political reality for what it is. They recognize that, beyond constitutional hierarchies, are real people. People make laws, people construe them and people give them meaning. To take account of the needs and interests of those people, courts move from literal to non-literal methods of interpretation. To effect pragmatic ends, they move from static to dynamic constructions of *Charter* rights. They acknowledge, openly, as Chief Justice Dickson did in *Big M Drug Mart*,[77] that strictly analytical methods of interpreting the *Charter* succumb to constructive methods of interpretation. They appreciate that, to secure for individuals the full benefit of the *Charter's* protection, they are bound to construe the *Charter* "generously", not restrictively.[78] To provide equal protection of the law to pregnant women from both Southern Ontario and Prince Edward Island, they cannot help but realize that abortion-on-demand is not uniformly available to women across Canada. To recognize diffuse constructions of *Charter* rights, they develop formulae for mediating among them; and in mediating among rights, they rely upon suppositions about fact as distinct from fact *per se*.

Thus, the notion that a constitutional hierarchy is scientifically prescribed runs full circle. In place of the hierarchy rises its social context. In place of constitutional principle, judges consider the social effect of State action upon different social needs, interests and wants. In lieu of a uniform moral discourse, they discover and react to disparate moral precepts.

---

72   *R. v. Big M Drug Mart Ltd.*, [1985] 1 S.C.R. 295, at 344.
73   *R. v. Oakes*, [1986] 1 S.C.R. 103.
74   *Morgentaler 1988*, at 110 *per* Beetz J.
75   *Ibid.*
76   See *Big M Drug Mart, supra*, note 72, at 344, cited in *Morgentaler 1988*, at 52 *per* Dickson C.J.
77   *Supra*, note 72, at 344.
78   *Ibid.*, at 344 *per* Dickson C.J.

A PRIORI SOCIAL RIGHTS

> An individual is not a totally independent entity disconnected from
> the society in which he or she lives. Neither, however, is the individual
> a mere cog in an impersonal machine in which his or her values,
> goals and aspirations are subordinated to those of the collectivity.[79]

Judges sometimes illuminate the pathway from constitutional rights
to social justice through an individualized as distinct from a social conception of rights. They do so in the inherent guarantee that the *Charter*,
supposedly, grants to pregnant women under s. 7. It is depicted in Madam
Justice Wilson's contention that

> . . . liberty . . . in s. 7 guarantees to every individual a degree of
> personal autonomy over important decisions intimately affecting their
> private lives.[80]

Pregnant women are entitled to express their reproductive freedom as
individuals, not as a group. To provide them with security of the person
is to entitle each woman to express her rights in her democratic private
sphere, not in some public domain beyond it.[81] Her reproductive freedom
is not an incident of public kindliness, empathy or tolerance towards her,
but the result of a freedom that attaches to her right itself.[82] In effect, the
social context that surrounds reproductive rights is limited to the pregnant
woman as an individual, not to social groups. For the individual to protect
her reproductive rights is to maintain her private sphere, not social aspirations beyond it. To preserve her security is not to respond to the
political sentiment of pro-lifers and pro-choicers towards the unwanted
foetus. To enforce her individual rights is to suppose that the social
worth of those rights is given.[83] It is not to place a protective public fence
around her by insisting that the status of pregnant women, as a group,
subserve to her rights as an individual woman.

Yet, individual rights have a determinative meaning under the *Charter*
as much because courts insist that they ought to, as for any other reason.
For judges to suppose that they protect the individual rights of pregnant
women, not women as a *genus*, is merely to conceptualize a more restrictive form of democracy in place of a broader one. In asserting that

---

[79]   *Morgentaler 1988*, at 164 *per* Wilson J.
[80]   *Ibid.*, at 171 *per* Wilson J. That Wilson J. is a primary source of such *a priori* liberties
         contrasts, quite distinctly, with her singular readiness to comment upon the substance
         of reproductive rights. See further, *infra*, at 189.
[81]   *Ibid.* I discuss this as part of the public-private schism. See, *supra*, Chapter 4.
[82]   In fairness to Madam Justice Wilson, her traditional view of liberal rights is tempered
         by her open vision of women's rights as a social, as distinct from an individual
         phenomenon. Moreover, she alone among the *Morgentaler 1988* judges is willing to base
         the pregnant woman's right directly upon liberty. See esp. *Morgentaler 1988*, at 171-72.
         See too, *infra*, at 189.
[83]   For an extensive discussion of such principled private rights in the context of modern
         liberalism, see, *supra*, Chapter 2.

Canadian courts must ensure "that the legislative initiatives pursued by our Parliament and legislatures conform to the democratic values expressed in the *Canadian Charter of Rights and Freedoms*",[84] Chief Justice Dickson seemingly confines democracy to a particular manifestation of individual rights. That rights have a distinctly communal context is another democratic alternative. Those who reduce democratic rights to the individual's isolated state, to the exclusion of the alternative, reduce the content of democracy itself. Each woman has in common with other women only her desire to be shielded from a State that otherwise might diminish her private autonomy. Her private rights, duly constitutionalized, acquire no normative content beyond their private characteristics. They remain abstract in nature, and neutral in application. Her communal life is fixed in her private status, not in her common identity with other women.

Certainly, the content of individual rights is prescribed by individual conscience. As Chief Justice Dickson and Madam Justice Wilson would have it:

> The values that underlie our political and philosophic traditions demand that every individual be free to hold and to manifest whatever beliefs and opinions his or her conscience dictates . . .[85]

However, in construing the reproductive rights of pregnant women privately, judges sometimes impede meaningful discourse into social conceptions of rights. They raise individual rights above countervailing social policies by maintaining that "the basic theory underlying the *Charter* . . . [is] that the state will respect choices made by individuals".[86] They insist that to do otherwise would constitute "profound interference with"[87] each woman's autonomy over her body. The rights discourse ends where it began, in the neutral camp of the habituated individual. In passing over the social context surrounding reproductive rights, Mr. Justice Beetz supposes that security of the person under s. 7 of the *Charter* "must include" the pregnant woman's "right of access to medical treatment".[88] He so concludes as a matter of principle, not in light of the desirability or expediency of reproductive freedom. Constitutional rights, it would seem, are prescribed wholly by law. A *Charter* right is "to be understood . . . in the light of *the [legal] interests it was meant to protect*".[89] All this presupposes that the legal interests which the *Charter* was meant to protect

---

84 In *Morgentaler 1988*, at 46 *per* Dickson C.J.
85 *Big M Drug Mart, supra*, note 72, at 346 *per* Dickson C.J. (emphasis added), cited with approval in *Morgentaler 1988*, at 177 *per* Wilson J.
86 *Morgentaler 1988*, at 166 *per* Wilson J.
87 *Ibid.*, at 57 *per* Dickson C.J.
88 *Ibid.*, at 90 *per* Beetz J.
89 *Big M Drug Mart, supra*, note 72, at 344 *per* Dickson J. (emphasis added). See too, *Hunter v. Southam Inc.*, [1984] 2 S.C.R. 145; *R. v. Therens*, [1985] 1 S.C.R. 613.

somehow rise above social justice. It suggests, further, that any reflection upon the social character of those interests undermines their constitutional value.[90]

Why judges do not wish to recast private into social rights is quite understandable. To insist that reproductive rights are wholly private is to risk being accused of the very sin judges wish to avoid: being guided by an unprincipled construction of rights in conflict with the principles of democratic government. In addition, judges who engage in social law reform hazard manipulating gender relations in the interests of a biased conception of the "public good". By treating the reproductive rights of pregnant women as abstract, principled and private, they avoid having to balance the social interests of warring groups of pro-choicers and pro-lifers. By allowing fundamental rights to rise above social interests, they avoid being labelled unprincipled, or being accused of adopting one vision of social morality above all others.[91]

Yet, judges who opt out of the social life of pregnant women as a *genus*, assume that they have no obligation towards the *genus*, only towards the individual. They sometimes overlook the fact that liberty and security of the person are as communal as they are private. They disregard the observation that pregnancy, instead of being an isolated state, is a communal condition that embraces groups in which individuals, including pregnant women, participate.[92] In addition, they risk isolating the individual woman from the common weal, as from other pregnant women. They play down her communality of interest in favour of her abstract and decontextualized self. They assume that, for her to be unrestrained in her human relations, she must be subject to a law that "has long recognized that the human body ought to be protected *from interference by others*."[93] They insist upon her solitary status, even though in doing so they possibly undermine an important part of her interest as a woman, namely, her communal identity.[94]

RECONSTRUCTING COMMUNAL RIGHTS

A communal conception of rights extends fundamental freedom beyond the abstract right-holder. Judges who apply it conceive of liberty and security of the person according to communal properties that supersede, yet still include, private rights. They entertain a diverse social programme

---

90   See *Morgentaler 1988*, at 53 *per* Dickson C.J.
91   This desire to avoid controversy is often reformulated as a judicial wish not to engage in complex social reform. See further hereon, *infra*, at 196.
92   On the communal division of rights, see, *infra*, Chapter 3. See too, W. Kymlicka, "Liberalism as Communitarianism" (1988), 18 Can. J. Phil. 181.
93   *Morgentaler 1988*, at 53 *per* Dickson C.J. (emphasis added).
94   On such human associations, see esp. Chapter 3.

that embodies the biological, religious and cultural character of pregnancy and foetal life. Their programme is discursive, reflective, and functional. They engage in social discourse about the quality of reproductive life. They reflect upon disparate communal impressions of it; and they propose functional accommodations to such disparities. At their most aggressive, they identify reproductive freedom with the emancipation of women from an intolerant male image of them as childbearers and mothers.[95] At their most proactive, they assert reproductive rights as the means of ensuring the mutual respect of women for women, and hopefully, of men for women too. At their most far-sighted, they justify treating women differently from men on grounds that women are different in fact. As Madam Justice Wilson would have it,

> [i]t is probably impossible for a man to respond, even imaginatively, to such a dilemma not just because it is outside the realm of his personal experience . . . but because he can relate to it only by objectifying it . . .[96]

Thus, Madam Justice Wilson links social unity to the distinctiveness of the pregnant women's voice. Each woman is galvanized into unity with others through her discourse into freedom-as-choice and freedom-from-choice. A subject and an object of conversation about reproductive rights, she politicizes rights as much as she is politicized by them. Her politicization of reproductive autonomy takes the form of communicative discourse about rights. Her physical autonomy consists of an organic condition that she shares with other women. Her personal security evolves into an integral part of her struggle against the debilitating effect of domination over her.[97] Thus, she finds virtue in identifying with others as much as in disassociating from them.[98] No longer a classless person, she acquires standing according to the quality of treatment which they accord her and others like her. Her reproductive freedom evolves into an

---

95 See esp., C.A. MacKinnon, "Privacy v. Equality: Beyond *Roe v. Wade*", in *Feminism Unmodified: Discourses on Life and Law* (Cambridge: Harvard University Press, 1987), pp. 93-102. See too, S.B. Boyd and E.A. Sheehy, "Feminist Perspectives on Law: Canadian Theory and Practice" (1986), 2 Can. J. Women & L. 1; A.C. Scales, "The Emergence of Feminist Jurisprudence: An Essay" (1986), 95 Yale L.J. 1373; A. Bottomley, S. Gibson and B. Meteyard, "Dworkin; Which Dworkin? Taking Feminism Seriously" (1987), 14 J.L. & Society 47.

96 *Morgentaler 1988*, at 171 *per* Wilson J.

97 *Ibid.* See, in general, S.A. Gavigan, "Women and Abortion in Canada: What's Law Got to Do with It?", in *Feminism and Political Economy: Women's Work, Women's Struggles*, H.J. Maroney and M. Luxton, eds. (Toronto: Methuen, 1987), p. 263.

98 See, *e.g.*, H. Lessard, "The Idea of the 'Private': A Discussion of State Action Doctrine and Separate Sphere Ideology" (1986), 10 Dalhousie L.J., No. 2, p. 107. See too, S.M. Okin, "Justice and Gender" (1987), 16 Phil. & Pub. Aff. 42; M.J. Mossman, "Individualism and Community: Family as a Mediating Concept", in *Law and the Community: The End of Individualism?*, A.C. Hutchinson and L.J. Green, eds. (Toronto: Carswell, 1989), p. 205.

expression of her worth as a social being, not simply as one "human being" separated from all others.[99]

Whether or not women actually agree upon the social significance of their legal rights, difference in viewpoint is part of their discourse. It solidifies their debate over the limits to which they should tolerate stereotype images that others, men or women, impose upon them. It gives social significance to their assertion that they are a disadvantaged group. It is part of their social agenda. Through it, they assert their interests as women, no matter how differently they conceive of them.

The *Morgentaler* majority, consciously or otherwise, appreciates this social sphere that surrounds reproductive autonomy. Both Chief Justice Dickson and Madam Justice Wilson treat the right to security of the person as part of the shared heritage of pregnant women.[100] Even Mr. Justice McIntyre, in dissent, supposes that access to abortion facilities transcends narrow *a priori* rights to personal security.[101] Each judge evaluates reproductive freedom in light of its social justification. Each treats the individual's autonomy from physical and mental invasion in light of its communal ramifications. Each identifies reproductive freedom with the social context in which it arises;[102] and each avers that "the proper approach to the definition of the rights and freedoms guaranteed by the *Charter* [is] . . . purposive, not rationally self-evident."[103]

Judges who favour such a social conception of reproductive freedom engage in a communal discourse about the relationship between pregnant women, as a group, and the life of the polity. They root reproductive rights in political conversation about the rights of pregnant women to autonomy over their bodies.[104] They suppose, at their most assertive, that the compulsion to reproduce enslaves women. They argue, at their most formal, that to deprive women of their s. 7 rights "*cannot* be in accordance with the principles of fundamental justice."[105] This social conversation about the impact of reproductive autonomy upon the status of women is implicit in much of *Morgentaler 1988*. For Mr. Justice Beetz, security of the person is linked to the distinctly public threat to the life and

---

[99]   On feminist characterizations of women's experience, see esp., R. West, "Jurisprudence and Gender" (1988), 55 U. Chi. L. Rev. 1; D. Greschner, "Feminist Concerns with the New Communitarians: We Don't Need Another Hero", in *Law and the Community, supra*, note 98, at 119.

[100] *Morgentaler 1988*, at 53-63 *per* Dickson C.J., and at 173-74 *per* Wilson J.

[101] *Ibid.*, at 142-49.

[102] The indeterminacy of rights is discussed in detail, *supra*, Chapter 5.

[103] *Reference re Section 94(2) of the Motor Vehicle Act (B.C.)*, [1985] 2 S.C.R. 486, at 499, referring with approval to *Hunter v. Southam Inc.*, [1984] 2 S.C.R. 145. See too *R. v. Therens*, [1985] 1 S.C.R. 613.

[104] See hereon esp., C. MacKinnon, "The Male Ideology of Privacy: A Feminist Perspective on the Right to Abortion" (1983), 17 Radical America 23. See B. Cossman, "The Precarious Unity of Feminist Theory and Practice: The Praxis of Abortion" (1986), 44 U.T. Fac. L. Rev. 85.

[105] *Morgentaler 1988*, at 175 *per* Wilson J. (emphasis added).

health of pregnant women.[106] For Chief Justice Dickson and Madam Justice Wilson, *Criminal Code* restrictions upon reproductive autonomy threaten the security of women as a *genus*, beyond the security of the individual.[107] For each, the legal character of fundamental rights and freedoms is the product of social history and political experience. It is reflected in religious traditions and social attitudes, in the sexual revolution and the political characterization of bodily integrity.

This publicization of private rights by the *Morgentaler* judges is singularly unavoidable. Those judges who trust in a strictly private autonomy perpetuate the facade of personal freedom in the face of the distinctly public context that surround them. They pretend to say "as little as possible to dispose of the case",[108] all the while employing public gamesmanship to say more. Private illusion is an important part of their fairytale world. However, for them to suppose that reproductive freedom is a private beacon high in the sky, is to build a stairway to nowhere. Judges who insist upon a "generous rather than [a] legalistic"[109] construction of reproductive rights inject a communal notion of "generosity" into them. They avoid "manufactur[ing] a constitutional right out of whole cloth"[110] only by choosing a social context in which to frame that right. In no case do they link liberty inextricably to one unified conception of "fundamental justice". In no case do they allow s. 7 rights to weave their own private web in the presence of their public character.

Certainly, judges can insist that the legitimation of a public interest in reproductive autonomy is likely to invite injudicious capriciousness in relation to human rights. However, they cannot avoid politics entirely in construing rights. Chief Justice Dickson embraces constitutional politics in *Morgentaler 1988*, albeit negatively, when he alleges that "courts are *not* the appropriate forum for articulating complex and controversial programmes of public policy."[111] Mr. Justice Beetz engages in politics when he insists that the court accord the legislature "a certain latitude to make

---

106   *Ibid.*, at 90 *per* Beetz J.

107   *Ibid.*, at 53-63 *per* Dickson C.J., and at 173-74 *per* Wilson J.

108   See D. Pothier, "Developments in Constitutional Law: The 1987-88 Term" (1989), 11 Supreme Court L.R. 41. Dianne Pothier summarizes the multiple decisions in *Morgentaler 1988*: "Each of the four judgments takes quite a different approach to s. 7. Justice McIntyre, in dissent, finds no deprivation of any of the interests protected by s. 7, nor any infringement of the principles of fundamental justice. Justice Beetz finds a limited deprivation of security of the person, and identifies a contravention of the principles of fundamental justice by focusing on procedural aspects. The Chief Justice finds a substantial interference with security of the person, but limits his discussion of fundamental justice to the identification of procedural defects. Madam Justice Wilson finds a deprivation of both liberty and security of the person, as well as a violation of both procedural and substantive principles of fundamental justice" (at 46).

109   *Re B.C. Motor Vehicle Act*, *supra*, note 103, at 500 *per* Lamer J. See too *Hunter v. Southam Inc.*, *supra*, note 103, at 156 *per* Dickson J.

110   *Morgentaler 1988*, at 141 *per* McIntyre J.

111   *Ibid.*, at 46 (emphasis added).

choices regarding the type of administrative structure that will suit its needs".[112] In each case, judges devise a political bridge between private rights and governmental schemes. They do so when they observe, as Madam Justice Wilson did in *Singh*, that, under s. 7 of the *Charter*, "everyone has the right to life, liberty and security of the person, and the right not to be deprived thereof except in accordance with the principles of fundamental justice".[113] They do so too when they allege, as Mr. Justice McIntyre did in *Morgentaler 1988*, that "[a] court is not entitled to define a right in a manner unrelated to the interest which the right . . . was meant to protect."[114]

This is not to suggest that the socialization of rights beyond the self-serving individual necessarily protects women as a *genus*. Groups are every bit as negatively stereotyped as child-bearers or sex partners for their spouses as are individuals. However, their "right to reproduce or not to reproduce . . . [is] an integral part of [their] *modern woman's* struggle".[115] It is directed at a shared, not a private identity. It embraces the individual woman in relation to others in society, not as distinct from them. The struggle for reproductive autonomy.

> . . . deeply reflects the way the woman thinks about herself and her relationship to others and to society at large . . . it is a profound social and ethical [decision] . . .[116]

Consequently, it is precisely because women often are isolated as a *genus* that their constitutional rights should be socialized. It is for that reason, too, that courts need to recognize the collective self-determination of women, beyond their individual rights.

CONTINGENT RIGHTS

> Rights are those conditions of social life without which no man can seek, in general, to be himself at his best. For since the State exists to make possible that achievement, it is only by maintaining rights that its end may be secured.[117]

Certainly, judges can idealize objectivity in construing *Charter* rights. They can declare, as Mr. Justice Dickson did in *Big M Drug Mart*, that "[t]he task of the [Supreme] Court is not to choose between substantive or

---

[112]   *Ibid.*, at 109-10, citing *R. v. Jones*, [1986] 2 S.C.R. 284, at 304.
[113]   *Singh v. Minister of Employment & Immigration*, [1985] 1 S.C.R. 177, at 201.
[114]   *Morgentaler 1988*, at 140.
[115]   *Ibid.*, at 172 *per* Wilson J. (emphasis added).
[116]   *Ibid.*, at 171 *per* Wilson J.
[117]   H.J. Laski, *A Grammar of Politics*, 5th ed. (London: G. Allen & Unwin, 1948). In liberal rhetoric, the common good is attained, first, by supposing that the central role of social regulation is to protect private rights, and secondly, by assuming that the State is duty-bound to fulfil this function. See J.S. Mill, *Utilitarianism, Liberty, Representative Government* (London: Everyman's Library, 1968).

procedural content [of rights] *per se*, but to secure for persons 'the full benefit of the *Charter's* protection'."[118] However, they cannot help but define that "full benefit" in normative terms. They cannot give meaning to life, liberty and security of the person without rejecting alternative meanings. To determine that "[t]he interpretation [of the Charter] should be . . . a generous rather than a legalistic one"[119] they decide against a stricter method of construction. To "guarantee and secure for individuals the full benefit of the *Charter's* protection"[120] they choose the substantive content and means of effecting that "guarantee".

Judges who raise fundamental human rights into manna from heaven, ultimately undermine their own stance. They suppose that the *Charter* provides a perfected mechanism through which courts exhaust constitutional rights. They aver, all too emphatically, as Mr. Justice McIntyre did in *Morgentaler 1988*, that "[i]t is not for the courts to manufacture a constitutional right out of whole cloth."[121] They sometimes miss an essential point, that legislation is a vehicle of law-making, not a conclusive determinant of it. They forget that, in striking down legislation that undermines security of the person, they cross the procedural threshold between parliamentary sovereignty and the judicial reconstruction of rights. They disregard the fact that no legislated principle clearly circumscribes the reach of reproductive autonomy for all time. They ignore the extent to which Parliament is unable to unravel such complex human rights issues without judicial coaxing.[122]

Judges who claim to be guided by scientific reason cannot completely displace the impact of normative thought upon their decisions. No matter how extensive medical study into foetal life, medical science cannot give exact weight to foetal life. No matter how extensive the medical examination of pregnant women, it cannot predict the exact effect of psychological and emotional trauma upon them. Like legal opinion, medical opinion is based upon satisfactory, not conclusive opinion. No perfect syllogism establishes the exact biological or legal moment at which foetal life comes into existence. Scientific investigation, like legal analysis, commences with diffuse suppositions about the quality of foetal life and maternal stress in nurturing "life". Medical analysis reflects selected suppositions and propositions about the nature and quality of life. No medical belief is wholly self-inspired. No scientific supposition or proposition is determinative by itself.[123] Judges, too, are motivated by normative suppositions when they decide upon the constitutional rela-

---

[118]   *Re B.C. Motor Vehicle Act, supra,* note 103, at 499. See too, *R. v. Big M Drug Mart Ltd.,* [1985] 1 S.C.R. 295, at 344.

[119]   *Big M Drug Mart, supra,* note 118, at 344.

[120]   *Ibid.*

[121]   *Morgentaler 1988,* at 141.

[122]   See further, *supra,* Chapter 5.

[123]   For a critique of "obvious" truths, see, *supra,* Chapter 5.

tionship between the *Criminal Code* and *Charter* rights. They are influenced by belief when they decide what weights to attribute to the medical opinions expressed in the Powell[124] and Badgley Reports.[125] They explore medical opinion equally normatively when they debate the harmful effect of delayed abortion procedures.

Certainly, judges can defer to medical expertise. They can allude to their limited ability to arrive at the exact intensity of the pregnant woman's psychological stress in being denied access to abortion facilities. However, they cannot ignore the fact that doctors have no magic formula by which to access the pregnant woman's feelings of stress and indignity. Doctors do not agree upon the mental and physical effect of stress upon pregnancy, just as judges do not concur in the constitutional significance of such stress. No opinion, medical or legal, is sacred in itself. No medical or legal principle tells its own tale. Judges themselves decide when abortion procedures are manifestly unfair, and when those procedures "contain . . . many potential barriers" that render abortions "practically unavailable to [some] women".[126] They gauge the mental and physical state of women. They decide, too, upon the extent to which each woman suffers harm in the face of barriers to abortion services. They cannot be neutral towards reproductive rights and still balance those rights against the interests of government. They cannot regulate reproductive rights, without attributing a preferred meaning to them. They cannot arrive at a proportionate relationship between governmental objectives and means of fulfilling them without attributing weights to those proportions themselves.[127]

Certainly, courts can contend that life, liberty and security of the person have obvious worth, and further that this worth is evident for all rational persons to observe. They can conjure up a loosely causal connection between so-called fundamental rights and those who hold them. They can balance the woman's "psychological stress" and "trauma" in not receiving an abortion against her stress and trauma in having one. They can also attach rational properties to the observation that 58% of all Canadian hospitals cannot muster abortion committees,[128] that most women must travel at least some distance to obtain abortion services,[129] and that delay in receiving an abortion increases the risk of medical complications.[130] They can suppose, too, that their observations favour

---

[124]   Ontario, *Report on Therapeutic Abortion Services in Ontario* (Toronto: Ministry of Health, 1987) (Powell Report).

[125]   Canada, *Report of the Committee on the Operation of the Abortion Law* (Ottawa: Minister of Supply & Services, 1977) (Badgley Report).

[126]   *Morgentaler 1988*, at 72-73.

[127]   But *cf.*, D. Beatty, *Talking Heads and the Supremes: The Canadian Production of Constitutional Review* (Toronto: Carswell, 1990).

[128]   *Morgentaler 1988*, at 66 *per* Dickson C.J.

[129]   *Ibid.*, at 70-72 *per* Dickson C.J.

[130]   *Ibid.*, at 59 *per* Dickson C.J.

reproductive freedom; and they can identify that determination with the autonomy of the individual. In Chief Justice Dickson's opinion,

> . . . the right to life, liberty and security of the person [represents] a wide-ranging right to control one's own life and to promote one's individual autonomy. The right would therefore include . . . a right to make unfettered decisions about one's own life.[131]

Nevertheless, no matter how rational reproductive rights might appear to be, judges cannot *know* whether and how the *Charter* defines its own scope of operation. They cannot move, with perfect ease, from constitutional rights to juristic truth.[132] Reproductive rights acquire their authority, not simply from s. 7 of the *Charter*, but from each judge's vision of the impact of social interests upon them. Judges who construct a relationship between fundamental justice and s. 7 rights give a diffuse meaning to both. When they argue, as Beetz J. did, that "s. 251(4), taken as a whole, does not accord with the principles of fundamental justice",[133] they conjure up a selective explanation for fundamental justice.[134] When they insist that "some" procedural requirements of s. 251 "are manifestly unfair",[135] they choose those social conditions under which, they believe, unfairness arises. Far from treating substantive justice as a conclusive fact, they identify justice with distinctly human subjects. To their wants and needs, they add their own expectations, along with the expectations of others. They do all this through an open, not a closed discourse, through debate, not simply observation.

Those courts that admit openly that they influence the substance of *Charter* rights accept the presence of contingent truth. They realize that reproductive rights are contingent upon preferred premises and satisfactory means of justifying them.[136] They appreciate the normative underpinnings of access to abortion facilities. They recognize, too, the variable extent to which pregnant women who are denied such access suffer. In short, judges do far more than interpret legislative action: they guide it too. They treat legislation that restricts abortion services as "complex and controversial"[137] largely in light of the manner in which they understand, and ultimately judge, "public policy" that surrounds those services. They render administrative schemes tenable according to the perceived quality of social discourse into those schemes.

In truth, judges can no more avoid contextualizing reproductive rights than they can bypass the political hierarchy that surrounds humanity

---

131 *Ibid.*, at 51.
132 See, *supra*, at 156.
133 *Morgentaler 1988*, at 110.
134 On judicial understandings, see, *supra,* Chapter 5.
135 *Morgentaler 1988*, at 110 *per* Beetz J.
136 See, *e.g., Morgentaler 1988*, at 162-63 *per* Wilson J.
137 *Ibid.*, at 46 *per* Dickson C.J.

itself. It is judges who transform the right of pregnant women to make unfettered personal decisions into contingent truth. It is judges who risk dehumanizing pregnant women by denying them their reproductive autonomy as a group. It is judges, too, who reflect upon the social value of foetal life in propogating the human species, and reproductive autonomy in foiling attempts to reduce women into public chattel.

CONCLUSION

Reproductive autonomy personifies more than sycophantic individualism. It embodies more, too, than archetypical private properties which are imputed, somewhat mechanically, to individuals. Reproductive rights reflect a social interest in reproductive life itself. That interest is both personal and public. It transcends yet includes the individual. It is a very essence of communal life. Marked by discourse into social practice, it is determined by the understandings of those who engage in communicative dialogue, as well as by those who draw inferences from it.[138] Thus, each woman's right to have an abortion is justified in light of the social conditions that are deemed to affect the pregnancy of women as a *genus*. Her rights are the product of judicial constructions of the public debate into the unequal access of pregnant women to abortion services, the reason for that inequality, and its perceived effects upon pregnant women in general. That some women have limited resources to defray abortion costs, while others are not so limited, is itself a social consideration. That some abortion procedures give rise to greater risk than others is equally a public concern. Each concern likely impacts upon the manner in which judges, in *Morgentaler 1988* as elsewhere, form their opinions.

Judges who emphatically deny that they engage in substantive law-making about reproductive rights engage in dubious reasoning. They ignore the fact that they themselves construct "democratic values" in carrying out "legislative initiatives".[139] They decide which application of rights ought to be treated as "fundamental". They decide which rights ought to succumb to State action. That their construction of rights differs is evident from the different opinions in *Morgentaler 1988*. That they cannot agree upon the precise nature of reproductive autonomy demonstrates that they, like the rest of us, have imperfect vision.

I do not suggest that individual rights are mere appendages to social life. To believe in social action is also to believe that one manifestation of it resides in the individual. However, to isolate the rights of pregnant women from the social milieu in which they are exercised is to displace the very interdependence that exists between those rights and the polity beyond them. It is to marginalize the common plight of pregnant women,

---

[138]   This public nature of rights is discussed, in considerable detail, *supra*, Chapter 5.
[139]   *Morgentaler 1988*, at 46 *per* Dickson C.J.

indeed, to undermine the social struggle to promote the dignity of women as a *genus*.[140] Reproductive rights are dynamic. They evolve both singularly and collectively. They are diffuse in social effect. They add force to private life through, rather than to the exclusion of, the society that surrounds each individual.

Both fundamental rights and substantial justice are contingent upon normative properties that a diverse discourse instils in them.[141] Neither doctors nor judges are the sole determinants of those properties. Both are participants within a far wider discourse that includes myriads of others.[142]

---

[140] See *Morgentaler 1988*, at 171-72 *per* Wilson J. See further, *supra,* Chapter 4.
[141] On this communicative discourse, see, *supra*, Chapter 3.
[142] On conceptions of community in difference, see, *supra*, at 78.

CHAPTER 7

REFLECTIONS

One problem with negative conceptions of individual rights is that they are construed as excluding other visions of liberty. The individual, free to isolate herself from others, gives no normative content to civil society beyond her negative self. The result is a private realm that is no greater than the plurality of individuals who function within it; and a public realm that acquires meaning only through a monolithic State, not through the citizens who empower it.

This book seeks two primary ends: to extend judicial discourse beyond individual rights; and to highlight the relationship between social action and judicial decisions that impact upon that action. Thus, the freedom to speak and associate encompasses the collective rights of women, aboriginal peoples and Jehovah's Witnesses. It takes account of the distributive suffering of, *inter alia*, indentured labourers, exploited consumers, and abused children. It extends beyond the individual's negative rights under ss. 2 and 7-14 of the *Charter.* It encompasses communal justifications for rights and freedoms.

Judges who endorse this extended interpretation of constitutional rights evaluate them in light of their social properties. Rather than trust in pre-existing qualities that are embedded in rights themselves, they construct those qualities in light of communal — including judicial — practice. Thus, they endorse the right to advertise, strike, pray, or trade on Sundays selectively, in light of social dissonance or harmony which they attribute to it. They do not simply choose between foetal and reproductive rights: they take account of the perceived public harm that arises from constrained pregnancy and unwanted life. They do not formally legitimate the rights of disadvantaged aboriginal peoples: they consider the social costs of doing so. So motivated, judges do not treat French Canadians, First Nation Peoples, blacks and Asian Canadians as plural right-holders. They evaluate their rights in light of the treatment accorded them historically and conventionally. They apply more than predetermined principles of law to them: they engage in communicative discourse about them.

This wider sphere of public life, arguably, is embedded in the spirit of the *Charter*, notably in s. 1. It is explicit in the endorsement of bilingualism under s. 23, multiculturalism under s. 27, aboriginal rights under s. 25 and the rights of the disadvantaged under s. 15(2). It is also implicit in the realization that *Charter* rights are expressions of communal interest, however privately they are framed.

Some will argue that, to affirm rights and freedoms so communally, I have advanced an unrealistic hope that is unlikely to come to fruition. Indeed, if cases like *Morgentaler*[1] and *Borowski*[2] depict anything, it is that the Supreme Court of Canada is likely to evaluate human rights as a contest between individual and intruding government, less as a normative condition underlying social life itself. However, these critics likely fail to appreciate that human rights are not composed wholly individualistically, or totally competitively. They are as positive as they are negative. They are as open to variable discourse about human rights as to the objective verification of those rights. Thus, courts deal with rights, less as abstract entitlements, than as social and ultimately, judicial constructions. They identify the right to pray, not only with the isolated individual, but also with the impact of religion upon piety, atheism and agnosticism. They construct rights imaginatively in their social context, not in a communicative void. They subject those rights to mediation as much as they constrain themselves in light of them.

One can hardly castigate judges for claiming that they ought not to engage in normative decision-making about rights and freedoms. Injudicious law-making by judges may well regress into selective thumb-sucking. However, judges cannot hide their interpretation of fundamental rights and freedoms behind the bushel of "obvious" meaning. Nor can they construct the meaning of *Charter* language by wholly objective means. Courts cannot be apolitical and yet participate in political discourse. They cannot be wholly neutral towards private rights and State interests, yet find some pre-arranged division between private and public life that remains wholly consistent over time. Judges do not dwell within an "empty promised land".[3] They face — indeed, endure — inconsonant ideologies and sentiments, not least of all their own. Their explanations for human rights, far from being carved in stone, reflect the incompleteness of their understanding about the nature of rights and freedoms, along with everyone else's limited understanding. The reliability of their decisions depends upon the manner in which popular — and unpopular — conceptions of rights and freedoms are conveyed to them.

However neutral and objective judges claim to be, they cannot arrive at decisions in a social vacuum. They cannot pretend that an imperfect process of social discourse evolves that excludes them. Nor can they

---

[1]   *R. v. Morgentaler*, [1988] 1 S.C.R. 30.
[2]   *Borowski v. Canada (A.G.)*, [1989] 1 S.C.R. 342.
[3]   A. Camus, *The Rebel*, trans. A. Bower (New York: Knopf, 1971), p. 305.

render that discourse principled without reconstructing it. For judges to devise an aloof juridical science that somehow excludes political and moral discourse, is not only for them to pretend. It is for them to hide that discourse *within* the very rules and principles which they employ to exclude it.

Judges who earnestly deny that they engage in social conversation about *Charter* rights merely disguise their sentiment as principled reason. They recast political conceptions of rights into self-explanatory rights and freedoms. At their most mysterious, they interpret the *Charter* in light of decontextualized principles that lead inevitably to clear and predictable results. At their most realistic, however, they construct those principles within an open conversation. They exchange thoughts, sentiments and opinion with others, not limited to judges. They are informed — and they inform others — in light of social history, communicative experience and normative practice. They listen, just as they speak, understand, just as they convey understanding. They arrive at mediated solutions, without negating the value of difference.

I end as I began. My goal is to confront the illusion of the autonomous individual who possesses fixed rights. My aim is to challenge the myth of a determinative State that displaces human rights at will. Both extremes are not only in conflict. They are mutually destructive. The State is far from a monolithic intruder that undermines the fundamental rights and freedoms of individuals. Individuals are far from unified subjects who stand together against the State. The position of each is the product of sentiment as much as reason, conviction as much as fact. Judges who raise objective reason above sentiment create only the illusion of legal certainty. Those who raise sentiment above reason open the door to judicial despotism. The alternative is to deny absolute reign to both.

EPILOGUE

Several days after I had completed this book, the Supreme Court of Canada handed down two important decisions: *McKinney v. Bd. of Governors of the University of Guelph*[1] and *R. v. Keegstra*.[2] I have briefly integrated comments about both these decisions in the text. However, as *Keegstra*, a race hatred case, is central to my analysis, I highlight additional aspects of it here. The goal is to evaluate the reasoning used, not the result.

In *R. v. Keegstra*, the Supreme Court of Canada, in overruling the Alberta Court of Appeal,[3] upheld s. 319 of the *Criminal Code* of Canada, rendering the wilful promotion of hatred criminal.[4] The Court maintained that, while s. 319 violates s. 2(*b*) of the *Charter*, it was saved by s. 1.[5] This analysis of ss. 1 and 2 of the *Charter* is not wholly novel. However, the Court does transcend its more traditional method of reasoning in a number of respects.

First, the Supreme Court emphasizes that freedom of association addresses, not the isolated individual, but communal values beyond her. In particular, the majority states that "self-autonomy stems in large part from one's ability to articulate and nurture an identity derived from membership in a cultural or religious group".[6] This proposition accords with my central contention, that autonomy is associated as much with communal interaction as with the rights of individuals.[7]

Second, the majority explicitly recognizes that the State is not the sole determinant of public life. In particular, it proposes that the State should not be viewed as "the sole arbiter of truth".[8] In orienting truth around social practice, the Court transcends the narrow public-private divide in which private is associated wholly with the individual's sphere and public with the State. This expanded vision of public life is central to Chapter 4 of this work.

---

[1]   (1990), 76 D.L.R. (4th) 545.
[2]   (1990), 61 C.C.C. (3d) 1.
[3]   (1988), 43 C.C.C. (3d) 150.
[4]   *Supra*, note 2, at 72-73 *per* Dickson C.J.
[5]   *Ibid.*, at 27-73.
[6]   *Ibid.*, at 49.
[7]   See, *supra*, Chapters 2 and 3.
[8]   See, *supra*, note 2, at 49.

Third, both the majority and minority in *Keegstra* acknowledge the significance of contingent truth in judicial reasoning. For example, the majority states that "it [is] impossible to know with *absolute* certainty which factual statements are true, or which ideas obtain the greatest good".[9] In a similar way, the minority argues that freedom of expression provides "no *guarantee* that truth will *always* prevail."[10] This conception of contingent knowledge and truth is central to the critique of rational discourse in Chapter 5.

Fourth, the Court treats freedom of expression as contingent rather than absolute in nature. Thus, the majority "balances" competing rights and freedoms, rather than simply finds them.[11] The minority adds that "different justifications for freedom of expression may assume varying degrees of importance in different fact situations".[12] This contextualizing of rights and freedoms is central to the analysis in Chapters 2 and 3.

Finally, the court does not place unbridled faith in strict principles of rationality, notwithstanding its resort to the *Oakes'* test.[13] The majority claims, quite explicitly, that "it is dangerously misleading to conceive of s. 1 as a rigid and technical provision".[14] In arguing for a less categorical vision of rationality, it stresses further, that the court should not "overplay the view that rationality will overcome all falsehoods in the unregulated market-place of ideas".[15]

Undoubtedly, *Keegstra* stands for a great deal more than the issues addressed above. However, it is heartening to find the Supreme Court shifting, in that case, from unflinching faith in private rights towards a more open conception of communal norms. Equally heartening is the perception of both majority and minority, that objective truth, rationally conceived, is false and misleading.

Hopefully the reasoning in *R. v. Keegstra* represents a judicial trend, not an aberration.

---

[9] *Ibid.*, at 48-49 (emphasis in judgment).
[10] *Ibid.*, at 79 *per* McLachlin J. (emphasis in judgment).
[11] *Ibid.*, at 81.
[12] *Ibid.*, at 80 *per* McLachlin J.
[13] *Ibid.*, at 27 *et seq.*
[14] *Ibid.*, at 28.
[15] *Ibid.*, at 49.

CANADIAN CHARTER OF RIGHTS AND FREEDOMS

Being Part I of the Constitution Act, 1982
Enacted by the Canada Act, 1982 (U.K.), c. 11, Schedule B

Whereas Canada is founded upon principles that recognize the supremacy of God and the rule of law:

Guarantee of Rights and Freedoms

Rights and freedoms in Canada

1. The *Canadian Charter of Rights and Freedoms* guarantees the rights and freedoms set out in it subject only to such reasonable limits prescribed by law as can be demonstrably justified in a free and democratic society.

Fundamental Freedoms

Fundamental freedoms

2. Everyone has the following fundamental freedoms:
- (*a*) freedom of conscience and religion;
- (*b*) freedom of thought, belief, opinion and expression, including freedom of the press and other media of communication;
- (*c*) freedom of peaceful assembly; and
- (*d*) freedom of association.

Democratic Rights

Democratic rights of citizens

3. Every citizen of Canada has the right to vote in an election of members of the House of Commons or of a legislative assembly and to be qualified for membership therein.

Maximum duration of legislative bodies

4. (1) No House of Commons and no legislative assembly shall continue for longer than five years from the date fixed for the return of the writs at a general election of its members.

Continuation in special circumstances

(2) In time of real or apprehended war, invasion or insurrection, a House of Commons may be continued by Parliament and a legislative assembly may be continued by the legislature beyond five years if such continuation is not opposed by the votes of more than one-third of the members of the House of Commons or the legislative assembly, as the case may be.

Annual sitting of legislative bodies

5. There shall be a sitting of Parliament and of each legislature at least once every twelve months.

Mobility Rights

Mobility of citizens

6. (1) Every citizen of Canada has the right to enter, remain in and leave Canada.

Rights to move and gain livelihood

(2) Every citizen of Canada and every person who has the status of a permanent resident of Canada has the right

(a) to move to and take up residence in any province; and

(b) to pursue the gaining of a livelihood in any province.

Limitation

(3) The rights specified in subsection (2) are subject to

(a) any laws or practices of general application in force in a province other than those that discriminate among persons primarily on the basis of province of present or previous residence; and

(b) any laws providing for reasonable residency requirements as a qualification for the receipt of publicly provided social services.

Affirmative action programs

(4) Subsections (2) and (3) do not preclude any law, program or activity that has as its object the amelioration in a province of conditions of individuals in that province who are socially or economically disadvantaged if the rate of employment in that province is below the rate of employment in Canada.

Legal Rights

Life, liberty and security of the person

7. Everyone has the right to life, liberty and security of the person and the right not to be deprived thereof except in accordance with the principles of fundamental justice.

Search or seizure

8. Everyone has the right to be secure against unreasonable search or seizure.

Detention or imprisonment

9. Everyone has the right not to be arbitrarily detained or imprisoned.

Arrest or detention

10. Everyone has the right on arrest or detention

(*a*) to be informed promptly of the reasons therefor;

(*b*) to retain and instruct counsel without delay and to be informed of that right; and

(*c*) to have the validity of the detention determined by way of *habeas corpus* and to be released if the detention is not lawful.

Proceedings in criminal and penal matters

11. Any person charged with an offence has the right

(*a*) to be informed without unreasonable delay of the specific offence;

(*b*) to be tried within a reasonable time;

(*c*) not to be compelled to be a witness in proceedings against that person in respect of the offence;

(*d*) to be presumed innocent until proven guilty according to law in a fair and public hearing by an independent and impartial tribunal;

(*e*) not to be denied reasonable bail without just cause;

(*f*) except in the case of an offence under military law tried before a military tribunal, to the benefit of trial by jury where the maximum punishment for the offence is imprisonment for five years or a more severe punishment;

(*g*) not to be found guilty on account of any act or omission unless, at the time of the act or omission, it constituted an offence under Canadian or international law or was criminal according to the general principles of law recognized by the community of nations;

(*h*) if finally acquitted of the offence, not to be tried for it again and, if finally found guilty and punished for the offence, not to be tried or punished for it again; and

(*i*) if found guilty of the offence and if the punishment for the offence has been varied between the time of commission and the time of sentencing, to the benefit of the lesser punishment.

Treatment or punishment

12. Everyone has the right not to be subjected to any cruel and unusual treatment or punishment.

Self-crimination

13. A witness who testifies in any proceedings has the right not to have any incriminating evidence so given used to incriminate that witness in any other proceedings, except in a prosecution for perjury or for the giving of contradictory evidence.

Interpreter

14. A party or witness in any proceedings who does not understand or speak the language in which the proceedings are conducted or who is deaf has the right to the assistance of an interpreter.

Equality Rights

Equality before and under law and equal protection and benefit of law

15. (1) Every individual is equal before and under the law and has the right to the equal protection and equal benefit of the law without discrimination and, in particular, without discrimination based on race, national or ethnic origin, colour, religion, sex, age or mental or physical disability.

Affirmative action programs

(2) Subsection (1) does not preclude any law, program or activity that has as its object the amelioration of conditions of disadvantaged individuals or groups including those that are disadvantaged because of race, national or ethnic origin, colour, religion, sex, age or mental or physical disability.

Official Languages of Canada

Official languages of Canada

16. (1) English and French are the official languages of Canada and have equality of status and equal rights and privileges as to their use in all institutions of the Parliament and government of Canada.

Official languages of New Brunswick

(2) English and French are the official languages of New Brunswick and have equality of status and equal rights and privileges as to their use in all institutions of the legislature and government of New Brunswick.

Advancement of status and use

(3) Nothing in this Charter limits the authority of Parliament or a legislature to advance the equality of status or use of English and French.

Proceedings of Parliament

17. (1) Everyone has the right to use English or French in any debates and other proceedings of Parliament.

Proceedings of New Brunswick legislature

(2) Everyone has the right to use English or French in any debates and other proceedings of the legislature of New Brunswick.

Parliamentary statutes and records

18. (1) The statutes, records and journals of Parliament shall be printed and published in English and French and both language versions are equally authoritative.

New Brunswick statutes and records

(2) The statutes, records and journals of the legislature of New Brunswick

shall be printed and published in English and French and both language versions are equally authoritative.

Proceedings in courts established by Parliament

19. (1) Either English or French may be used by any person in, or in any pleading in or process issuing from, any court established by Parliament.

Proceedings in New Brunswick courts

(2) Either French or English may be used by any person in, or in any pleading in or process issuing from, any court of New Brunswick.

Communications by public with federal institutions

20. (1) Any member of the public in Canada has the right to communicate with, and to receive available services from, any head or central office of an institution of the Parliament or government of Canada in English or French, and has the same right with respect to any other office of any such institution where

(*a*) there is a significant demand for communications with and services from that office in such language; or

(*b*) due to the nature of the office, it is reasonable that communications with and services from that office be available in both English and French.

Communications by public with New Brunswick institutions

(2) Any member of the public in New Brunswick has the right to communicate with, and to receive available services from, any office of an institution of the legislature or government of New Brunswick in English or French.

Continuation of existing constitutional provisions

21. Nothing in sections 16 to 20 abrogates or derogates from any right, privilege or obligation with respect to the English and French languages, or either of them, that exists or is continued by virtue of any other provision of the Constitution of Canada.

Rights and privileges preserved

22. Nothing in sections 16 to 20 abrogates or derogates from any legal or customary right or privilege acquired or enjoyed either before or after the coming into force of this Charter with respect to any language that is not English or French.

Minority Language Educational Rights

Language of instruction

23. (1) Citizens of Canada

(*a*) whose first language learned and still understood is that of the English or French linguistic minority population of the province in which they reside, or

(b) who have received their primary school instruction in Canada in English or French and reside in a province where the language in which they received that instruction is the language of the English or French linguistic minority population of the province,

have the right to have their children receive primary and secondary school instruction in that language in that province.

Continuity of language instruction

(2) Citizens of Canada of whom any child has received or is receiving primary or secondary school instruction in English or French in Canada, have the right to have all their children receive primary and secondary school instruction in the same language.

Application where numbers warrant

(3) The right of citizens of Canada under subsections (1) and (2) to have their children receive primary and secondary school instruction in the language of the English or French linguistic minority population of a province

(a) applies wherever in the province the number of children of citizens who have such a right is sufficient to warrant the provision to them out of public funds of minority language instruction; and

(b) includes, where the number of those children so warrants, the right to have them receive that instruction in minority language educational facilities provided out of public funds.

Enforcement

Enforcement of guaranteed rights and freedoms

24. (1) Anyone whose rights or freedoms, as guaranteed by this Charter, have been infringed or denied may apply to a court of competent jurisdiction to obtain such remedy as the court considers appropriate and just in the circumstances.

Exclusion of evidence bringing administration of justice into disrepute

(2) Where, in proceedings under subsection (1), a court concludes that evidence was obtained in a manner that infringed or denied any rights or freedoms guaranteed by this Charter, the evidence shall be excluded if it is established that, having regard to all the circumstances, the admission of it in the proceedings would bring the administration of justice into disrepute.

General

Aboriginal rights and freedoms not affected by Charter

25. The guarantee in this Charter of certain rights and freedoms shall not be construed so as to abrogate or derogate from any aboriginal, treaty or other rights or freedoms that pertain to the aboriginal peoples of Canada including

(*a*) any rights or freedoms that have been recognized by the Royal Proclamation of October 7, 1763; and

(*b*) any rights or freedoms that now exist by way of land claims agreements or may be so acquired. [Am. S1/84-102, Sch.]

Other rights and freedoms not affected by Charter

26. The guarantee in this Charter of certain rights and freedoms shall not be construed as denying the existence of any other rights or freedoms that exist in Canada.

Multicultural heritage

27. This Charter shall be interpreted in a manner consistent with the preservation and enhancement of the multicultural heritage of Canadians.

Rights guaranteed equally to both sexes

28. Notwithstanding anything in this Charter, the rights and freedoms referred to in it are guaranteed equally to male and female persons.

Rights respecting certain schools preserved

29. Nothing in this Charter abrogates or derogates from any rights or privileges guaranteed by or under the Constitution of Canada in respect of denominational, separate or dissentient schools.

Application to territories and territorial authorities

30. A reference in this Charter to a province or to the legislative assembly or legislature of a province shall be deemed to include a reference to the Yukon Territory and the Northwest Territories, or to the appropriate legislative authority thereof, as the case may be.

Legislative powers not extended

31. Nothing in this Charter extends the legislative powers of any body or authority.

Application of Charter

Application of Charter

32. (1) This Charter applies

(*a*) to the Parliament and government of Canada in respect of all matters within the authority of Parliament including all matters relating to the Yukon Territory and Northwest Territories; and

(*b*) to the legislature and government of each province in respect of all matters within the authority of the legislature of each province.

Exception

(2) Notwithstanding subsection (1), section 15 shall not have effect until three years after this section comes into force.

Exception where express declaration

33. (1) Parliament or the legislature of a province may expressly declare in an Act of Parliament or of the legislature, as the case may be, that the Act or a provision thereof shall operate notwithstanding a provision included in section 2 or sections 7 to 15 of this Charter.

Operation of exception

(2) An Act or a provision of an Act in respect of which a declaration made under this section is in effect shall have such operation as it would have but for the provision of this Charter referred to in the declaration.

Five year limitation

(3) A declaration made under subsection (1) shall cease to have effect five years after it comes into force or on such earlier date as may be specified in the declaration.

Re-enactment

(4) Parliament or the legislature of a province may re-enact a declaration made under subsection (1).

Five year limitation

(5) Subsection (3) applies in respect of a re-enactment made under subsection (4).

Citation

Citation

34. This Part may be cited as the *Canadian Charter of Rights and Freedoms*.

. . . . .

PART VII
GENERAL

Primacy of Constitution of Canada

52. (1) The Constitution of Canada is the supreme law of Canada, and any law that is inconsistent with the provisions of the Constitution is, to the extent of the inconsistency, of no force or effect.

Constitution of Canada

(2) The Constitution of Canada includes
   (a) the *Canada Act 1982*, including this Act;
   (b) the Acts and orders referred to in the schedule; and
   (c) any amendment to any Act or order referred to in paragraph (a) or (b).

Amendments to Constitution of Canada

(3) Amendments to the Constitution of Canada shall be made only in accordance with the authority contained in the Constitution of Canada.

INDEX

Belief
  nature of
    conviction, 7-76, 180, 201
    decision-making, in, 2-3, 22-35, 61-72, 79-82, 89-92, 128-133, 162-168, 195-196
    desire, 52, 187-188
    mythology, 68, 201
    political instrument, 3-5, 74-76, 115-125, 133-138, 162-168
    predilection, 117, 173
    prejudice in, 79
    sentiment, 67, 78, 81, 136-140, 177-179, 200-201
    spirituality, 5, 24, 39-46, 49-52, 71-72, 84, 199
    truth, 67-68, 73-78, 100-103, 145-153, 192-196, 203-204
    virtue, 18-24, 87-88, 143, 149-155, 170
  subject matter
    race
      antisemitism, 150
      hate literature, 21, 49, 101, 203
      the holocaust, 68, 74, 75, 167
      neo-Nazi, 21-23, 25, 65-66
      racism, 23-25, 49-51, 79-83, 133
      volksgeist, 34, 78
      Zionism, 68
    religion
      atheism, 39, 200
      Catholicism, 38, 47, 52, 70, 139
      Christianity, 72-74, 78-80, 166
      church and state, 139
      Mormon, 70, 171

      practice, in, 29-50, 68-74, 81-94, 133-136, 152-156, 160-172
Canadian identity
  aboriginal peoples, 45, 67, 77, 88, 139-140
  bilingualism, 40, 61, 133, 145, 199
  constitutionalism, 1-5, 12-13, 40-41, 47-49, 57-60, 77-79, 110-115, 131-133, 153-156, 187-192
  denominational schooling, 27, 134
  federalism, 24-25, 28, 35, 81, 127, 133, 163
  multiculturalism, 40, 80-81, 133-134, 140
  Meech Lake Accord, 1-2, 40, 53, 78, 82, 119
Censorship, 29, 74
Communal relations
  consensual, 22, 62, 100, 124, 147, 171
  discrete, 64-66, 80, 95, 123, 131
  gender, 51, 85, 129-130, 188-190
  reciprocal, 55, 61-62, 95, 99, 121, 148
Communicative discourse
  ability to engage in, 122
  comprehension of 72, 93, 135, 143-145
  conception of, 63-65, 73-78, 119-120, 133-134, 201
  discursive communication, 56-61, 67-88, 92-96, 143-146, 156-159
  experience in, 31-33, 71, 80-82, 143-145, 189-191
  friendship in, 39, 101, 123
  interaction, 41-44, 52-54, 64-88, 92-96, 189
  interdependence of, 41, 52, 96, 196

Communicative discourse, *cont'd*
  mediating through, 69-70, 93-96,
    139, 184-185, 200-201
  nature of
    conversation, 55-56, 72, 88, 94,
      167, 172
    debate, 1-5, 31-34, 53, 70-78, 86-
      89, 160-171, 194-197
    dialectic, 42, 91, 94, 140, 196
    jargon, 14
    observation, 69-72, 92-94, 169,
      181-188, 194-195
Community, conceptions of
  communal values, 76-79, 133-138,
    168-171, 186-188, 203-204
  communicative action, 41-46,
    72-82, 92-96, 133-142, 197-201
  cooperative, 43, 53, 96, 108, 146
  cultural, 39-41, 76-79, 86-89, 113-
    114, 129-138, 147-148, 168-172
  ethnic, 21, 44-45, 92-93, 133-135
  harmony in, 33, 59, 66, 79, 118-122,
    138-140
  popular, 22-25, 41-44, 166, 175-179
  relational, 66-72, 104-110, 113-129,
    133-138
  situational community, 59, 109,
    115, 128, 184
  spontaneous community, 70, 76-
    79, 92
  theory of community, 35-45, 55-72,
    83-89, 120-123, 133-138
Competition, nature of
  adversarial, 38-39, 43, 49, 70, 85, 88
  antagonistic, 50, 88, 89, 131
  theory, 35-37, 48-58, 77-83, 117-
    121, 155-157
Contractual relationships
  adhesion, 100, 104
  bargaining, 104-109, 123-125, 137-
    138
  compensation, 106-108
  theory, 37-38, 61-62, 104-108, 120-
    126
  unbargained, 125
Decision-makers, attitudes towards
  activism, 14-16, 19, 22-23, 26-29,
    33-34, 38, 44, 51, 120

detachment, 81, 130, 146, 152, 162
dualism, 8, 140, 152, 168
equity, 64
ethics, 74, 84, 95, 151, 166, 170, 192
morality, 43, 80, 168
neutrality, 10-16, 60-62, 72-74, 121-
  128, 162-166, 200-201
partiality, 12, 28, 33, 46-47, 143,
  155, 163, 175-176, 185
precedent, 151, 160, 172
predilection, 11, 143, 152, 156, 193
realism, 86, 95, 100, 111, 118, 145,
  161, 168
standing, 12, 56, 87, 91, 189
subjectivity, 22, 31, 78, 81, 86, 132,
  145, 148-152, 162, 166
subordination, 96, 116, 129, 186
symbolism, 104, 118, 143
Democracy, nature of
  participatory, 37-41, 43-45, 60-63,
    84-88, 124-126
  representative, 18, 24, 29, 43-46,
    69, 80, 97-100, 176-177
  undemocratic element, 31, 105,
    184
  voting, 10, 43-44, 99, 117, 136, 176
Dominance, sources
  abuse of power, 46, 49-52, 55-60,
    79-82, 116-119, 130-132
  arbitrariness, 74, 105, 108, 113, 149,
    157
  bourgeois values, 24, 131, 140
  corporate power, 11-14, 28-33, 100-
    107, 111-117, 121-129, 137-141
  denial of choice, 15-18, 110-114,
    136-140, 154-157, 175-181, 186-
    189
  hierarchy, 55-59, 87-90, 121-126,
    152-154, 173-177, 180-185
  supremacy position, 8-12, 26-30,
    85-91, 100-108, 146-156, 176-187
Freedom of action
  assembly, 55, 62, 80, 115, 148, 150
  association, 13-14, 45-47, 61-63, 84-
    88, 98-106, 118-126
  expression, 8-9, 13-14, 20-23, 65-69,
    72-76, 98-104
  religion, 41-43

Freedom of action, *cont'd*
  speech, 13-14, 20-22, 48-51, 72-75,
    86-87, 150-151
  voluntariness 105, 135
Government
  bureaucracy, as, 103, 121, 123, 135,
    140
  executive, as, 17-19, 23-26, 117,
    121, 124, 127, 149, 166
  majoritarian, 27, 35, 45, 63, 66, 86,
    90, 92, 114, 174
  militaristic, 26, 80, 91, 143, 166
  municipal, 135, 140
  national, 37, 46, 49, 77-81, 87-89,
    114-120, 129-130
  parliamentarian, 16-22, 27, 39, 41,
    58, 83, 110, 158, 173-176, 184
  sovereign, 57-58, 86, 117, 126, 139,
    173, 182-184
  totalitarian, 102
Identity, Canadian. *See* Canadian
  identity
Inequality, aspects
  abuse of power, 15-19, 48-50, 95-
    108, 113-117, 122-126, 133-138
  disadvantaged status, 7-10, 26-36,
    41-48, 87-92, 117-118, 131-132
  discrimination, 36, 48-50, 90 94,
    98, 101, 105, 118-119, 131, 134
  enslavement, 35, 167, 190
  exploitation, 11, 77, 80, 87, 104, 140
  injustice, 20, 35-36, 49-50, 93, 102,
    108-110, 124-125
  marginalization, 60, 130, 172, 197
  oppression, 49-50, 72, 89, 105, 130,
    133
  patronage, 61
  racial inequality, 36, 44-45, 50, 78-
    81, 101-103, 119-120, 140, 159
  sexism, 44, 50, 61, 81, 119, 159, 166
  social practice, 9-10, 27-28, 45, 49,
    86-90, 104-114, 130-132, 180
  suffering, 44-45, 86-87, 103, 111-
    118, 131-133, 185, 194
Interests, social
  balancing of, 26, 80-83, 110-114,
    155-158, 164, 181, 194
  collective, 7-10, 36-39, 41-51, 62-64,
    115-119, 130-139, 151-154

constituent, 30, 39, 88, 92, 171
consumer, 13, 29-30, 58-59, 103-
  108, 117-127, 133-137, 163-165
contingent, 23, 55-57, 86-88, 126,
  143-148, 162, 165, 192, 195-197
heterogeneous, 88, 171
imbalance in, 35, 104
incommensurate, 87, 114, 143, 155,
  156, 164, 184
possessory, 40, 56, 88, 116, 120, 132
reconcilatory, 34, 49-53, 57-59, 80-
  85, 121, 140, 157, 169, 172
Interpretation, methods of
  constructive, 60-66, 81-88, 93-95,
    109-112, 146-157, 180-185, 191-
    196
  contextual, 31-33, 41-42, 57, 63, 83-
    87, 93-95, 136-137, 151-159, 179-
    180, 185-187, 190-192, 203
  empirical, 161, 172
  evidentiary, 78-79, 91-93, 135-138,
    147-151, 156-158, 168-173
  extrinsic, 159, 195
  flexible, 107
  linguistic, 21-22, 49-50, 152-155,
    171, 180
  literal, 3, 180, 185
  significance of, 17-21, 31-35, 143-
    146, 151-162, 171-173, 182-185
  teleologic, 146
Juries, 10, 105, 106, 153
Justice
  conceptions
    equality, 8-14, 19-26, 30-36, 43-
      45, 61-63, 78-84, 88-92, 104-
      105, 109-119, 121-135, 147-
      150
    injustice, 91, 104, 138
    morality, 20-25, 47-49, 85-89,
      137-139, 144-148, 150-152,
      170, 174-185
    punishment, 21, 29, 42, 81, 106,
      108, 127, 136-138, 166-169
    reasonableness, 68-70, 107, 111-
      112, 124, 154-163, 169-172,
      183-185
    welfare, 15, 22-23, 33, 48, 64, 81,
      89-94, 111, 129, 163, 170

Justice, *cont'd*
  forms of,
    criminal, 18-19, 26-27, 43, 47, 104-107, 127, 136, 148, 165, 174-175, 178-183
    demonstrable, 48, 154
    distributive, 20, 36, 105, 126-129, 131-134, 140-142, 199
    evenhanded, 138
    exemplary, 106, 108, 137-138
    formal, 17, 34, 72-74, 90, 123-125, 138, 139, 151, 177
    mechanical, 66, 90, 155, 160-162, 172, 196
    practical, 9, 27, 61, 87, 148, 183, 186, 194
    rectificatory, 35, 36, 137
    redistributive, 8, 9, 36, 63, 88, 128
    retributive, 30, 81, 133, 165
    unprincipled, 146, 152, 188
Legal categorization
  nature
    certainty, 11, 144, 152, 161, 169
    conceptual clarity, 17-19, 42-46, 146, 150-152, 159-161, 165-167, 170-172, 176-178, 184-191
    connectedness, 48, 104, 133, 148, 154-158, 160, 163-172, 179, 183, 194
    idealism, 40-45, 52, 82-84, 90, 95, 137, 152, 160, 175, 179
    legalism, 116, 191, 193
    professionalism, 70, 85-87, 100-101, 129, 137
  purposive ends, 21, 43, 66, 76, 89-92, 110, 157
  results
    contradiction 33, 48, 59, 61, 67, 73, 89, 91, 116, 128, 138, 157-158, 169
    deduction 159-161, 171
  sources
    causation, 23, 24, 106, 158, 179, 194

    characteristic, 32, 41, 56, 99, 149-150, 158, 175
    classification, 101, 112
    structure, 55-57, 75, 78, 99, 123-129, 141-142, 143-145, 181-185
Legal obligation
  fiduciary, 101, 106, 107, 138
  general, 8-9, 13-16, 32-33, 60-62, 103-108, 135-139, 148-153, 188
Legal philosophy
  analytic, 5, 11, 67, 146-152, 157-162, 164-168, 171, 174, 178, 180-182, 185
  capitalistic, 13, 78, 99, 114-116, 129, 141
  conservative, 22, 34, 44, 141, 152, 184
  critical, 24, 28, 33, 41, 48-51, 59-61, 75-76, 83-86, 95, 100-101, 109-111, 116, 123-125, 129-132, 146-149, 158, 161-162, 173-175, 178, 193
  deontologic, 48, 62
  egalitarian, 30, 42, 49, 51, 128
  etymological, 153
  formalistic, 16-20, 35-39, 66-67, 75-76, 90-93, 101-102, 120, 134-135, 141, 145-146, 150-156, 175-177, 186, 189, 190
  functional, 2-4, 17-19, 41, 58, 60-64, 70, 83-87, 93-95, 114, 119-120, 126, 138-139, 181-182, 187-192, 199
  general, 26-27, 31-33, 70-74, 91, 94, 101, 146-148, 170-177
  liberal, 1-3, 9-17, 24-31, 40-44, 48-53, 57-73, 86-91, 98-101, 111, 118-125, 140-145, 147-152, 184-188
  liberationist, 7, 52, 53, 133
  libertarian, 8, 101, 111, 141
  Marxist, 13, 72, 116, 123, 126, 145
  metaphysical, 67, 157, 167
  modernist, 24, 31, 43, 77, 99
  neoclassical, 118

Legal philosophy, *cont'd*
 nihilistic, 13, 24, 146, 147, 162
 ontological, 69
 positive, 7, 10, 15-16, 22-24, 27-29,
  40-47, 53-54, 99-100, 146-150,
  174-178, 192, 200
Meech Lake Accord, 1, 2, 40, 53, 78,
 82, 119
Politics in law
 apolitical judgement, 175, 200
 deconstruction, 24, 140, 162
 decontextualised reason, 34
 decriminalization, 174
 depoliticization, 112, 115, 118, 131
 enfranchisement, 60
 influence, 9-14, 22-31, 39-45, 60-66,
  71-74, 84-90, 98-100, 103-106,
  127-140, 144-152, 158-161, 163-
  167, 186-189
 practices
  empowerment, 23, 33, 63, 69,
   110, 116, 154, 199
  repoliticization, 131
Race
 Aryan, 21-23, 49
 Chinese, 134
 German, 25, 41, 50, 86, 130, 138
 Jew, 21-23, 25, 49-50, 65-66, 70, 74-
  75, 78, 80, 126
 Mohawk, 45, 86, 120, 171
Rationality, aspects
 axiomatic reason, 15, 149, 182, 193
 concept, 2-3, 17, 55-56, 98-100, 145-
  150, 153-157, 171-172, 179-183,
  204
 logical determination, 23-24, 111,
  114, 150, 156-161, 167, 179, 183
 objective truth, 14-18, 34, 48-52,
  78-81, 143-145, 148-166, 180-184
 programmatic response, 22, 27, 47-
  48, 156, 173, 188, 191-192
Reasoning, methods of
 algorithmic, 144
 ambiguous, 31
 antecedent, 69, 88
 antithetical, 101
 assumption, 10, 30, 57, 62, 78, 153,
  164, 165, 173, 196

authoritative, 57, 58, 103, 112, 174,
 207
commensurate, 114, 155
consistent, 67, 103, 150, 161, 165,
 167, 183, 184, 200
creative, 15, 22, 34, 95, 151, 155,
 168, 184
depersonalized, 13, 129
determinative, 11-14, 16-18, 23-26,
 47-48, 53, 58-63, 78-84, 88-90,
 111-114, 134-139, 149-156, 158,
 166-170, 174-177, 191-197, 203
diagnostic, 137
dialogic, 2-5, 72-73, 78, 87, 133,
 140, 143, 145
disparate, 20, 31, 71, 85-88, 92-93,
 133, 156, 160, 172, 185, 189
distinction, 43, 110, 112, 125, 129,
 151, 157, 180
distinctive, 16-19, 22-24, 74, 77, 92,
 100-101, 110-113, 151, 161-163,
 174, 180, 189-192
doctrinal, 24, 106, 150, 158, 162-
 163, 189
dogmatic, 23, 142, 163
exhaustive, 76, 78, 83, 91, 121, 138,
 143, 193
expansive, 70-71, 101, 140-142,
 155, 180, 184
foundational, 11, 104, 123, 138,
 141, 143, 146, 150, 162, 184, 193
imaginative, 34, 95, 106, 144, 189,
 200
incoherent, 31
indeterminate, 32, 161, 171, 190
inference, 40, 55, 63, 77, 148,
 152, 153, 158-159, 163, 183, 184,
 196
instrumental, 28, 51, 56, 105, 119,
 131-133, 146, 157, 174, 178
irrational, 24, 149, 162
justification, 20-21, 23-25, 42-46,
 56-57, 93-94, 108-113, 137-139,
 152-158, 161-172, 174-175
methodological, 34-35, 47, 93-94,
 130-131, 145-146, 149-152, 155-
 161, 168-172, 183-185

Reasoning, methods of, *cont'd*
> natural, 31, 36, 56, 110-116, 146-
> > 147, 179
>
> paradigmatic, 172
>
> paradoxical, 15, 53
>
> practical, 64, 163, 185
>
> pragmatic, 24, 147, 152, 161, 162,
> > 172, 185
>
> presupposition, 12, 79, 80, 145,
> > 170, 176, 188
>
> principled, 12, 17-18, 31, 58, 104-
> > 105, 121, 126, 145-158, 163, 174-
> > 177, 181-186, 204
>
> progressive, 72, 166, 188-192
>
> proportionate, 11, 17, 155, 180, 183
>
> propositional, 12, 50, 93-94, 144-
> > 145, 150, 168-171, 181, 193, 203
>
> reactive, 50, 52, 64, 71-79, 86-87,
> > 94, 133, 155, 166-168, 185, 191
>
> reconstructive, 22, 92, 101, 134,
> > 142, 177, 188, 193, 201
>
> relative, 10, 41, 42, 101, 105, 116,
> > 119, 128, 135, 143-149
>
> sceptical, 111, 138, 143, 161, 184
>
> simulated, 22, 48, 84, 148, 156, 165,
> > 194
>
> situational, 60, 66-69, 93-95, 126-
> > 128, 138-139, 187-188, 197
>
> speculative, 165, 182
>
> supposition, 20-21, 50, 79, 91, 144-
> > 147, 150, 155-159, 169-173, 180-
> > 187, 194-196, 204-205
>
> syllogistic, 172, 193
>
> systematic, 29-30, 73, 76, 79, 104,
> > 111, 146-156, 176
>
> uncertain, 162, 165, 168, 169
>
> uniform methods of, 14, 67, 78, 81,
> > 84, 138-140, 183-185, 191, 201
>
> universalized, 24-25, 82, 121, 138-
> > 140, 145, 148-149, 157-158
>
> unreasonable, 15, 130, 206

Rights
> quality of
> > affirmative, 15-16, 29, 35-41, 45,
> > > 50-51, 192
> >
> > correlative, 56, 65-72, 74, 75, 83-
> > > 88, 94, 95

> > democratic, 15-18, 22, 32-35, 37,
> > > 57-58, 98-101, 112-114, 150,
> > > 154, 175-177, 182, 187, 196
> >
> > derivative, 50, 62, 73-75, 82,
> > > 126, 145-146, 153, 168-171,
> > > 179-180
> >
> > entrenched, 15, 58, 62, 177
> >
> > feminist, 61, 114, 124, 130, 147,
> > > 189, 190
> >
> > foetal, 46, 50, 68, 86, 89, 120,
> > > 131, 136, 147, 150, 167, 176-
> > > 178, 186-188, 193
> >
> > freedom to enjoy, 8-14, 31-38,
> > > 67-69, 71-76, 133-141, 156-
> > > 164, 185-192, 199-201
> >
> > fundamental, 21-26, 57-59, 86-
> > > 89, 101-103, 111-113, 148-
> > > 151, 180, 183, 190-192
> >
> > gay, 23, 38, 44, 50, 91, 122
> >
> > individual, 10-16, 21-24, 46-54,
> > > 58-62, 71-73, 83-90, 97-103,
> > > 115-128, 137, 145-150, 199-
> > > 201
> >
> > labour, 9, 37-39, 56, 63-65, 69,
> > > 80, 97-98, 100, 115, 126-129,
> > > 165
> >
> > minority, 35-36, 90-92, 133, 166
> >
> > negative, 7-8, 10-12, 46-49, 199-
> > > 200
> >
> > practice, in, 7-8, 26-35, 78-83,
> > > 131-153, 173-181, 199-201

theories
> *a priori*, 9-10, 19-24, 55-56, 93,
> > 126, 145-153, 173, 186-190
>
> behavioral, 28, 78, 80, 93, 95,
> > 128, 138, 145, 147
>
> coherence, 5, 90, 94, 138, 144,
> > 147-148, 161, 163, 169
>
> compliance, 26-32, 63, 109, 116
>
> deterrence, 30, 106, 108, 133,
> > 165-168
>
> elitist, 27, 31, 115, 124, 130, 163,
> > 176
>
> humanist, 25, 33, 50, 60, 69, 71,
> > 160, 184, 195
>
> pluralist, 45, 51-55, 60-63, 84,
> > 90, 139, 199

Rights, *cont'd*
  theories, *cont'd*
    postmodern, 24, 60
    radical, 111, 118, 124, 140, 141,
      143, 146, 190
    socialist, 12, 21, 52, 116, 141,
      142
    sociological, 75, 109, 115, 130,
      145, 155
    utilitarian, 41, 99, 120, 148, 192
Scope
  demonstration, 21, 63, 151-152, 165
  equality, 14-16, 19-20, 25-26, 36,
    43-45, 51, 90-92, 109-115, 128-
    129, 131-140, 163, 196-197
  personhood, 11, 51, 75, 172
  reproductive freedom, 46-48, 50-
    51, 89-92, 147, 173-182, 184-196,
    199

Status, legal
  class, 3, 19, 80, 88, 90-92, 109, 119,
    124-125, 128-130, 140
  classlessness, 109, 189
  deference to, 13, 15, 112, 128, 135,
    149, 176, 184, 194
  effect of, 9, 11, 14, 17, 20, 30, 37-38,
    45-46, 57-59, 63, 89-92, 95, 104-
    106, 112, 115-119, 126, 129-134,
    180, 186-188
  privileged, 13, 28, 33, 56, 64, 112,
    116-121, 126, 138, 140
  stereotyped, 4, 61, 76-79, 81, 129,
    190, 192
  typecast, 25, 78, 128, 134, 188
Unity in difference, 20-24, 31-32, 44-
  52, 82-84, 144-148, 162-169, 176-187